Exploring the Toxicity of Lateral Violence and Microaggressions

Christine L. Cho · Julie K. Corkett
Astrid Steele
Editors

Exploring the Toxicity of Lateral Violence and Microaggressions

Poison in the Water Cooler

Editors
Christine L. Cho
Schulich School of Education
Nipissing University
Brantford, ON, Canada

Astrid Steele
Schulich School of Education
Nipissing University
North Bay, ON, Canada

Julie K. Corkett
Schulich School of Education
Nipissing University
North Bay, ON, Canada

ISBN 978-3-030-09071-5   ISBN 978-3-319-74760-6   (eBook)
https://doi.org/10.1007/978-3-319-74760-6

Cover design by Emma Hardy

Printed on acid-free paper

This Palgrave Macmillan imprint is published by the registered company Springer International Publishing AG part of Springer Nature
The registered company address is: Gewerbestrasse 11, 6330 Cham, Switzerland

To my daughter, Quinlan, may the road you travel in life be more open and accepting.
—Christine L. Cho
To my sister who took the risk of entering a male dominated profession and had to face aggression every single day because of it.
—Julie K. Corkett
To the women with whom I paddle, we continue to teach each other how to navigate in a world not of our making.
—Astrid Steele
We dedicate this book to all those who have been impacted by social hostility, those working for change and those on the road to discovery.

PREFACE

Given the rise in racial tensions in the United States, the #MeToo out-pouring, combined with unfolding concerns regarding exclusion and nationalism around the globe, we have sought input from contributors, who use a variety of lenses, to make sense of some disturbing phenomena that goes by many terms in the literature: "lateral or horizontal violence"; "microaggressions"; "incivility"; "counter-productive work behavior" and "social undermining" amongst others. What all these terms have in common is the concept of ambiguous intentionality. That is to say, there is a perception on the part of the victim that another's actions have hostile or negative undertones, but the acts are so subtle they are often dismissed and the instigator often denies any negative intent. This is a growing conversation which explores the ways in which interlocking systems of oppression appear in innocuous and often covert ways.

In the summer of 2016, we, the editors, came together following a graduate student information session at our institution. Christine had presented a paper on microaggressions experienced by immigrant teachers and Julie had just attended a workshop presented by the Canadian Mental Health Association on lateral violence and mental health. Astrid began to make connections between lateral (horizontal) violence, incivilities, and microaggression. We planned an informal "retreat" and began to discuss the linkages between intra-professional aggressions displayed within disciplines and were curious about its occurrence in a range of professions and communities.

We read with interest newspaper articles from the *Chicago Tribute* and the *Ottawa Citizen* on the prevalence of incivility in the workplace. Lateral (or horizontal) violence is overtly discussed in the field of nursing and, more recently in Aboriginal communities. We found incivility to be increasingly discussed in law and business. Microaggressions is the term of choice to explain slights and subtle hostilities that are racist, sexist, homophobic, etc. in nature. However, we also found the terms themselves can be difficult to explain, particularly to those not versed in the discipline-specific language, which awakens a defensiveness in individuals. Some people may feel threatened, either by virtue of being an involuntary participant or as a bystander who did not voice objection to an affront.

The terms "microaggression" and "lateral/horizontal violence" are challenging for some, most likely because they use the language of conflict to name experiences some people would rather dismiss as trivial. The terms are not self-defining, rather, they expose hostility and viciousness. Those with privilege do not always recognize the subtleness of the infractions for what they are: ways of maintaining power and exerting control—they strongly contest that no harm or malice was intended. Others may lash back with a criticism that interactions are becoming overly policed; all words and actions are not said or done with malice and perhaps we as a society are becoming "too sensitive". Asking a person of color "where are you from?", for example, is just a polite conversation starter, one may argue, a way to get to know someone, not a microaggression that reveals a bias that you must not be from *here*. This is just one argument heard repeatedly in defense of this particular racial slight which is a microaggression that questions people's nationality and sense of belonging. Incivility seems to be more easily understood, perhaps because it references social norms and softens pugnacious language. While what is considered uncivil by one person may be permissible to another, there seems to be a continuum rooted in both context and perception, which further troubles already difficult conversations.

To be sure, as three professional women working in education and academia, there were certainly moments of resonance, as we considered our own past experiences with colleagues through the lenses of microaggression and incivility. We work in an environment in which having a resilient spirit and a thick skin seem to be taken-for-granted requirements in the workplace. Unfortunately, to claim that one has never been witness to, or involved in an uncivil exchange at work would be remarkable indeed. Rather, we are forced to navigate mandated forms of civility in the workplace. Mean-spirited sarcasm might be explained away as 'humor'; harsh criticism might be viewed as thinly veiled collegial 'critique'. Whether verbal or digital, face to face, or rumored, such exchanges seem to be embedded in many of our experiences over the years. It seems far too easy to accept such behaviors as inherent in the human workplace. Thus, by considering ways of hearing multiple voices on these phenomena, we are seeking a more humane approach to working together.

And so, we decided to both put out a call for chapter submissions and also contact authors directly, based on the important work many were already doing in these fields. We reached out to people in education, law, business, native studies, and political science, amongst others. We sought a variety of voices from a range of communities (LGBTQ, Aboriginal, cisgender and gender nonconforming, multiple ethnicities and races). What we have collected are some very unique perspectives on the toxicity that is affecting the proverbial watercooler of workplaces, institutions and our communities. The contributors expose the ways in which lateral/horizontal violence, incivility, and microaggressions are wide spread phenomena on a continuum that ranges from the uncomfortable to the dangerous.

Optimistic at the start, we thought perhaps we could determine a unified phrase or coin a term that would adequately express our interrogation of lateral/horizonal violence, incivility, and microaggression in the literature. While what is common is an uncritical acceptance of time-worn practices, traditions, approaches, and concepts, which ultimately limit transformative and communicative possibilities in our professions and institutions, each term, microaggression, lateral/horizontal violence, and incivility are distinct and speak to particular aspects of exclusion or ways in which people are rendered vulnerable. What we can offer is a broadening of the conversation of workplace and community aggression by exploring its occurrence in a variety of spaces and places.

We also reflected on the concept that forms of aggression tend to extend beyond the initial trigger and can wear away at an individual for a long time after the transgression is over. Some of the counter-stories shared here are raw. In many instances, the contributors are personally invested in bringing the stories to light, and their own social locations are embedded in their critiques. This is difficult work but it is work that cannot be done alone. We hope that the counter-stories contained here provide new perspectives and perhaps even bring clarity to some long-held beliefs. There is an emotional cost to doing this work and it is hoped that, just as our conversation and lived experience was the impetus for this book, the chapters herein will provide an avenue for conversations to continue and, ultimately for change and a greater acceptance for all, to occur.

Brantford, Canada   Christine L. Cho
North Bay, Canada   Julie K. Corkett
North Bay, Canada   Astrid Steele

CONTENTS

EDITORS AND CONTRIBUTORS

About the Editors

Christine L. Cho is an Associate Professor at Nipissing University's Schulich School of Education. As a practicing visual artist and former classroom teacher, her research in teacher education contributes to current educational conversations on racial, ethnic, and linguistic representation in schools and explores the constructions and understandings of teacher identity within the structures of schools. Her work challenges educators through critical consciousness-raising to examine their own social location and trouble "the way things are" in schools.

Julie K. Corkett has worked for the Canadian Federal government, and as an intermediate and high school teacher. Dr. Corkett is currently a tenured Assistant Professor at the Schulich School of Education who teaches special education, educational psychology, diversity and inclusion, and religious education. Her research interests pertain to literacy, pedagogy, technology, special education, and educational psychology. Julie has been invited guest lecturer at Beni Suef University, in Egypt and at Sino-Canadian International College, Guangxi University, Nanning, China.

Astrid Steele is an Associate Professor in the Schulich School of Education at Nipissing University. She has taught in both the elementary and secondary panels in Ontario, on a reserve in Northern Ontario, in adult education at the college level, and has worked with youth at risk in outdoor education settings. At Nipissing University Astrid teaches science education and provides environmental and sustainability education opportunities for teacher candidates.

Contributors

John Antoniw is a student in the Master of Social Work program at the University of Windsor. John also holds a Master of Education in Curriculum Studies, a Master of Arts in Sociology, a Bachelor of Education, a Bachelor of Arts in Sociology, and a Bachelor of Arts in Psychology. John's research interests investigate the barriers that minorities face when engaging with curriculum, specifically in regards to representation and inclusion. John also has an extensive background with volunteer work within the realm of social justice, specifically with a feminist focus. John also recently served as a research associate on a three year SSHRC funded research endeavor titled *The Tikkun Project*.

Renée E. Mzinegiizhigo-kwe Bédard is of Indigenous Anishinaabeg ancestry and a member of Dokis First Nation. She holds a Ph.D. from Trent University. Currently, she is an Assistant Professor at Nipissing University in the Department of Native Studies. Her area of publication includes work related to topics involving Indigenous culture and traditions relating to Indigenous women's issues, mothering traditions, philosophy, environmental issues, Elders, and artistic expressions.

Michelle Bothwell is an Associate Professor of Bioengineering at Oregon State University. Her teaching and research bridge ethics, social justice, and engineering with the aim of cultivating an inclusive and socially just engineering profession. Michelle serves as a co-PI for two NSF-funded institutional transformation awards: *OREGON STATE ADVANCE* and *Revolutionizing engineering Departments*.

Lorraine M. Carter is the Director of the Centre for Continuing Education at McMaster University in Hamilton, Ontario, Canada. In addition to serving as the Director of the School of Nursing at Nipissing University in North Bay, Ontario, Canada, she has played an important role in advancing online education in nursing and the broader health education field in Northern Ontario. Dr. Carter is an active national and international scholar, and has served as President of the Canadian

Network for Innovation in Education and the Canadian Association for University Continuing Education.

Yvette Daniel is an Associate Professor in Educational Leadership and Policy Studies at the Faculty of Education, University of Windsor, Canada. Dr. Daniel has extensive experience in teacher education as course instructor and faculty advisor. She has developed a new service-learning program for teacher candidates. She is PI on a three-year SSHRC and University of Windsor funded cross-cultural research and partnership development project that explores youth civic engagement for healing and reconciliation (*Tikkun*) in their communities.

Natalie Davey began her career as an educator in the public secondary school environment, then moved into the realm of higher education, and today bridges those two worlds on the college campus. Natalie's doctoral research was a place-based memory-driven investigation of education as it occurred inside a youth detention center in Toronto. Her research is always philosophical at its core, but Natalie's work consistently makes forays into narrative and other arts-based methodologies, with the belief that such interdisciplinary practices strengthen educational stories.

Tanya Erazo is a New York City transplant hailing from the Bay Area in California. She has two master's degrees and is completing her Ph.D. in clinical psychology. She is also a certified alcohol and substance abuse counselor in training (CASAC-T) in New York State.

Chassitty N. Fiani is a doctoral candidate in clinical psychology at the CUNY Graduate Center. She works to alleviate disparities faced by marginalized social groups through understanding the role of microaggressions, applying techniques from Acceptance and Commitment Therapy, and exploring the fluid nature of self and identity.

Heather Han received her Bachelor of Arts in Psychology from State University of New York (SUNY) Stony Brook and is currently working on the Master of Arts in Forensic Psychology from John Jay College of Criminal Justice. Her research interests include discrimination, implicit bias, and microaggression.

Louise Hard was an early childhood teacher before joining academia in 1994. Her career spanned teaching, research, and administrative responsibilities. She was the Head of the Murray School of Education at Charles Sturt University for ten years and moved to the Faculty of

Business to become the Associate Dean in 2012. In 2016 she joined the new Faculty of Arts and Education as the Deputy Dean and retired in mid 2017.

Roberta Hunte is an Assistant Professor in Women Gender and Sexuality Studies at Portland State University where she teaches on gender and race inequality and equity. She is a cultural worker and develops her narrative research into theater and film pieces including the plays My Walk Has Never Been Average, We are BRAVE, stories of reproductive justice and a short film Sista in the Brotherhood. She is a mama to a beautiful boy.

Diane P. Janes is an Instructional Designer with the Faculty of Extension, University of Alberta. She has consulted on distance education/e-learning, instructional development, and program evaluation in Canada, Mexico, and New Zealand. Her research focuses on faculty development, collaborative online learning, online teaching pedagogy, e-research, e-policy, program evaluation, and instructional design. Diane has served as President of the Canadian Network for Innovation in Education (CNIE). She currently sits a Director of the AMTEC Trust.

Toivo Koivukoski is an Associate Professor of Political Science at Nipissing University and Director of the Nipissing University Peace Research Initiative. He is author of *The New Barbarism and the Modern West: Recognizing an Ethic of Difference* (2014), *After the Last Man: Excurses to the Limits of the Technological System* (2008), and co-editor with David Tabachnick of a series of books on classical regimes theory, including *On 'Oligarchy* (2011), *Enduring Empire* (2009), and *Confronting Tyranny: Ancient Lessons for Global Politics* (2005), along with *The Question of Peace in Modern Political Thought* (2015) and *Globalization, Technology and Philosophy* (2004). His current research and teaching are focused on the topics of love and justice through a comparative study of Plato's *Symposium* and *Republic*.

Karey D. McCullough is the Director of the School of Nursing at Nipissing University in North Bay, Ontario. She has taught courses primarily at the undergraduate level in the areas of pharmacology, trauma/emergency nursing, preceptorship, and global health. Dr. McCullough is the recipient of the Chancellor's Award for Excellence in Teaching at Nipissing University as well as the 2017 Preceptor Recognition Award from the Council of Ontario University Programs in Nursing. Her major area of research interest is in international preceptorship, teaching and learning strategies in undergraduate nursing education, and curricula development.

Mónica Christina Murillo Parilla born in Bogota Colombia, is a first-generation graduate from the forensic psychology program at John Jay College of Criminal Justice. She's passionate about using academia and grassroots activism to advocate for social change. She's interested in multicultural psychology, the effects of immigration on youth, multiculturalism, gender studies, and microaggressions.

Kevin L. Nadal, Ph.D. is a Professor at the City University of New York. He is president of the Asian American Psychological Association; former Executive Director of the Center for LGBTQ Studies; founder of the LGBTQ Scholars of Color Network, a leading expert on the study of microaggressions, and author of 8 books.

Anne Nelun Obeyesekere has her Honors. B.A. in International Relations/Peace and Conflict Studies, and her B.Ed., from the University of Toronto (UofT). She is a teacher at an alternative secondary school where she engages in the implementation of anti-racist pedagogy. Anne is presently working towards an M.A. in Social Justice Education at UofT focused on race and identity politics.

Laurie Peachey is an Assistant Professor in the School of Nursing at Nipissing University. She has practiced in perinatal and pediatric nursing while also working in various roles in nursing education since 2004. As a professor, she integrated the classroom and simulation lab to prepare students for a two-day maternal child simulation combined with their traditional practicum hours. Laurie is currently working on her dissertation in the Ph.D. program in Education at Nipissing University. Her research interests are rooted in practice education to include the use of maternal child simulation, and the transition of new graduates entering practice.

Dwaine Plaza is a Professor of Sociology and the Associate Dean in the College of Liberal Arts at Oregon State University. He teaches a wide slate of classes both at the undergraduate and graduate levels. He has written extensively on the topic of Caribbean migration within the international diaspora. His current research focuses on gender and race issues in the NSF funded OREGON STATE ADVANCE grant.

Ramona Pringle is an Associate Professor in the RTA School of Media at Ryerson University and Director of the Transmedia Zone, an incubator for innovation in media and storytelling. Ramona's work examines the evolving relationship between humans and technology, and has been featured at Hot Docs, SXSW, NXNE, Social Media Week, TEDx, and in the New York Times, Mashable, and CBC. Ramona has a Master's Degree from NYU's Interactive Telecommunications Program.

Stephanie M. Reio is a Program Supervisor, Pretrial Services in Jefferson County, Louisville, KY. She earned her B.S. degree is Justice Administration from the University of Louisville. Her research interests include workplace attitudes and behaviors and the effectiveness of pretrial release.

Thomas G. Reio, Jr. is an Assistant Dean of Graduates Studies and Professor of Adult Education and Human Resource Development in the Department of Leadership and Professional Studies at Florida International University in Miami, Florida. His research concerns workplace incivility, curiosity and risk-taking motivation, workplace socialization processes, and workplace learning. His work has been published in leading journals in education, business, and psychology.

Lorna E. Rourke is the Librarian at St. Jerome's University in the University of Waterloo, Canada. She has been an instructor in the Master of Library Science program at Western University and in the Library Techniques program at Mohawk College. Rourke is a past recipient of the Ontario College & University Library Association Lifetime Achievement Award. Her areas of research include generational differences, mental health issues in universities, and the relationship between information, politics, and democracy.

Bonnie Ruder is a Ph.D. candidate in biocultural anthropology at Oregon State University. Her research interests include equity and inclusion in STEM fields, systems of oppression, and maternal and reproductive health. She currently serves as the graduate research assistant for *OREGON STATE ADVANCE*. Bonnie is also a licensed midwife and has attended births in Oregon since 1997.

Anver Saloojee is currently Professor in the Department of Politics and Public Administration, and is Assistant Vice President (International) at Ryerson University. Between 2005 and 2008 he was a Special Advisor in the Presidency, Government of South Africa. In the past, he has served as President of the Laidlaw Foundation, President of The Community Social Planning Council of Toronto and as Vice President of the Canadian Association of University Teachers.

Zubeida Saloojee is currently Professor in the Child and Youth Program in the School of Social and Community Services at George Brown College. For over 20 years she worked in the fields of family counseling and community engagement. Between 2005 and 2008 she worked as a consultant to the United Nations, the Government of South Africa, the South African Management Development Institute, and the Africa Institute.

David Starr-Glass is a mentor with the International Programs (Prague) of SUNY Empire State College and a research fellow at the University of New York in Prague. He has master's degrees in business administration, organizational psychology, and education. He has multiple research interest and has published more than a hundred journal articles and book chapters. When not in Prague, he lives in Jerusalem (Israel) and teaches economic and business-related courses with a number of local colleges.

Rebecca Warner is a Professor of Sociology at Oregon State University. From 2009 to 2015 she served as Senior Vice Provost for Academic Affairs advancing both faculty and student success. Becky is PI for *OREGON STATE ADVANCE*. Funded by NSF, this grant serves to recruit and retain women in STEM disciplines.

LIST OF FIGURES

LIST OF TABLES

CHAPTER 1

Introduction

Christine L. Cho, Julie K. Corkett and Astrid Steele

We appreciate the numerous voices that have been raised in our exploration of microaggression, lateral (horizontal) violence and incivility. As a result of our contributors' chapters, we have come to a deeper understanding of how nuanced this work is. The ways in which aggression is manifested can take many forms and is dependent upon context. It is not always easy to name. Overt acts of violence can overshadow and, perhaps, even trivialize the daily violence and aggression that many experiences within the workforce and in their communities. This oversight may be embedded in the cyclical nature of microaggression and lateral/horizontal violence, which enables seemingly innocuous acts to go unnoticed and simply be accepted as "part of the job" (Ceravolo, Schwartz, Foltz-Ramos, & Castner, 2012). Microaggression, lateral/ horizontal violence and incivility can be overt and/or covert manifestations of social exclusionary tactics. The violence and discomfort that is exhibited and/or understood is enacted through the perception and reception of biased interactions. The chapters contained herein build on Augoustinos and Every's (2007) description of modern subtle and covert forms of discrimination: "discursive strategies that present negative

C. L. Cho (✉)
Schulich School of Education, Nipissing University, Brantford, ON, Canada

J. K. Corkett · A. Steele
Schulich School of Education, Nipissing University, North Bay, ON, Canada

© The Author(s) 2018
C. L. Cho et al. (eds.), *Exploring the Toxicity of Lateral Violence and Microaggressions*, https://doi.org/10.1007/978-3-319-74760-6_1

1

views of out-groups as reasonable and justified while at the same time protecting the speaker from charges of racism and prejudice" (p. 124). As you read the chapters, it becomes apparent the relationship between silence and trauma. This relationship exposes the ways in which aggressive acts impact an individual's vulnerability, as a strategy to undermine a person's legitimacy. There is a cumulative effect to repeated transgressions. Power is the central vortex around which all these forms of harassment circulate.

TERMINOLOGY

While various authors offer definitions in their respective chapters, the following are our common understandings of the terminology used in the book:

Microaggression is a term coined by psychiatrist Chester Pierce in the 1970s to describe acts of racism so subtle that neither the perpetrator nor the victim is even fully conscious of what is happening. As Sue et al. explain, microaggressions are "brief and commonplace daily verbal, behavioral, or environmental indignities, whether intentional or unintentional, that communicate hostile, derogatory, or negative racial slights and insults toward people of colour" (Sue et al., 2007, p. 273). Several authors extend this definition to include gender, ability, sexual orientation, nationality and religious affiliations and refer to Sue et al. subcategories of microinsults, microassaults, microinvalidations.

Lateral violence and Horizontal violence are terms used interchangeably to explain workplace incivility or "collegial" conflict. As McKenna, Smith, Poole, and Coverdale (2003) explain, horizontal violence is, "psychological harassment, which creates hostility, as opposed to physical aggression. This harassment involves verbal abuse, threats, intimidation, humiliation, excessive criticism, innuendo, exclusion, denial of access to opportunity, disinterest, discouragement and the withholding of information" (2003, p. 92).

Incivility is often defined as social behaviours that show a lack of respect for societal norms. As Andersson and Pearson (1999) suggest, incivilities are "low intensity deviant behavior with ambiguous intent to harm the target, in violation of workplace norms for mutual respect. Uncivil behaviors are characteristically rude, discourteous, displaying a lack of respect for others" (p. 457). Be it as an instigator, target or onlooker, a person's perception of an event as being uncivil, is impacted by their cultural and social location.

THE ORGANIZATION OF THE BOOK

We have organized the contributions in this book according to three interrelated themes: *Explorations of Disruption, Hierarchical Layers and Practices;* and *Towards Systemic Change.* As we worked to determine the organization, we were interested in the ways in which the contributors spoke from their social location and how the chapters related and conversed with each other and revealed what Augoustinos and Every (2007) refer to as "recurring and pervasive patterns of talk" (p. 125). Intersectionality (Crenshaw, 1991) is a theme that runs throughout the book and so it was difficult to impose categorization as we know that readers will come to this book with a variety of purposes and outlooks. We did not wish to fall into an essentialist portrayal of the viewpoints; rather, we were compelled to consider the ways in which the chapters gave insights into various perspectives: how bodies disrupt the status quo (*Explorations of Disruption*); insights into how institutions are structured and practices that may cause harm are maintained (*Hierarchical Layers and Practices*); and finally, we wished to end on an optimistic note, considering progressive and proactive alternatives (*Towards Systemic Change*). The thread that runs throughout all the chapters is the notion of power. In the first section, *Explorations of Disruption*, we hear the voices of historically oppressed individuals in relation to the White hegemonic narrative and have the opportunity to explore the ways in which, to draw from Wetherell and Potter (1992), some individuals work to "dodge the identity" of privilege.

EXPLORATIONS OF DISRUPTION

We begin this section with David Starr-Glass's chapter, which provides a framework of key terminology. Starr-Glass examines the shift in prejudice-based and discriminatory aggression, which has also been accompanied by a spiral of general workplace incivility. Starr-Glass suggests that racism, sexism, homophobia, etc. remain rooted in societal interactions but have undergone a metamorphosis which makes recognizing, describing, and/or denouncing such acts more problematic as they now occur under the guise of microaggressions, lateral violence and incivility. As Starr-Glass explains, "the violence that lies at the heart of prejudice-based violence remains present and potent, but has undergone a *metamorphosis*" (Chapter 2, p. 13). We lead with this chapter as it offers a global overview of how historical "racism" has morphed into contemporary microaggressions. The shift from blatant forms of prejudice to more subtle and covert expressions of negativity is at the heart of understanding contemporary social hostilities (Augoustinos & Every, 2007). As Starr-Glass argues, the form may change but the substance remains constant.

We follow with Roberta Hunte's chapter as she explores the experiences of Black women in nontraditional roles as tradeswomen, some of whom have been in the industry for many decades. Hunte uses Black Feminist Theory to offer an examination of nontraditional roles and the ways in which microaggressive acts arise to subvert and undermine workers. She asks the compelling question: "is it your race or your gender" when exploring microaggressions in the construction industry, as she draws from the subtle and not so subtle ways in which power and control are exercised in a field that is White male-dominated. Recognizing how multiple layers of identity impact the ways in which women work to navigate challenging work environments, despite an exclusionary climate, sheds new light on the importance of understanding intersectionality in relation to experiences of microaggressions.

Continuing to share historically unrepresented voices and counter-stories, in Chapter 4, Nadal, Eraxo, Fiani, Murillo Parilla and Han focus on the types of discrimination and bias transgender and gender nonconforming (TGNC) people encounter and how those experiences impact their perceptions and interactions with different sectors of the criminal justice system. This chapter also presses the reader to consider intersectionality when exploring experiences of microaggression and considers the links between physical and mental health as related to the effects of microaggression.

As Canadians work through the trauma of residential schooling and move towards reconciliation with Indigenous people, Renée Mzinegiizhigo-kwe offers us insights into the tensions between the push to Indigenize higher education institutions and the microaggressions experienced by Indigenous academics trying to forge new paths. Mzinegiizhigo-kwe Bédard considers her responsibility as an

Anishinaabe-kwe woman, as a keeper or protector of the water, and what this means when there is poison in the metaphorical water cooler in the form of lateral violence in the academy. Using the imagery of the "Indian in the Cupboard", she argues, "I could be brought out on special occasions as long as I had the appropriate attire (beads, feathers, and buckskin)" (Chapter 5, p. 75). As institutions of higher learning work to build capacity with the Indigenous population, this chapter offers an important and relatively unheard perspective.

In Chapter 7, Nelun Obeyesekere continues the conversation of identity in relation to the diasporic, negatively racialized urban teacher and student. She explores how shadeism informs identity and, in particular, how negatively racialized people perceive themselves and how others perceive them as a result of colonization and White hegemony. Nelun Obeyesekere offers analysis into the more nuanced aspects of colour and its impact on teachers and students.

Finally, as we consider the role of the institution, particularly institutions of higher education, we turn to Ruder, Plaza, Warner, and Bothwell to expose the White, male hegemonic culture in STEM departments. The authors discuss the institutional and derisive betrayal of women, and expose the myth of meritocracy in the field of science research. The concept of "institutional betrayal" comes in many forms including, but not limited to, different understandings of work assigned, tenure and promotion processes, and/or a lack of formal reporting mechanisms for grievances between leadership and faculty. We end this section with this chapter as it serves to make linkages between the concepts of identity and the role of the institution, which is taken up in greater detail in the next section.

HIERARCHICAL LAYERS AND PRACTICES

In the second section, *Hierarchical Layers and Practices*, the contributors explore the ways in which power is played out in institutions and serves to maintain systemic patriarchal structures. What stands out for us as we organized this section is the amount of hostility and negative interactions found in what are typically considered "helping" or "caring" professions: nursing, teaching, early childhood care and even those working to rehabilitate young offenders. Instead, these places of care become sites of aggression where backstabbing, putdowns and culture of harassment are propagated.

Reio and Reio begin this section with a chapter that exposes how stress in the workplace, particularly in K-12 schools, results in uncivil behaviours which, if allowed to fester, can escalate into bullying, forms of intentional aggression and physical violence. What was touched upon in Nadal et al.'s chapter is further explored here, namely, the link between social hostility and physical and mental health. The authors discuss professional burnout and turnover as related to lateral violence. The concept of professional burnout is explored by many of the contributors in this section and speaks to ways in which self-esteem, professional aspirations and community can be eroded by experiences of microaggressions, lateral/horizontal violence and incivility.

In Chapter 9, concepts of power are further teased apart as Daniel and Antoniw ask if lateral violence is a necessary rite of passage for student teachers. That is, is being in a subservient role a required aspect of the progression to becoming a teacher? The contributors argue, that, "although power dynamics between novice and veteran teachers cannot be totally eradicated (nor is it advisable to do so), the dynamic, although hierarchical to some extent, must allow for non-threatening spaces for crucial conversations to occur as part of this repertoire of education and training" (Chapter 9, p. 169). We often think of teaching and nursing professions as caring professions and so it can be difficult to understand and ascertain why these professions seem wrought with instances of lateral violence. What is at the heart of many of the negative interactions described in the section is the wearing away of self-confidence and self-esteem.

Over a decade ago, Louise Hard wrote about the lingering discourse of niceness and a culture which condones behaviours that marginalize and excludes some individuals. Her piece, reprinted in this book, stands as a testament to the glacial pace at which change is (or is not) occurring. This chapter focuses on the examples of horizontal violence in spaces that some might consider to be the height of caring and compassion, the profession of childhood education and care (ECEC). Hard is exploring aspects of leadership enactment and the ways in which horizontal violence limits and constrains leadership.

Next, Janes and Carter continue the leadership conversation by examining the ways in which leadership opportunities for women are thwarted through what they introduce as DIM (dissonance, incivility and microaggression). The authors delineate the contrasting tensions between perceptions and the lived experiences of women in leadership.

Optimistically, they write, "women's capacity for relation, facilitative, and collaborative leadership foreshadow an important place for women in the 21st century university" (Chapter 11, p. 209). We hear sentiments echoed in this chapter that were explored by Ruder, Plaza, Warner and Bothwell in Chapter 7, namely the ways in which institutions of higher education continue to be bastions of male normed behaviours and practices, diminishing the leadership potential of women.

This section concludes with a chapter by Davey, who broaches the concept of hierarchies and reciprocal learning through the lens of micro-aggression, as she explores experiences of youth interactions with prison guards. Davey dissects and interrogates the language prison guards' use with inmates and with each other, and the ways in which microaggressions can be recognized. As she writes, "These stories point to the benefits of positive *micro-messaging* in spaces of containment, a potentially powerful tool to disrupt incivilities experienced by those who work on the inside" (Chapter 12, p. 231).

Towards Systemic Change

Finally, section three, *Towards Systemic Change*, examines strategies for progressive transformation. Here, the contributors explore the potential for a culture of opportunity and the ways in which to work towards systemic, collegial and interpersonal restructuring.

This section begins with a chapter by Saloojee and Saloojee who offer an analysis of race, racism and the everyday experiences of people of colour in the academy. The authors challenge Canadian researchers to build upon critical race theory frameworks and to enhance the taxonomy of racial microaggressions. The authors write, "If we argue that racist and sexist microaggressions are to be understood in the context of the multiple forms of systemic and structural discrimination then it is important to separate anti-discrimination policies and procedures from these civility policies" (Chapter 13, p. 249).

In Chapter 14, Peachey and McCullough explore the ways in which new nursing graduates might be better prepared to deal with lateral violence and build a comportment of resilience through international preceptorships. From a pragmatic approach, nursing graduates need to identify, understand and face the complexity of health care and the high likelihood of workplace adversity as they gain professional experience.

Rourke and Carter continue the discussion of hierarchical layers and practices through their exploration of building multigenerational teams and add a new dimension to the conversation: the ways in which age and experience impact, preserve and exacerbate experiences. The disparities between baby boomer leaders and millennial staff can create unique challenges for both groups. This circumstance may derive from different visions of leadership and workplace structure and is not unique to universities.

In our rapidly growing age of technology, building off of the millennial/baby boomer debate in the previous chapter, Pringle examines the online environment and "digital infractions" and the ways in which social infrastructure can be developed for the online world in order to provide a framework by which we can start to mitigate microaggressions online. As she writes, "these shared digital spaces have become hijacked by the toxic minority, whose vitriolic presence often overwhelms any attempt at dialogue or debate" (Chapter 16, p. 309).

Finally, this section closes with an essay by Koivukoski, which draws from classical literature and political science to offer insights into the human condition in relation to violence. As he writes, "For human societies get it wrong sometimes; they encode patterns of domination into the very structures of state and institutions, making objects, slaves, and resources of human beings where respect and recognition ought to be the hallmarks of civility" (Chapter 17, p. 327).

CONCLUSION

This book serves to extend and broaden the conversation of microaggressions, lateral violence and incivility by exploring its occurrence in a variety of professions and across various sectors—work environments, social and institutional systems. While each chapter can stand alone, we believe the narrative threads are stronger when read as a whole. Some contributors begin a conversation that is deepened by another. We believe this book will serve as a strong source of general information about lateral (horizontal) violence, microaggressions and incivility and as such will spur current research and thinking in professional workplace aggression and conflict resolution as well as encourage research in new directions in the field. We also expect that this book will be incredibly useful in supporting thinking and planning to address workplace aggression and to enable organizations and communities to understand that microaggression, incivility and lateral violence should not be accepted as a standard operating procedure but rather are evidence of social hostilities that diminish everyone's capacity to fully participate in society.

REFERENCES

Andersson, L. M., & Pearson, C. M. (1999). Tit for tat? The spiraling effect of incivility in the workplace. *Academy of Management Review, 24*(3), 452–471.

Augoustinos, M., & Every, D. (2007). The language of "race" and prejudice: A discourse of denial, reason, and liberal-practical politics. *Journal of Language and Social Psychology, 26*(2), 123–141.

Ceravolo, D. J., Schwartz, D. G., Foltz-Ramos, K. M., & Castner, J. (2012). Strengthening communication to overcome lateral violence. *Journal of Nursing Management, 20*(5), 599–606.

Crenshaw, K. (1991). Mapping the margins: Intersectionality, identity politics, and violence against women of color. *Stanford Law Review, 43*(6), 1241–1299.

McKenna, B. G., Smith, N. A., Poole, S. J., & Coverdale, J. H. (2003). Horizontal violence: Experiences of registered nurses in their first year of practice. *Journal of Advanced Nursing, 42*(1), 90–96.

Sue, D. W., Capodilupo, C. M., Torino, G. C., Bucceri, J. M., Holder, A., Nadal, K. L., & Esquilin, M. (2007). Racial microaggressions in everyday life: Implications for clinical practice. *American Psychologist, 62*(4), 271.

Wetherell, M., & Potter, J. (1992). *Mapping the Language of Racism*. London: Harvester Wheatsheaf.

PART I

Explorations of Disruption

The Metamorphosis of Prejudice-Based Discourse: Change of Form, Continuity of Being

David Starr-Glass

Introduction

In the United States of America, Title VII of the 1964 Civil Rights Act is often seen as the legislative centerpiece in attempts to significantly reduce—if not to totally eliminate—racial and gender-based discrimination in the workplace. Although Title VII had a somewhat checkered history, it did contribute greatly to the elimination of blatantly discriminatory practices in workplace hiring, promotion, and advancement (Carle, 2011; Hirsch & Youngjoo, 2017). Yet, despite the reduction of discriminatory practices in the work-world, everyday prejudice-centered aggression still remains a common feature of many social and organizational settings (Namie, 2014; Nielsen, Notelaers, & Einarsen, 2011).

Although aggression continues to exist, it is generally observed that there has been a shift in the tenor of the post-Title VII discourse—a move toward more muted and nuanced forms of abuse and toward more surreptitious and insidious forms of implied racism and sexism.

D. Starr-Glass (✉)
International Programs, SUNY Empire State College,
Prague, Czech Republic

© The Author(s) 2018
C. L. Cho et al. (eds.), *Exploring the Toxicity of Lateral Violence and Microaggressions*, https://doi.org/10.1007/978-3-319-74760-6_2

13

In turn, some have seen this shift in the nature of discriminatory and prejudice-based discourse as mirroring a move away from old confrontational racism toward a newer *aversive racism*, in which open hostility and hatred ended, only to be replaced by "discomfort, uneasiness, disgust, and sometimes fear" (Dovidio & Gaertner, 2004, p. 4).

Many prejudice-based remarks are subtle in nature, have a seemingly inconsequential content, and are made by those who "believe they are acting free from prejudice and may be unaware that their decision-making negatively impacts black workers" (Ritenhouse, 2013, p. 98). Indeed, it is common for contemporary prejudice-based discourse to be framed in ways that suggest—or which explicitly declare—that it is grounded in a denial of ethnic prejudice or in a repudiation of racism or sexism, even though an objective analysis of its content would indicate quite the opposite (Augoustinos & Every, 2007; Mitchell, Every, & Ranzijn, 2011). Most perpetrators insist there is no racist or sexist agenda; however, they may concede that they have inadvertently created the impression of *microaggressions, micro*assaults, *micro*insults, and *micro*invalidations in the minds of the targets. But, they argue, even if this has occurred: (a) the perceived offense lies more in the sensitivities and sensibilities of the targets than in the words of the suspected perpetrators; and (b) that in any case, even the targets involved concede that these are only "micro" incivilities—where "micro" reasonably and objectively represent the magnitude of the damage caused and the inconsequentiality of the incivility employed (Caplan & Ford, 2014; Forrest-Bank & Jenson, 2015; Sue, Bucceri, Lin, Nadal, & Torino, 2009).

This chapter argues that prejudice-based aggression and incivility have neither fundamentally changed nor simply accommodated to evolving social norms. Confrontational prejudiced aggression—whether grounded in ethnicity, racism, sexism, ageism, or sexual orientation—has not been replaced by microaggression through a process of linear change that disconnects, separates, and distances current microaggression from cruder historic forms of prejudiced aggression. Instead, the violence that lies at the heart of prejudice-based violence remains present and potent, but it has undergone a *metamorphosis*—a change of form and substance, but a change that has left its virulent essence intact.

Drawing on the process and dynamics of metamorphoses, it is argued that metamorphic changes—unlike discrete and progressive linear changes—are always associated with ambiguous boundaries, contradictory perceptions, and perplexing liminalities. The unresolved and cognitively troubling qualities that resonate within all metamorphic changes contribute toward the lingering, but curiously unspecific, sense of hurt and damage produced by repeated microaggression assaults.

The first section considers the shift from what has been termed *old-fashioned* prejudice to its modern form. The second section analyzes the processes and dynamics of metamorphosis, and argues that these are helpful in reconsidering the present nature of prejudice-centered discourse. The third section explores the consequences, ambiguities, and the disruptive nature of this metamorphosis in contemporary prejudice-based aggression. The concluding section briefly reviews some of the main issues presented in the chapter and looks at an alternative metamorphic system that may well become increasingly important in understanding future political, social, and organizational contexts within which prejudice-based aggression occurs.

Shifting Patterns and Manifestations of Prejudiced Discourse

Reviewing the 25-year-course of federal statutory law and US Supreme Court decisions designed to eliminate racial discrimination, Freeman (1978) divides the period into three eras: (a) 1954–1965—the era of uncertainty (the jurisprudence of violations); (b) 1965–1974—the era of contradiction (the jurisprudence of remedy); and (c) post-1974—the era of rationalization (the jurisprudence of cure). This analysis points to a sequence—perhaps even to a progression—and may also contain the implicit hope that a rational process led from an era of *uncertainty* to a period of *judicial cure*. And yet, even in this apparently hope-filled progression, there lurk a number of unanticipated consequence and unwanted outcomes. As Freeman (1978) warns:

> for just as surely as the law has outlawed racial discrimination, [so too] it has affirmed that Black Americans can be without jobs, have their children in all-black, poorly funded schools, have no opportunities for decent housing, and have very little political power, without any violation of antidiscrimination law. (p. 1050)

It would seem that legislation, by focusing on manifest behavior that is confrontational, personal, and blatantly discriminatory has left untouched—and in that sense has implicitly affirmed—a deep racial sentiment that is submerged, societal, and systematic.

Adopting a critical analysis and assuming what he terms a *victim's perspective*, Freeman (1978) further suggests that this sequentially divided trajectory of anti-discrimination law—irrespective of its contradictory and perverse ending—is a common and inevitable feature of all attempts to reconstruct the history of a socially embedded judicial system. In reaching his conclusions, Freeman (1978) notes that he "cannot regard the Court as autonomous and separate from the society that orchestrates it and therefore cannot regard that one institution as the villain of the tale" (p. 1119). Many regard Freeman's linear trajectory of anti-discrimination law as particularly telling and predict that similar conflicting and pernicious outcomes will also be associated with current LGBT anti-discrimination legislation (Chang, 2016; Kang & Banaji, 2006).

Despite the significant impact of Title VII of the 1964 Civil Rights Act and the legal decisions that surrounded it, racial discrimination has not been eliminated even though discriminatory workplace practices have been curtailed. However, many believe that there has been a shift in the *nature* of racist and similar prejudice-based discourse, and in the ways in which it is communicated. For example, it has been argued that *old-fashioned* racist and sexist bigotry, which involved "unconcealed contempt, endorsement of offensive stereotypes, and support for blatant discrimination against women and people of color... underwent a *radical decline* in the United States in the latter half of the 20th century" (Cortina, Kabat-Farr, Leskinen, Huerta, & Magley, 2013, p. 1583, emphasis added).

Similarly, it has been argued that confrontational and belligerent prejudice-based racism has morphed into an *aversive racism* that is grounded in negative attitudes toward people of color, but which is now espoused by those who claim they abhor such attitudes, hold egalitarian perspectives, and denounce racial prejudice (Dovidio & Gaertner, 1998; Dovidio, Gaertner, Niemann, & Snider, 2001). Likewise, in its present form, *modern sexism* projects a "denial of continued discrimination, antagonism toward women's demands, and lack of support for policies designed to help women" (Swim, Aikin, Hall, & Hunter, 1995, p. 199).

Many consider that the recasting of discriminatory-based prejudice is a response to shifts in social understandings and cultural norms that make blatant sexist and racial assaults unacceptable, indefensible, and generally illegal (Barreto, Ryan, & Schmitt, 2009; Brief, Dietz, Cohen, Pugh, & Vaslow, 2000; Yamada, 2013). Strangely, this shift in prejudice-based and discriminatory aggression has also been accompanied by an increasing spiral of general *workplace incivility*, defined as "low-intensity deviant behavior with ambiguous intent to harm the target, in violation of workplace norms for mutual respect... behaviors [that] are characteristically rude and discourteous, displaying a lack of regard for others" (Andersson & Pearson, 1999, p. 457). Although workplace incivility has been considered a general disposition, when targeted toward women and people of color it often represents itself more unequivocal as specific and *selective incivilities* grounded in racial and sexist prejudice, resentment, and hostility (Cortina et al., 2013; Kabat-Farr & Cortina, 2012).

Further, in the workplace—and in other organizational and social setting—many aggressive prejudice-based behaviors take the form of what have been termed *microaggressions*. Microaggressions can take a number of forms and have been defined in different ways:

- Subtle, stunning, often automatic, and non-verbal exchanges which are "put downs" (Pierce, Carew, Pierce-Gonzalez, & Willis, 1978, p. 66).
- Subtle insults (verbal, nonverbal, and/or visual) directed toward people of color, often automatically or unconsciously (Solórzano, Ceja, & Yosso, 2000, p. 60).
- Brief, everyday exchanges that send denigrating messages to people of color because they belong to a racial minority group (Sue et al., 2007, p. 273).

Although originally put forward to designate negative and offensive behavior in racist contexts, the construct of the microaggression has also been associated with—and has shed light on—other forms of discriminatory-based abuse centered on gender, ethnicity, and sexual orientation (Wong, Derthick, David, Saw, & Okazaki, 2014). The following examples, provided by Sue (2010a), are microaggressions that have been casually made and which contain a hidden, but not particularly subtle, prejudice-based message:

- I mean, you got the first mainstream African-American who is articulate and bright and clean and a nice-looking guy. I mean, that's a storybook, man (p. 11, referring to U.S. presidential candidate Obama).
- A lesbian client in therapy reluctantly disclosed her sexual orientation to a straight male therapist by stating that she was "into women." The therapist indicated he was not shocked by this disclosure because he once had a client who was "into dogs" (p. 14).

- A blind man reports that, when people speak to him, they often raise their voices. A well-meaning nurse was actually "yelling at him" when giving him directions on taking his medication. He replied to her: "Please don't raise your voice, I can hear you perfectly well" (p. 14).

Microaggressions and microinvalidations are "usually delivered by well-intentioned individuals who are unaware that they have engaged in harmful conduct toward a socially devalued group" (Sue, 2010b, p. 3). Perpetrators are usually left perplexed and annoyed, since they genuinely believe themselves to be free of gender, racial, or ethnic animosity. For them, the very accusation of microaggression is interpreted as a form of abusive victimization in which *they* are cast as the victims of duplicity, deceit, and ill-intent (Campbell & Manning, 2014; Wells, 2013). Further, the targets of microaggression also have to deal with the persistent and ambiguous nature of intent. Are they *really* the targets of this veiled and uncalled for hostility? Are they imposing upon themselves a reflexive victimhood and—albeit unwittingly—*complicit* in the pain and psychic discomfort that they experience?

Overt hostility is distinctly unpleasant, but it is in plain view and can be recognized and responded to. However, *latent abuse* (which might or might not have been intended) and *ambiguous prejudiced discourse* (which might or which might not have been expressed) can generate persistent self-doubt, debilitating anxiety, and personal damage that may be even more significant than overt discriminatory-based violence and explicit bigoted venom. For the targets of microaggression, their confusion and discomfort are understandable because they consider that the crude expression of prejudice-based violence is a thing of the past—a condition that has been contained, isolated, and frozen in a linearly constructed and historically envisaged past.

A linear change perspective recognizes a progression from what was to what is: the past is separated and isolated from the present. In a linear change narration, we make sense of the present by seeing it as an outcome or consequence of what has come before. The present is connected to the past through a chain of change-events in which each link possesses its own integrity and separateness. Just as the linear chain of change connects present and past, so too it distances them. From this perspective, microaggression may have been rooted in blatant prejudice-based hostility but those roots lie in a distanced past, have withered, and have no substantial connection with the present. From this perspective, linear change is reassuring because it represents an advance—a *moving forward* that distances us from what may have been a troubled past; a *shifting position*, in which the present is unfettered from what went before and in which "what went before" is no more than a historical footnote, not a part of active memory.

The Process and Dynamics of Metamorphosis

Metamorphosis has a long history, originating in Greek mythology and being somewhat reformulated and advanced in the works of the Roman poet Ovid some two thousand years ago, particularly in his epic *Metamorphoses*, which contains more than two hundred examples of metamorphic change. In its Ovidian sense, metamorphosis is a dramatic and enduring transformation from one state of being to another through which "a departure from the norm—often a transgression—is fixed forever by a change into a non-human state, frequently one… appropriate to the nature of the transgression or abnormality" (Buxton, 2013, p. 49).

In the ancient Greek view of the created world, there was no hermetic seal between the realms of mortals and immortals. There was an assumed hierarchy between mortals and immortals—and certainly among immortals—with different characteristics attributed to each, but there was also a great fluidity in terms of contact, communication, and interaction between deities and humans. One key difference between mortals and immortals was that the wishes of the gods, once expressed, could neither be rescinded nor changed. The conduct of mortals was more predictable, often preordained, and irrevocably linked to their assigned fate. However, not infrequently, the deities realized that the enduring nature of their own actions could have unanticipated and disturbing consequences for mortals.

For example, when the god Apollo encountered the nymph Daphne he was consumed by lust and pursued her with rape in mind. Once set in motion, the intended sexual violence and the resulting degradation of Daphne were inevitable—in worldly terms the outcomes could not be stopped, in mythical terms the skeins of fate could not be untangled. However, these seemingly inevitable outcomes offended and angered the gods, particularly Daphne's father. So, in order to prevent the offending act, the gods intervened by *freezing the moment* in time and not allowing the event to materialize. When it seemed inevitable that the rape would occur, the nymph Daphne was metamorphosed into a laurel tree. In this, as in all metamorphoses:

> There is a radical change in category, from god to man, from divine being to tree, or from human being to animal, there nevertheless remains a continuity of identity... [even though] the protagonists changed his or her outward appearance, the core of their being, the inside, remained unchanged. (Takács, 2008, pp. 73–74)

Metamorphosis is a process, not simply an outcome or an event. To appreciate the process of metamorphosis, its internal logic, and its operating dynamics the following points are useful.

Preservation of original identities: Metamorphosis changes the external form of the entity but preserves its original identity as an internal quality of the new object. Metamorphosis rearranges the boundaries that define and categorize the living Daphne, and uses these altered boundaries to redefine and recategorize what is apparently a quite different entity: a tree. However, Daphne does not *become* a tree nor does she lose her former being. Rather, the essential identity of Daphne *remains present* and is accessible in the flowers, leaves, bark, and aromatic pungency of the laurel. Metamorphosis preserves and perpetuates original identity. In the classical Greek worldview, metamorphosis was considered a form of immortality that guaranteed continuity of existence, and—through shared narratives and collective remembrance—an enduring cultural presence.

Persistence of original traumas: Although metamorphosis constitutes a means of obtaining immortality, what is recognized and remembered is not simply the generality of the individual's existence but the specifics surrounding the transformation. The immortality gained through metamorphosis is neither desired nor blissful. What endures is *the fateful moment*—often charged with terror, despair, and significant trauma—that precipitated the metamorphosis. Ovidian metamorphoses are not a collection of quaint myths that explain the natural world or which provide colorful and otherwise hidden meanings of that world. Instead, they shock us into peeling back the layers of ordinariness that surround the familiar and exposing an unexpected and disturbing interiority. Metamorphosis insists that preserved within familiar forms there is a hidden core that resonates with our deeper being, emotions, and humanity. The laurel does not preserve a youthful and ephemeral nymph; it embodies the moment of Daphne's anguish, pain, and trauma.

At first glance, metamorphosis seems to involve people and natural objects. However, what it really deals with is the continuing and accessible presence of personal experiences, feelings, and emotions—usually dark, painful, and at the limit of endurance.

Insistency on liminality: At its core, metamorphosis involves an excursion into *liminality*—that is, into a zone of betwixt and between that joins the before and the after, separates the before from the after, and yet belongs to neither. As Turner (1969) put it, liminality is "a cultural realm that has few or none of the attributes of the past or coming state" (p. 94). Liminality is a moment that is passively lived in—a moment in which the past, present, and future are perpetually present but equally unreachable. It is true that with some *linear changes* a liminal zone can exist between what came before and what will come later. Van Gennep (1960/1909) observes that social life is itself a "series of passages from one age to another and from one occupation to another... life comes to be made up of a succession of stages with similar ends and beginnings" (p. 3). This succession is tripartite, with each stage having: (a) an initial phase, which represents a clear and discernable break from the past; (b) a liminal phase (L. *limen* = threshold), which is indeterminate and belongs to neither past nor future; and (c) a terminal phase, in which the new role, social status, or changed identity are recognized.

In linear change, what presently exists may have a remembered past—a history that has shaped it and in which it is embedded—but there is a discontinuity between the present and the past. If there is liminality in linear change it exists as a bounded zone, not as a permanent feature. However, in a metamorphic change there is *only* an ongoing and irrevocable assumption of liminality—there is neither a separated initial phase nor a resolution through an equally separated terminal phase. Metamorphosis ruptures the presumed continuities and established logics of linear change. It is an invitation—more properly, it is an insistence— to enter into the unsettling realm of ambiguity, disruptive possibility, and fluid liminality where past and present coexist without resolution. Liminal experiences can provoke surprise and liberation; more often, they generate a sense of perplexity, disorientation, and unease.

Invitation to continuous reimagination: Metamorphosis challenges us to consider what we encounter in the world through the recognized lens of our own limitations, expectations, and imagination. Metamorphic narratives invite us to encounter forces that are independent of us—forces that shape and change, but which are beyond our locus of control. The world of ancient Greece recognized that there were potent supernatural and theological forces that might be recognized. In our contemporary world there is often an understanding that what we encounter is shaped by powerful social and cultural forces that we recognize, barely understand, and cannot alter. Metamorphosis contains more wonder than reason, more questions than answers. Buxton (2009) sees metamorphosis as expressing the "astounding, destabilizing irruption of divinity, and the existence of remarkable continuities between human life and the natural environment. Stories told in this tradition were a way of articulating, and perhaps even partially coping with, the astonishing strangeness of life's outcomes" (Buxton, 2009, p. 252).

In metamorphic changes, the past is continuously present even though it is partially obscured by a novelty of form. In metamorphosis, there is a constant fluidity between what was and what is—both past and present are contiguous states, not separated ones. Metamorphosis provides us with a present in which the past is copresent, perpetually accessible, and incapable of being distanced—even from a past that is not apparent. The narratives of metamorphosis lead us into unexpected continuities, liminal zones, and re-formations of the present. These nonlinear complexities provide different modes of sense-making and unexpected ways of coping with the astonishing strangeness of life's outcomes.

THE CONSEQUENCES AND DISRUPTIVENESS OF METAMORPHOSIS

The forms of racism and the expressions of racial aggression have changed; however, these changes are not part of a linear sequence but rather of metamorphosis. Fleras (2016), reviewing the changes from direct racism—which he terms "Racism 1.0"—to indirect racism (Racism 2.0), and then to the microaggression (Racism 3.0), notes that there has been a shifted "burden of proof in defining how racialized information is perceived, processed, and communicated—namely, from a type of condition that is experienced to a claims-making process in defining the problem" (p. 12). In this repositioning from an existing condition to a problematic process, Fleras (2016) also detects "a sharp reminder that neither racism nor the war on racism are hardly over.... they just keep reinventing themselves" (p. 15). In this chapter, the process of *reinvention* is understood from a perspective of metamorphosis—the creation of an apparently new and distinct form that incorporates, preserves, and vitally sustains a previous identity.

The core quality of racism and other prejudice-based behavior is aggression. Within the context of the workplace, aggression takes multiple forms that include organizational bullying, managerial hostility, worker incivility, abusive supervision, and more. Indeed, a significant problem associated with understanding aggression in the workplace is that it has been splintered into such a broad range of seemingly distinct, separate, and independent constructs. These multiple perspectives, expressions, and consequences of aggression tend to draw attention away from its core quality and to obscure the centrality of the aggressive violence that produces all forms of prejudice-based discourse. However, despite the complexity and confusion of aggressive splintering, "meta-analytic research that compares these constructs against a series of consequences has found that, by and large, there is little to no difference in the magnitude of consequences from these different constructs" (Hershcovis, Reich, & Niven, 2015, p. 4).

In the workplace setting, aggression is understood as behavior directed toward another with the intent to cause *harm*, even though the perpetrator who initiates such behavior might be: (a) personally unaware of the specific nature of the harm produced; (b) personally unconcerned or ignorant about the extent, or the consequential impact, of the harm caused; and (c) equally ignorant, unaware, or unconcerned about the personal identity of the target (Anderson & Bushman, 2002; Barling, Dupré, & Kelloway, 2009).

In these definitions and expressions, aggression is not a reified object—a *thing* that exists independently in an external world—but a personally and socially constructed phenomenon. Aggression initially comes into being in the mind and is subsequently expressed, communicated, and directed toward others who then construct their own meaning of that behavior. Aggression is the outcome of an actively interpreted process, not a passively existing condition. Viewed from a social constructivist perspective, racial aggression is ultimately "defined as racist and worked into existence as a lived reality through meaningful interaction and interpretive practices" (Fleras, 2016, p. 15).

Prejudice-based aggression has often been understood in linear terms. In that understanding, prejudice-based aggression has undergone irrevocable shifts in its nature and, viewing the progression of these stages and epochs, the progression is seen as moving toward its reduction, if not extinction. It has shifted from its overt and confrontational manifestations to more subtle and nuanced microaggressions, in which racism (and other prejudice-based hostility) is "increasingly framed as banal—even boring—rather than egregious, routine rather than exceptional, mundane rather than extraordinary, insidious rather than invidious, implicit rather than explicit, consequential rather than intentional, constructed rather than inherent, and fundamental rather than accidental" (Fleras, 2016, p. 15).

As Jeannine Bell (2015) notes:

> In an era in which no one admits to being a racist, white supremacists who engage in hate murders seem weirdly *anachronistic*. In some ways, we only have ourselves to blame for our shock that such incidents can occur. It is our *denial of the existence* of racism which makes such incidents seem as if they are wholly out of place in contemporary American society. (p. 376, emphasis added)

Anachronism (Greek: *ana-chronismós =* backward + time) comes into play from a linear change perspective, in which there is a constructed temporal sequence that has a past distanced from the present. Anachronism is *never* a feature of metamorphosis, because past and present are copresent, not artificially or arbitrarily distanced, and cojoined in what has been termed the perpetual present tense. Metamorphosis preserves liminality by freezing the crossing from one border to another, from what was to what is. The essence of Daphne—specifically her enduring fear and her unresolved anguish—is presently accessible in the aromatic leaves of the laurel. It is this unexpected fluidity and unresolved shift in form, but not in the essence of existence, that is so bewildering, disconcerting, and troubling for those who encounter metamorphic narratives—and for those who encounter microaggression beside the watercooler.

Old-fashioned prejudice and contemporary microaggression may seem to have different forms, but each form contains prejudice-based aggression as an active and palpable reality. In metamorphosis there may be a sense of surprise and wonderment, but there is also the recognition of a transcending—and often an unwished for—continuity that provides a new expression for an unforgotten past. This is unlike linear change, where the recognition of fractured links in the chain, or troublesome regressions back toward what has been, can elicit a sense of shock and even a sense of misplaced self-blame. But if there is any blame in linear change, it is not connected with the *acknowledgement* of the hurt of microaggression or with its unexpected occurrence. Rather, any blame needs to be attached to our *failure to acknowledge* that prejudice-based hostility and hatred can flourish in the present.

AFTERTHOUGHTS: OVIDIAN METAMORPHOSIS OR NONNIAN SHAPE-SHIFTING?

The argument in this chapter is that changing forms of prejudice-based aggression and incivility are better considered as metamorphic rather than as linear. In this argument, the processes and dynamics of metamorphosis are drawn from the mythical narratives of Ovid. Ovidian metamorphoses—which are a familiar part of Western literature and culture—all possess the same underlying logic and all feature what the ancient Greek world considered aberration of behavior and violations of justice. However, there exists an older set of metamorphoses that were recorded by the Greek poet Nonnus in his *Dionysiaca*. Indeed, in *Metamorphoses*, Ovid retold and recast a number of these older Nonnian metamorphoses.

In Ovid, the compelling rationale for metamorphosis was that a sequence of events, if allowed to run their course, would cause affront to the sensibilities of the immortals or would disrupt the notions of social order and natural justice that they had embedded in their created world. However, if Ovidian metamorphosis is about *justice*, it must be kept in mind that it was a very particular concept of justice because "in the epic world of the *Metamorphoses*, in which divine power determines all, there is little purpose in discussing justice in human terms" (Hawes, 2008, p. 24).

Nonnian metamorphoses have a different underlying logic and purpose: (a) they were generally prompted by strategic necessity and advantage, rather than by traumatic events; (b) they occurred in a deliberate and premeditated manner, rather than spontaneously; (c) they were temporary and usually reversible, rather than permanent; (d) they were almost always restricted to the lives and worlds of the immortals, rather than mortals; and (e) perhaps most spectacularly, they were self-initiated, rather than externally imposed. In sum, Nonnian metamorphoses accentuate deliberate, calculated, and repeated *shape-shifting* (Paschalis, 2014).

In Nonnian shape-shifting, the reason for transformation is not rooted in the justice of the immortals or even in the considerations of mortals. Instead, Nonnian shape-shifting is actively brought into play to deceive, to gain strategic advantage, or to evade. For example, Proteus, the ancient sea deity, had the ability to answer any question that was asked of him. However, he was reluctant to provide answers and avoided questioning by dramatically changing his shape and escaping in the resulting bewilderment. Shape-shifting was a deliberate and transitory act, initiated by Proteus himself and designed to confuse, baffle, and evade possible interrogation. Perhaps understandably, Proteus was viewed as a deceiver, a rogue, and a source of deliberate inconsistency and deception—an image widely perpetuated in Western literature and culture (Pesic, 2010).

During the course of writing this chapter, shifting political and rhetorical landscapes—in the United States and in Europe—have raised significant questions about the nature of the change in dynamics of prejudice-based discourse and behavior. It seems inescapable that the present manifestations of racism, xenophobia, sexism, and other prejudice-based hostilities are again changing and that they have not been permanently replaced by more muted and attenuated variants such as microaggression. This might strengthen arguments for metamorphosis. It might suggest that the change from blatant hostility and violence to microaggression was a change in form but not substance, and that a *second* metamorphosis is now underway that is again changing the form of prejudice-based microaggression while at the same time continuing to preserve its enduring violent essence. It might make sense, as has been argued, to see these change patterns as occurring at the surface, not at the core—as metamorphic sequences, not as linear discontinuities.

But two issues have not been addressed. In the dynamics of Ovidian metamorphosis, the triggering events were moral outrage and assertions of justice and the initiation was undertaken by the immortals. These are understandable in the context and worldview of Ovid, but if metamorphic change is a contemporary phenomenon why might it be presently triggered and by whom?

- Does metamorphosis occur at the level of the individual, where it provides the individual with a psychological mechanism for freezing what has become a painful and traumatizing situation?
- Is metamorphosis in some way a collective or social response to cope with socially destructive events or forces?
- In what circumstances is metamorphosis triggered and is it possible to identify the antecedents so that such changes can be anticipated?
- In what manner, and to what degree, might shape-shifting be self-initiated and used to confuse and disorientate the other?
- Are shifts in contemporary prejudice-based behavior and discourse more convincingly approached through the change-dynamics of Ovid or of Nonnus?

These are all open questions and they might promote further research within the scholarly community. Answers to them—and more especially the process of arriving at those answers—may also be of particular importance and concern for those confronting increased prejudice-based aggression, and more, besides the watercooler.

REFERENCES

Anderson, C. A., & Bushman, B. J. (2002). Human aggression. *Annual Review of Psychology, 53,* 27–51. https://doi.org/10.1146/annurev.psych.53.100901.135231.

Andersson, L. M., & Pearson, C. M. (1999). Tit for tat? The spiraling effect of incivility in the workplace. *Academy of Management Review, 24*(3), 452–471. https://doi.org/10.2307/259136.

Augoustinos, M., & Every, D. (2007). Contemporary racist discourse: Taboos against racism and racist accusations. In A. Weatherall, B. Watson, & C. Gallois (Eds.), *Language, Discourse and Social Psychology* (pp. 233–245). London, UK: Palgrave Macmillan. https://doi.org/10.1057/9780230206168_10.

Barling, J., Dupré, K. E., & Kelloway, E. K. (2009). Predicting workplace aggression and violence. *Annual Review of Psychology, 60,* 671–692. https://doi.org/10.1146/annurev.psych.60.110707.163629.

Barreto, M., Ryan, M. K., & Schmitt, M. T. (2009). *The Glass Ceiling in the 21st Century: Understanding Barriers to Gender Equality.* Washington, DC: American Psychological Association.

Bell, J. (2015). There are no racists here: The rise of racial extremism, when no one is racist. *Michigan Journal of Race & Law, 20*(2), 349–376.

Brief, A. P., Dietz, J., Cohen, R. R., Pugh, S. D., & Vaslow, J. B. (2000). Just doing business: Modern racism and obedience to authority as explanations for employment discrimination. *Organizational Behavior and Human Decision Processes, 81*(1), 72–97. https://doi.org/10.1006/obhd.1999.2867.

Buxton, R. (2009). *Forms of Astonishment: Greek Myths of Metamorphosis.* Oxford, UK: Oxford University Press.

Buxton, R. (2013). *Myths and Tragedies in Their Ancient Greek Contexts.* Oxford, UK: Oxford University Press.

Campbell, B., & Manning, J. (2014). Microaggression and moral cultures. *Comparative Sociology, 13*(6), 692–726. https://doi.org/10.1163/15691330-12341332.

Caplan, P. J., & Ford, J. C. (2014). The voices of diversity: What students of diverse races/ethnicities and both sexes tell us about their college experiences and their perceptions about their institutions' progress toward diversity. *Aporia, 6*(4), 30–69. Retrieved July 11, 2017, from http://www.oa.uottawa.ca/journals/aporia/articles/2014_10/Caplan_Ford.pdf.

Carle, S. D. (2011). A new look at the history of Title VII disparate impact doctrine. *Florida Law Review, 63*(1), 251–300.

Chang, R. S. (2016). Will LGBT antidiscrimination law follow the course of race antidiscrimination law? *Minnesota Law Review, 100,* 2103–2151.

Cortina, L. M., Kabat-Farr, D., Leskinen, E. A., Huerta, M., & Magley, V. J. (2013). Selective incivility as modern discrimination in organizations: Evidence and impact. *Journal of Management, 39*(6), 1579–1605. https://doi.org/10.1177/0149206311418835.

Dovidio, J. F., & Gaertner, S. L. (1998). On the nature of contemporary prejudice: The causes, consequences, and challenges of aversive racism. In J. L. Eberhardt & S. T. Fiske (Eds.), *Confronting Racism: The Problem and the Response* (pp. 3–22). Thousand Oaks, CA: Sage.

Dovidio, J. F., & Gaertner, S. L. (2004). Aversive racism. *Advances in Experimental Social Psychology, 36,* 1–52. https://doi.org/10.1016/S0065-2601(04)36001-6.

Dovidio, J. F., Gaertner, S. L., Niemann, Y., & Snider, K. (2001). Racial, ethnic, and cultural differences in responding to distinctiveness and discrimination on campus: Stigma and common group identity. *Journal of Social Issues, 57*(1), 167–188. https://doi.org/10.1111/0022-4537.00207.

Fleras, A. (2016). Theorizing microaggressions as racism 3.0: Shifting the discourse. *Canadian Ethnic Studies, 48*(2), 1–19. https://doi.org/10.1353/ces.2016.0011.

Forrest-Bank, S., & Jenson, J. M. (2015). Differences in experiences of racial and ethnic microaggression among Asian, Latino/Hispanic, Black, and White young adults. *Journal of Sociology & Social Welfare, 42*(1), 141–161.

Freeman, A. D. (1978). Legitimizing racial discrimination through antidiscrimination law: A critical review of Supreme Court doctrine. *Minnesota Law Review, 62,* 1049–1119.

Hawes, G. (2008). Metamorphosis and metamorphic identity: The myth of Actaeon in works of Ovid, Dante and John Gower. *Iris, 21,* 21–42. Retrieved July 11, 2017, from https://classicsvic.files.wordpress.com/2014/01/hawesvol21.pdf.

Hershcovis, M. S., Reich, T. C., & Niven, K. (2015). *Workplace bullying: Causes, consequences, and intervention strategies.* White Paper, International Affairs Committee of the Society for Industrial and Organizational Psychology. Bowling Green, OH: SIOP. Retrieved July 11, 2017, from http://www.siop.org/WhitePapers/WorkplaceBullyingFINAL.pdf.

Hirsch, E., & Youngjoo, C. (2017). Mandating change: The impact of court-ordered policy changes on managerial diversity. *ILR Review, 70*(1), 42–72. https://doi.org/10.1177/0019793916668880.

Kabat-Farr, D., & Cortina, L. M. (2012). Incivility: Gender, race, and the discriminatory workplace. In S. Fox & T. R. Lituchy (Eds.), *Gender and the*

Dysfunctional Workplace (pp. 107–119). Cheltenham, UK: Edward Elgar. https://doi.org/10.4337/9780857932600.00014.

Kang, J., & Banaji, M. R. (2006). Fair measures: A behavioral realist revision of affirmative action. *California Law Review, 94*(4), 1063–1118. https://doi.org/10.2307/20439059.

Mitchell, M., Every, D., & Ranzijn, R. (2011). Everyday antiracism in interpersonal contexts: Constraining and facilitating factors for "speaking up" against racism. *Journal of Community and Applied Social Psychology, 21*(4), 329–341. https://doi.org/10.1002/casp.1077.

Namie, G. (2014). *U.S. Workplace Bullying Survey*. Workplace Bullying Institute, Retrieved July 11, 2017, from http://www.workplacebullying.org/multi/pdf/WBI-2014-US-Survey.pdf.

Nielsen, M., Notelaers, G., & Einarsen, S. (2011). Measuring exposure to workplace bullying. In S. Einarsen, H. Hoel, D. Zapf, & C. L. Cooper (Eds.), *Bullying and Harassment in the Workplace: Developments in Theory, Research, and Practice* (2nd ed., pp. 149–174). Boca Raton, FL: CRC Press. https://doi.org/10.1201/EBK1439804896-9.

Paschalis, M. (2014). Ovidian metamorphosis and Nonnian poikilon eidos. In K. Spanoudakis (Ed.), *Nonnus of Panopolis in Context: Poetry and Cultural Milieu in Late Antiquity With a Section on Nonnus and the Modern World* (pp. 97–122). Berlin, Germany: De Gruyter. https://doi.org/10.1515/9783110339420.97.

Pesic, P. (2010). Shapes of Proteus in Renaissance art. *Huntington Library Quarterly, 73*(1), 57–82. https://doi.org/10.1525/hlq.2010.73.1.57.

Pierce, C., Carew, J., Pierce-Gonzalez, D., & Willis, D. (1978). An experiment in racism: TV commercials. In C. Pierce (Ed.), *Television and Education* (pp. 62–88). Beverly Hills, CA: Sage. https://doi.org/10.1177/001312457701000105.

Ritenhouse, D. (2013). Where Title VII stops: Exploring subtle race discrimination in the workplace. *DePaul Journal of Social Justice, 7*(1), 87–116.

Solórzano, D., Ceja, M., & Yosso, T. (2000). Critical race theory, racial microaggressions, and campus racial climate: The experiences of African American college students. *Journal of Negro Education, 69*(1/2), 60–73.

Sue, D. W. (2010a). *Microaggressions in Everyday Life: Race, Gender, and Sexual Orientation*. Hoboken, NJ: Wiley.

Sue, D. W. (2010b). *Microaggressions and Marginality: Manifestation, Dynamics, and Impact*. Hoboken, NJ: Wiley.

Sue, D. W., Bucceri, J., Lin, A. I., Nadal, K. L., & Torino, G. C. (2009). Racial microaggressions and the Asian American experience. *Asian American Journal of Psychology, S*(1), 88–101. https://doi.org/10.1037/1948-1985.S.1.88.

Sue, D. W., Capodilupo, C. M., Torino, G. C., Bucceri, J. M., Holder, A. M. B., Nadal, K. L., & Esquilin, M. (2007). Racial microaggressions in everyday life: Implications for clinical practice. *American Psychologist, 62*(4), 271–286. https://doi.org/10.1037/0003-066X.62.4.271.

Swim, J. K., Aikin, K. J., Hall, W. S., & Hunter, B. A. (1995). Sexism and racism: Old-fashioned and modern prejudices. *Journal of Personality and Social Psychology, 68*(2), 199–214. https://doi.org/10.1037/0022-3514.68.2.199.

Takács, S. A. (2008). Initiations and mysteries in Apuleius' metamorphoses. *Electronic Antiquity, 12*(1), 73–87. Retrieved July 11, 2017, from http://scholar.lib.vt.edu/ejournals/ElAnt/V12N1/takacs.pdf.

Turner, V. W. (1969). *The Ritual Process: Structure and Anti-Structure*. Chicago, IL: Aldine Publishing Company.

Van Gennep, A. (1960/1909). *The Rites of Passage*. Chicago, IL: University of Chicago Press.

Wells, C. (2013). Microaggressions in the context of academic communities. *Seattle Journal for Social Justice, 12*(2), Article 3. Retrieved July 11, 2017, from http://digitalcommons.law.seattleu.edu/sjsj/vol12/iss2/3.

Wong, G., Derthick, A. O., David, E. J. R., Saw, A., & Okazaki, S. (2014). The what, the why, and the how: A review of racial microaggressions research in psychology. *Race and Social Problems, 6*(2), 181–200. https://doi.org/10.1007/s12552-013-9107-9.

Yamada, D. (2013). Workplace bullying and the law: A report from the United States. In *Workplace Bullying and Harassment* (pp. 165–185). Tokyo, Japan: Japan Institute for Labor Policy and Training. Retrieved July 11, 2017, from http://www.jil.go.jp/english/reports/documents/jilpt-reports/no.12.pdf.

CHAPTER 3

"You Can Show a Person Better Than You Can Tell 'em": Black Tradeswomen Mitigate Racial and Gender Microaggressions in Construction

Roberta Hunte

Microaggressions are dehumanizing and contribute to a culture that dismisses the presence and potential of stigmatized identity groups. Microaggressions can be minor or major events in the life course of an employee. Such acts have a cumulative impact on the targeted person and microaggressions speak to the overarching environment of an institution or organization where the act occurred. Underlying microaggressions are attitudes and perceptions of the 'other' as less than or inferior to dominant groups. Stigmatized groups navigate these attitudes in the workplace and seek to continue employment despite an exclusionary climate. The following essay seeks to explore some of the ways microaggressive assumptions manifest in the lives of Black women in their careers as construction workers in the United States. Drawing from a narrative study I completed in (2012) (Hunte & Senehi), I will explore

R. Hunte (✉)
Child, Youth, and Family Studies, Portland State University,
Portland, OR, USA

© The Author(s) 2018
C. L. Cho et al. (eds.), *Exploring the Toxicity of Lateral Violence and Microaggressions*, https://doi.org/10.1007/978-3-319-74760-6_3

microaggressive themes and experiences at different points in Black tradeswomen's careers; some of the strategies women employed to mitigate the impacts of microaggressions; and discuss the role of management, including foremen, supervisors, training centers, and contractors in challenging or maintaining microaggressive attitudes and behaviors. From the narratives of Black tradeswomen, I am particularly interested in the potential opportunities for intervention that could foster a healthier work environment for women and people of color in an environment where both groups have experienced racism and sexism.

In 2008, I became a career counselor for Ready Tradeswomen (a pseudonym), a Northwestern US preapprenticeship construction training center whose mission was to bring more women into the construction workforce. Preapprenticeship programs are job training initiatives that teach people basic construction skills, introduce them to the industry, and prepare them for the competitive application process for apprenticeships. I worked with women and people of color to enter our program and to place them in construction-related jobs. Construction apprenticeships are the pathway to become a commercial construction worker, such as a plumber, laborer, carpenter, or cement mason. Preaapprenticeship programs have been used in the United States and Canada to prepare youth, people of color and women for the building trades. Apprenticeships range between two to five years of classes and thousands of work hours logged on the job. Apprentices increase their wage dependent on the hours of study and on-the-job training hours completed. An apprentice becomes a journeyman, or journey-level worker, upon completing their apprenticeships. Becoming a journeyman allows one to work nationally and internationally on commercial construction projects.

The United States opened construction apprenticeships to women in 1978 with Executive Order 11246, which prohibited discrimination against women on projects using federal monies. Prior to this the US construction industry was all male and predominately White. Men of color entered formal apprenticeships with the Civil Rights Act of 1964, which prohibited discrimination in the workplace based on race and sex. Women were to initially comprise 6.8% of construction apprentices on federal jobs with a goal of increasing this number over time. However, a combination of workplace sexism and racism, lack of commitment on the part of apprenticeships, unions, and employers to support the success of tradeswomen, and reduced federal oversight over affirmative action compliance have limited the numbers of tradeswomen to 2.6% of the construction workforce (National Women's Law Center, 2013).

Women of color make up less than one percent of the overall US construction workforce. Black women are 0.2%; Hispanic women account for 0.4%; Asian/Pacific Islander and American Indian/Alaska Native women respectively are 0.1% of all construction workers (National Women's Law Center, 2013). Obstacles for women and people of color in the building trades include overcoming structural and cultural barriers to their entrance into apprenticeship programs, conflict in the workplace, and long-term job retention. Working in the trades as a minority is a complex experience. Mastering the trade itself is challenging. Learning to negotiate the realities of racism, sexism, and at times heterosexism further complicates the experience.

In 2010, I began a narrative study of fifteen Black tradeswomen about the course of their trades careers as they navigated issues of race, gender, and sexuality over their careers. I focused on Black women as the nuanced experience of Black women are often lost in the women's movement and the broader movement for racial justice (Crenshaw, 1989). Study participants were carpenters, laborers, a cement mason, a sprinkler fitter, electricians, contractors, and technicians from different parts of the country. Their careers spanned six to thirty plus years. The women were at different points in their careers—retirement, mid-career, or recently journeyed out of apprenticeship. The majority of the women interviewed completed formal apprenticeships.

The methodology for this study is grounded in Black feminist thought, which is developed from an Afrocentric epistemology and based on Black women's self-definition (Collins, 1989). A core theme of Black women's struggle is an awareness of the experience at the intersection of race and gender oppression (Collins, 1989). I used narrative inquiry to analyze data. Women were interviewed. Data was coded to mark different stages of career progress. From this coding tightened to focus on race and gender-related experiences, and strategies employed to address these challenges. I shared my initial analysis of individual interviews with each participant and shared my final analysis of the collective data with all of the participants. This reflexivity deepened my analysis and contributes to Black Feminist theorizing as it brings the voices of Black women into conversation around their specific experiences of race and gender in the United States. As my data analysis continued, my leading research questions became: (1) What can we learn from the strategies Black tradeswomen use to negotiate race and gender in non-traditional work? (2) How does this deepen our understanding of the intersections of social identities in non-traditional labor? (3) How does intersectional analysis advance our understanding of individual responses to structural violence?

The following is a table listing the women interviewed, their trade, duration in the trades at the time of our initial interview, the highest position attained, and the regions of the United States where they worked. Women will be referred to according to pseudonyms throughout the chapter, with the exception of Kareema. I received specific Human Subjects approval to use Kareema Ali's real name in this study. She asked that her real name, and the name of her tradeswomen advocacy group, The National Coalition of Women of Color in Construction, be used.

Table 3.1 A table of interviewees

Name	Trade	Years in trade at interview	Highest position held in career	Position at time of interview	U.S. regions worked
Keisha	Carpenter (bridge construction)	30+	Superintendent	Superintendent (20 years with company)	NW and SW
Z	Carpenter (commercial)	6	Journeyman Crew Lead	Laid off (longest job 1 year)	NW
Shonda	Electrician (Inside Wireman)	30+	Foreman (commercial construction); Municipal Planner (Municipal Worker)	Municipal Planner (15 years with Municipality)	NW, SE, and NE
Sharla	Electrician (Low Voltage Electrician)	12	Special Projects Lead (commercial construction)	Special Projects Lead	NW, SW, NE, SE, and MW
Sandra	Electrician (Inside Wireman)	10	Journeyman Worker	Laid off (longest job 1 year)	MW
Debra	Electrician (Inside Wireman)	6	Sixth Term Apprentice	Laid off (longest job 1 year)	SW
Wanda Lou	Welder (entered the trades during WWII)	30+	Crew Lead	Retired from shipyards after 30 years of service	NW
Grace	Welder	30+	Crew Lead	Retired from shipyards after 30 years of service	NW

(continued)

Table 3.1   (continued)

Name	Trade	Years in trade at interview	Highest position held in career	Position at time of interview	U.S. regions worked
Crystal	Laborer	6	Journeyman Crew Lead	Laid off (longest job 2.5 years)	NW and SW
Danielle	Laborer	6	Journeyman	Laid off (longest job 1 year)	NW
Darnita	Laborer	10	Journeyman, Safety Coordinator, Traffic Control Supervisor, Compressed Air Worker	Safety Coordinator (longest job 5 years)	NW
Veronica	Utility Worker and Mill Worker	30+	Pump Technician	Pump Tech (with Municipality for 20 years	NW
Kareema*	Cement Mason	25+	Commercial Contractor	Family Owned Concrete Business throughout career	MW and S
Patricia	Sprinkler Fitter	20+	Commercial Contractor	General Construction Business Owner for over 12 years	NW
Sue	Electrician	6	Sixth Term Apprentice	Recruiter of minorities for Trades Careers and Contractor	NW

* Kareema asked that I use her real name, as opposed to a pseudonym in the study

OVERLAPPING MICROAGGRESSIONS

Sue's microaggression framework (2010) offers a way to categorize the covert and overt discriminatory incidents that people experience based on membership in a stigmatized group. Microaggressions come in the form of (a) microinsults which are often unconscious communications that are rude, insensitive, and demeaning of one's race, ethnicity, gender, sexual orientation, or ability status; (b) microassaults which are usually conscious, explicitly demeaning aggressions against one's race, gender, and/or sexual orientation in the form of discriminatory acts, violent verbal, nonverbal or environmental attack and its purpose is to harm the intended victim; and (c) microinvalidations which are communications which exclude, nullify, or negate the thoughts, feelings, and experiences of a person of color, woman, or sexual minorities (Sue, 2010). All of these serve the function of maintaining an oppressive and exclusionary system that promotes the stigmatization of people based on their identity group.

The Black women in my study revealed complex experiences of overlapping racial and gender-based microaggressions that occurred as episodic and at times chronic experiences throughout their careers. Though all of the women were Black they did not experience racism or sexism in the same way. There were similarities in their struggles as they came onto the job, and had interactions with supervisors, and/or coworkers.

The racial and gender microaggressive themes that emerged from Black women's narratives were: the assumption of inferiority, the myth of meritocracy, color- and gender-blindness, treatment as second-class workers, the denial of individual instances of racism and sexism, sexist and racist humor, invisibility, and being sexualized in the workplace. A handful of women in my study talked about microaggressions due to their sexual orientation—specifically the microaggressions of heterosexism, and the assumption of abnormality based on one's sexual orientation. I will highlight the dominate microaggression themes that emerged from my study and explore the impact of these incidents on tradeswomen's careers. I will then discuss the implications of this in terms of institutional responses to address racism and sexism in the building trades.

All of the women in my study worked the majority of their careers in predominately White environments. This created its own stress where women often felt hyper-scrutinized, and judged both for their race and gender. Women said they needed to demonstrate their worth to make space for other Black women to follow suit. In a study of Black women in various work environments, Hughes and Dodge (1997) found that Black women working in predominately White environments reported more racial and gender-based discrimination than Black women in predominately Black or more integrated workplaces. The presence of institutional discrimination and interpersonal prejudice were overarching indicators of job quality, more so than other stressors such as poor supervision, heavy workloads, and mundane work. This was true for the women I interviewed as well. Women encountered hostility during their apprenticeships, as journey-workers, as they moved into leadership roles, and as they became contractors. Women described the complexity of overlapping microaggressions. At times it was clear that the microaggressions were directed towards their race or gender, but often the intent behind the microaggressions was less clear. Women said what was clear was the familiarity of the encounters, and the negative impact these interactions had on their experience in the workplace.

Microaggressions and the Challenge of Invisibility

Each time a new apprentice comes onto a job they are to work with a new journeyman or journey-level worker. Journeyman is the term for a licensed construction worker. It is a gendered term, which in and of itself can be a form of gender microaggression. There is a movement to move towards gender-neutral terms, such as journey-level worker or journeyperson in the industry. Some tradeswomen welcome this as a challenge to patriarchy. Some feel they worked hard to become journeymen and that is what they are. In my study, this was not a major discussion, but it is one that training centers and unions are seeking to address.

The apprentice-journeyman relationship is the foundation of on-the-job training, whereby "on-the-job training" is the practical skills learning component of formal apprenticeships. Apprentices work for roughly 2000 hours a year alongside journey-level workers on construction sites. On the job apprentices apply the skills they have learned in apprenticeship classes and it is in this relationship that apprentices gain the work experience they need to be proficient in their work. Working alongside a journeyman who does not want to work with an apprentice, or does not know how to train an underling, can mean that the apprentice does not learn the skills they need to move through their apprenticeship. Racism and sexism can hinder that relationship and prevent women and men of color from developing in the industry. Critical points related to the apprenticeship process, which made Black women vulnerable to the direct and indirect impacts of microaggressions were: (1) at the application process; (2) entrance onto a jobsite as a new apprentice; (3) when working with a new journeyperson or crew; (4) getting trained and evaluated fairly; and (5) during efforts to complete the apprenticeship and continue working.

Becoming journeymen did not necessarily mean Black women were more accepted in the workplace than they were as apprentices. As journey-level workers, Black women had challenges similar to those of an apprentice, including: (1) working with coworkers who may be hostile to working with them; (2) being given marginal tasks; (3) safety concerns, such as being assigned tasks without the proper safety precautions in place or working with a peer who is acting in ways that can endanger the physical safety of other workers; (4) struggles to stay employed and continue with the same employer; and (5) limited avenues to challenge unfair working conditions and hiring practices.

Tradeswomen described encountering varying levels of aversion from colleagues to working with them. This aversion came in the form of indifference or blatant hostility. Z relays the following narrative about her experience as a carpenter apprentice. As an apprentice Z was treated as a second-class worker; she was given menial tasks for much of her first few years on the job. When a new superintendent came onto the job-site she was threatened with termination for the assumption of incompetence. Z said:

> I was working for a company, and my first two months of working there, they switched superintendents. We had progress reports that we had to fill out and turn in every month for the apprenticeship program. I've never gotten a bad written report. The first time that this new superintendent did my report, everything was bad. I'm looking at it and thinking, "We've never even worked together. How can you give me a bad grade and we don't even know each other?" [...] He said, "Well, the other carpenters say, you are lazy or you do this or do that."
>
> I said, "Okay, I hear what you're saying, but this isn't a third-party piece of paper. This piece of paper is based on what you think, and what you have observed. Have you observed me not doing my part out here?" [...] I have to answer to somebody about this. Somebody is going to ask me, "What is going on at the jobsite where you are not getting it right! We train you here, and you go out on the jobsite and you're still not getting it right? What is the problem?" You haven't put me alongside a journeyman to work with on a consistent basis enough for me to get everything. When we have a concrete pour and we're building forms and they're wondering why I don't know where to position stuff, it's because I've been under the bridge all day stacking wood."
>
> I think it resonated with him, because the next day, I was up on deck, working alongside a carpenter, doing what everybody else was doing. [...] If I hadn't said anything to him [...] I wouldn't know anything.

As a new apprentice Z was unaware that the tasks she was assigned were less technical than others on the site. Z's example demonstrates institutional and cultural discrimination that is faceless. As someone new to the culture she did not know it was happening. Though Z was able to advocate for herself and subsequently was given tasks that directly improved her skill-level, her story is indicative of how apprentices, especially non-traditional apprentices, can be consistently overlooked and stereotyped as inferior. This has a push-out effect that causes them to eventually leave the apprenticeship due to termination for underperformance or on their own volition.

The consistent experience of not being trained can also mean that people complete their apprenticeships without the appropriate skill knowledge to hold their own as journeymen. Training is an issue throughout the apprenticeship system, however the experience of being overlooked is amplified for women of color. Jones and Shorter-Gooden (2003) describe this experience of being *invisible* as a common feature of Black women's experience on the job. Z's story demonstrates the vulnerability of Black women when faced with an employer or journeymen who do not want them on the job or care about their success. Further her story demonstrates how the assumption of inferiority contributed to the superintendent's belief that Z was "lazy" based on the comments of anonymous journeymen. To counter the assumption of inferiority women in this study took construction classes to deepen their trades skills. Greater knowledge helped them feel competent at work, it did not always interrupt invisibility or the assumption of inferiority.

When entering a new jobsite tradeswomen may find that they are facing workers who are consciously or unconsciously hostile to working with them. The assumption of inferiority and treatment as second-class workers are microaggressions tradeswomen anticipate and strategize to combat as they move onto a jobsite. The following narrative speaks to both the ability to build relationships despite opposition, and the challenges of group hostility.

Breaking Through Resistance, One by One

Shonda, an electrician, described her experiences of trying to integrate into new crews as an electrical apprentice. Shonda was among the first women of color to become a journey-level electrician in her union. Confronting male aversion to working with her was a challenge, from meeting the contractor, to the foreman, to the journeyman she was to work alongside. Shonda found she could win over racist or sexist attitudes in one-on-one situations, but when working with a group of tradespeople this became impossible. Shonda's career has spanned over

25 years. She has an extensive track record to demonstrate her skills and has moved up the ranks on the construction jobsite, however, within the municipality where she worked, and within the union, the collective racism and sexism of her male colleagues often impacted her reputation and the way she was perceived. Throughout her career, she actively net-worked with her male colleagues as a type of damage control against men who publicly ridiculed her and tried to discredit her leadership within the union and on the job. Shonda related some of her challenges with male coworkers during her apprenticeship.

> They put me with this White guy who knew that the foreman was fucking with me. [...] He hated Black people so he really thought I was screwing with him. Well, I'm being myself and within four weeks this man was invit-ing me home for rabbit to meet the family. [...] One-on-one I can get you. I can connect with you. They can see my value system, my work ethic.

Shonda did not think all White people were out to get her; though she was sensitive to signs of discriminatory behavior. Shonda noted that her efforts meant that White men were more open to her, but not neces-sarily more open to other Black people and women.

If Shonda had not successfully won over her colleagues she would have lost her job. This was not about her skill as an electrician, but rather her ability to soften the attitudes of hostile colleagues. Shonda said she could not have progressed in her career without the men who were will-ing to give her a chance on the job. During her career, at times she had been an accepted member of the group and at other times not. Shonda credited career longevity in the same place as helping her build real rela-tionships with male coworkers. Mid-career she transitioned from com-mercial construction to a Municipal Electrical Department. Working for the municipality allowed relationships to be formed over time. This is in contrast to shorter jobs in commercial construction where people may work together for a few hours to a couple years depending on the work.

Learning to assess the cultural climate of the workplace and the actors involved is a subtle skill that Black tradeswomen describe as necessary for self-preservation in a competitive environment. Sandra, a fellow electrician, learned to "play psychologist" to understand her male coworkers. She said:

> So, besides trying to learn what I need to do and what I need to know [to stay] on the job I had to play psychologist so many times. You kind of feel people out, you know. You gotta get them to feel like they are comfortable

with you. They'll let you do what you need to do, learn from them. [...] I had to try to figure out how I was going to get past this so I could learn something.

In both Shonda and Sandra's cases, their approach was to build individual relationships. This meant analyzing individual coworkers and learning to overcome their resistance to them as tradeswomen and apprentices on the jobsite.

Keisha acknowledges the humanity of working for different supervisors. She says: "I figured out it's not the contractor that you work for. It's the person. They are humans, too. They make mistakes. They are incompetent. [...] You just can't judge people. I mean, you can show a person better than you can tell 'em." The comment, "You can show someone better than you can tell them," was a recurring comment among the participants. The default comment throughout the interviews was "let my work speak." Tradeswomen on commercial construction projects said they often faced a scarcity mentality on jobs where the presence of only a handful of women would be tolerated.

Intragroup Sexism

Study participants stated that gender microaggressions were nuanced and came from other women, White men, and men of color. With the high numbers of White men in construction, women expected to experience sexism from White men. They did not necessarily expect it from other women or Black men. The following seeks to explore this dynamic.

Black women have historically fought with Black men against racism. This remains true in the trades. However, Black male privilege in relation to women in general and Black women in particular is also present. Black patriarchal attitudes weaken the relationships between Black men and women, which are already affected by racial and class oppression (Woods, 2010). Women in my study said that their relationships with Black men were at best mutually supportive, and at worst Black men tried to sabotage their careers. Eisenberg (1998) in her study of tradeswomen described an alliance between men of color and White women on the jobsite. She found that men of color tended to treat the White women on site with respect, and support them against discriminatory behaviors from White tradesmen. She noted that this alliance was also built out of a history of men of color experiencing retaliation if they were perceived as harming White women. However, she noticed in her study that this alliance of mutual support was not necessarily extended from Black tradesmen towards Black tradeswomen. Similarly, Moccio (2009) found in her study of women in an electrical union that Black men were more inclined to collude with White men against Black women than to join in racial solidarity with Black women.

In her experience as a cement mason, Kareema found that Black tradesmen's fear that she was taking their jobs, or was more qualified than they, was a barrier at times in her career. Kareema moved to the Southern United States and joined one of the only predominately Black cement locals in the country. She thought that Black men would be more supportive of her than the White men she encountered in the Northern United States. Though highly skilled, Kareema was unable to find work as a journeyperson within her Southern cement union. Similarly, as a superintendent, Keisha observed that when Black men could benefit from joining with White men against her leadership, they would. Women were not immune to sexist thinking when faced with other women on the job.

Women observed that intense competition on the jobsite to remain working heightened tensions between women. Women also discussed the phenomenon of either distancing themselves from other women, or having other women do this to them. One woman shared that this distance from other women was a desire to not be categorized with them as inferior. Black women shared that this phenomenon impacted their relationships with other Black women and across race with White women.

Z relayed her worst experience of aggression between women on the jobsite. While a carpentry apprentice, she encountered a fellow tradeswoman on site. Z was excited as this was a rare occurrence. Instead of validating each other, the White tradeswomen told Z she would not make it as a carpenter. This assumption of inferiority undermined Z's abilities and right to be on the jobsite. The insulting experience had a lasting impression on Z's apprenticeship. She said:

> I knew she didn't want me there. It went from her being the only woman on the jobsite and her being babied, to me being another woman, a minority [Black person] on the jobsite. But I wasn't babied that much. I needed to work just as hard as everybody else. I ended up lasting longer in that company than she did.

Efforts Towards Intragroup Solidarity

For the Black tradeswomen in this study, intentional networks with other women and with Black men contributed to their long-term retention in the trades. Tradeswomen relayed experiences where Black men intentionally supported their presence in the trades. They did this by hiring Black tradeswomen, supporting their leadership, and sharing their knowledge as journeymen. They also worked with Black tradeswomen in their workplaces to challenge discrimination. In an environment with only a handful of men of color Darnita, a laborer, said of the Black tradesmen she encountered: "They're trying to hold onto their jobs. They're just lucky to be working." She acknowledged that Black men continued to struggle to advance up the leadership ladder. She gave the example of a colleague who worked for the same company for ten years and was continually passed over for promotion by White males newly brought into the company: "He's been with these cats for so long. They take these guys and make them foreman, right before him. I mean [White men are] just trying to help themselves. We all got to eat."

During the study, Darnita's job ended due to lack of work. She networked with a Black tradesman who owned his own business. She talked with him about joining his crew on an upcoming job. She said mainstream White contractors "are only hiring [Black people] because they have to. This brother is hiring me because he can." Her efforts were stymied by limited work from this contractor.

To counter mistrust between women some of the women discussed networking with tradeswomen outside of work through tradeswomen organizations. This gave women the opportunity to meet and connect in a neutral setting before they met at work. Creating networks is a key strategy to keep working in the trades. Two of the tradeswomen worked for the same employer for the majority of their careers. Their workplace had more than a handful of women on the job and women worked consistently for years on the site. These two factors lessened the competition between women. Having more women on the job meant that women were not interloper hires; more women on the job shifted the culture of the organization to be less resistant to the presence of women.

JOKES, SLURS AND GENDERED LANGUAGE

Sexist or racist jokes are a reality on jobsites. Wanda Lou had little patience with jokes. She said:

> You had a few prejudiced people. There's always going to be a few. I knew how to set them straight. [...] If they said something to me, I knew how to answer them back. I didn't let them get away with anything, period. I stopped them right then. As I said, I worked with men and I did not allow them to tell me jokes. If they were telling me a joke, I may say "Well, what did they want to do that for?" Kill the joke, you know. There wasn't anything to laugh at when I got through with them, because I made it stupid. I did not allow them to tell me jokes.

In preventing people from telling racist and sexist jokes Wanda Lou interrupted oppression and put a hard boundary around herself. Each woman had to figure out how she would negotiate these comments. Some women maintained rigid boundaries to support their authority among their crews. They did not fraternize with crewmates or employees. Distance from male crews prevented them from being taken advantage of by subordinates or becoming the butt of jokes or pranks from their peers.

Danielle, a laborer shared that sexist or racist attitudes were communicated by the use of stereotypes. For example, at a work picnic a fellow White laborer made a stereotypical comment about the Black people on crew liking watermelon and chicken; or driving to a job site and being chastised by a Latina boss for playing loud music in her car. She also talked about racial and sexual slurs drawn on the portable toilet of jobsites; the most offensive being a sexually explicit drawing of a naked woman on the wall of the toilet. Danielle acknowledged these experiences as potentially harmful and contributed to people leaving the industry. She said supervisors and contractors needed to address these microaggressions and failed to do so.

Veronica said the willingness of organizations and supervisors to dismiss explicitly racist behavior as jokes left employees with little recourse. She shared an overt hostile act of racism that happened at the Municipal Utility where she worked. A noose was left in the locker of a Black male employee. The employee's supervisor trivialized the microassault by publicly laughing about what happened and treated the incident as a joke. The supervisor's treatment of this incident as a joke gave the institutional message that there would be little to no recourse for the victim of this racist assault. People of color offered each other group solidarity to encourage the Black employee to not be silent about what happened. Human resources did not act on this discrimination claim. Human resources failure to act in this instance points to a climate where overt discriminatory behavior is maintained. It is within this climate that the placing of a noose, a symbol of racial terrorism against Black people in the United States, could be dismissed as a joke. Five of the women in the study brought gender or racial legal disputes or human resources grievances to their employers with mixed success. Retaliation and the challenge of proving the intent of covert microaggressions limited the effectiveness of grievances or legal suits.

Sexual Harassment and Heterosexism

The inability of human resource departments to respond effectively when people bring forward discrimination claims contributes to a "code of silence" from victims of harassment. Veronica noted that a "code of silence" among women prevented them from speaking out about sexual harassment for fear of retaliation. She said breaking the code required women to speak when something happened but also for human resources, supervisors, and crew leads to act. Veronica was verbally sexually harassed by a male peer. She initially asked to be transferred to another crew to get away from the perpetrator. Her supervisor dismissed her concerns and told both herself and the perpetrator to "work it out" and "get along." The response of her supervisor gave the perpetrator license to increase his harassment of Veronica. This was done privately and in front of other colleagues to humiliate her. Eventually, she worked with other women who worked for the Municipal Utility to bring a claim to Human Resources about sexual harassment. Human Resources took the claim of sexual harassment seriously, but were ultimately ineffective in removing the perpetrator from the organization. Her story highlights the need for greater training of managers regarding their responsibilities in terms of keeping workers safe from physical harm and bullying; and for human resources to make known and enforce procedures to address sexual and racial harassment.

Breaking the code of silence also requires the participation of tradesmen. Veronica's harassment experience was witnessed by her male colleagues. The witnessing of harassment and failure to speak out is a form of collusion with the perpetrator against the target. Bystander intervention is crucial to interrupt sexual and racial harassment of women and people of color.

A bystander witnessed a fellow tradesperson make a homophobic comment towards Z, a lesbian. The bystander told the foreman, who told the contractor. This particular job was on the grounds of a large manufacturer with strict guidelines around conduct. The institutional mandate for compliance around higher safety behaviors, including higher codes of conduct in regards to racism and sexism, compelled Z's contractor to call a meeting of all those working on the jobsite, and announce that anyone making homophobic or racist comments on the jobsite would be fired. In contrast to Z's experience with her employer, Crystal was fired when she told a coworker she was gay. Employees cannot trust that an employer will protect their rights.

LEADING WITHIN A MICROAGGRESSIVE CULTURE

The assumption of inferiority, and expectations of failure, undermine Black tradeswomen's competence on the job, and hinder their willingness to step into leadership roles. Black women in leadership roles on construction jobsites are few and far between. Superintendent Keisha spoke of challenges to her leadership by male subordinates who held sexist beliefs that men knew best, of battling stereotypes that women's decisions were inefficient and their crews substandard, and of potential sabotage by male peers. Keisha said:

> Yet, it never fails, the testosterone in these guys that "they are construction workers," you know? They come out there and they've got their tools and stuff, and they're gonna work. You're gonna pick up behind them. I just felt like I was constantly paying my dues. [...]
>
> I was just like, "Naw, I'm not going to do it like that. We are gonna do it like this, because I didn't buy my card ["Buying your card" is a term used when people buy their journey card from the union hall without going through the formal apprenticeship. Buying a card is a less rigorous path towards attaining a journey card and qualifies individuals to earn journey-level wages]. You might have bought your card, and then you brought your brother-in-law in. He's getting journeyman scale [wages], and he didn't even go through the apprenticeship. He doesn't know what he's talking about. [...] I'll take the blame if it's wrong. But I am confident that it's right. I know it's right." [...]
>
> This is my constant fight. The guys don't like giving me a chance. I'm not trying to prove my stuff or myself, or whatever. I'm just trying to do what works for me because at the end of the day, especially if I am a journeyman, and they are the apprentice, I am responsible for it being right.

As a woman, Keisha faced gender-based challenges to her leadership on a regular basis. She spoke to the irony of having males come onto the jobsite, underestimate her wealth of knowledge and offer less credible ways to problem-solve on the job. She also noted that males could be promoted based on their networks rather than their skill. As a superintendent, she had to assertively challenge men to respect her decisions.

Keisha worked on bridge building projects around the United States for over 20 years at the time of our interview. Though her resume was impressive, she noted that male subordinates had to get past their bias against working for a woman before they would work effectively for her. She said once they did so they would work for her "in a heartbeat." She felt that she was a fair boss and set a high standard. Over her career, she had had three complaints lodged against her by male subordinates. The complaints did not stand up to scrutiny. However, complaints by subordinates can cause women in leadership to be removed from their position. Keisha walked a fine line around when to speak up, and when to let men figure out for themselves whether their ideas worked.

LIMITED INSTITUTIONAL COMMITMENTS TO INCLUSION

All of the tradeswomen interviewed at some point in their careers were brought onto construction projects through affirmative action efforts to bring more women and people of color into the trades. These efforts have been beneficial, however commitment to greater inclusion of women and people of color in the industry has waxed and waned depending on institutional will for diversity, and the political and economic climate. Wanda Lou noted that after her 30 years on the shipyards the numbers of women and Black people working on the yards dropped drastically. She attributed this to a lack of concerted effort on the part of her former employer to cultivate and maintain a diverse workforce. Wanda Lou said:

> [The yard] has changed since we've been there. I retired in 1988. But when we went back [...] I didn't see that many Black people there, period. And I didn't see that many women there. [...] You see, there were a lot of Black people there when we were there. But as we retired, I don't think they hired many more Black people.

Hiring went from targeted outreach to women and people of color towards a more color and genderblind approach, which contributed to the absence of people of color and women in the workforce. Colorblindness supports race-neutral policies, and has been used to undermine affirmative action efforts to bring people of color into apprenticeships. Genderblindness supports gender-neutral policies, and operates similarly to colorblind policies. Without long-term commitments to hiring women and people of color racial and gender diversity at all levels of the construction workforce will not be achieved.

As a laborer apprentice, Danielle said she had regular work. The economy was booming and apprentices were attractive to employers because they earned a lesser wage. As a Black woman, Danielle said contractors were incentivized to hire women and people of color to meet their affirmative action goals. Danielle sought to extend her apprenticeship by not rushing to submit her hours to graduate from each level of her apprenticeship. To her chagrin once her apprenticeship finished she found she was unemployed for ten months. She said:

> A lot of people told me to stay working, try to stretch out your apprenticeship as long as possible. It was very true. In the laborer's trade [...] they are accepting apprentices still to this day and they are the ones that are still working. [...] It's like they used you while you were an apprentice and then when you're done they just toss you aside. Yeah. That's how they stand. I'm really fed up with them.

Danielle spoke to the tension between the rhetoric of inclusion that she heard from the union, and the precarious experience of being a woman and a racial minority in the industry. She said: "I know that [women] have come a long way in this industry. But I don't think we get the respect. [...] They always say they want us to be in it and stuff like that, and still we're like the first ones to go."

Moving Forward

Women experienced microaggressions when they applied for their apprenticeships, when entering jobsites, while working alongside other men and women in the industry, as journey-level workers, as they attempted to move into leadership positions, and at the pinnacle of their careers. Microaggressive themes that impacted all of the women interviewed were the assumption of inferiority, colorblindness and genderblindness, racial and gender-based jokes, language, and slurs. Women experienced sexual harassment and heterosexism directly and indirectly. All of the women worked to address the resistance of coworkers and the industry as a whole to their presence as Black women.

If more women and people of color are to enter the construction industry and thrive in long-term careers the experiences of the Black tradeswomen offer key points of intervention. Affirmative action efforts to bring women and people of color into the industry are important. Many of the women in this study got their first jobs because of affirmative action goals on large construction projects. These efforts need to be consistent and industry wide. Without industry wide commitment to the inclusion of women and people of color into the workforce, gains made in bringing more people into the industry will continue to lag.

Bringing women and people of color into the trades is not enough. Foremen, supervisors, owners, apprenticeship centers, and human resource departments need to directly challenge microaggressive attitudes and behaviors that create a microaggressive culture within the trades. It is important for leadership at all levels to uphold a high standard of professional conduct on jobsites that promotes the inclusion of all workers. This is challenging. In interactions with major construction employers, I found some were interested in changing the culture, and some felt they could not set such a high standard for their employees as they would face opposition. Culture change is hard work, and is crucial for the construction industry to integrate in a meaningful way.

For all of the women in the study, working with other women on the jobsite was rare. I hypothesize that when women are hired in greater numbers and for longer timeframes there is a greater opportunity for solidarity to form among women. Tradeswomen who had the opportunity to remain with the same company for decades found it easier to establish a presence on the job, and to build lasting relationships across race and gender. In addition, there is a need to increase the numbers of women and people of color on the job at all levels of employment to normalize the presence of women and people of color in the workplace.

Supervisors who know the skills of their workers is key to mitigate the impact of invisibility of Black women. The awareness of supervisors can help ensure that as apprentices Black women are being trained, and as journey-level workers are being assigned meaningful work. The microaggressive culture of the US building trades can change. Failure to change this microaggressive culture will continue to waste the potential and contributions of valuable workers. As the US building trades face a workers' shortage in the coming decades due to the aging out of the current workforce, addressing gender and race-based microaggressions is an economic necessity.

References

Collins, P. (1989). The social construction of black feminist thought. *Signs: Journal of Women in Culture and Society, 14*(4), 745–773.

Crenshaw, K. (1989). Demarginalizing the intersection of race and sex. In *Scratching the Surface: Democracy, Traditions, Gender* (Vol. 20). Chicago, IL: University of Chicago.

Eisenberg, S. (1998). *We'll Call You if We Need You: Experiences of Women Working Construction.* Ithaca, NY: ILR Press.

Hughes, D., & Dodge, M. (1997). African American women in the workplace: The relationships between job conditions, racial bias at work, and perceived job quality. *American Journal of Community Psychology, 25*(5), 581–599.

Hunte, R., & Senehi, J. (2012). *"My Walk Has Never Been Average": Black Tradeswomen Negotiating Intersections of Race and Gender in Long-Term Careers in the U.S. Building Trades.* ProQuest Dissertations and Theses.

Jones, C., & Shorter-Gooden, K. (2003). *Shifting: The Double Lives of Black Women in America.* New York: Perrenial.

Moccio, F. (2009). *Live Wire Women and Brotherhood in the Electrical Industry.* Philadelphia, PA: Temple University Press.

National Women's Law Center (NWLC) calculations using Miriam King et al., Integrated Public Use Microdata Series, Current Population Survey 2013: Version 3.0, IPUMS-CPS: Minnesota Population Center (March 2013), available at http://cps.ipums.org/cps/index.shtml (Machine readable data).

Sue, D. W. (2010). *Microaggressions in Everyday Life: Race, Gender and Sexual Orientation.* Hoboken, NJ: Wiley.

Woods, J. (2010). The black male privileges checklist. In M. Kimmel & A. Ferber (Eds.), *Privilege: A Reader* (2nd ed., pp. 27–38). Boulder, CO: Westview Press.

CHAPTER 4

Navigating Microaggressions, Overt Discrimination, and Institutional Oppression: Transgender and Gender Nonconforming People and the Criminal Justice System

Kevin L. Nadal, Tanya Erazo, Chassitty N. Fiani,
Mónica Christina Murillo Parilla and Heather Han

Throughout American history, lesbian, gay, bisexual, transgender, and queer (LGBTQ) people have been targets of violence. As the United States formed, LGBTQ people (or individuals who were suspected of being LGBTQ) were killed, assaulted, or harassed for their presumed sexual orientations or gender identities; if they were granted a trial and found guilty of sodomy, they were jailed or suffered violent punishments (Crompton, 1976). In the early 1900s, police officers in metropolitan cities regularly raided gay bars and arrested LGBTQ people for sodomy (i.e., the act of engaging in oral sex, anal sex, or sex with an animal); cross-dressing (wearing clothes considered untraditional for one's birth sex); or for no illegal reason at all (Bronski, 2011; D'Emilio, 2014).

K. L. Nadal (✉) · T. Erazo · C. N. Fiani · M. C. Murillo Parilla · H. Han
City University of New York, New York, NY, USA

© The Author(s) 2018
C. L. Cho et al. (eds.), *Exploring the Toxicity of Lateral Violence
and Microaggressions*, https://doi.org/10.1007/978-3-319-74760-6_4

The uprisings at Compton's Cafeteria in San Francisco in 1966 and Stonewall in New York City of 1969 (which were led predominantly by transgender women of color) marked the beginnings of the LGBTQ Civil Rights Movement in the United States (D'Emilio, 2014; Nadal, 2013). For the first time in history, LGBTQ people organized themselves—declaring their right to exist and to express their sexual orientations and gender identities without tyranny or persecution.

While many LGBTQ people have become more visible and vocal over the past five decades, both individuals who are out and those who are closeted continue to live in fear. Coming out publicly has elicited fears of rejection, harassment, or violence—particularly due to the number of hate crimes committed towards LGBTQ people. The murders of people like Marsha P. Johnson, Harvey Milk, Brandon Teena, Matthew Shepard, Sakia Gunn, Gwen Amber Rose Araujo, Mark Carson, and Islan Nettles have signaled a need to be hypervigilant, to conceal one's sexual or gender identity, or both. While transgender and gender nonconforming (TGNC) people in general are targeted most by hate violence, Black and Latina transgender women are targeted most and at disproportionate rates (Dinno, 2017).

Systemically, there have been many federal, state, and local laws that directly affected the rights of LGBTQ people. Sodomy was viewed as illegal under federal law until the *Lawrence vs. Texas* Supreme Court (2003) decision, which ruled that state sodomy laws were unconstitutional. LGBTQ people could be fired from their jobs if their sexual identities were discovered; in fact, President Eisenhower signed Executive Order #10450 in 1953—which called for LGBTQ people to be fired from jobs in the federal government (Hillman & Hinrichsen, 2014). Sexual orientation and transgender identity were not protected classes under federal hate crime law until President Obama signed the Matthew Shepard and James Byrd Jr. Hate Crimes Act in 2009. Lesbian and gay people were not allowed to serve in the military until President Obama repealed Don't Ask, Don't Tell; and same-sex couples were not legally allowed to get married across all fifty states until the Supreme Court Decision of 2015 (Nadal, 2018).

While many laws have changed to protect LGBTQ rights, and though public opinions about LGBTQ people have become generally more favorable, research has found that LGBTQ people are still susceptible to various types of microaggressions—or subtle, more unintentional forms of discrimination (Nadal, 2013; Nadal, Rivera, & Corpus, 2010). Over the past ten years, multiple scholars have described the various micro-aggressions faced by LGBTQ people, as well as the negative impact of these microaggressions on LGBTQ people's mental health (see Nadal, Whitman, Davis, Erazo, Davidoff, 2016 for a review). Several themes of LGBTQ microaggressions have been identified including: (a) the use of heterosexist or transphobic terminology; (b) the endorsement of heteronormative or gender normative culture and behaviors; (c) the assumption of sexual pathology, deviance, or abnormality; (d) exoticization; (e) discomfort with/disapproval of LGBTQ experience; and (f) the assumption of a universal LGBTQ experience.

Further, numerous studies (e.g., Nadal, Skolnik, & Wong, 2012; Nadal et al., 2016) describe common microaggressions encountered by TGNC people. Examples of these types of microaggressions include:

a. the use of transphobic terminology (e.g., a colleague misgenders a TGNC person with an incorrect pronoun or uses a transphobic slur to describe someone);
b. the endorsement of gender normative culture and behaviors (e.g., a cisgender family member proclaims that a TGNC person should conform to gender expectations of their assigned sex at birth or should identify as binary);
c. discomfort with or disapproval transgender experience (e.g., a stranger stares at a TGNC person in disgust or uneasiness);
d. exoticization (e.g., someone wants to date or be friends with a TGNC person only because of their gender identity);
e. assumption of sexual pathology, deviance, or abnormality (e.g., an acquaintance presumes that a TGNC person is a sex worker or is sexually promiscuous);
f. assumption of universal transgender experience (e.g., someone presumes that all transgender people must transition into the gender opposite to their sex assigned at birth);
g. denial of the reality of transphobia (e.g., a professor or supervisor says that transgender people are too sensitive or paranoid about discrimination);
h. denial of bodily privacy (e.g., an acquaintance or stranger asks transgender people about their genitalia or whether they have had any medical surgeries).

Specific to the criminal justice system, emerging studies have uncovered different types of heterosexist and transphobic discrimination within the criminal justice (CJ) system, as well as how those perceptions impact how people perceive or experience the CJ system. Nadal, Quintanilla, Goswick, and Sriken (2015) describe the many ways that lesbian, gay, bisexual, and queer (LGBQ) perceive the police, courts, and other legal venues. Participants revealed issues related to gender presentation, intersections with race and class, and microaggressions they encounter as a result of their sexual orientation and other identities. Results indicate that stereotypes and perceived bias affect whether LGBQ people would feel comfortable seeking help from police officers, as well as how much they would trust different sectors of the justice system. One limitation to this study is that it focused solely on LGBQ people, without understanding how gender identity may impact one's perception of, and experiences within, the CJ system.

In order to investigate transgender experiences in the criminal justice system, Fiani and colleagues (2017) used a qualitative method with a group of 11 self-identified TGNC adults in the US. Participants shared several themes of microaggressions within the CJ system, including:

1. Dehumanization (e.g., a correctional officer who refers to a TGNC person as "it" instead of her gender pronoun);
2. Assumptions of Criminality, Pathology, or Abnormality (e.g., a trans woman who is presumed to be a sex worker for no other reason than her gender identity);
3. Use of Derogatory Language (e.g., being referred to as a "she-male" or a "tranny");
4. Second-Class Citizenship (e.g., a TGNC person who is put into solitary confinement or denied healthcare because the prisons refuse to validate their gender identities);
5. Intentional Misgendering (e.g., a prosecutor who intentionally calls a trans woman "Mr." during a trial, despite being corrected numerous times on her pronouns);
6. Microinvalidations (e.g., officers who laugh at a TGNC person who file a police report or discourage TGNC from seeking help);
7. Invasion of Bodily Privacy/Exoticization (e.g., a TGNC person who is groped or excessively frisked during an arrest); and
8. Systemic Microaggressions (e.g., a TGNC person whose legal identification cards are not viewed as valid because they list their assigned sex at birth, instead of their current gender presentation).

While Fiani and colleagues (2017) describe the microaggressions or subtler forms of discrimination TGNC people encounter, it is important to explore TGNC people react to, or cope with microaggressions, overt discrimination, and institutional discrimination.

The purpose of this chapter is to uncover how TGNC people perceive and experience the criminal justice system. We will primarily focus on the types of discrimination and bias TGNC encounter and how those experiences impact their perceptions and interactions with different sectors of the CJ system. Utilizing a Qualitative Secondary Analysis (QSA) from the data from Fiani and colleagues (2017), we employed the following exploratory research questions:

1. How do TGNC people react to microaggressions and other forms of discrimination in the CJ system?
2. How do TGNC cope with microaggressions in the CJ system cognitively, emotionally, and behaviorally?
3. What recommendations do TGNC people have for improving the CJ system?

METHOD

Participants

Participants ($N = 11$) included adults who self-identified as transgender or gender nonconforming (TGNC); their reported ages ranged from 23 to 51 (Mean = 32.9). Participant demographic characteristics were assessed via a free response self-report format. One participant responded to socio-demographic items describing race/ethnicity, sexual orientation, gender identity, and religion/spirituality as "All," and self-reported an occupation of "Mystic." The majority of the remaining 10 participants self-identified their race as White ($N = 7$), followed by Black ($N = 2$) and Latina/o/x ($N = 1$). Diverse ethnic identifications were reported, including Jewish-American, White, African-American, Puerto-Rican/Sephardi, American, Irish/Italian, and African. Sexual orientation comprised a similarly diverse distribution, including identifications of Queer ($N = 3$), Bi/Queer ($N = 1$), Gay ($N = 2$), Bisexual ($N = 2$), and Heterosexual/Straight ($N = 2$). Participants described and reported a number of gender identities, including Male $(N=1)$, Female $(N=1)$, Transgender $(N=2)$, Trans $(N=1)$, and FTM or female-to-male $(N=1)$ as well as composite identifications including GNC Queer Woman, Male/Neutrois, and Transmasculine Genderqueer. See Table 4.1 for detailed socio-demographic information.

Participant recruitment drew from a community sample in a metropolitan region of the Northeastern United States. To participate, volunteers responded by email to posts in the volunteer section of the website Craigslist.com, as well as a series of e-mails sent to the research team's networks. Participants were each provided with $20 at the conclusion of the focus groups as an appreciation for their time and contributions. To protect participant confidentiality and promote feelings of safety, participants provided either pseudonyms or their initials throughout the research process, rather than their names or other identifiable information. In our results section, we removed any identifiable demographic information.

Table 4.1 Participant socio-demographic self-identifications

Age	Race	Ethnicity	Sexual orientation	Gender identity	Occupation	Religion
51	White	Jewish-American	Queer	GNC Queer Woman	Writer	Jewish
31	White	White	Gay	Male	Student	Jewish
34	White	–	Gay	Female	Chef	Atheist
28	All	All	All	All	Mystic	All
28	Black	African-American	Heterosexual	Transgender	Student	Buddhist
30	Latino	Puerto-Rican/Sephardi	Bi/Queer	Male/Neutrois	Freelance writer/artist	Jewish
27	White	–	Queer	Transmasculine Genderqueer	College writing instructor	Unitarian Universalist
39	White	American	Queer	Trans	Student	Agnostic
25	White	Irish/Italian	Bisexual	FTM	Government	Wicca
23	Black	African	Straight	Transgender male	Customer service rep	Christian
46	White	–	Bisexual	–	–	Jewish/Buddhist

Researchers

The research team included five research assistants trained and experienced in conducting qualitative research and in data analysis using Consensual Qualitative Research (CQR) (Hill, Thompson, & Williams, 1997). This team was comprised of one cisgender male professor, two cisgender female doctoral students, two genderqueer/gender nonbinary Master's students, and one cisgender female undergraduate student. Additionally, coders reported sexual orientation identities including queer, gay, asexual, pansexual, and heterosexual. The racial/ethnic distribution of coders included White, Asian, Asian-American, Latina, and Mixed. All researchers and research assistants were members of the same university psychology department, studying Clinical and/or Forensic Psychology. As per the recommendations of Hill et al. (1997), coders met prior to coding inception to explore their own personal reference groups, expectations, and biases related to TGNC identities and experiences and related to the criminal justice system. This preliminary exploration occurs in hopes of minimizing the later impacts of researcher bias upon data analytic processes and results.

Measures

Participants engaged in a semi-structured, in-person, focus group interview in addition to completing the aforementioned demographic questionnaire. After informed consent was acquired, the demographic questionnaire was completed, followed by the focus group interview. The demographic questionnaire assessed the following characteristics: age, race, ethnicity, sexual orientation, gender identity, occupation, and religion.

The semi-structured focus group interview protocol included 14 facilitator-directed questions, each with two identical prompts for elaboration: (1) "Tell me more about that" and (2) "How do you feel about that?" Structured interview items pertained to participant experiences with and perceptions of the criminal justice system (i.e., police, prison systems, juvenile detention centers, courts, and government and state agencies). Participants were asked to describe both their beliefs regarding the criminal justice system (e.g., thoughts on its effectiveness and safety) and personal experiences with this system.

The semi-structured nature of the focus group interview allowed for the generation of novel themes and concepts not previously demonstrated in extant research or hypothesized by the researchers. It also gave participants a chance to express themselves in their own words as opposed to canned/multiple choice responses via a survey. The degree to which participant discussions deviated from the structured portions of the protocol varied by focus group. This semi-structured protocol is exploratory and appropriate—given the preliminary nature of this research, and the sparse nature of such investigations in extant literature. Thus, the present investigation allowed for the generation of both novel and hypothesis-driven conclusions, therefore providing a foundation upon which future research may readily expand.

Procedure

This study utilized a qualitative methodology comprised of semi-structured focus group interviews. Based on the convergence of participant and research team availability, three focus groups were held. Each group was attended by 1–2 (co)facilitators, one observer from the research team, and 3–5 TGNC participants. The observer identified non-verbal behaviors (e.g., gestures, facial expressions, and body language) and dimensions of group dynamics (e.g., conformity, dissent, and processes of groupthink) which qualitative methodology experts have asserted is often not readily apparent to the facilitator(s) (Krueger & Casey, 2014). Each focus group lasted 60–90 minutes, and took place in a private conference room at an urban public college. Participants reviewed and signed the informed consent document, and they were made aware of and agreed to audio recording of the group discussion to aid in the later stages of the research process. The audio recording began as the facilitator(s) reiterated a brief summary of the informed consent information, highlighting the importance of confidentiality and the voluntary nature of the study.

A semi-structured interview protocol was utilized, beginning with the prompt: "How do you feel about the police?" Subsequent questions focused on other sectors of the criminal justice system—including courts, prisons, and others. To encourage group discussion and secure robust research, participants were prompted to elaborate upon their responses with open-ended directives (e.g., "Tell me more," "How did you feel about that?", etc.). Participants were asked about their beliefs on the effectiveness, safety, and treatment of LGBTQ victims and incarcerated

LGBTQ people within the criminal justice system. Upon conclusion of the last structured discussion item, the facilitator(s) prompted participants to provide closing thoughts. After participants gave their final thoughts, a brief concluding discussion took place in which the facilitator(s) attempted to summarize the groups' sentiments and asked for their corrections or agreement of the summation. When the concluding discussion ended, the audio recording was stopped. Participants then received their monetary compensation ($20) as well as a document listing TGNC-competent, identity-affirming, counseling referrals. After participants departed from the focus group location, the facilitator(s) and observer met to process reactions to the focus group and their discussions. These research team reactions were not transcribed or coded, but rather informed later research investigations and research team training protocols.

Analyses

Because we were interested in further understanding how TGNC people coped with microaggressions in the CJ system, we utilized both a QSA and CQR approach (see Hill et al., 1997). Utilizing the data collected by Fiani and colleagues (2017), we used a QSA—which is used when previous data is reanalyzed to investigate new questions, to apply a fresh perspective to unanswered questions, or to expand on existing phenomena (Gladstone, Volpe, & Boydell, 2007; Heaton, 2004). We also used a CQR approach to ensure that multiple coders and analysts were considered in understanding our data.

All focus group discussions were audio recorded to maintain the accuracy of data analysis. Research assistants within the primary investigator's lab transcribed each audio recording into a distinct focus group transcript, from which the coding team drew their conclusions. Data analysis consisted of four research assistants meeting on five separate occasions to analyze the three transcripts via CQR. As previously mentioned, the first meeting consisted of a discussion and self-reflection among the coding team regarding assumptions and expectations about the research and TGNC experiences and identities.

Prior to the second team meeting, coders individually examined all three transcripts, and sorted participant quotes into preliminary sets of coding domains. This starting list, composed by the research coordinator to reflect existing empirical frameworks, yielded five categories:

Criminal Justice Category (e.g., police, courts, government agencies, etc.); Affective Experiences Related to Discussion; Reactions to Criminal Justice Experiences (Cognitive, Affective, and Behavioral); Categories of Experiences (e.g., random searches, microaggressions, etc.); and Intersectionalities (e.g., grasping how one's experiences were related to one's gender identity, race, socioeconomic status, age, and other identities).

During meetings three through five, the coding team discussed individual preliminary classifications, and constructed novel domains as appropriate. The remainder of the coding process consisted of discussion and revision of domains (both the conceptualization of each domain's contents and sorting of all participant responses into appropriate domains). Consistent with CQR, all coding decisions required group consensus. Thus, group dissent produced a discussion of the rationale of each party's perspective, which continued as long as necessary to reach consensus. Group consensus produced seven descriptive domains of TGNC experiences with the criminal justice system as well as one domain of TGNC reactions to personal experiences with said system.

Following final consensus among the coders, an external auditor reviewed the aforementioned eight domains of experiences with the criminal justice system and various reactions to those experiences. The auditor (an expert in both CQR methods and research with TGNC populations), is an expert in both qualitative research and CQR; the auditor's role was to manage potential biases that may have emerged within the original coding team (e.g., groupthink and group polarization). Moreover, the auditor provided feedback to the coding team regarding the naming and conceptualization of domains as well as the quotes which comprised them. He also provided recommendations for the organization of the final coding document. After the coding team received this feedback, they met to review and address said recommendations, again reaching consensus for each decision. The final four domains and subsequent themes presented were approved by the external auditor.

RESULTS

Fiani and colleagues (2017) described the most robust domain that emerged from the data—the types of microaggressions TGNC people encounter in the CJ system. For this study, we describe the four other domains that emerged from the participants' narratives. These domains include: (1) Points of interactions with the CJ System; (2) Beliefs/ Thoughts About the Police; (3) Reactions to Experiences with CJ System; and (4) Intersectionalities. Themes emerged under each domain, and original and representative quotes are provided to elucidate each theme.

Domain 1: Points of Interactions with Criminal Justice System

The first domain encompasses participants' narratives about their interactions with different law enforcement agents, agencies, or both. Among others, some of the agencies mentioned include police departments, prisons, and jails. Three themes emerged under this domain: (1) Arrests, Apprehensions, and Custodies; (2) Seeking Assistance from Police; and (3) Protests and Demonstrations.

Theme 1: Arrests, apprehensions, and custodies. Participants shared narratives of being arrested and being held in custody in prison or jails—describing the overt and subtle discriminatory treatment that they had received. Some participants shared incidents during the booking process. Others described the experience of being an inmate in these facilities. Stories about microaggressions, trauma, marginalization, violence, and prejudices were shared. One participant said, "I was arrested, like falsely arrested, and instead of asking me anything, when I finally said to them 'I'm Trans,' all the cops said was 'Yeah, I thought there was something weird about you.'" Participants who were arrested and held in custody shared anxiety and constant worry surrounding the idea of gendered cells and bathrooms at these facilities, as well as anxiety regarding potential violence that may occur.

Theme 2: Seeking assistance from police. Some participants discussed instances in which they felt it necessary to reach out to law enforcement for help. Consistently, participants recognized the negative effects that having to reach out to these systems to get support or assistance had on their lives. An example of one of these incidents was being a witness to or survivor of a hate crime. Participants shared an array of emotions regarding help-seeking with police, with one participant who revealed: "I've had experiences where I've had to call the police to diffuse situations and it felt like they were always turning it, somehow, against me as being the aggressor." Across all groups, participants revealed their experiences with police officers to be consistently negative—sharing hesitance about engaging with police officers; most participants disclosed past histories of maltreatment and injustice by officers when reaching out for support. Despite these negative encounters, the majority of participants vocalized that reaching out to the authorities was considered the legitimate formal process. Even if they felt harassed or invalidated, they continued to engage with police in order to seek justice.

Theme 3: Protests/demonstrations. Some participants shared narratives about interacting with police officers as a result of their involvement in collective actions, political protests, and other demonstrations related to social justice activism. In these encounters, many participants mentioned narratives of maltreatment and injustice towards civilians. Participants perceived that the police held animosity towards protestors and activists engaged in organizing and attending these events—which often resulted in aggressive or hostile actions towards protestors.

Domain 2: Beliefs/Thoughts About the Police

Participants reflected upon their personal ideas, judgments, and opinions about the police, focusing specifically on the functionality and efficiency of police departments. Four themes emerged from this domain: (1) Police as ineffective, (2) Police as selectively effective, (3) Police as discriminatory, and (4) Police as unjust.

Theme 1: Police as ineffective. Participants shared narratives and anecdotes related to incidents or moments in their lives when the police underserve them as civilians. The intersection of social class, race, and sexual orientation were discussed in connection to the treatment certain people receive. Participants expressed negative emotions and opinions about the police and police treatment in their communities. One participant shared: "...in my community—in the GBLT community and my community in the south Bronx they are, in fact, ineffective."

Theme 2: Police as selectively effective. Across groups, participants endorsed the idea that the police protect and serve only a specific group of people, and if one is not part of that group, one does not benefit the same way from police protection. In some cases, this theme explored the idea that privilege fuels how people will treat you and the fair treatment you will receive from the police or the criminal justice system. Participants expressed that this inequality is a systemic issue stemming from social stratification where the police is but one party implicated in upholding and protecting the status quo. One participant described,

"They are they are incredibly effective doing what the system is set up for the police to do, which is to protect White privilege, White power... I think they are doing a great job doing that." This quote exemplifies the beliefs that many of the participants shared in regard to the systemic influence over individual police officers' behaviors—particularly in acknowledging how biased beliefs exist within a larger social system and are manifested through policing.

Theme 3: Police as discriminatory. Participants identified more overt and undisguised beliefs in regard to how police officers maltreat, marginalize, underserve, and exclude certain groups of people based on their perception of group identification. Participants discussed the beliefs they have seen police officers express towards marginalized groups. For example, participants shared blatant and microaggressive instances of how racist, sexist, cissexist homoantagonist, and transantagonist that police have been. One participant shared: "I feel that they discriminate a lot with the LGBT community and I know a few years ago some [transgender people] died from bashing and the police, um, you know, sometimes they joke about it." This participant's quote speaks to the idea that police officers are insensitive or invalidating of TGNC people and that systems of transphobia perpetuate and even fuel these beliefs.

Theme 4: Police as unjust. Participants discussed the unjust and unfair treatment that TGNC people experience with the police. This theme again explores both overt and blatant forms of injustices perpetuated by the police, as well as microaggressions. For example, one participant described feeling dehumanized by police, when trying to file a report:

> I'm treated like a number. I'm treated like an individual who can't afford anything. I'm treated like an individual who has to take what is in fact being given to them. Um. Whatever deal is in fact being given to them because I don't have anyone to fight for me.

Many participants discuss the intertwining of the systemic and individual perpetuation of injustice, with some recognizing the underlying problems of systemic transantagonism and transmisogyny. One participant shared: "It makes me physically sick to think that this is a system that's supposed to protect us and it's doing the complete opposite." Another added, "Your mouth got busted open and because you are in fact transgender...it almost feels like the police officers give the other individual—the one that committed the assault—a thumbs up." Through these quotes, participants identify how systemic transphobia is both insidiously and overtly infused into how police treat TGNC people.

Domain 3: Reactions to Experiences with CJ System

Participants shared narratives or past lived experiences involving how they reacted when they encountered aspects of the CJ system. Most of these reactions were negative or ambivalent—filled with wariness and skepticism. Three themes emerged: (1) Loss of Trust; (2) Cognitive and Behavioral Reactions (with four subthemes: Cognitive Avoidance, Behavioral Avoidance, Learned Helplessness, and Self-Reflection); and (3) Emotional Reactions (with three subthemes: Unsafe/Vulnerable, Anger/Frustration, and Mixed Emotional Response).

Theme 1: Loss of trust. Participants described how they lost faith in the criminal justice system, specifically describing a level of disconnect and lack of discomfort in the presence of police officers and a larger system. Their reactions to confronting the criminal justice system seem to be very cynical and cautious, with sample quotes including: "You know we cannot trust the police," "It's sad that I have to go in…assuming that I can't trust them," "I don't trust that justice would be served," and, "If you can't trust the police then who can you trust, you know?"

Theme 2: Cognitive and behavioral reactions. Participants shared ideas or behaviors when they interacted with law enforcement and other sectors of the CJ system, with four major subthemes that emerged.

Subtheme 1: Cognitive avoidance. Many participants shared how they tried to repress or disassociate from any memory regarding their experiences with police and how they intentionally try not to think about certain possibly traumatic experiences. One participant shared: "I'd rather not go into that because it doesn't serve a purpose other than to disturb me."

Subtheme 2: Behavioral avoidance. Some participants described how they altered behavior to evade any violence or discomfort. They avoided certain practices or circumstances they imagined could lead to awkward or distressing situations for them and others. Participants constantly made decisions to avoid confrontations in the face of politically incorrect (and sometimes even aggressive) language or behavior. If they reacted in the way they wanted to, they felt their safety would be compromised and could lead to more trouble. One person revealed:

It challenges my safety because I want to defend myself... but in the same sense, like, my own personal safety means, like, at some points you have to pick and choose your battle... I [tend to] just kind of like shrink and curl up. And just like act very defensive and just like to be self-protective, instead of, even though I want to be kind of defiant. I think I'm usually just kind of like more concerned about both of our wellbeing.

This quote demonstrates how participants were changing their behavior and their actions in order to avoid uncomfortable or potentially hostile situations; TGNC people often choose not to confront these issues in order to avoid more dire and serious consequences.

Subtheme 3: Learned helplessness. Some participants revealed a sense of losing their personal power because of the continuous obstacles they face. Some participants seemed to have been pushed so far that they give up hope and optimism, as they see the systemic issues as being too deeply embedded and engrained to endure or change. One participant stated:

I feel like, do we spend our energy trying to mend the system that we can't get rid of or trying to over throw it. And what like, what, what do um these small steps—like you know getting rid of solitary confinement for youth—like what does that really do in the long run?

Subtheme 4: Self-reflection. Participants identified ways they increased their own awareness and consciousness about the contributing factors affecting their lived experiences, as well as how they cope with systemic oppression. Most participants acknowledged that privilege, or lack of privilege, modifies how they navigate the world. One participant opined, "Before this whole stuff happened... I was almost like, what's the phrase, willfully ignorant. I really wanted to believe it wasn't this systemic or as systemic as it is." This illuminates some participants' desire to keep self-reflection at bay because of the emotional burden of acknowledging the perceived inequality of the CJ system. However, participants reported that self-reflection allowed them to cope with the reality of and actual engagement in this unfair system.

Theme 3: Emotional reactions. Participants described an array of feelings and emotional reactions they experienced when interacting with the CJ system. Three major subthemes emerged.

Subtheme 1: Feeling unsafe/vulnerable. This subtheme described the lack of safety and constant vulnerability participants faced when navigating a heteronormative world. Participants discussed everyday issues they understood could potentially be threatening to their wellbeing and safety; they described ways in which they have learned to be hypervigilant when living their lives, particularly in relation to police officers. One participant disclosed, "Every day, I see the police. I feel as if... I'm being...if—not that I'm being protected, that I'm being the one who is, in fact, looked at to be the suspect." This feeling of lack of safety relates to the hesitation around police injustice and discrimination as well as how the police have perpetuated these systemic "isms" that affect transgender gender nonconforming people.

Subtheme 2: Anger/frustration. When describing the injustices of the CJ system, feelings of anger and frustration were frequently expressed. While one participant expressed specific instances in which they feel "rage and anger," another described how they constantly "feel pissed. I just feel really angry." This highlights the development of consistent, negative emotions participants must navigate when interacting with an unfair CJ system.

Subtheme 3: Mixed emotional responses. Participants expressed many other emotions—predominantly negative or ambivalent at best—with some responses conveying two or more feelings. Some participants shared disdain, anxiety, and sadness in thinking about the current status quo. When failing to confront a microaggression, one participant shared: "I really do feel like, I don't know, like disappointed—a little ashamed of myself for not doing something." These mixed emotional responses show the complexity of reactions TGNC individuals have regarding microaggressions and overt discrimination in the CJ system. There is not just one, singular reaction to employ, but a myriad of emotional reactions TGNC people grapple with.

Domain 4: Intersectionalities

Similar to the various emotional reactions elicited by microaggressions and overt discrimination, intersectional identities are at play too. Participants discussed how their multiple identities affected their interactions with the CJ system—including the police and the CJ system as a whole. Four themes arose from this domain: (1) Gender identity/presentation and multiple identities; (2) Gender identity/presentation and race; (3) Gender identity/presentation and age; and (4) Gender identity/presentation and class/socio-economic status.

Theme 1: Gender identity/presentation and multiple identities. Participants expressed their different experiences with the criminal justice system when they were perceived to have many identities or belonging to many groups (e.g., being a Black, transgender, queer male with a physical disability). Participants also shared their beliefs that these multiple identities shaped how they were treated by the CJ system. They believed that multiple identities could yield greater victimization via discrimination or microaggressions. One participant shared a stark conversation with their father:

> [It] has just been my own personal experience growing up with being transgender and or identifying as homosexual at one time in my life where my dad would tell me you got three strikes against you kid. I'm letting you know that right now at the door. You are black, and you're gay, and you want to be a girl. Oh My God. They are going to destroy you.

Moreover, participants also agreed that the roots of overt discrimination and covert biases (via microaggressive remarks or actions) were harder to decipher, as it is confusing to disentangle which identity was being attacked. However, they also believed that some identities were more present than others. For example, one participant explained, "You know it depends a lot on your wealth. And being gay is a factor. Being queer or trans is a factor. But, I feel like maybe money and skin color is more of a factor there."

Another participant echoed these sentiments. They elaborated, "The court system... I believe is just as biased as the police officers. And you—I know I keep referring to my ethnic background—you know me being African American, it doesn't even matter what judge it is that you get; I cannot afford an attorney and based on that I am often railroaded by the judicial system." While it is sometimes unclear which identity is being discriminated against within the CJ system, participants agreed that their multiple identities coalesce to elicit many types of discrimination and microaggressions. So, while many of their identities can be targeted, it appears that some identities are more prominent than others.

Theme 2: Gender identity/presentation and race. Another theme that emerged under the Intersectionality domain was that race was a salient identity that affected one's experiences. Race was something most participants could pinpoint as clear reasons for discrimination when traversing the CJ system. For example, one participant revealed that while detained by police, their racial identity was part of their experience: "Just like earlier in the week I was taken in for prostitution and I was treated with racial slurs and all of that."

White participants were also able to recognize how their racial identity may give them privilege in how they are treated. A White participant was in accordance with the aforementioned belief that race is a prominent marker of treatment in the CJ system. They stated, "I think that um, like, racial privilege somehow trumps cis privilege in a way. So, like I feel like as, like, as a White, genderqueer person, like, I'm still safer than a cis-person of color." However, despite a feeling of safety in being White, other identities can arouse feelings of impending discrimination by the CJ system. One White participant explained this well:

> I was at a street fair and we passed like, my girlfriend and I passed... five cops. And I whispered to her and I was like: "Why am I so fucking angry right now, what do I have to be afraid of, I am White. She turned to me and she is like what? You are something to be afraid of, you are gender nonconforming. I was like, "Yeah but, like, the intersections of like vulnerability, you know, do not cross as thickly for me as for others.

Theme 3: Gender identity/presentation and age. Age was another prominent identity that affected one's experiences. Most participants agreed that age was a significant factor in how they were treated- particularly regarding discrimination. Participants believed that younger— or seemingly younger—people were targeted by police than older ones. One participant opined, "In my experience they seem to target people who are younger, people who dress a little differently."

Further, some participants claimed that their age presentation was more of a targeted identity. For example, one participant clearly articulated this when they said: "I get picked on my age more you know my appearance as far as age is concerned more than my identity." These statements further illuminate the compounding and complex effects of intersectionality on discrimination within the criminal justice system.

Theme 4: Gender identity/presentation and class/socioeconomic status. Lastly, participants also acknowledged how the interplay of gender identity and socioeconomic status (SES) affected their interactions with the CJ system. They were quick to describe ways in which they are treated like second-class citizens by police and the judicial system based on their economic standing and gender. For example, one person shared "I feel like within the LGBT community, [police] are more helpful towards some people than others. You know, like the wealthier people out here in [this posh neighborhood] maybe have a better time with the police." Relatedly, another participant shared a personal struggle regarding government identification: "I don't have the money to change my documents right now or even my name so it's so frustrating you know, like there is this discrepancy." Most participants described beliefs regarding how they would be treated if they had more money. Many participants seemed troubled that SES could so greatly affect their treatment, particularly when formerly believing that government and other systems should offer equal protection for all citizens.

DISCUSSION

The purpose of this study was to gain a better understanding of the TGNC people's perceptions of the criminal justice system, particularly in exploring how they respond to microaggressions and other forms of discrimination. As hypothesized, many people held unfavorable opinions regarding the police; including perception of police as largely ineffective, unjust, discriminatory, and selectively effective dependent upon specific circumstances. Many TGNC people shared how unpleasant interactions with the police led them to hold unfavorable views about them. This finding is consistent with extant study regarding how people are more likely to hold negative opinions of the police after an unpleasant interaction with them (Brown & Reed Benedict, 2002; Weitzer & Tuch, 2005).

The majority of participants reported direct, first-hand experiences with the criminal justice system and could identify a number of microaggressions that typically occur. These experiences are in agreement with past research findings which suggest that TGNC people report relatively higher levels of contact with the criminal justice system in comparison to the national statistic (Grant et al., 2011; Stotzer, 2009). Participants engaged in contact with the police through three main ways in our study: (1) seeking help; (2) being arrested/apprehended; and (3) participating in protests and demonstrations. Extant findings suggest TGNC people come into contact with the criminal justice system through much more diverse means than cisgender people- via courts, prisons, jails, immigration, and streets (Grant et al., 2011).

With regards to orientation toward seeking assistance, many participants shared that they did not want to report to the police and many stated they would only contact the police conditionally. Because TGNC people are often discriminated against in the criminal justice system, it is understandable as to why many would be hesitant to contact them for help. Studies conducted on crime reporting behaviors suggest that people who hold unfavorable views of the police are much less inclined to report crimes (Tyler & Fagan, 2008).

Our findings bolster past research findings regarding discrimination from the police as a common shared experienced between TGNC people, especially for LGBTQ people of color. Results indicate that we must continue to consider intersectionality when examining experiences of microaggressions and discrimination with TGNC people. In our study, themes regarding the intersectionalities between gender identity and race, age, gender identity presentation, and class socioeconomic status all emerged—supporting past studies that suggest intersectional identities affect peoples' experiences with microaggressions (Nadal, Davidoff, et al., 2015, Nadal, Quintanilla, et al., 2015).

Our study also demonstrated the stress of microaggressions and discrimination on TGNC people's mental health. In some ways, TGNC and other historically marginalized people must undergo several psychological processes to evaluate microaggressions or discriminatory acts; to modulate their reactions; and to respond in a way that enhances their safety. Our research team interpreted this process to be both draining and demoralizing; TGNC people are forced to gracefully navigate microaggressions for their safety and comfort, while also being mindful of how others will react. Meanwhile, perpetrators of microaggressions are given free rein to unapologetically express themselves, offend, or both.

Finally, our study aligns with previous studies which have found that enduring microaggressions and other forms of discrimination can have deleterious effects on individuals' mental and physical health (Anderson, 2012; Nadal, Griffin, Wong, Hamit, & Rasmus, 2014; Pascoe & Smart Richman, 2009). While not all of the participants articulated this directly, most of our TGNC participants described their feelings of anger, exhaustion, and defeat when dealing with microaggressions and other forms of discrimination in the criminal justice system. Participants seemed more burdened when they held multiple marginalized identities, demonstrating the need to further examine intersectionalities in understanding the physical and mental health effects of microaggressions.

Implications

This study yielded various implications for future research regarding TGNC people and the criminal justice system. Findings from this study affirm how TGNC people are highly marginalized and are systemically discriminated against. In addition, the current study suggests that many TGNC people are largely distrustful of the police and of the CJ system. Results point to the need for transgender-affirmative competency training programs for police officers and other liaisons of the legal system. Studies on police legitimacy suggest that people's perceptions of fairness engender their opinions about them (Hinds & Murphy, 2007). Thus, future steps can be taken to identify TGNC specific factors that increase police legitimacy and increase their perception of procedural justice which in turn can help improve the relationship between two parties. Current study also identified many different forms of microaggressions that TGNC people experience from contact with the criminal justice system. Since there are many different ways in which TGNC people experience microaggressions, police training programs can incorporate findings from this research to lower the prevalence of such microaggressions.

Based on our findings, future studies can examine how various factors such as appearance and gender expression can affect one's experiences with microaggressions. Further, because it is largely unknown what factors affect individuals' perceptions of others' gender expressions and identities, future studies can provide insight into how transphobic biases are developed and how they can be prevented. Educational and training programs that affirm transgender and nonbinary experiences can be created to assist in minimizing biases and microaggressions across various sectors—school systems, work environments, and CJ systems. Finally, our study briefly touched upon the role of media and how media can affect police perception and perception of TGNC people. Future studies can explore the mediating effects of media on cisgender people's perception of TGNC people, while also understanding how media may influence TGNC people's own feelings of internalized oppression.

Limitations

While this study improves our understanding of TGNC people and their experiences of the CJ system, we note some limitations. Due to a relatively small sample size ($N = 11$) and majority being White, participants' experiences may not be generalizable to the entire population. Because this study explores the intersectionality of multiple identities, participants' experiences may differ from TGNC people of color. Other factors (e.g., race, age, appearance, perceived gender identity and expression) also could have influenced the participants' experiences and shaped their perceptions of the CJ system. While there is a dearth of literature examining the relationship between gender identity, gender expression and perceptions of the police, past studies suggest that diverse factors such as race, age, past contact with the police, and neighborhood can affect police perception (Brown & Reed Benedict, 2002; Weitzer & Tuch, 2004). Further, our participants were recruited from the New York City area which may limit generalizability across the US and beyond. For instance, extant literature on perceptions of police suggest how geographical contexts such as crime rates and neighborhood culture can shape and influence people's opinions (Schafer, Huebner, & Bynum, 2003). Finally, due to its focus group semi-structured format, group dynamics may have influenced participants' behaviors and responses, while the established questions may have limited the type of data collected. Despite these limitations, we hope our study assists in further understanding how microaggressions in the CJ system and across all other environments are toxic and harmful for TGNC people and individuals of many other historically marginalized identities.

Acknowledgements Funding for this study was provided by the John Jay College of Criminal Justice Office for the Advancement of Research.

REFERENCES

Anderson, K. F. (2012). Diagnosing discrimination: Stress from perceived racism and the mental and physical health effects. *Sociological Inquiry, 83*(1), 55–81.

Bronski, M. (2011). *A Queer History of the United States*. Boston: Beacon Press.

Brown, B., & Reed Benedict, W. (2002). Perceptions of the police: Past findings, methodological issues, conceptual issues and policy implications. *Policing: An International Journal of Police Strategies & Management, 25*, 543–580.

Crompton, L. (1976). Homosexuals and the death penalty in *colonial* America. *Journal of Homosexuality, 3*, 277–293.

D'Emilio, J. (2014). *Making Trouble: Essays on Gay History, Politics, and the University*. London: Routledge.

Dinno, A. (2017). Homicide rates of transgender individuals in the United States: 2010–2014. *American Journal of Public Health, 107*, 1441–1447.

Fiani, C. N., Nadal, K. L., Han, H., Mejia, D., Deutsch, T., & Murillo, M. (2017). A system of transphobic injustice: Microaggressions toward transgender and gender nonconforming people in the criminal justice system. *New York State Psychologist, 29,* 5–15.

Gladstone, B., Volpe, T., & Boydell, K. (2007). Issues encountered in a qualitative secondary analysis of help-seeking in the prodrome to psychosis. *The Journal of Behavioral Health Services & Research, 34*(4), 431–442.

Grant, J. M., Mottet, L., Tanis, J. E., Harrison, J., Herman, J., & Keisling, M. (2011). *Injustice at Every Turn: A Report of the National Transgender Discrimination Survey.* Washington, DC: National Center for Transgender Equality.

Heaton, J. (2004). *Reworking Qualitative Data.* London: Sage.

Hill, C. E., Thompson, B. J., & Williams, E. N. (1997). A Guide to conducting consensual qualitative research. *The Counseling Psychologist, 25,* 517–572.

Hillman, J., & Hinrichsen, G. A. (2014). Promoting an affirming, competent practice with older lesbian and gay adults. *Professional Psychology: Research and Practice, 45,* 269–277.

Hinds, L., & Murphy, K. (2007). Public satisfaction with police: Using procedural justice to improve police legitimacy. *Australian and New Zealand Journal of Criminology, 40,* 27–42. https://doi.org/10.1375/acri.40.1.27.

Krueger, R. A., & Casey, M. A. (2014). *Focus Groups: A Practical Guide for Applied Research.* Sage Publications.

Lawrence v. Texas, 539 U.S. 558. (U.S. June 26, 2003). Retrieved January 14, 2016, from https://www.law.cornell.edu/supct/html/02-102.ZS.html.

Nadal, K. L. (2013). *That's So Gay! Microaggressions and the Lesbian, Gay, Bisexual, and Transgender Community.* Washington, DC: American Psychological Association.

Nadal, K. L. (2018). *Microaggressions and Traumatic Stress: Theory, Research, and Practice.* Washington, DC: American Psychological Association.

Nadal, K. L., Rivera, D. P., & Corpus, M. J. H. (2010). Sexual orientation and transgender microaggressions in everyday life: Experiences of lesbians, gays, bisexuals, and transgender individuals. In D. W. Sue (Ed.), *Microaggressions and Marginality: Manifestation, Dynamics, and Impact* (pp. 217–240). New York: Wiley.

Nadal, K. L., Skolnik, A., & Wong, Y. (2012). Interpersonal and systemic microaggressions toward transgender people: Implications for counseling. *Journal of LGBT Issues in Counseling, 6,* 55–82.

Nadal, K. L., Griffin, K. E., Wong, Y., Hamit, S., & Rasmus, M. (2014). Racial microaggressions and mental health: Counseling clients of color. *Journal of Counseling and Development, 92,* 57–66.

Nadal, K. L., Quintanilla, A., Goswick, A., & Sriken, J. (2015). Lesbian, gay, bisexual, and queer people's perceptions of the criminal justice system: Implications for social services. *Journal of Gay & Lesbian Social Services, 27,* 457–481.

Nadal, K. L., Davidoff, K. C., Davis, L. S., Wong, Y., Marshall, D., & McKenzie, V. (2015). A qualitative approach to intersectional microaggressions: Understanding influences of race, ethnicity, gender, sexuality, and religion. *Qualitative Psychology, 2,* 147–163.

Nadal, K. L., Whitman, C. N., Davis, L. S., Erazo, T., & Davidoff, K. C. (2016). Microaggressions toward lesbian, gay, bisexual, transgender, queer and genderqueer people: A review of the literature. *Journal of Sex Research, 53,* 488–508.

Pascoe, E. A., & Smart Richman, L. (2009). Perceived discrimination and health: A meta-analytic review. *Psychological Bulletin, 135*(4), 531–554.

Schafer, J. A., Huebner, B. M., & Bynum, T. S. (2003). Citizen perceptions of police services: Race, neighborhood context, and community policing. *Police Quarterly, 6,* 440–468.

Stotzer, R. L. (2009). Violence against transgender people: A review of United States data. *Aggression and Violent Behavior, 14,* 170–179.

Tyler, T. R., & Fagan, J. (2008). Legitimacy and cooperation: Why do people help the police fight crime in their communities. *Ohio St. Journal of Criminal Law, 6,* 231–275.

Weitzer, R., & Tuch, S. A. (2004). Race and perceptions of police misconduct. *Social Problems, 51,* 305–325.

Weitzer, R., & Tuch, S. A. (2005). Racially biased policing: Determinants of citizen perceptions. *Social Forces, 83,* 1009–1030.

CHAPTER 5

"*Indian in the Cupboard*" Lateral Violence and Indigenization of the Academy

Renée E. Mzinegiizhigo-kwe Bédard

Boozhoo! Aaniish inaa akawe ninga-gaagiizomaag aadizookaanag miiniwaa indinawemaaganidog. Anishinaabe-kwe ndaw. Waabzheshii ndoondem. Mzinegiizhigo-kwe ndizhinikaaz. Waabzheshii indibendaagoz ndoondem. Iwidi Waabnoong Bemjwang ndoonjibaa miinwaa North Bay ndaa.

Greetings! Well now, first of all, I honour the spirits and my all relatives (human beings, animals, birds, fish, the celestial beings, the plants, and other animate beings). I am an Anishinaabe woman. I am member of the Marten Clan. My Spirit name is Woman-Who-Paints-Like-the-Sky. Over there by the "Place where the waters flow from the East") is where I come from and I currently live in North Bay (Ontario, Canada). The Anishinaabeg always begin with introductions to set the tone or energy of a space within an Indigenous idiom. When Anishinaabeg speaks in Anishinaabemowin we are speaking to all of Creation in the good way *Gzhe-Mnidoo* (The Great Spirit; the Creator) instructed

R. E. Mzinegiizhigo-kwe Bédard (✉)
Department of Native Studies, Nipissing University, North Bay, ON, Canada

© The Author(s) 2018   75
C. L. Cho et al. (eds.), *Exploring the Toxicity of Lateral Violence and Microaggressions*, https://doi.org/10.1007/978-3-319-74760-6_5

in the *Kiimiingona manda Giikeedaasiwin* or Original Instructions. Beginning this way, I control the dialogue and syncopate readers within an Anishinaabeg paradigm. I also begin in the language as a way to draw strength from Spirit, so that I can talk about subject matter that makes me feel vulnerable. I call my ancestors to guide my words so that I offer the world good ideas. *Aambe maajtaadaa!* (Lets start!)

I Am Not a Powwow Dancer: The Politics of Indigenization

A colleague once informed me that university administrators thought it would be a good idea if I, as their new hire, could lead the grand entry for the annual powwow. At first, my colleague and I thought it was funny considering I am not a powwow dancer. But after some time I understood the darker implications of this supposed well-intentioned request. Here, I was witness to the notions of what my role as an Indigenous faculty member should be without my input, and that role was one in which I was becoming the metaphorical *Indian in the Cupboard*. I could be brought out on special occasions as long as I had the appropriate attire (beads, feathers, and buckskin). By doing this, I would be conforming to that which non-Indigenous society expects of Indigenous peoples—a façade without a voice. If I had spoken my concerns about being a stereotype, I likely would have evoked an equally troubling stereotype—that of the angry Indian.

Over the past several years, universities across Canada have been working toward making post-secondary education a more inclusive environment through Indigenization. The movement to indigenize the university is a conscious effort to attract Indigenous peoples, as well as bring their philosophies, pedagogies, and cultural knowledges into university strategic planning processes, governance roles, faculties, research, and recruitment practices. These pathways to opportunity and transformation are crucial to eliminating embedded racism, and they facilitate the removal of institutional barriers to success faced by many Indigenous people who want to either attend or work at the university.

This chapter is an explorative work that seeks to point out the realities, issues, and challenges that come with indigenizing the academy so that awareness can be raised to facilitate a more culturally safe environment for teaching and learning. Indigenous academics working in universities have interactions that have the potential to be laced with racism, sexism, classism, ageism, and heterosexism. Scholars like Fyre Jean Graveline, Taiaike Alfred, Devon Abbot Mihesuah, Angela Cavender Wilson, and many others document the challenges faced by Indigenous academics, and warn that Indigenization is a part of the antidote. Following the recommendations outlined by the Truth and Reconciliation Commission (TRC), universities are seeking to find paths towards Indigenization. For this process to take place, there needs to be recognition and reconciliation by the institutions that have a past of intra-professional aggressions towards Indigenous faculty.

Integration of Indigeneity and decolonization of the university is taking place despite lateral resistance to proposed changes to the university structure to be inclusive of Indigenous knowledge, people, culture, and community involvement. In my experience, examples of lateral resistance can manifest in minor arguments or the extreme tactics of funding cuts or withholding hiring opportunities. Lateral resistance tends to arise by those non-Indigenous administrators, faculty, and staff who feel threatened, are ignorant, might hold racist attitudes towards Indigenous peoples, fear change, or are ambivalent to Indigenous faculty members' needs in the university setting. As an Indigenous academic, I see that the road ahead for us will likely not be easy nor welcome to change. For change to take place, we have to recognize the intra-professional aggressions towards the Indigenization movement. From this discussion we can chart new paths, heal, and begin conversations about how to coexist in the university.

Water is Life, Mni Wičoni: Cleaning out the Poison in the Water Cooler

Mni Wičoni is Lakota for "water is life," and it is the rallying cry for Indigenous water protectors across the continent of Turtle Island, or North America, as non-Indigenous peoples call it. The phrase *Mni Wičoni* became the rallying call for the 2016 protests against the Dakota Access Pipelines at the Standing Rock Sioux Reservation. The pipeline jeopardizes the drinking water and lands of the Standing Rock Sioux. Indigenous and non-Indigenous allies from around the world descended on the lands at Standing Rock; the protesters were called *water protectors*, and their job was to defend and speak out for the lifeblood of Mother Earth. The message to all Indigenous peoples generated out of these peaceful protests was to give voice against pollution of water on the Earth.

Anishinaabe-kwe Elders Edna Manitowabi and Shirley Williams, both from Wikwemikong Unceded First Nation, taught me that as an Anishinaabe-kwe woman, my responsibilities are to the water and to act as a keeper or protector of the water. When I saw the title of this book was *Poison in the Water Cooler*, I thought of my responsibilities as an Indigenous woman to speak for the water, and to stand up against the poison in the water, even if metaphorical. The university, as the water cooler, is a place rife with the poison resulting from lateral violence and intra-professional aggressions rooted squarely in racism, discrimination, and sexism. The target of the poison includes both current Indigenous faculty and the new Indigenous hires from Indigenization initiatives. It is my job as an Anishinaabe-kwe academic to stand up and speak out on injustices, but also to educate the university community about the challenges that Indigenous peoples are facing due to entrenched colonialism and intellectual imperialism.

I argue that lateral violence and intra-professional aggressions against Indigenous academics in the university is rooted in racism, sexism and more importantly as a tool for continued colonization of Indigenous peoples. Moreover, it is manifested in manipulation and control that diminish and at times negate all sense of agency held by Indigenous people in the university. Additionally, I feel that lateral violence and intra-professional aggressions perpetuate colonization of Indigenous academics because such actions silence, isolate, violate, and negate our rights as Indigenous peoples.

My fellow Indigenous academics provide ample evidence of this kind of poison in the water cooler. For decades now, Indigenous academics have been suffering and are continued to be colonized by the bureaucracy of the university as an institution created to support the diffusion of Eurocentric culture. These scholars are increasingly voicing their protests against the challenging nature of the university's bureaucratic and institutional society which seems mired in injustice for its Indigenous faculty, but which is recruiting them to join the ranks in greater and greater numbers. Angela Cavender Wilson (Wahpetunwan Dakota) acknowledges that Indigenous scholars have now had decades of experience being, "exposed to intellectual imperialism … by those who consistently wish to denigrate them" (Wilson, 2004, p. 69). The late Vine Deloria Jr. (Standing Rock Sioux) noted that since the end of the nineteenth century, Indigenous academics have been forced by the non-Indigenous academics to serve the agenda of the institution. He states that "[t]he

Indian professor will always be on a variety of committees so the university can claim that Indians were consulted and represented in whatever harebrained scheme the administrators have conceived" (Deloria, 2004, p. 28). Further, he says that the criteria used to judge Indigenous academics is conceived within a Western ideology and unfairly critiques the work of Indigenous faculty members through the lens of stereotypes and false concepts of authenticity (Deloria, 2004).

Similarly, Keith James (Onondaga) feels that the Indigenous experience in the university setting is one grounded in stereotypes, competitiveness, discriminatory behaviour, and preconceived prejudicial thinking (James, 2004). James explains that colleagues single out Indigenous academics for being different and are thus excluded based on those differences. He contends that universities,

> are controlled and populated largely by people who differ from Natives genetically, in values, and in the sense of identity that both of the latter underlie. This predisposes members of the majority and the institutions that they control to a fundamental lack of sympathy, support, or understanding of Native individuals or communities. (James, 2004, p. 51)

Also, James notes that a "genetic and value-based identity" results in advantages for those of similar cultural heritage. However, Indigenous academics who are different from the norm experience exclusion from certain benefits, such as professional "...encouragement, nonverbal and verbal support, information, and resource and opportunity access" (James, 2004, p. 51). James describes how lateral violence and intra-professional aggressions (both micro and macro) are present and arise against Indigenous academics when,

> Individuals who do not fit the surface image of profession or unit sub-cultures can be seen as threatening all of the functions they serve for the members. Such a threat promotes stereotyping of both in-group members (including self) and out-groups. Perceived differences are exacerbated, and negative feelings about and behaviors toward out-groups become likely. (James, 2004, pp. 51–52)

Highlighting the injustice of these actions, Devon Abbott Mihesuah (Comanche) calls out those who perform acts of lateral violence towards their fellow Indigenous academics. She refers to these individuals as "sentries" of the university. She notes that they use, "…gatekeeping strategies that keep Indigenous voices subsumed so that the gatekeepers' opinions representing the status quo emerge at the forefront of discussions about how Indigenous histories and cultures should be written and for what purpose" (Mihesuah, 2004, p. 32). The gatekeeper strategies that these oppressors utilize are a reminder of the Indian Act and Canadian governmental policies of assimilation, like the Residential School system, that sought to eliminate our humanity and instead saw Indigenous peoples as instruments to craft a Canadian identity and economy. Mihesuah reveals that evidence of this behaviour in the modern university found in those individuals:

> guarding the gates of academia double as standard-bearers of the status quo and are in essence the "rulers" [who] . . .. They take advantage of the oppression of Indigenous peoples, and from their positions of power, they decide who is amiable enough to be hired, neutral enough in their writings to be published, and Euroamerican enough in their outlooks to earn awards to qualify for grants and fellowships. In other words, to be acceptable to the gatekeepers, Indigenous scholars and their work must be non-threatening to those in power positions. (Mihesuah, 2004, pp. 31–32)

Mihesuah notes that challenging this behaviour fosters retribution and punishment for Indigenous academics and their non-Indigenous allies within the faculty. The result is the isolation of Indigenous faculty from non-Indigenous faculty who see any alliance with them, or defense of their fellow Indigenous colleagues, as damaging to their reputation and possibly their prospects at tenure (Mihesuah, 2004). Instead, Indigenous academics become marginalized in the institution, in what David Newhouse (Onondaga) characterizes as being metaphorical, "at the wood's edge" (Newhouse, 2016, n.p.).

Mihesuah, along with Indigenous scholars like Daniel Heath Justice (Cherokee) and Taiaiake Alfred (Kanien'Kehaka), contends that Indigenous academics' assertions of rights to express and defend our different Indigenous worldviews have met with targeted aggression. Mihesuah states that as Indigenous faculty, "we often search for rational justifications to defend our cherished worldviews against attack by those who consistently wish to denigrate them" (Mihesuah, 2004, p. 69). The fact that Indigenous scholars have to justify the use of our worldviews reveals that we are still at the lower end of the hierarchy of power within the university structure. If we are always asking permissions to assert our culture and ways of knowing on an equal footing with other cultural worldviews, we thus agree to partake in our institutionalized colonization. Speaking to this dilemma, Justice believes that, "Native wholeness is a threat to white dominance, as it evades the allotment of our lives and lands and faces the threat directly. Our fight is that of all Indigenous peoples: to remain whole, unbroken, and adaptive through tradition" (Justice, 2004, p. 100). Alfred adds to this statement by saying that the modern university society is an environment that is,

> adamantly and aggressively opposed to *Indigenous ways*. Our experiences in universities reflect the tensions and dynamics of our relationships with Indigenous people interacting with people and institutions in society as a whole: an existence of constant and pervasive struggle to resist assimilation to the values and culture of the larger society. (Alfred, 2004, p. 88 [Italics added])

Additionally, he warns that while universities praise their efforts as being safe spaces for education, he counters instead that, "universities are not safe ground ... they are microcosms of the larger societal struggle. But they are the places where we as academics work - they are our sites of colonialism" (Alfred, 2004, p. 88).

Reflecting on the words of my fellow Indigenous academics leads me to feel that I am not alone in my discomfort of the embedded colonialism surrounding me on a daily basis as I go about working in the modern university society. My fellow non-Indigenous faculty and students remind me that I am an alien on unfamiliar terrain. The irony is that terrain is on top of my people's ancestral territory. The university where I now work lies on the hill that my ancestors used as scout posts, and overlooks the lake that my family lived on, traded on, and paddled upon for generations. As I seek to fight injustice in the university society for Indigenous peoples, Cherokee scholar Daniel Heath Justice (Cherokee) reminds me that all university institutions owe us more than the violence and sociocultural aggression they have aimed at us. He shares that, "[t]he Academy is the privileged center of meaning-making in this hemisphere dominated by imperial nation-states; as such, its primary history is one that has served colonialist cultural interests, both directly and covertly. This reality - the creation of institutions of learning erected on the lands and the literal bodies of Native people" (Justice, 2004, p. 101).

INDIAN IN THE CUPBOARD

Indigenous academics working in universities face both overt and subtle forms of lateral violence and intra-professional aggressions based on their Indigeneity, as well as gender. Over the years, as an Indigenous academic, I often used the phrase *Indian in the Cupboard* to refer to the adverse treatment of Indigenous faculty. Being an *Indian in the Cupboard* is a reference to the 1995 film of the same name, directed by Frank Oz, which is based on the children's book *Indian in the Cupboard* (1980) by Lynne Reid Banks. In the movie, a diminutive Indigenous male character named Little Bear lives in a cupboard and is let out at the whim of the boy in the film. Little Bear is allowed to share his "Native American" wisdom as a guide to the child but then is put away in the cupboard when it is inconvenient for him to be seen by others. Little Bear is a slave to the whims of his master. This concept appropriately embodies the term *tokenism* or *Indian tokenism*, which has been a concept popularized in North American consciousness and culture. Universities like to hire us to be their token Indians, like cigar store Indians standing quietly inside their institution, but we are not welcome to have a voice, opinion, or thought that articulates our worldviews.

In the 1700s, tokenism became connected with the Indigenous population in the hearts and minds of North Americans. Elyse Bruce (2015) explains that Thomas Jefferson wanted commercial enterprises to give financial credit to Indigenous peoples in the United States of America to cause those Indigenous people to accumulate a debt that would then force them to pay it by ceding their lands to the government. She notes that,

> When an *Indian* did *not* have a debt, but rather, had a credit coming to him, he received a *token* since there was a shortage of coins in circulation during this era. . . . These *tokens* were meant to prove good faith trading and when accusations of unfairness by commercial enterprises surfaced, it was the *Indian* with the *token* or *tokens* who was named as proof that the commercial enterprise in question was fair to all, including Indians. In other words, the *Indian* with the *token* became the known as the *token Indian*. (Bruce, 2015, n.p. [original italics]).

Today, the term still borrows from its roots and reflects the underlying connotations of using Indigenous peoples and manipulating them for gain by non-Indigenous peoples. Bruce describes it as follows:

If you hear someone talking about the token Indian in the group, it's an offensive comment. It means that there was need for at least one person to be included regardless of qualifications, and so someone was chosen to be that token person. The reason for having a token person in a group is to give the appearance of being inclusive and to deflect any allegations of discrimination. The bottom line, however, is that it's extremely discriminatory and not inclusive in the least. (Bruce, 2015, n.p.)

In his post, "I was a Token Indian," Tsimshian blogger Theo Collins details his ideas and personal experiences concerning Indian tokenism. His post frames tokenism within modern contexts relating to Indigenous professionalism in the realms of government and academic culture. He writes:

I've known them. I've been one. I suspect it is an almost inevitable rite of passage for any Aboriginal professional. What I am talking about is the role of token Indian. You'd be able to unearth a token Indian position in almost any government department at one time or other, often in response to the panicked realization by some bureaucrat that they are not even close to meeting their First Nations hiring quota, but sometimes because departments that have a lot to do with Aboriginal people just want to put a brown face up front in order to disguise their essential Whiteness from their clients. No one is fooled by tokens, really. (Collins, 2012, n.p.)

Further, he adds,

You see, that's the essential thing about token Indian positions, one of the reasons you know they are token. They are not there to do anything except serve as a public relations front. Their purpose is to sell whatever an institution is selling, to recruit customers for that institution, to put a brown face on an institutional product. (Collins, 2012, n.p.)

Collins warns of the dangers of the psychological and ideological implications of falling into the trap of participating in tokenism. He calls on Indigenous professionals to recognize that tokenism at these levels is racism born out of notions of "White superiority racism" [or "White narcissism") as Lindsay calls this phenomenon (Lindsay, 2015, n.p.)].

Lindsay notes that "white superiority" and "white narcissism" occur when some individuals of White European descent engage in actions to generate a positive story that bolsters their poor self-image. For instance, voluntourism has become a vehicle for some individuals of White European descent to go out in the world and volunteer within Indigenous communities in places like Peru. As Meaghan Brittini explains, she went to Peru with fellow university students to perform labour in exchange for accommodations and a glimpse into Indigenous culture (Brittini, 2014, n.p.). She admits that their desire to do good was broken by the reality that the Indigenous Peruvian peoples were being exploited by "voluntourism" programmes that were, "catering more to the needs of volunteers than the communities they claim to help, or for operating more like a for-profit business rather than an organisation that's genuinely concerned about development." Brittini admits that they wanted to appear as helpful volunteers, but that the reality was they were intrusive. She highlights that the positive benefits of the encounter were primarily felt by the foreigners (Brittini, 2014). Unfortunately, the lives of Indigenous peoples have "become tokenized entertainment for foreigners whose intent is to swoop in and save the Indigenous populous from poverty, gawk at the culture, and then leave without being burdened with prolong expose or commitments for the future" (Biddle, 2014, n.p.; Machado, 2014, n.p.). Overall, some of these voluntourists will only end up pursuing an overly Eurocentric narcissistic enterprise of collecting tidbits of knowledge and feel-good impressions associated with of their own actions. Why do some foreigners of largely White descent do this? Lindsay acknowledges that the answer lies in her own "White guilt," which can be connected back to colonization and the "White privilege" is built from the fragmentation of Indigenous culture and rights.

Lindsay explains further that,

> Someone who secretly believes she is a *bad* person will be more motivated to do things to convince herself she's a good person. Additionally, when confronted with evidence that something she did makes her a bad person, she is likely to act out in rage or denial (...narcissistic rage). The big problem with white narcissism, is while it may motivate some positive behavior, it also serves as a massive defense system that preserves subconscious racist behaviors. (Lindsay, 2015, n.p. [original italics])

Thus, I feel that Indigenization, along with efforts to join the reconciliation movement, can easily fall into a similar state of tokenism when large numbers of Indigenous professionals are hired merely to bolster a university's profile. Rushing to join the bandwagon of Indigenization or reconciliation, universities are hiring Indigenous academics in record numbers. I will admit that I have benefited from the indigenization initiatives, but it also leaves me uneasy and scared about what I have willingly walked into. I am left asking the question, is it tokenism and does that make me the token Indian?

For me, the concept of the *Indian in the Cupboard* is just another phrase born out of Indian tokenism—what Daniel Francis coined "the imaginary Indian" phenomenon (Francis, 1992) described as follows:

> Every generation claims a clearer grasp of reality than its predecessors. Our forebears held ludicrous ideas about certain things, we say confidently, but we do not. For instance, we claim to see Indians today much more clearly for what they are. . . . Much public discourse about Native people still deals in stereotypes. Our views of what constitutes an Indian today are as much bound up with myth, prejudice, and ideology as earlier versions were. If the Indian really is imaginary, it could hardly be otherwise. (Francis, 1992, p. 6)

In the North American consciousness, stereotypes of the imaginary Indian, including the savage, noble Indian, Indian princess, or squaw whore, have become the possession of the conqueror and inform how non-Indigenous peoples relate to Indigenous peoples. Like a favourite toy, pet, or tool, the imaginary Indian stereotypes underlie all contemporary interactions with Indigenous peoples despite the change of time or education.

Indigenous academics who accept teaching positions in universities continue to be haunted by the mythos of the "Indian" in their day-to-day interactions with the bureaucracy, peoples' attitudes, and ignorance. Deloria warns new generations of Indigenous academics about the efforts of universities to hire academics without first addressing the need for decolonization of the institutionalized racism and oppressive policies towards Indigenous cultures (Deloria, 2004). Deloria rallies Indigenous academics against the token efforts of universities to offer only a shred of visibility or a hint of racial parity, and rails against those Indigenous academics who become complicit with people or systems that erase and ignore Indigenous intellectualism (Deloria, 2004, pp. 29–30). Using the label "pet," Deloria describes the token Indian qualities of those academics that agree to take a passive role, to be the Indian voice of approval for the whims of the predominantly White administration and faculty found at most universities. He writes, "When I criticized anthropologists in *Custer Died for Your Sins*, there was an outcry of unfairness by scholars, Indian and non-Indian. The Indians were the most vocal, and they accused me of trying to destroy the good relationships they had with white scholars. They were content to be good house pets in anthropology" (Deloria, 2004, p. 29). Mihesuah offers that universities employ Indigenous academics as "window dressing" or passive objects with no humanity, needs, or intellectual opinions (Deloria, 2004). David Newhouse refers to this phenomenon of tokenism as the university using Indigenous faculty as "decorations" (Newhouse, 2016, n.p.). On many occasions, when asked to give lectures, speak at events, show up to graduations, or give opening words, I felt like a decoration—what I like to call being the *Indian in the Cupboard*.

INDIGENIZATION OF THE WATER COOLER

Indigenization is part of a new Canadian consciousness in the academy, particularly in universities that are seeking to build new relationships with Indigenous peoples, and are additionally willing to acknowledge the impacts of colonization. Canadian universities are reaching out to Indigenous people in this country as part of a larger movement towards reconciliation of past injustices carried out against the Indigenous population. Those same universities are also asking Indigenous peoples to direct the way forward as we all come to terms with what has happened to Indigenous nations as a result of colonization. A new national consciousness for reconciliation between Indigenous and non-Indigenous peoples has started to enter the rhetoric of the country, and more specifically, among Canadian universities. However, while the needs for reconciliation have been articulated by Indigenous people via the Commission for Truth and Reconciliation, it has to be accepted by Canadians, and the realization of future relations must have guidance by Indigenous peoples in order manifest in ways that do not perpetuate colonization. In universities, Indigenous academics are being hired in record numbers to aid universities in this pursuit of reconciliation and to establish further racial and cultural parity.

As discussed earlier, until recently, the university has been accommodating of a limited Indigenous presence but has not been very hospitable to "Indigenous intellectual and institutional heritage" (Newhouse, 2016, n.p.). To date, Indigenous faculty and staff have predominantly been hired by universities to satisfy multicultural requirements (Newhouse, 2016). Newhouse contends that,

> We help universities to chalk up the diversity and equity points. And in many places, in many ways, Indigenous cultures are present and visible. This *cultural representation project* is important. However, it risks being only decoration. The real work of the academy is about knowledge and its production and transmission from one generation to another. (Newhouse, 2016, n.p. [italics added])

Newhouse notes that for decades he has been working on a "visioning exercise" to bring the university to a point where Indigenous knowledge is recognized within the university society as a valid means of understanding and expressing the world (Newhouse, 2016). He offers that such efforts are aimed at creating, "a good rebuttal to the denial of the last few centuries. It's a small action, but our futures are built from thousands of small actions" (Newhouse, 2016, n.p.).

Proceeding with the radical *Idle No More* movement in 2012, Indigenous peoples and our non-Indigenous allies are now seeking radical decolonization of those institutions, like the modern university, which continue to foster Indigenous oppression and threaten the survival of our cultures. Heavily pregnant at the time the *Idle No More* movement marches were taking place, I chose not to march. Rather, I watched in support as my friends, fellow Indigenous and non-Indigenous faculty, students, and community leaders left their homes or jobs to walk in protest. *Idle No More* educated the public about a modern Indigenous society arising to, "use ideas from Indigenous cultures and intellectual traditions to build better lives, better families, clans, and houses, leaders, communities and nations" (Newhouse, 2016, n.p.). In turn, as Newhouse notes, we also aimed our radical gaze directly at the universities as sites of change. That movement laid the seeds for the Indigenization movement spreading across Canada's universities.

Then, in early May of 2016, the Liberal government's Indigenous Affairs Minister, Carolyn Bennett, announced that Canada was removing its objector status to the United Nations Declaration on the Rights of Indigenous Peoples (UNDRIP). In 2007, the previous Conservative government had opposed UNDRIP, which followed on the heels of the earlier rejection of the Kelowna Accord of 2005 that had promised Indigenous people $5 billion for education and social welfare programmes. In Article 14 of the UNDRIP, Indigenous peoples have the "right to all levels and forms of education of the State without discrimination" delivered "in a manner appropriate to their cultural methods of teaching and learning," which should also be "in their own culture and provided in their own language" (Cultural Survival, 2017, n.p.). The endorsement of the UNDRIP by the Liberal government raised the expectations that focus would again be put towards improving educational opportunities for Indigenous peoples.

On June 2, 2015, Justice Murray Sinclair presented the Truth and Reconciliation Commission of Canada's (TRC) 94 Calls to Action (Truth and Reconciliation Commission of Canada, 2015). The Commission released and acknowledged the dark truth of the Residential School System, and it opened the door to reconciliation efforts between Indigenous and non-Indigenous people. The TRC made clear that universities have fundamental roles to play in educating the next generation about Indigenous peoples, and beginning to foster right relations between Canada and the Indigenous nations within its borders. The *Calls to Action* triggered Canadians to join those who had already mobilized to support Indigenous peoples in Canada to make necessary changes, particularly to education. The final report of the TRC called on post-secondary institutions to act as spaces to support Indigenous languages and cultures as part of a broader societal movement to heal, disseminate information, and build a more tolerant society (CAUT Bulletin, 2016, n.p.).

Many universities across Canada have responded to the UNDRIP and the *Calls to Action* by releasing public statements, and also inwardly examining their institutions. Before the TRC release, "some universities had already recognized a need to make Indigenous cultures, histories, languages, and knowledge systems" a strategic priority in their institutions (MacDonald, 2016, n.p.). However, the *Calls to Action* increased momentum for the changes already taking place. Introspection is required, but most importantly, there needs to be action taken on multiple fronts in universities across Canada. If Canada is truly going to seek the path of healing and reconciliation with the Indigenous population of Canada, education is the key to beginning to inform all Canadians of a new narrative about and with the Indigenous population. Indigenization has become the mantra for meeting the *Calls to Action*.

If the *Calls to Action* are going to be realized in universities, increasing the number of Indigenous scholars builds the capacity of universities to meet these goals. We need Indigenous academics, but not just any Indigenous academics with a Ph.D. at the end of their name. Instead, we need Indigenous academics of quality and substance that are in it for reasons related to improving the lives and bettering the wellbeing of Indigenous communities. Hiring Indigenous people who are only in the university for their own self-interest does not meet the goals of the *Calls to Action*, rather it is hiring more token Indians and what Deloria calls pets. I recognize the value of those non-Indigenous academics who have been trained, guided, mentored, and fostered on the path towards right relations with Indigenous peoples. I have taught them in Indigenous Studies programs and Departments, sat with them in ceremony, and watched Elders inform them how to uphold their Treaty responsibilities. Indigenous academics, Elders, community leaders, and knowledge keepers have now spent several decades training non-Indigenous academics to become allies and advocates for Indigenous peoples' rights, so to dismiss the work we put into these individuals by not including them into the fold of reconciliation or Indigenization is to perpetuate racism/exclusion and dismiss the rights of Indigenous people to self-determine who we can ally with in our efforts towards decolonization. I want to work with qualified Indigenous and non-Indigenous allies and see that the best candidates get hired in universities. Only when this type of parity is a realized can reconciliation and decolonization truly begin in the academy.

What does Indigenization of the university mean? Further, who is benefiting from Indigenizing the academy? Taiaiake Alfred feels that Indigenization means:

> we are working to change universities so that they become places where the values, principles, and modes of organization and behaviour of our people are respected in, and hopefully even integrated into, the larger system of structures and processes that make up the university itself. In pursuing this objective. . . . as faculty members attempting to abide by a traditional ethic in the conduct of our relations in fulfilling our professional responsibilities, we as Indigenous people immediately come into confrontation with the fact that universities are intolerant of and resistant to any meaningful "indigenizing". (Alfred, 2004, p. 88)

Alfred explains that within the project of Indigenizing the academy, we must all "work to defeat the operation of colonialism within the university and reorder academe" (Alfred, 2004, p. 88). Similarly, Rainey

Gaywish (Cree/Anishinaabe) offers that within the University, "[t]he stories that are being told to us are that we are the deficit of Canada's future.
We are not. We are the hope of Canada's future" (CAUT Bulletin, 2016,
n.p.). Jacqueline Ottmann challenges that Indigenization should offer a
radical and systematic change solution that can "lead to the disciplining
of the disciplines" and begin to offer a shift in the narrative to address the
concrete needs of Indigenous peoples (Ottmann, 2013, n.p.). A radical
change process towards Indigenization of the university must be rooted
in decolonization of the colonial structures (such as university governance, policies, curriculum, spaces, and the majority representation of
non-Indigenous faculty); otherwise, any efforts to Indigenize (including
the hiring of qualified Indigenous and non-Indigenous academics, more
Indigenous designated space, professional development and training for
staff, faculty and administration, along with inclusive policies towards the
use of Indigenous knowledge, to name just a few examples) become a
hollow pursuit and easily manipulated as tokenism.

President of CAUT James Compton notes that the Universities
Canada's website and publications offer little in the way of substantive
discussion on the TRC or UNDRIP, but instead articulates Indigenous
education as a path towards bolstering the Canadian labour market
and economy (Compton, 2016, n.p.). Thus, unfortunately, the culture of universities appears to offer only window dressing on how to
accommodate reconciliation and Indigenization, and only if it leads to
increased student enrolment, and in turn increased profit. Achieving
Indigenization in the university will be challenging because "The strategic plans of most Canadian universities continue to reflect the policies
of the "managed university," with an emphasis on austerity budgets, and
the micro-management of faculty through the use of metrics and other
forms of "audit culture"" (Compton, 2016, n.p.). Jacqueline Ottmann
refers to the university institution as a "closed system," which is rooted
in traditions that have experienced few changes (Ottmann, 2013,
n.p.). The "managed university" poses a threat to substantive efforts at
Indigenization and reconciliation. This model can essentially be used
to manipulate efforts of Indigenization and reconciliation as strategies
to entice students and new faculty to come to a university, thus increasing the bottom line of profit, but offer no real depth of change from
the status quo. Indigenization under the managed university model will
not deliver a positive direction for Indigenous peoples because it further
makes us "Indians" within the Eurocentric worldview. The university

tradition is a European tool rooted in creating and managing the narratives on Indigeneity for the benefits of Western culture. In other words, the managed university should never control the formation of the discourse on Indigenization or it has nothing to do with Indigeneity, but is instead a ruse for perpetuating continued colonization. Compton warns universities that Indigenization of the academy should not be a mere "exercise" or it will "simply result in tokenism, distortion, or cultural appropriation" (CAUT Bulletin, 2016, n.p.).

A great deal of the literature generated in this post-TRC period focuses on the need for hires of Indigenous faculty members, increasing rates of Indigenous enrolment, infusing Indigenous content into the curriculum, as well as more support for Indigenous researchers and research initiatives. However, there is limited discussion on the mounting needs of Indigenous faculty within efforts to Indigenize the academy. In order for authentic Indigenization to occur, Indigenous faculty needs a community of Indigenous faculty, Elders, and community members to guide them, funding, support staff, space, and most importantly, open-mindedness among the non-Indigenous university staff, faculty, and administration. The project of Indigenization can be isolating when surrounded by those who reject changes to the status quo or perceived loss of power or importance within the university bureaucracy. Further, there is continued debate of how to resolve the past and present difficulties faced by Indigenous faculty working within university institutions entrenched with colonial paradigms and Euro-Canadian patriarchal governing structures. The question I am left asking is whether Indigenization is part of decolonization or if it is an assimilation?

INDIGENIZATION OR ASSIMILATION?

Microaggressions come at me in the multiple words that label my ethnicity within the national rhetoric and the legal system. The words used to name the Indigenous peoples of Turtle Island have been changing every decade in order to achieve a sense of political correctness, authenticity, and mutual accord. Yet, it leaves both Indigenous and non-Indigenous heads spinning. What are we as the first peoples of Turtle Island? Indian, Native, Aboriginal, First Nations or Indigenous? Are we all of the above or none of them at all? When I went to Trent University for graduate school, I was informed by a White professor that Indians no longer existed, but my response of "*I am pretty sure my relatives would disagree,*" was met with a frown and a very low end of term grade. The term Indian was no longer my identity but a weapon used against me for political and social advantage by a White professor.

My fear of Indigenization is that it is, in fact, assimilation. I wonder if Indigenization just feeds the narcissism of the modern university society. Alfred, Ottmann, and Newhouse caution against Indigenization as a solution to decolonizing the university (Alfred, 2004; Newhouse, 2016; Ottman, 2013). Newhouse adds, "If we are not careful, Indigenization can repeat the mistakes of the past" (Newhouse, 2016, n.p.). Politics around verbiage in connection with Indigeneity, such as decolonization, foreshadow problems for the use of Indigenization. For instance, Celia O. Rodríguez states, "[h]ow rapidly phrases like 'decolonize the mind/heart' or simply 'decolonize' are being consumed in academic spaces is worrisome" (2017, n.p.). Indigenization, like decolonization, is a mystery as to what it is or looks like exactly. One might ask who gets to set the agenda for Indigenization in universities when the majority of faculty in universities is primarily non-Indigenous? Further, I fear that Indigenization could increase instances of lateral violence and intra-professional violence against Indigenous academics. Increases in lateral violence could stem from a backlash to changes to existing structures, planning, polities, and ideologies held by the university. Lateral violence could look like outright rejection of participation in Indigenization efforts, isolation, lack of support, verbal or physical assaults, and sabotage, to name a few. Having witnessed other colleagues' efforts with design and implementation of Indigenization, I can report Indigenous participants are often strategically isolated within their faculties and the university community, ignored or avoided by faculty unreceptive to change, receive insufficient staffing requirements, are underfunded, and face verbal attacks, belittling, and dismissals. I find myself asking if there truly is potential for Indigenization to occur at any meaningful level in the academy without Indigenous participants facing lateral violence.

Words have power over Indigenous peoples to either colonize or to liberate. Many are undecided about the word "Indigenization," but I fear how the term might evolve and how our non-Indigenous colleagues in the university will use it (to support or hinder). In his short essay, "Indigenosity, Aboriginality, and the Dubious Concept of Indigenization," Clyde L. Hodge articulates the fears that I hold for the use of the word Indigenize:

The verb "to indigenize" is . . . a lie in any form that comes out of the pen or mouth of someone not Native American Indian. In my mind, the use of such a word changes the meaning: It becomes a synonym to "patronize," (literally, to act like our father, implying we are children). Being Indigenous, I cannot "indigenize" someone or a group, either, because we already have been indigenized, not by any human being, but by Turtle Island's Mother Nature. We breathe the dust of our ancestors with every step we take. We are one with every relative; every plant, animal, and rock of this continent. We are not aboriginal, and we cannot be indigenized, for we are Indigenous: Period. (2013, n.p.)

Similarly, Terry Hansen (Winnebago/Cherokee) offers that we need to first negotiate old terms that we find problematic and then come to terms with the legacy of how these words inform societal views on Indigeneity. She offers that,

Terms such as savage were invoked to justify the claiming of our lands. Theories of racial superiority were invoked to force the transferring of our children under a genocidal legal framework. The problem with this is the colonial society and people that created these laws and policies have never addressed why they do such destructive things against other peoples and nations. The denial that goes with the truth behind these destructive behaviors is paramount. The colonizer needs to look inward and examine its own conduct as to why these are catastrophic problems. When it gets real with itself, we can begin to build peace on our great Turtle Island and the world. (Hansen, 2016, n.p.)

Her words illustrate the need for overcoming the closeted denial and pushback on substantive reconciliation of past crimes by merely slapping on another new term when Indigenous peoples and non-Indigenous peoples have not reconciled the use of the old ones. Rodríguez, Hodge, and Hansen are just a few who are sounding warnings.

As an Anishinaabe academic who has worked as a faculty member in universities since 2008, I posit that Canadian universities harbour a climate of narcissism regarding their cultural identity and the placement of Indigenous peoples within university spaces. Canadian universities have a long history of being an unwelcoming space for Indigenous peoples, and while they are indeed motivated to change, I wonder if that change will be one that asks us as Indigenous people to once again forfeit who we are so we can fit within an alien and alienating system that reflects policies of colonization. One of the dangers within the university environment can be the potential response when the institutional bureaucracy confronts with issues of systemic racism. In her blog post "White Guilt is actually White narcissism," Emma Lindsay warns those of us confronting narcissism that we should not expect "people acting out of White narcissism" to empathize with peoples who have experienced the violence of racism and intolerance (Lindsay, 2015, n.p.). She warns us that our very presence, let alone our radical calls for change, will "trigger a massive immune response," and for us as Indigenous academics, will lead to further barriers to Indigenization, ultimately perpetuating emotional pain, discrimination, and forced assimilation.

Gaywish and the *CAUT Bulletin* acknowledge, "[t]he challenge, however, is that Indigenization of the academy remains an often murky and even contested concept" (CAUT Bulletin, 2016, n.p.). Ultimately, universities are businesses focused on selling education to students, with hefty price tags attached. The focus of universities is vested in satisfying its needs of clients, donors and the popular sentiments of Canadian social culture. Currently, universities are focused on appearing to generate a more hospitable environment for Indigenous students, Indigenous issues, and knowledge. As a response to the *Calls of Action*, universities are employing Indigenous faculty members in record numbers. These universities, however, are not generating new culturally appropriate working environments for these new Indigenous hires. Instead, the same academic status quo of old is meeting Indigenous academics. The workplace setting that Indigenous academics enter is ripe for lateral violence laced with racism and discrimination. From personal experience, and as a witness to the high turnover among my Indigenous colleagues at multiple universities throughout their careers, Indigenous faculty are repeatedly dispersing to new universities in search of safe work environments. Indigenization faces challenges if it does not integrate Indigenization strategies for both faculty enrolment and retention. To name just a few examples, Indigenous faculty retention hinges on factors related to including Indigenous beliefs into the collective agreements, such as: opportunities for professional development centred on Indigeneity; the right to smudge in a personal office; inclusion in programme development; and inclusion on key administrative committees. Therefore, it falls on Indigenous academics to try to voice the need for Indigenization that is defined, designed and patterned after Indigenous worldviews and meeting the job requirements. Only when Indigenization is an

Indigenous-centred path forward will both Indigenous academics and the universities even begin to experience authentic change.

THE PATH FORWARD: MINO-BIMAADIZIWIN

Over the course of my career in the university, I have endured moments of intra-professional aggressions displayed and interwoven with general notions of racism, discrimination, and sexism. These intra-professional aggressions have included: being ignored, being isolated, tokenism, verbal affronts, withholding information, scapegoating, infighting, backstabbing, and undermining activities. For example, in the past, I have been instructed by administration to watch what I say because my words might make other faculty members feel threatened, which could lead to them filing a complaint about me. Such a statement characterized me as the "Angry Indian" stereotype. Further, it cut me off from verbal communication with other faculty and removed my Indigenous voice from participation in university affairs. Another example is the time I was instructed to tone down my "Aboriginalness" because it was making non-Indigenous students feel uncomfortable. Being instructed by non-Indigenous faculty members to play "White" only served to drive me away from those particular working environments. Unfortunately, events like this are not isolated. On numerous occasions, I have also been informed by both Indigenous and non-Indigenous faculty to edit or filter my language to be more accommodating to non-Indigenous students, faculty, and staff, and to conform or omit my spiritual beliefs, or alter how I enact Indigenous traditions in ways that accommodate university policies or procedures. I recall one incident where I was warned (or threatened) by a male non-Indigenous senior faculty to watch how I talked to other faculty because they could interpret my words as a threat, which could jeopardize my prospects at tenure or even my job position. This was not the first time I had heard this warning, but it was the first time I took it seriously. From that point on I wondered, do other non-Indigenous faculty fear speaking to other non-Indigenous faculty? I carry those words and, to this day, I have been silenced in order to protect myself. This is a very difficult thing to explain because I tend to go on both experience and intuition in order to navigate my use of words. Other Indigenous people will understand what I am saying, but it is difficult to put into words the fear of speaking your opinions, sharing ideas and feeling or offering a contrary view. I am guarded and do not trust other non-Indigenous faculty not to make me into the stereotype of the angry Indian if I speak my truth because the angry Indian stereotype gets the police called for causing a disturbance and loses her job.

So, how do I cope with the poison in the water cooler? I turn to the teachings of my ancestors and I look to stories of my people to realign my compass and remind myself of the moral path of the Anishinaabeg. Speaking from a Blackfoot worldview, Leroy Little Bear (Blackfoot) teaches that Indigenous learners who seek to understand their place in the world must look to the old stories of our ancestors who saw the world with much clearer eyes. Little Bear explains story and storytelling as a

> very important part of the educational process. It is through stories that customs and values are taught and shared. In most Aboriginal societies, there are hundreds of stories of real-life experiences, spirits, creation, customs, and values. For instance, most Aboriginal cultures have a trickster figure. The trickster is about chaos, the unexpected, the "why" of creation, and the consequences of unacceptable behaviour. (Little Bear, 2002, pp. 81–82)

Little Bear advises that story and storytelling facilitate a transcending, shape-shifting, transformation, and a metamorphosis of knowing, which for victims of colonization (i.e. lateral violence) enables healing. Therefore, through Indigenous' stories Indigenous academics can learn how to contextualize our place in this world and begin to situate our everyday experiences within an Indigenous worldview, ethics, and teachings. From there we can learn to make sense of and navigate interactions within the university using our knowledge system as a way to anchor our Indigenous identity and cultural integrity.

By following the original teachings of the Creator, Anishinaabe-kwewag[1] and Anishinaabe-niniwag[2] find our moral compass and a sense of being as Anishinaabeg.[3] The Elders refer to this path as following *mino-bimaadiziwin*. In his book *Honoring Elders: Aging, Authority, and Ojibwe Religion*, Michael D. McNally (2009) describes the philosophy of *mino- bimaadiziwin* as an ethical attainment that all Anishinaabeg work to manifest in their lives. He states that for the Anishinaabeg, *mino-bimaadiziwin* is representative of "our way of life" or "our way" (p. 48). In other words, *mino-bimaadiziwin* describes the pursuit of maintaining moral ground and living the ethical teachings of the ancestors despite the rigours of life in a colonized world, and while working in the institutions that seek to enforce those Eurocentric foundations that uphold the pillars of colonization in this country. As *mino-bimaadiziwin* is my goal, I look to the stories of my ancestors to formulate contemporary solutions for how best to identify and dismantle the effects of lateral violence on my life within the university. I look to Anishinaabeg teachings, ceremonies, and Elders to educate myself on how to not just survive, but also how to live as Anishinaabe-kwe, and live out *mino-bimaadiziwin*. Following the teachings of *mino-bimaadiziwin* means that I must work to identify lateral violence and microaggressions against me as sites of colonization and assimilation that seek to separate me from my identity and sense of place here on Turtle Island. Moreover, *mino-bimaadiziwin* teachings protect me from accepting that all I am is an *Indian in the Cupboard*. When I get trapped in the *Cupboard* as the university's pet *Indian*, I can lean on the teachings of my ancestors to shape-shift out and find my true form as an Anishinaabe-kwe.

In 2005, I had a young Cree woman in my office crying as she explained to me that she was so tired of going to every class and being asked to teach non-Indigenous students and faculty about being Indigenous. She felt berated, threatened, drained, and abused by the process. We cried together about the pain of being Indigenous in the academy. I told her that has become our burden as Indigenous peoples because non-Indigenous have been taught to not see us as human beings, but that they want to change and learn. Today, I see that non-Indigenous academics are hungry to build good relations with Indigenous academics entering the academy, but it is really difficult for them to stop colonizing Indigenous academics through the cultural, social, and political power they wield within the bureaucratic environment of the university. Non-Indigenous administration, faculty, and staff have an addiction to the power colonization affords them. Many of them think that colonization is something that has happened and that they have changed, but they still think, speak, and act through the mechanisms of colonization every time they interact with Indigenous academics. I rarely ever tell them this, and maybe I should, yet then again, I would probably be labelled the "Angry Indian." It is so easy to shut me down because they hold the power. I am always reminded that in the minds of some people I will only ever be an "Indian." My words of advice to non-Indigenous academics wanting to change is to begin to look within and begin to decolonize their minds, their words, and their actions. Susan Dion offers the advice that non-Indigenous peoples should begin by exploring their own personal understandings of Indigeneity for memories of the embedded "Indians we have in mind," so that, "opens the possibility for... alternative ways of knowing, to imagine new relationships, and to think about how they might want to work toward transforming," new ways of thinking about Indigenous peoples as merely "Indians" (Dion, 2007, p. 330). Because, as Thomas King (Cherokee/Greek) states, "[i]n the end, there is no reason for the Indian to be real." (King, 2003, p. 54).

As Indigenous intellectuals, we have to engage with questions about our obligations and responsibilities in our struggle for survival and freedom from oppression. I look to other Indigenous academics, like Taiaiake Alfred, whose words bring clarity to my struggle to decolonize the academy. Alfred warns us that the "the university is contentious ground" (2004, p. 92) and that it should make us seriously consider how we can exist within environments designed to perpetuate our colonization. Alfred calls on Indigenous academics to be "warriors of the truth" and to speak out against what Albert Memmi called "the colonizer's disease" (as cited in Alfred, 2004, p. 97). From an Indigenous perspective, that "colonizer's disease" is found in the culture of privilege that perpetuates colonization and Alfred explains that in order to survive we have to be insurgents and train both Indigenous and non-Indigenous allies to deliver the cure. Alfred states that the cure comes in cultural and political forms:

> *Solidarity*—We need to disentangle ourselves from state-imposed identities (tribal or patriotic) and reorient ourselves on traditional Indigenous identities, which inherently reflect the "independency" needed for effective political cooperation toward change. The most important aspect of this is the development of a sense of accountability to Indigenous values and community in conscious opposition to the imperial accountability enforced in academe (academic disciplines, departmental and university committees, tenure processes, etc.).
>
> *Organize*—We need to develop effective structures to mobilize the power of Indigenous identity and values. This means an association of Indigenous faculty with independent resources (human, cultural, and financial) to apply in contentious situations, and with the ability to represent an authentic Indigenous voice in academe and to shape the public's view on the rights and responsibilities of Indigenous peoples.

Empower—The need for action. There is no change without conten-tion. And for Indigenous peoples today, change (movement off the path of assimilation) is essential to our survival. Power will come from the resto-ration of connection (among ourselves and to the sources of strength: tra-ditional teachings, land, and community) and the respect that will emerge as we engage imperial power with dignity in a struggle for justice. (Alfred, 2004, pp. 96–97).

To conclude, once we recognize how to cure ourselves of colonization we can begin on this difficult path to Indigenization, but we should not try to Indigenize before we decolonize. Over the years, I have faced instances of lateral aggressions and the way I get through it is to inter-nally root myself in my Anishinaabe-kwe identity, reconnect with land, territory, and spirit. I find my sense of self in my customs, ceremonies, listening to the guidance of Elders, and finding wisdom in the ancient stories of the *Gete-Anishinaabeg* (the ancestors). Afterwards, the external application of the cure comes with enacting those parameters of engage-ment described by Alfred (2004). From there, Indigenous academic and our non-Indigenous allies can begin the insurgency of Indigenizing the university.

Mii sa iw. Miigwech (That is it. Thank you). *Baanimaa miinawaa odisaabandamang giga-waabandimin* (The spirits will decide when we will meet each other again. If we do not see each other in this world then we will see each other in the next).

NOTES

1. Anishinaabe-kwewag mean Anishinaabeg women.
2. Anishinaabe-niniwag means Anishinaabeg men.
3. Anishinaabeg is plural for more than one Anishinaabe person and can also refer to the Confederacy of the Ojibwe, Odawa and Potawatomi nations. Together, we form the larger umbrella nation of the Anishinaabeg.

REFERENCES

Alfred, T. (2004). Warrior scholarship: Seeing the university as a ground of contention. In D. A. Miheusuah & A. C. Wilson (Eds.), *Indigenizing the Academy: Transforming Scholarship and Empowering Communities* (pp. 88–99). Lincoln: University of Nebraska Press.

Banks, L. R. (1980). *Indian in the Cupboard*. Garden City: Doubleday and Co.

Biddle, P. (2014). *Little White Girls Aren't the Problem with Voluntourism: Privilege Is*. Retrieved from https://www.huffingtonpost.com/pippa-biddle/little-white-girls-arent-_b_6062638.html.

Brittini, M. (2014). *Voluntourism: More Hindrance than Help?* Retrieved from https://www.aquila-style.com/focus-points/voluntourism-more-hindrance-than-help/54925/.

Bruce, E. (2015, February 3). Token Indian. *Historically Speaking: Making Sense of it All*. https://idiomation.wordpress.com/2015/02/03/token-indian/. Accessed April 20, 2015.

CAUT Bulletin. (2016). *Indigenizing the Academy: The Way Forward*. Retrieved from http://www.caut.ca/bulletin/articles/2016/06/indigenizing-the-academy-the-way-forward.

Collins, T. (2012, August 5). *I Was a Token Indian*. [Web log post]. Retrieved from https://fathertheo.wordpress.com/2012/08/05/i-was-a-token-indian/.

Compton, J. (2016). *Contextualizing Indigenizing the Academy*. Retrieved from https://www.cautbulletin.ca/en_article.asp?ArticleID=4217.

Cultural Survival. (2017). *UN Declaration on the Rights of Indigenous Peoples*. Retrieved from https://www.culturalsurvival.org/undrip.

Deloria, V., Jr. (2004). Marginal and submarginal. In D. A. Miheusuah & A. C. Wilson (Eds.), *Indigenizing the Academy: Transforming Scholarship and Empowering Communities* (pp. 16–30). Lincoln: University of Nebraska Press.

Dion, S. (2007). Disrupting molded images: Identities, responsibilities and relationships—Teachers and indigenous subject material. *Teaching Education, 18*(4), 329–342.

Francis, D. (1992). *The Imaginary Indian: The Image of the Indian in Canadian Culture*. Vancouver, BC: Arsenal Pulp Press.

Graveline, F. J. (2004). *Healing Wounded Hearts*. Halifax: Fernwood Publishing.

Hansen, T. (2016). *Reconciliation is the New Assimilation: New NAIPC Co-chair*. Retrieved from https://indiancountrymedianetwork.com/news/politics/reconciliation-is-the-new-assimilation-new-naipc-co-chair/.

Hodge, C. L. (2013, February 3). *Indigenosity, Aboriginality, and the Dubious Concept of Indigenization*. [Web log post]. Retrieved from https://www.indybay.org/newsitems/2013/02/03/18731268.php?show_comments=1.

James, K. (2004). Corrupt state university: The organizational psychology of native experience in higher education. In D. A. Miheusuah & A. C. Wilson (Eds.), *Indigenizing the Academy: Transforming Scholarship and Empowering Communities* (pp. 48–68). Lincoln: University of Nebraska Press.

Justice, D. H. (2004). Seeing (and reading) red: Indian outlaws in the ivory tower. In D. A. Miheusuah & A. C. Wilson (Eds.), *Indigenizing the Academy: Transforming Scholarship and Empowering Communities* (pp. 100–123). Lincoln: University of Nebraska Press.

King, T. (2003). *The Truth About Stories: A Native Narrative*. Toronto: House of Anansi Press.

Lindsay, E. (2015). *White Guilt is Actually White Narcissism*. Retrieved from https://medium.com/@emmalindsay/white-guilt-is-actually-white-narcissism-ac6a29e9e995.

Little Bear, L. (2002). Jagged worldviews colliding. In M. Battiste (Ed.), *Reclaiming Indigenous Voice and Vision* (pp. 75–85). Vancouver, BC: UBC Press.

Machado, M. (2014). *The Privilege of Doing Development Work: Voluntourism and Its Limitations*. Retrieved from https://www.huffingtonpost.com/mario-machado/the-privilege-of-doing-de_b_4832836.html.

MacDonald, M. (2016). *Indigenizing the Academy: What Some Universities are Doing to Weave Indigenous Peoples, Cultures, Knowledge into the Fabric of Their Campuses*. Retrieved from http://www.universityaffairs.ca/features/feature-article/indigenizing-the-academy/.

McNally, M. D. (2009). *Honoring Elders: Aging, Authority, and Ojibwe Religion*. New York: Columbia University Press.

Mihesuah, D. A. (1998). *Natives and Academics: Researching and Writing About American Indians*. Lincoln: University of Nebraska Press.

Mihesuah, D. A. (2004). Academic gatekeepers. In D. A. Miheusuah & A. C. Wilson (Eds.), *Indigenizing the Academy: Transforming Scholarship and Empowering Communities* (pp. 31–47). Lincoln: University of Nebraska Press.

Mihesuah, D. A., & Wilson, A. C. (2004). Introduction. In D. A. Miheusuah & A. C. Wilson (Eds.), *Indigenizing the Academy: Transforming Scholarship and Empowering Communities* (pp. 1–15). Lincoln: University of Nebraska Press.

Newhouse, D. (2016). *The Meaning of Indigenization in Our Universities*. Retrieved from http://www.caut.ca/bulletin/articles/2016/06/the-meaning-of-Indigenization-in-our-universities.

Ottmann, J. (2013). *Indigenizing the Academy: Confronting Contentious Ground*. Retrieved from http://mun.ca/educ/faculty/mwatch/vol40/winter2013/indigenizingAcademy.pdf.

Oz, F. (Director). (1995). *Indian in the cupboard* [Motion Picture]. United States: Paramount Pictures.

Rodríguez, C. O. (2017). *How Academia uses Poverty, Oppression, and Pain for Intellectual Masturbation*. Retrieved from http://racebaitr.com/2017/04/06/how-academia-uses-poverty-oppression/#.

Truth and Reconciliation Commission (TRC). (2015). *Truth and Reconciliation Commission: Calls to action*. Retrieved from http://www.trc.ca/websites/trcinstitution/File/2015/Findings/Calls_to_Action_English2.pdf.

Wilson, A. C. (2004). Reclaiming our humanity: Decolonization and the recovery of indigenous knowledge. In D. A. Miheusuah & A. C. Wilson (Eds.), *Indigenizing the Academy: Transforming Scholarship and Empowering Communities* (pp. 69–87). Lincoln: University of Nebraska Press.

CHAPTER 6

Implications of Shadeism on Teacher Perceptions and Practices: Racial Microaggressions in Schools

Anne Nelun Obeyesekere

INTRODUCTION

In my position as a high school English teacher, I assign my students a task of writing their own graphic novel which centres on a protagonist conceived of as a 'hero'. As part of their initial brainstorming activity, students are instructed to develop mind maps listing individuals, both real and fictional, that they believe represent what it means to be a 'hero'. Despite the majority of the students being negatively racialized bodies, the names they come up with are almost exclusively those of White people. I was both surprised and disappointed by this incident as I realized that students in 2017 still seem to associate qualities of goodness and heroism with Whiteness.

Internalized inferiority can be harboured by negatively racialized bodies regarding the perception of the self in relation to Whiteness. This negative perception is driven by the concept that the 'closer in proximity

A. N. Obeyesekere (✉)
University of Toronto (OISE), Toronto, ON, Canada

© The Author(s) 2018
C. L. Cho et al. (eds.), *Exploring the Toxicity of Lateral Violence and Microaggressions*, https://doi.org/10.1007/978-3-319-74760-6_6

to Whiteness one is, whether this be measured by physical attributes such as lighter skin or straight hair, or social/ideological characteristics such as speech, religion, systems of beliefs, etc., the greater their access to White privilege' (Obeyesekere, 2017, p. 2). It is important to acknowledge that all social categorizations intersect informing and influencing each other, and as a result, none exist in isolation. This chapter will explore issues of racial microaggressions in Ontario, Canada high schools, particularly as they pertain to how racism and shadeism are enacted explicitly and implicitly through the hidden curriculum.

Microaggressions are 'brief and commonplace daily verbal, behavioural, or environmental indignities, whether intentional or unintentional, that communicate hostile, derogatory, or negative racial slights and insults toward people of colour' (Sue et al., 2007, p. 273). As a negatively racialized teacher myself, I am acutely aware of the effects of various forms of racial microaggression on both my negatively racialized students and colleagues. An American study focused on graduate student experiences noted, 'racial microaggressions are often perpetuated by well-intended peers, faculty, and supervisors at individual and institutional levels' (Hubain, Allen, Harris, & Linder, 2016, p. 947). Though 'well-intended', these microaggressions are implicit acts of racism that make 'many students of colour feel unwelcomed, invisible, and stigmatized on campuses, leading to experiences of isolation' (Hubain et al., 2016, p. 947).

Although discussion around microaggressions is often focused on race alone, such microaggressions are also based on other factors such as proximity to Whiteness and shadeism within negatively racialized groups. Shadeism refers to both interracial and intraracial discrimination based on skin tone. Shadeism or colourism; the ascribing of positive qualities to lighter skin (attractiveness, intellect, and aptitude), and negative qualities to darker skin (ugliness, unintelligence, and inability), continues to permeate many spaces (Herring, Keith, & Horton, 2004).

In the Canadian education system, 'the valorizing of lighter skin over darker skin is representative of negatively racialized students' desire to reproduce and reflect the dominant White culture' (Obeyesekere, 2017, p. 1). This false sense of inferiority has a tremendous impact on the self-esteem and self-worth of individuals. The hegemonic nature of the Eurocentric education system in Canada continues to perpetuate a structure where the closer in proximity to Whiteness a person is, the greater their access to White privilege. There is insufficient anti-racism education in the secondary school system, particularly in recognizing shadeism and its impact on staff and students.

Although educational spaces, such as schools and classrooms, are often places where these ingrained beliefs and perceptions are displayed, these spaces can also act as sites of change and resistance. I believe that there must be a reimagining of schools in order for classrooms to become such sites of revolutionary change.

For the purposes of this article, I will explore the importance of skin tone, and its influence on teacher perception, beliefs, and actions in a heterogeneous, urban environment, and the consequent impact of this influence on students and colleagues. I will engage in a discussion of how shadeism is perpetuated in Ontario classrooms through the hidden curriculum. I will focus on the concept of identity in relation to the diasporic, negatively racialized urban teacher and student, and how shadeism informs their identity in terms of how they perceive themselves and how others perceive them as a result of colonization and White hegemony.

This article will be divided into two sections. In the first section, I will locate myself by examining my own experiences with shadeism, and establish its present day implications on teachers in Canadian schools. Through this analysis, I will attempt to resist the positivist paradigm that suggests that there is an objective way of knowing.

My objective is to offer analysis into the more nuanced aspects of racism and its impact on teachers and students, as well as to suggest integrative solutions to address this issue and create more inclusive classrooms. The second part of this article will conclude with thoughts on the implications of my findings and recommend strategies to address the consequences of various forms of microaggressions in schools. For the purposes of this article, my focus will be on how to improve teacher training in order to equip teachers with a sense of awareness and understanding of how to detect and reduce racial microaggressions towards students and colleagues. I argue that the same academic space should be given to the theorizing of race (and its complexity) as is given to such subjects as biology, chemistry, English, math, etc. Further, I assert that this space can only be created if teachers work to recognize and challenge their inherent biases.

The Enduring Effects of Shadeism and the Hidden Curriculum

Through the Gaze of Ms. Obeyesekere: Locating the Self

I am engaging in shadeism from my position as a South Asian/ cisgendered/hetero/middle-class/woman living in the global North. As such, I am approaching the issue of shadeism particularly as it pertains to teachers and students in an urban environment, from my experiences in two very distinct metropolises, Toronto, Canada and Colombo, Sri Lanka. John Dewey (1938) speaks of experiences in this profound way,

> If an experience arouses curiosity, strengthens initiative, and sets up desires and proposes that are sufficiently intense to carry a person over dead places in the future, continuity works in a very different way. Every experience is a moving force. Its value can be judged only on the ground of what it moves toward and into. (p. 38)

How then, do our past and present experiences inform our future actions and beliefs? In attempting to theorize my experiences in my previous work, I have addressed almost exclusively my childhood and adolescence. As much as shadeism has integrally affected my formative years, I often overlook its manifestation in adulthood. As I set out to collect and organize field notes pertaining to shadeism's effect on the experiences and identities of my students, I realized that I must address its internalization in their teachers—my colleagues—both negatively racialized and dominant. I noted countless instances of internalization of microaggressions from students regarding how shadeism influences whom they deem attractive, intelligent, desirable, or how it informs their actions, for example, their aversion to going out into the sun for fire drills. Nevertheless, it was only in acknowledging similar sentiments in their teachers that I recognized the challenges in expecting students to theorize and attempt to transcend race and racism while their teachers, despite their own best efforts are yet to, or unable to do so.

Notable is a recent encounter I had with a colleague I teach closely alongside, at an Alternative High School in Mississauga, Ontario. Joe,[1] a White middle-aged man, openly suggested that I date another colleague, Kwame. When I displayed discomfort at the suggestion and communicated that I was not interested, he asked, 'is it because he is Black?' My immediate impulse was to refute this, in an attempt to propel myself closer to 'my kind', in this case, our negatively racialized colleague. This desire, which Fanon (1986) calls 'ethical orientation', outlines the polarized elements of servitude or conquest. For Fanon, real love requires 'the mobilization of psychological agencies liberated from unconscious tensions' (Fanon, p. 24). In that moment, to communicate my lack of romantic interest in Kwame required a conscious separation of my feeling of disinterest, from race. My need to prove my solidarity with other negatively racialized bodies persisted as Joe pressed for further information, asking, 'have you ever dated a Black guy before?' I immediately reminded him that my last long-term and fairly significant relationship was with a Black man, almost pleased that I could dismiss the allegation of prejudice that I felt he was placing on me. Yet, just as quickly, he retorted, 'no I mean really Black. Peter, isn't really Black, he is so light-skinned'. This belief that the lighter pigment of my ex-partner removed him from his Blackness and brought him closer in proximity to Whiteness, despite both his parents being Black, called me to critical self-reflection. These racial microaggressions are examples of how well-intended efforts to connect socially with me by my colleagues led to feelings of isolation and 'othering'.

I had heard similar sentiments in the past, but mostly from other negatively racialized people. I believed these White hegemonic ideals were a direct result of internalized inferiority felt by many negatively racialized bodies, completely overlooking their effect on dominant bodies. In this space, my professional space, an educational space, I necessarily wondered how these ingrained beliefs held by White bodies—teachers, administrators, and support staff—can lead to microaggressions in their interactions with negatively racialized students and colleagues. The polarizing effect of race has unarguably created debilitating conflict and tension, 'the juxtaposition of the black and white races has resulted in a massive psycho-existential complex. By analysing it we aim to destroy it' (Fanon, xvi). I believe we must destroy it in order to shatter the servant-conqueror binary, in order to achieve freedom of mind and heart for ourselves as educators as well as for our students.

Teacher Perceptions of Shadeism: Enforcement of the Hidden Curriculum

The servant-conqueror binary is manifested in racial microaggressions, which are enacted through the hidden curriculum. The hidden curriculum in this context refers to 'the unintended outcomes of the schooling process' (McLaren, 1989, p. 212). In my experience both as a student and a teacher in Ontario's school system, these 'instructional norms and values not openly acknowledged by teachers or school officials' consequently 'other' and exclude negatively racialized bodies (Vang, 2006, p. 20). The curriculum as it is presented continues to preserve Eurocentric hegemony through the normalization of Whiteness. This is witnessed in the constant normalization of Whiteness explicit in the narrative that students are bombarded with in textbooks and lessons. As a friend's son proclaimed after science class, 'it seems that anyone who has ever invented anything is White' Thus, not only does Whiteness dominate the curriculum, the omission and silencing of issues of race and shadeism by not addressing such concepts in schools, serves as a microaggression itself and reinforces White hegemony.

David Knight (2015), a teacher himself, looks at multiple studies based in New York and California in his research around the effect of shadeism on the perceptions and attitudes of American teachers. Knight found that generally, students are aware that their teachers treat them differently because of their skin colour. Knight (2015) notes the observation of another teacher, an Asian American from Sacramento, California who reported, 'students say that the afterschool teachers, who happen to be black, prefer the lighter-skinned students, which is funny because some of our strongest students are dark-skinned' (p. 48). A New York University study conducted on Latino high school males found that Mexican and Puerto Rican students with 'white-looking' skin are often perceived as White and as a result are treated better in school, while those of the same ethnicity with darker skin are perceived as Black and are treated less favourably (Knight, 2015, p. 46). A University of California, Los Angeles (UCLA) study reports that teachers with unchecked implicit biases are likely to interpret student behaviour and performance through the prism of stereotypes, and this can have long-term effects on how students see themselves and on their opportunities (Knight, 2015). The results of these studies show a correlation between lighter skin and better treatment in school. This research is consistent with my experience teaching in Ontario high schools. My students have consistently communicated an aversion to darker skin, correlating attractiveness and intelligence to light skin, and feelings that teacher expectations favour those with lighter skin. This evidence furthers the notion that the hidden curriculum reinforces White hegemonic ideal, by rewarding proximity to Whiteness.

The UCLA study cited by Knight (2015) found that educators often cannot perceive their own biases. They frequently assume that they do not carry bias because they chose to enter a profession of 'helping others' (p. 47). The idea that teachers may not believe they hold such biases, or if they do, fail to acknowledge that these biases may affect their interactions with their colleagues and students, became clear to me through an encounter I had with another White male colleague a few weeks ago. During a lunchtime conversation in the staffroom, Jeff stated that though he found racialized women 'exotic' and 'attractive', he is not attracted to them if they are 'too dark'. He went on to say that people in general, with very black skin look alarming or 'creepy' to him and he often finds this off-putting.

As I replayed this conversation in mind, I wondered how this bias towards lighter skin, though communicated in the personal context, might inform Jeff's relationships and interactions in the professional sense—with students and colleagues. Do darker students and colleagues frighten him on some level? How does this internalized fear of the 'other' affect Jeff's connections, communications, and expectations of negatively racialized bodies in the school environment? Though Jeff did not share his 'preference' with malice or ill-intent, I was uncomfortable with this microaggression towards negatively racialized bodies. This experience made me feel 'othered' and exoticsized and I pondered the impact of Jeff's perspective on other negatively racialized bodies in the school. Jeff's feelings work to perpetuate the idea that all things good are White. Therefore, the closer you are to Whiteness the more likely you will be to achieve, be accepted, and succeed, according to the existing conventions already engrained into Euro-normative pedagogy.

According to Portelli (1993), 'the hidden curriculum is usually contrasted with the formal curriculum and may form part of the actual curriculum' (p. 343). Thus, applied to the nuances of race and Whiteness, the dominant White hegemonic narrative is continuously created and recreated and as a result becomes the essence of the curriculum that is taught to all students, whether dominant or marginalized. However, it reflects the stories, experiences, understandings, and beliefs of a few, without ever addressing the omissions or experiences of the oppressed—in this case, negatively racialized students and staff. Portelli argues two major points '(1) that the hidden curriculum always has a normative or "moral" component', in this case, White Euro-normativity, and (2) all things being equal, educators have the responsibility to make the hidden curriculum as explicit as possible (p. 343). I echo Portelli's sentiment in this regard, as I believe that we must create the same academic space for theorizing, teaching, and learning about race and racism as we do for any other subject. Once we as teachers and educators openly acknowledge that the curriculum as it is presented continues to preserve Eurocentric hegemony through the normalization of Whiteness (in textbooks, lessons, etc.), we can create a foundation and forum where negatively racialized students and professionals can deconstruct, articulate, and share their own experiences and beliefs. These counter-stories (Solórzano & Yosso, 2002) act as a form of resistance to the dominant narrative and serve to combat internalization of microaggressions. This call for the explicit acknowledgment of the hidden curriculum is the first step in dismantling Euro-normativity through the establishment of schools as sites of change.

IMPLICATIONS AND RECOMMENDATIONS OF WORK

Addressing Shadeism in Urban Schools: Teaching Teachers

School serves as an effective creator and sustainer of social myth because of its structure as a ritual game of graded promotions. Introduction into this gambling ritual is much more important than what or how something is taught. It is the game itself that schools, that gets into the blood and becomes a habit. A whole society is initiated into the Myth of Unending Consumption of services. (Illich, 1970, p. 44)

This sentiment articulated by Illich as justification for his notion of 'deschooling', is especially relevant in the consideration of race, in Ontario schools. Schools, classrooms, all educational spaces, have the potential to be sites of decolonization and change. Our classrooms are calling for a shift, a re-centring. In order to change the dominant Eurocentric narrative, those who govern educational spaces must hold themselves accountable. Teachers, administrators, and support staff must tap into their ability to address and acknowledge difference in order to affect change. Removing the expectation from student productivity and performance, to refocus on teacher growth, is an especially crucial point of interrogation for me as I engage in the creation and implementation of a Professional Development (PD) initiative around anti-racism for teachers within the school board for which I work.

According to what Freire (1970) calls the 'banking method', students are turned into 'containers' or 'receptacles' to be 'filled' by the teacher (p. 72). This notion is consistent with the reinforcement of Euro-normativity throughout the curriculum. Students are offered one narrative, the dominant White narrative, which is deposited into their brains by teachers. Freire further postulates that the more (information) a teacher is able to deposit the better teacher they are, in this case, the perpetuating of White supremacy through the curriculum, and the more a student is able to process and internalize, the better student they are. Thus, success in school for negatively racialized students necessarily means the internalization of European ideals, which manifests into internalized and externalized feelings of inferiority and a disconnection from the curriculum, and school.

Fanon (1986) describes the Eurocentric schooling of negatively racialized bodies during the years he calls, 'the period of most vulnerable formation', as an experience of 'traumatism' (p. 127). According to Fanon, during their schooling years, children are taught White superiority so that they internalize it. This fragments their being as they quickly come to understand themselves as inferior (p. 126). Similarly, mandating teaching this Eurocentric curriculum positions negatively racialized teachers as inferior as their Indigenous knowledges are undervalued. Fanon further posits that 'the individual who *climbs up* into, white, civilized society tends to reject his black, uncivilized family...' (p. 128). Thus, for negatively racialized bodies, to succeed school requires the internalization of someone else's story at the expense of the erasure or rejection of their own.

I believe that teacher training focused on the valuing of multiple ways of knowing can offset these feelings of inferiority projected onto negatively racialized bodies. Though the immanent platform for the development of these strategies will be the PD workshop that I am developing for my school board, my hope is that the explicit teaching of race and racism will become a ubiquitous aspect of both initial teacher training and professional development for experienced teachers.

The proposed PD workshop will be divided into three sections:

  i. Acknowledging privileges and oppressions
 ii. Centring an understanding of teacher and student identity and experience
iii. Language as a tool or tribulation

i. Acknowledging Privileges and Oppressions

In order for teachers to acknowledge the diverse positions and experiences of their students, they must first situate their own identities informed by the various privileges and oppressions attached to their bodies. As Cannon (2012) posits in relation to pre-service education for teacher candidates, 'no one is free from being an oppressor or being oppressed' (p. 26). Teachers must recognize and accept the myth of meritocracy in that the privileges attached to certain (dominant) bodies and not others allot the former more opportunities. As outlined by Ghabrial (2012), the term 'meritocracy' entered in the late-twentieth century as a counter to 'affirmative action' (p. 38). The acknowledgment of privilege for the dominant threatens their perceived 'right' to what they have, the notion that their successes—academic, economic, and societal—have been earned.

I encountered an example of this White fragility during a recent conversation with the Student Success Teacher assigned to my class. As a White woman working with a majority of negatively racialized students in the alternative education setting, Susan's role often leads her to have heart-to-heart conversations with students around how their identities inform their circumstances. Despite this frequent and intimate exposure to student experiences of oppression, during a personal conversation about her son, Susan demonstrated how the '"construction of white racial identities" has socialized whites to conceptualize their world in ways that favor their positions within it' (Solomon, Portelli, Daniel, & Campbell, 2005, p. 147).

Susan's son Christopher had recently begun his first year of Engineering Studies at the University of Toronto. In a discussion about the humanities breadth requirement mandated for all engineering students, Susan refuted the idea that Christopher was privileged, both in the particular instance of the course, and in the general navigation of the program, in comparison to the rest of his group members, all foreign students from China. Not only did Susan defensively stress Christopher's 'exceptionality' and 'intelligence', she went on to claim that the Chinese students in fact had an easier time as the programme was so saturated with them, it had become more, 'Asian than Canadian'. She insisted that Christopher had to forgo his previously 'well-balanced' lifestyle in order to 'study like the Asians'. Susan went on to cite an example of a professor addressing students in Mandarin as evidence of what Ghabrial (2012) calls 'Yellow Peril' (p. 46). The term refers to the fear from dominant bodies that Asian students' 'single-minded' approach to university focused only on academics threatens the vitality of campuses, thus 'turning off white potential applicants or else "stealing" their futures' (Ghabrial, 2012, p. 46).

Susan voiced this fear by affirming what Ghabrial reports is the critique of the 'University of Toronto for its "too Asian" reputation: a place where white students feel they cannot balance their studies with socialization' (p. 46). This experience was especially saddening for me, not only because Susan refused to acknowledge that, as Peggy McIntosh (1990) believes, 'white privilege put [her] at an advantage' but further that she projected blame and 'othered' Asian students as being a barrier to her son engaging in a full and happy undergraduate experience (p. 1).

According to McIntosh, 'whites are carefully taught not to recognize white privilege, as males are taught not to recognize male privilege' (p. 1). As evident by my experience with Susan, who I believe genuinely cares about the success and well-being of our students, it is clear that any threat to their own White privilege alarms even the most well-intended, sympathetic dominant body. Susan's claim that her own son is disadvantaged serves as a 'microinvalidation', whereby she is nullifying the 'psychological thoughts, feelings, or experiential reality of a person of color' (Sue et al., 2007, p. 274) and denying the existence of barriers facing negatively racialized bodies. Acknowledging White privilege threatens the very idea of meritocracy that works to preserve dominant bodies' sense of self-worth and value, their 'right' to be who they are and have what they have without ever questioning at whose expense.

Recognizing the crucial importance of acknowledging privilege, my recommendation is that the first step of a PD around anti-racism should begin with a *Privilege Walk*. Similar to Martin Cannon's (2012) pseudo-identity exercise whereby teacher candidates are 'assigned a pseudo identity, based on religious, ethnic, colonial, gender, sexual, social class, and ability differences', I want to encourage participants to 'realize that privilege and oppression varies according to context and/or circumstances—mediating our everyday experience of racism' (p. 26). My intention is to have teachers recognize their own, actualized privileges and oppressions by simply walking in a straight line. Teachers should be asked to take steps backward (to indicate oppressions attached to their bodies) and forward (to indicate privileges attached to their bodies), by the end of the exercise, teachers should be aware of their own positionality based on where they are physically standing in relation to others in the room.

For teachers to understand and believe that negatively racialized peoples are placed outside the 'norm' and that this is reinforced through the school system is crucial to their vital role in establishing schools as sites of change. Ideally, more of our classrooms should have teachers at the front who reflect the experiences of the students they teach. They should look like them, sound like them, and understand them. As we move towards this goal, we can only hope that the teachers who are presently at the front of the classroom strive for an understanding of their students and colleagues by first acknowledging their own positionality in the academic space.

ii. Centring an Understanding of Teacher and Student Identity and Experience

Once teachers have situated themselves, they are better positioned to contextualize the developing identities and experiences of their students and colleagues. As Dewey (1938) states,

> [t]he greater maturity of experience which should belong to the adult as educator puts him in a position to evaluate each experience of the young in a way in which the one having the less mature experience cannot do. It is then the business of the educator to see in what direction the experience is heading. (p. 38)

Dewey's words are especially applicable in the context of race and shadeism as they pertain to student experience and identity. Though teachers may not share the experiences and positionality of their students, they do have a responsibility to assist them in the contextualizing of these experiences. It is the role of teachers to explicitly discuss race and racism in the classroom and create an environment in which students not only feel safe but also feel encouraged to share and theorize their experiences of oppression based on skin colour. In doing so, students are better able to unpack their internalized and externalized feelings of inferiority rooted in White supremacy.

Important to note is that student experiences do not 'occur in a vacuum' (Dewey, p. 40). Dewey (1938) acknowledges the 'sources outside of an individual which give rise to experience', in this case, the experiences of negatively racialized students, which inform their identity and positionality in school are attributed to aspects of their identity that are outside of their control (p. 40). The colour of their skin is one element of their identity that places them outside of this 'norm'.

Centring the experiences of negatively racialized teachers and students will be a vital element of the proposed anti-racism PD. Allowing negatively racialized teachers to teach from their own unique perspective informed by cultural knowledges works to decolonize schools by opening dialogue for all students to share their own positionality and experiences. This works to combat racial microaggressions by creating a safe space for counter-narratives to be shared and learned.

I suggest that teachers be presented with testimonials written by students within the school board reflecting their experiences with race/racism/shadeism throughout their schooling careers. Teachers will be placed in small groups to explore one testimonial and discuss the issues, which arose from the student feedback, any feelings about the findings they may have, as well as potential ways they feel the issues could be addressed in their classrooms. This exercise should then be debriefed in the larger group context in order to give facilitators the opportunity to contribute formal, theoretical recommendations in the form of lessons, workshops, and reflection assignments that teachers may work through in their own classrooms. However, it is important to acknowledge that this strategy should not be understood or read as being dependent on empathy, but rather one that seeks to elicit structural changes in how teacher education is delivered. The intention of centring the experiences and identities of negatively racialized students through testimonial case studies is to combat the resistance often communicated by teachers that they, 'won't have time to teach everything else and multicultural education, too' and that, 'there's nothing multicultural about algebra, biology, geography, chemistry, calculus, or computer science' (Gay & Howard, 2000, p. 4). Teachers need to be made aware or simply be reminded of the fact that the colour of their skin is a demarcation that students carry from class to class. Skin colour has consequences on how a student is perceived and how they process the curriculum being delivered to them, regardless of the subject.

iii. Language as a Tool or Tribulation

As Dei (2000) emphasizes the colour of our skin is the one element of our identity that is impossible to mask or transcend. Thus, in their attempt to vie for Whiteness and all the privilege associated with it, negatively racialized bodies have been forced to engage in other methods to achieve proximity to the dominant. Historically, as evident in the privileging of the *métissage*, a social group made up of the children of White colonialists and Black and Indigenous people in North America, material advantages were given to those with lighter skin (Lane & Mahdi, 2013). The result was the fragmentation of negatively racialized bodies from each other. An environment was created in which there was little or no little solidarity between racialized communities as they were vying for proximity to Whiteness. Consequently, racialized people often do not think outside of this system, but rather attempt to get as close as possible to Whiteness. This is evident in the valuing of 'standard English' over colloquial or local dialects.

According to Christensen (1990), there is a 'bias against those who do not use language "correctly"' (p. 36). She critiques the denotations of 'Standard English' and 'nonstandard English' reflecting, quite correctly that the labels suggest that one is 'less than' (p. 36). Christensen goes on to note, 'English teachers are urged to "correct" students who speak or write in their home language' (p. 36). Growing up speaking only Standard English, it was not until I was an adult that I realized the racial and cultural capital I acquired by doing so. However, though my Canadian accent and language style allowed me to navigate my educational and professional spaces somewhat easily, this came at the direct expense of my Sri Lankan identity. The erasure of my identity was evident throughout my teenage years, not only in the fact that I could not communicate in my native language of Sinhala, in Sri Lanka but also in the distancing that I felt among the Sri Lankan community in Canada. I felt 'othered' by my diasporic community, as I was not able to fully understand many of the nuances of language and local colloquialisms used by other Sri Lankan teens in Toronto. According to Fanon (1986), 'the more the black Antillean assimilates the French language, the whiter he gets—i.e., the closer he becomes to being a true human being' (p. 2). In my teenage experience, the racial and cultural capital I accrued by speaking Standard English, through currying favour with teachers or success in job interviews over other negatively racialized peers, became a source of pain as I felt a distancing from my peer group to whom I wished to belong.

I attempted to problematize this emphasis on Standard English and the consequent erasure of identity during a PD session that I recently attended. The after-school PD was meant to be about language disability, however, there was an alarming focus on a term coined '*Teenage Language Disorder*'. The interpretation of this supposed disorder by the presenter, a White female teacher seconded to the board (who has been out of the classroom for over a decade), seemed to indicate that urban colloquialisms such as slang, up-speak, vocal fry, etc., were elements of student language that needed to be 'unlearned'. When I suggested that perhaps there should be some onus on us as teachers to make an effort to understand some of the language commonly used by our students, and even create a platform for them to speak and write in this language in order to engage their 'authentic selves', I was shut down from every angle. Teachers were emphatically proclaiming the 'disservice we are doing to our students by not teaching them how "we" speak "here"', and 'if "they" want to come to this country "they" should do things the way "we" do things here'. One colleague referenced his previous career in the private sector, mentioning that when he did business in Asia, he had to 'conform to the etiquette and language conventions of the East', and similarly, the 'students should conform to the etiquette and language conventions of the West if they want to "succeed"'. I reminded him that as an infant settler nation, the question of what Canada is and thus, what her conventions are, remain very contentious and uncertain points of debate.

Enforcing these standards of English puts pressure on negatively racialized teachers to speak, and establish the expectation that students speak using Standard English in order to be validated in school though they may not feel comfortable doing so. A Jamaican teacher with whom I worked was viewed as being 'unrefined' for speaking with her students in Patois. Colleagues told her that by attempting to connect with her students through language that is native to them, she was inappropriately 'befriending' them. This is an example of a microaggression that 'others' both the teacher and her students, positioning their language and culture as inferior.

My own conclusion from the above-mentioned experiences is that language and race are points of intersection that cannot be separated just as skin colour and race cannot be separated. In order for teachers to fully acknowledge the identities and experiences of their negatively racialized students, they must create a space for their language in the classroom. They must afford the authentic voices of their staff and students, value, and validity. This will be the third element of the proposed PD. Teachers will problematize the notion of language through a self-reflective critique of their own understanding and perception of language. They will be asked to question why they value certain modes of communication over others, and what they feel the implications of these beliefs are on their students and colleagues. In order for classrooms to truly be sites of social and political change, those who govern schools, as though each is its own autonomous nation, must critique the very concept of nationhood itself, so that its citizens, their diverse group of staff and students, may have the hope of freedom and love, where their voices are valued and their experiences cherished.

CONCLUSION

The revolutionary change that can take place in the classroom must take the form of what Boler (2004) calls 'critical hope', this hope, this desire, 'recognizes that we live within systems of inequality, in which privileges, such as White and male privilege comes at the expense of the freedom of others' (p. 128). The White European narrative normalized by Canadian schooling through both the explicit and hidden curriculums works to oppress negatively racialized students and teachers by perpetuating White supremacy established during colonization. In order to liberate negatively racialized bodies from this mental and emotional incarceration, teachers must mobilize themselves as agents of revolutionary change. Teachers cannot afford to espouse such sentiments as 'There are too many cultures and ethnic groups and I don't know enough to teach them all'; or fear 'inadvertently saying something stupid or hurtful and embarrassing themselves or offending people from other ethnic groups' (Gay & Howard, 2000, p. 4). We have a responsibility to attempt to shift the dominant narrative, to question it, and to challenge it, 'for apart from inquiry, apart from the praxis, individuals cannot be truly human' (Freire, 1970, p. 72).

   If as Dei (2013) suggests, schools can act as sites of change, what better place is there to engage in discourse around shadeism? My hope is that through critical anti-racist work in schools, the effects of shadeism can be dismantled and a culture of awareness created in its place. By situating shadeism through deconstructing its colonial roots and examining its implications today, the call to decenter Whiteness is clear. The saliencies of race and skin colour indicate that there is no objective way of knowing. Negatively racialized bodies, moving through space and time, each experience the consequences of their skin colour differently.

   Schools must be sites of hope and change rather than sites of oppression. The discussion of teacher training in this article outlines three elements—acknowledging privileges and oppressions, centring an understanding of student and teacher identity and experience, and language as a tool or tribulation—as fundamental components of creating anti-racist classrooms. By expanding the dialogue about race and racial microaggressions in schools, my aim is to create an academic space that values the experiences and knowledges of negatively racialized students and teachers. This is part of the process of decolonizing education necessary to create an authentically equitable learning and working environment in Ontario's schools.

In this supposedly postcolonial world, people are still bombarded with images, advertisements, music, and textbooks that continue to valorize Whiteness. It is imperative that they recognize the many ways in which racism is enacted in order to understand the false perceptions and consequences ascribed to negatively racialized bodies and actively resist them.

NOTE

1. All names from personal examples and anecdotes used in this article have been replaced with pseudonyms.

REFERENCES

Bodenhorn, H. (2006). Colorism, complexion homogamy, and household wealth: Some historical evidence. *American Economic Review, 96*(2). https://doi.org/10.1257/000282806777211883.

Boler, M. (2004). Teaching for hope: The ethics of shattering world views. In D. Liston & J. Garrison (Eds.), *Teaching, Loving and Learning: Reclaiming Passion in Educational Practice* (pp. 117–131). New York: Routledge.

Cannon, M. (2012). Changing the subject in teacher education: Centring indigenous, diasporic, and settler colonial relations. *Cultural and Pedagogical Inquiry, 4*(2), 21–37.

Christensen, L. (1990). Whose standard? Teaching standard English. *The English Journal, 79*(2), 36–40.

Dei, G. J. S. (2000). Towards an anti-racism discursive framework. In G. J. S. Dei & A. M. Calliste (Eds.), *Power, Knowledge and Anti-racism Education: A Critical Reader* (pp. 23–40). Halifax, NS: Fernwood.

Dei, G. J. S. (2013). Reframing critical anti-racist theory (CART) for contemporary times. In G. J. S. Dei & M. Lordan (Eds.), *Contemporary Issues in the Sociology of Race and Ethnicity: A Critical Reader*. New York: Peter Lang.

Dewey, J. (1938). *Experience and Education*. New York: Free Press.

Fanon, F. (1986). *Black Skin, White Masks*. London: Pluto Press.

Freire, P. (1970). *Pedagogy of the Oppressed*. New York: Bloomsbury.

Gay, G., & Howard, T. (2000). Multicultural teacher education for the 21st century. *The Teacher Educator, 36*(1), 1–16. https://doi.org/10.1080/08878730009555246.

Ghabrial, S. (2012). Pink panics, yellow perils, and the mythology of meritocracy. In R. J. Gilmour, D. Bhandar, J. Heer, & M. C. K. Ma (Eds.), *Too Asian? Racism, Privilege, and Postsecondary Education* (pp. 38–52). Toronto: Between the Lines.

Herring, C., Keith, V., & Horton, H. D. (2004). *Skin Deep: How Race and Complexion Matter in the 'Color-Blind' Era*. Chicago: University of Illinois Press.

Hubain, B. S., Allen, E. L., Harris, J. C., & Linder, C. (2016). Counter-stories as representations of the racialized experiences of students of color in higher education and student affairs graduate preparation programs. *International Journal of Qualitative Studies in Education, 29*(7), 946–963.

Illich, I. (1970). *Deschooling Society*. London: Marion Boyars.

Knight, D. (2015, Fall). What's colorism? Skin color bias has real effects, do you and your students know how to talk about it. *Teaching Tolerance*, (51), 45–48.

Lane, L., & Mahdi, H. (2013). Fanon revisited: Race gender and coloniality vis-à-vis skin colour. In *The Melanin Millennium* (pp. 169–181). Dordrecht: Springer.

McIntosh, P. (1990). White privilege: Unpacking the invisible knapsack. *Independent School, 49*(Winter), 31–36.

McLaren, P. (1989). *Life in Schools: An Introduction to Critical Pedagogy in the Foundations of Education*. New York: Longman.

Obeyesekere, A. N. (2017). The fairness of shadows: Implications of shadeism on urban secondary school students. In *New Framings on Anti-Racism and Resistance* (pp. 1–22). Rotterdam: Sense Publishers.

Portelli, J. (1993). Exposing the hidden curriculum. *Journal of Curriculum Studies, 25*(4), 343–358.

Solomon, P., Portelli, J., Daniel, B., & Campbell, A. (2005). The discourse of denial: How white teacher candidates construct race, racism and 'white privilege'. *Race Ethnicity and Education, 8*(2), 147–169.

Solórzano, D. G., & Yosso, T. J. (2002). Critical race methodology: Counter-storytelling as an analytical framework for education research. *Qualitative Inquiry, 8*(1), 23–44.

Sue, D. W., Capodilupo, C. M., Torino, G. C., Bucceri, J. M., Holder, A., Nadal, K. L., & Esquilin, M. (2007). Racial microaggressions in everyday life: Implications for clinical practice. *American Psychologist, 62*(4), 271.

Vang, C. T. (2006). Minority parents should know more about school culture and its impact on their children's education. *Multicultural Education, 14*(1), 20–26.

CHAPTER 7

STEM Women Faculty Struggling for Recognition and Advancement in a "Men's Club" Culture

Bonnie Ruder, Dwaine Plaza, Rebecca Warner and Michelle Bothwell

I mean, you just recognize that if you're going to go into a STEM meeting room, ninety percent of the people will be white males. And so that's just the way that it is. (Dr. Jordan)[1]

It's like white men just want everyone to fit into their mold. You know we've created this system, we're welcoming you into the system, but don't try and change it. (Dr. Sage)

They don't pay attention to you because they've already put you down on the bottom of the hierarchy.... If you try to get yourself into that hierarchy, you're going to lose. You don't cause problems....you behave like a guy and then you're just seen as a bitch. You can't win that hierarchy battle with men. (Dr. Garcia)

B. Ruder (✉)
School of Language, Culture, and Society, Oregon State University, Corvallis, OR, USA

D. Plaza · R. Warner
School of Public Policy, Oregon State University, Corvallis, OR, USA

M. Bothwell
School of Chemical, Biological and Environmental Engineering, Oregon State University, Corvallis, OR, USA

© The Author(s) 2018   121
C. L. Cho et al. (eds.), *Exploring the Toxicity of Lateral Violence and Microaggressions*, https://doi.org/10.1007/978-3-319-74760-6_7

INTRODUCTION

The three interviews' quotes above highlight a hegemonic male culture that continues to pervade STEM departments at many research institutions in the United States. In these spaces, STEM women faculty often feel unwelcome and alienated because of the existence of an overall climate that strongly preferences men and consigns women to be inferior STEM scientists. The purpose of this chapter is to use Oregon State University (OSU)[2] as a case study to examine the experiences of women faculty as they navigate and negotiate their careers in a male-dominated STEM environment. Despite having made a number of positive steps to advance diversity and provide support for women scientist in the past ten years, OSU, like other STEM research institutions, continues to be an environment where STEM women faculty face a kind of "patriarchal DNA[3]" that treats women scientists as subordinate to men. What becomes clear from this research, funded by the National Science Foundation (NSF), is that despite institutional interventions and concerted attempts to address gender equity through policy changes, an environment continues to exist where women faculty often feel unwelcome and unsatisfied in the rate of their accomplishments. Women scientists still are expected to, and do, more of the service work and emotional labor that all organizations require to survive. Yet, at the time of promotion and tenure, women can feel a sense of betrayal as their work is evaluated as being "less than" the work of men. To be successful in this derisive environment, many STEM women faculty report that they have developed coping strategies to "turn off" or "tune out" the culture that often excludes them from occupying senior leadership roles, diminishes their accomplishments, and makes them feel remorseful for trying to find a work–life balance with children and their spouse.

BACKGROUND AND METHODOLOGY

The data for this chapter come from an ongoing NSF- funded ADVANCE research project[4] at OSU entitled: Transforming the Institutional Culture for Women in STEM fields at OSU. This NSF research project was funded in 2015 and is designed to better understand why women continue to be significantly underrepresented and marginalized in STEM faculty positions at OSU. The degree of underrepresentation varies among STEM disciplines, although women's advancement to senior ranks and leadership is an issue in all fields. To address this, the ADVANCE grant at OSU seeks to catalyze sustainable climate change by having institutional leaders (senior faculty in STEM and senior administrators) take a two-week (54 hours) seminar that is designed to raise their consciousness about difference, power, and discrimination in STEM disciplines and in the academy, and to move their awareness to action. The theoretical underpinning of the seminar is a "systems of oppression" perspective developed by Patricia Hills Collins (2000). The ADVANCE seminar is facilitated by two tenured faculty members, one from a traditional STEM field and the other a social scientist with experience in teaching a systems of oppression perspective. Both instructors strive to provide an overview of the current research that highlights the historic nature of institutionalized and systemic practices of STEM-related discrimination in the United States. The seminar instruction is supplemented by faculty content experts in order to cover specific topics like race, gender, class, homophobia, religion, cognitive bias, and disability. All seminar graduates end the two weeks by coming up with an action plan. The action plan is a self-generated project where ADVANCE seminar graduates apply their new knowledge to a project that will bring about systemic or institutional change at the university, college, or department level.

All NSF ADVANCE grants require an associated research project, and the women's voices presented here come from just a portion of that research. The overall project includes interviews with participants in the seminar as well as purposively chosen "comparators." All participants are interviewed in the month prior to a particular seminar offering and then one year later. Comparators are faculty who do not attend the seminar but are matched with participants on rank, discipline, and social identities (as close as possible). The interviews were open-ended using a standard interview guide, lasted between 45 and 90 minutes, and were audio recorded with the participants' permission. The interviews were conducted by a graduate research student or a tenured faculty member on the ADVANCE research team. Our ultimate objective is to determine if after having taken the seminar, the participants would be moved to take direct action to implement structural changes at the institution, department, or in their own lab/work spaces because they better understand how systems of oppression affect STEM women faculty. We are also trying to access if participation in the summer seminar would give participants agency and a language to better understand the intersecting systems of their own and others' oppression.

The experiences shared in this chapter come from the "pre-seminar" interviews for thirteen women only. The sample includes both seminar participants ($n = 10$) and comparators ($n = 3$). Our decision to include only women in this chapter was made for two reasons: (1) our primary focus here is on the experiences of oppression in STEM units, (2) while the interviews with men did include some discussions about a gendered climate, they were more likely to be second-hand information. We hope that follow-up interviews and subsequent cohorts will reveal more information from men's perspectives in STEM units.

The voices we present here come from 13 women (Table 7.1). Seven held the rank of professor while the other six were associate professors. All have tenure at OSU. Nine of the women self-identified as White Euro-American, one each identified as Middle Eastern, Latina or Asian-American. Twelve self-identified as being heterosexual while one identified as being lesbian. With respect to their academic discipline there was some variation. All were STEM faculty. While we have not given the specific disciplines in the table to protect the confidentiality of our participants, three identified as being in Biology, three identified as being in STEM Education, two were in Agricultural Sciences, two were in Forestry, two identified as being in Biochemistry/Biophysics, one was in Geology, and one was in Wild Life Ecology. In terms of the years served at OSU, there was significant variation with the longest being employed thirty-one years and the shortest just two years. The women who have only been at OSU for five or fewer years all arrived via a tenure-line position at another institution.

The interview guide consisted of questions that began with their recruitment and hiring process. We then went on to talk about their pre- and post-tenure experiences. Throughout the interview, we asked subjects to reflect on their experiences and coping strategies as faculty. The interviews were transcribed and analyzed using a "constant comparative method of analysis," a strategy of data analysis that calls for the continual "making comparisons" and "asking questions" (Strauss & Corbin, 1998). Interviews were coded and sorted according to emerging themes using Nvivo version 11. These themes were then compared for generalizability. According to Strauss and Corbin (1998, p. 65), Patton (1992) inductive analysis allows for "categories or dimensions to emerge from

Table 7.1 Sample of STEM women in the ADVANCE study

Interviewee pseudonym	Sexuality self-identified	Ethnicity self-identified	No. years at institution	Current rank	Experienced microaggression	Experienced sexism	Had credentials questioned	Experienced institutional betrayal	Experienced invisible labor	Experienced emotional labor
Dr. Ryan	Hetero	Middle Eastern	13	P	X	X	X	X	X	
Dr. Jordan	Hetero	White	31	P	X	X			X	
Dr. Kelsey	Hetero	White	2	AP	X	X	X			
Dr. Sage	Hetero	White	16	P	X	X	X			
Dr. Garcia	Hetero	Latina	11	P	X	X	X			
Dr. Scott	Hetero	White	5	P		X	X		X	
Dr. Jones	Hetero	White	12	P	X	X	X		X	
Dr. Johnson	Hetero	White	22	AP	X	X	X		X	X
Dr. Chang	Hetero	Asian American	4	AP		X			X	
Dr. Walker	Lesbian	White	17	AP	X	X	X		X	
Dr. Smith	Hetero	White	2	AP	X	X				
Dr. Paul	Hetero	White	15	AP	X	X		X	X	X
Dr. Roberts	Hetero	White	17	AP	X	X			X	

P = Professor
AP = Associate Professor

open-ended observations as the inquirer comes to understand patterns that exist in the phenomenon being investigated." Essentially, as Strauss and Corbin (1998) note, this type of analysis involves identifying categories, patterns, and themes in one's data through one's interaction with the data. After this analysis, similarities and differences were documented based on our personal understanding, professional knowledge, and the literature.

Our review of the pre-seminar interviews reveals a number of trends. While not all women interviewed gave examples relevant to these trends, we found sufficient evidence that these are ongoing experiences and are not isolated in small pockets across campus. The themes emerging from our data include: the persistence of a "boys club" culture that often excludes women from important interactions; the experience of "microaggressions" from colleagues and students; ongoing questioning of women's qualifications as scientists; an environment unsupportive of maintaining a healthy work–life balance; expectations for more service overall but especially on committees with a focus on diversity; and some feelings of "institutional betrayal." We describe each of these after we review the relevant literature on women STEM faculty.

BACKGROUND LITERATURE ON WOMEN IN STEM

Women STEM faculty tend to be underrepresented at research facilities and being in the minority means they face more stress and competition than do women faculty in the social sciences where there is relatively more gender parity among faculty (Fox, 2001; Ward & Wolf-Wendel, 2004). Within STEM disciplines, women faculty tend to have heavier teaching loads than their male counterparts (Austin & Gamson, 1983) and also tend to be overburdened with service roles. Women faculty report doing more mentoring and advising for underrepresented students on campus and they serve on more committees that focus on race and gender-related issues compared to their male counterparts (Allen, Herst, Bruck, & Sutton, 2000). They also tend to be excluded from important committees and decision-making (August & Waltman, 2004). STEM women faculty tend to have their research trivialized (Johnsrud & Wunsch, 1991) and consequently receive less recognition than do their male peers (Clark & Corcoran, 1986). It is not surprising, then, that STEM women faculty are tenured and promoted less often than men in the same discipline and units (August & Waltman, 2004; Umbach,

2006). Over the previous twenty years, academic research has continued to find that STEM women faculty members experience structural inequities that can result in barriers to access, promotion, tenure, and retention especially at research one institutions (Allen et al., 2000; Frazier, 2011; Gardner, 2012). The norms, values, practices, beliefs, and assumptions that are part of the "DNA" of higher education institutions often serve as obstacles to women and other underrepresented faculty members particularly in the STEM disciplines (Aguirre, 2000; Jayakumar, Howard, Allen, & Han, 2009).

STEM women faculty tend to be significantly more likely than men to express the intention to leave the academy (Xu, 2008; Zhou & Volkwein, 2004) and also have higher rates of actual turnover when compared to men, both pre- and post-tenure (Johnsrud & Heck, 1994; National Science Foundation, 2006; Rothblum, 1988). At the same time, the decision to depart is complex and is influenced highly by a myriad of variables reflective of the context in which the faculty member is situated (Rosser, 2004), including institutional and disciplinary contexts. In STEM fields it is often expected that faculty spend long periods in the lab or the field, and gaining tenure depends on the output from this intensive process. Of course, this period of work typically occurs during the same years that adults form families. For STEM women faculty, the decision to depart is often made when these conflicting presses play out at the same time (Hagedorn, 2000; Ward & Wolf-Wendel, 2004; Wolf-Wendel & Ward, 2013). Researchers have found that higher ranked and higher prestige institutions in particular may have higher rates of attrition among women and faculty of color, and that faculty who spend more time on research activities are more likely to leave than are their primarily teaching-focused peers (Smart, 1990).

STEM women faculty members report experiencing interpersonal oppression, both directly and indirectly (Constantine, Smith, Redington, & Owens, 2008; Pittman, 2010). This is quite common in academia, a subset of which is referred to as racial microaggression. Racial microaggression is defined as "a form of systemic, everyday racism used to keep those at the racial margins in their place" (Pérez Huber & Solorzano, 2015). Racial microaggression leads to negative experiences for STEM women of color in the workplace, adversely impacting their physical and psychological well-being. It also creates an unwelcoming campus climate for STEM women faculty members in the classroom, the department, and the institution. STEM women of color faculty members tend to experience isolation, invisibility, marginalization, unequal treatment, and the devaluing of credentials, qualifications, and scholarly expertise by colleagues, administrators, and students (Pittman, 2010).

According to Essed (1991), the everyday STEM experiences of sexism, racism, and homophobia involve those naturalized events perceived by the majority to be typical and neutral. This can include putdowns and demotions that are disproportionally experienced by minority women and men (Fleras, 2016). The English language has many words in the popular vernacular that perpetuate everyday sexism, homophobia, and racism (Augoustinos & Every, 2007; Hill, 2009; Kubota, 2015; Shoshana, 2015). The potency of language as power and social control is often undervalued. Words and language are "loaded" with values and preferences that draw attention to some aspects of reality as being normal and acceptable yet diminish other dimensions as inferior, irrelevant or threatening, thereby naturalizing a prevailing status quo (Fleras, 2016). Examples of this type of language are found in our everyday lexicon of conversations. It might include a derogatory way of describing and sexualizing a female STEM faculty member by referring to her as a MILF, a bitch or a slut.

Related to this, Essed (1991) points out that everyday discrimination is entrenched within mainstream institutions so that patterns of dominance are largely invisible to those in power and passively tolerated by the majority. The concept of everyday sexism, racism, and homophobia encompasses those subtle but significant forms of normalized bias that are perpetuated against women, racialized, and sexual minorities through language and actions, often unconsciously, and stealthily by members of the dominant group without eliciting much attention in the process (Shin, 2015). These expressive acts tend to be unpremeditated instead of being coldly calculating, ostensibly triggered by a perceived insult, a grievance, or a transgression rooted in the incivilities of everyday social life (Fleras, 2016). Acts and words of everyday sexism, racism, or homophobia become normalized through incorporation into daily interactions (from name calling to racist jokes to avoidance of close contact) in ways that reinforce the powers of privilege (Barnes, 2000).

Women STEM faculty experience their professional and personal lives across intersecting identities, and attending to this more complex understanding of experiential knowledge will give voice to women who have been marginalized along other axes of domination (Gardner, 2012).

For example, it is well documented that women of color in STEM fields face unique challenges due to their gender and ethnicity (Ong, 2005; Turner, 2002; Turner & González, 2011), including isolation, invisibility, tokenism, not belonging, discrimination, and disconnects from external social and cultural networks (Turner, 2002; Turner & González, 2011).

Changes in life stage, particularly for STEM women faculty, can trigger positive or negative feelings toward one's job. The academic careers of STEM women faculty are more likely to be affected by changes in life or familial status than are male faculty (Grant, Kennelly, & Ward, 2000; Ward & Wolf-Wendel, 2004). Women faculty tend to be tenured and promoted less often (e.g. August & Waltman, 2004; Umbach, 2006) and changing rank can also play a role in research interests or faculty career satisfaction (Hagedorn, 2000). Women faculty may wait longer to have children or marry/partner (Etzkowitz, Kemelgor, & Uzzi, 2000).

Women in the STEM fields today face a minefield that often prevents their success as faculty. These women want a sense of work–life balance in order to pursue a successful STEM career along with children and a happy equal domestic relationship. Despite their desire, STEM women scientists at OSU continue to feel a sense of betrayal by their department and the institution because the tenure and promotion process articulates the value of preparing students and providing service to units and colleagues, yet it rarely, if ever, recognizes the invisible labor or department service work women STEM scientists are often disproportionately required to do in the name of teaching and service. This work is left unrewarded when attention is paid only to their scientific discoveries.

Institutional betrayal that women face comes in the form of a service taxation that is expected of them. The family-friendly policies that have been put in place over the past ten years do not address the realities of service taxation that women STEM faculty often bear. In our study, women reported disappointment when their academic trajectory was not the same as their male counterparts. They realize that they were fighting an uphill battle with many cultural barriers in place that prevents their success, including being a mother, a wife, a supportive emotional caregiver to friends and family, all while they are expected to do the lion's share of domestic and emotional chores in their unit.

The following figure captures the sense of institutional betrayal felt by women STEM faculty in general. While we heard from junior and senior

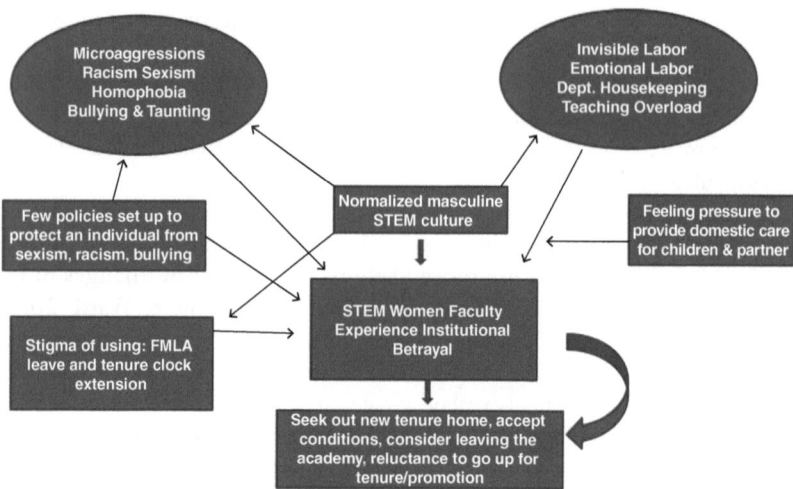

Fig. 7.1 STEM women faculty experiencing everyday department culture at tier-one research institution

women faculty about the experiences of gendered oppression, the group most likely to report it as a betrayal in their lives are those in newer cohorts of faculty because they have come to believe that the academic system is objective and compassionate towards women having children or other needs. Their disappointment often comes when they realize that the overall institutional system is stacked against them having an academic career that is fair, balanced, and equitable (Fig. 7.1).

We turn now to the lived experiences of the women in our sample. As already mentioned, women still see STEM as a "boys club" that excludes them from full participation in departmental affairs, but also reminds them of their gender through daily interactions.

A MALE WORKPLACE—IT STILL FEELS LIKE A "BOYS CLUB"

Eleven of the 13 women in our study reflected on their experiences working and functioning in STEM disciplines where male-dominated humor is punctuated by prejudices, sexist, racist, and homophobic banter. Their male colleagues treat the workplace at times like a "man cave" where the expectation was different wry forms of taunting, teasing, and ridiculing. This was further accentuated by after-work socializing, often at a bar, that acted as another location where male bonding and solidarity were naturalized. This was all considered as part of an extended playground exclusively for male STEM scientists. To be considered successful in this environment, a STEM scientist would often be required to be near or around their lab for 10–15 hours per day. Essentially, the "ideal type" scientist was premised on being a cisgender male who was backed up by a stay-at-home wife who does the domestic chores and fulfilled the emotional labor for their family.

It was this environment that early STEM women had to quickly adapt to or else face taunting, teasing, exclusion or ridicule from the "boys club." This was certainly the culture that Dr. Jordan, a professor who has been at OSU for 30 years, recalls having to function within. Despite her efforts to tolerate and be successful in this environment, Dr. Jordan reported feeling inadequate and unprepared as it conflicts with the way in which she was socialized. She tells us:

> You need many hours in the lab, 20 hours a day, or 60 hours per week—you're competing with them, you have to do it their way. But it's not like they're forcing you, but you're competing, what else can you do? So you have to do it, even though you think that there are other things one should do. You see in this way, I think you have to do what everybody does. So even though we don't think that everybody in the lab should not be working this much. The pressure is on and you have to do what other people do or else you won't survive. White males can afford the time more than the women, they can have it easier than ethnic people because they know the system. So you have to work harder than they are, and if they are working a lot of hours then you have to do more... If you want to be accepted in a man's world, you act like men.

In a similar sentiment, Dr. Jones (professor) notes that when she arrived at OSU in 2002, she had to conform to a particular "old White boys" way of doing things or else face ridicule. Ironically she noted that her training in a laboratory on the East Coast where she completed her doctorate had a similar White patriarchal culture. So coming to work at OSU was actually not a huge culture shock for Dr. Jones. She says:

> I'm just going to sound like a broken record, but the social construction is that there is a certain way to do STEM. There's a right way to do STEM

and that right way is the way that all the old, White boys have been doing it forever. And as long as we have that be the way that it's set up, we're going to have others, whatever they are, you know, if they're 40 year old White guys verses 60 year old White guys or they're women or, you know, women of color... You know, that's a barrier...this whole binary setup that there's...this is the right way and this is the wrong way, I mean there's so many binaries.

Over the previous 20 years, academic research has continued to find that STEM women faculty members experience structural inequities that can result in barriers to access, promotion, tenure, and retention especially at research one institutions (Allen et al., 2000; Gardner, 2012). The norms and practices among those working in STEM disciplines that appear as a kind of "boys club" are pervasive in higher education institutions and can serve to privilege men while at the same time disadvantaging women and other underrepresented faculty members particularly in the STEM disciplines (Aguirre, 2000; Jayakumar et al., 2009). Gaining access to the club, or getting rid of the club, is especially challenging when daily interpersonal interactions work to continue a feeling of being "less than" among women.

EXPERIENCING MICROAGGRESSIONS AT WORK

An experience that many STEM women faculty reported in their labs, departments, and on the university campus in general was different forms of everyday microaggressions. The term "microaggression" was developed by Columbia professor Derald Sue to refer to "brief and commonplace daily verbal, behavioral, or environmental indignities, whether intentional or unintentional, that communicate hostile, derogatory, or negative racial slights and insults toward people of color." Dr. Kelsey, a recently arrived associate professor, explains her experience thus far at OSU. She says:

A lot of this stuff is subtle now, and that's actually what makes it in some ways worse than when it's blatant. When it's blatant, you see it, you go, "Okay, we can deal with it." But when it's subtle and it just kind of picks at you, you don't realize you're bleeding until afterwards. I would think "What happened? How come I feel so awful today?" And so it's those...it's subtle in those pieces.

Microaggressions were reported by women from associate to full professors, in teaching or administrative leadership roles. However, participants who had been socialized into their STEM fields earlier did not
use the term microaggression in describing the many incidents that they
were exposed to at OSU during their career—mainly because the term
microaggression is relatively recent and has not permeated the cultural
lexicon of STEM culture. We include them here as they are consistent
with how we understand microaggressions to exist in academic work settings. Dr. Jordan, a senior professor, described a situation when a male
colleague dismissed her accomplishment when she was chosen for a prestigious national award. Upon getting the news that she was selected for
the award her male colleague stated, "Oh yeah, you got one of those
pink money NSF awards, but it is one of those women things." Dr. Sage,
a professor and head of a STEM department, recalled a time when she
was told by a male colleague, "You are thinking with your "X" chromo-
some instead of your brain."

The everyday naturalized "locker room" language of male STEM
faculty contributed to the respondents experience of microaggressions.
Dr. Roberts, an associate professor, shared this example:

> We'll be sitting in a meeting, with friends you know, people in my depart-
> ment that I socialize with. Everything is like, "my guys do this" and actu-
> ally one time I said, "but you have women in your group." And he just
> looked at me and gave me the dirtiest look. Another time, I was trying
> to hire for a field crew and the other person on the hiring team, a White
> male, he kept referring to the female applicants as girls.

One microaggression six women faculty experienced was being called
"Mrs." rather than "Dr." or "Professor." This often occurred with
undergraduate or graduate students. Dr. Jones (professor) tells us:

> With students, you know I get the emails that start off with "Hey Jane"
> as opposed Dr. or even Professor. I know some of my male colleagues- the
> same students will address them very formally. ... I tell my advisees always
> default to those professional norms. Don't assume that just because it's a
> woman that the person is a secretary, which is often the assumption.

However, it was also noted by five of our interviewees that STEM male
faculty would belittle women scientists in public spaces or when students

were present. Dr. Johnson, an associate professor reflected on a 22-year career at OSU where this practice was normalized in her unit:

> So, we were just noting the other day about how often we are in meetings, particularly a graduate committee meeting or something like that…often if the graduate committee chair is a male, they will go around the table and introduce everybody as Dr. so and so, and then they get to you and they call you by your first name if you are female.

Another microaggression that nine women reported was that their ideas were ignored or discounted until the same idea with a slightly different title was presented even during the same meeting but by a STEM male colleague. Ideas put forth by male colleagues magically become eureka moments. Dr. Walker (an associate professor at OSU for 17 years) describes the way this subtly happens in her department. She says:

> So I will say something and it is perceived as the dumbest idea since dirt. Then in the same meeting a male colleague would re-voice the idea and its considered brilliant.

Several women reported intentionally engaged in strategies to get their ideas heard in department meeting. This often came at the expense of sacrificing personal credit for their ideas. Dr. Sage explained her strategy to get ideas on the table during department meetings. She says:

> I certainly have been in situations where I felt like my opinions or suggestions were not taken seriously. But I've learned pretty early on how to make suggestions in those situations, how to make suggestions in a way that ended up being somebody else's idea so they still happened. [laughing] It's a strategy, you know.

The sentiments that were voiced by Drs. Johnson, Sage, Walker, and Jones above are reflected in earlier literature (Augoustinos & Every, 2007; Kubota, 2015; Shoshana, 2015). This earlier research found that language in the work environment is often used as a powerful tool of social control and as a way to value or undervalue an individual's accomplishments. Words and language are often "loaded" with values that draw attention to some aspects of what is "normal and ideal" while at the same time diminishing other dimensions as inferior, irrelevant or threatening, thereby naturalizing a prevailing status quo (Fleras, 2016). This was true for six of the STEM women interviewed in this ADVANCE study. When women's experiences or actions were not labeled as "normal" or "traditional," we heard that they often were questioned about their legitimacy.

QUESTIONING OF CREDENTIALS AND LEGITIMACY

Another theme that emerged from the narratives of our women participants was one of "doubting their qualifications." Participants reported that both colleagues and students, particularly males, made derogatory, debasing sexual comments or shrewd remarks that diminished and called into question the qualifications or competence of women STEM faculty members. Participants expressed that colleagues usually commented about their rank and alluded to their academic unworthiness as faculty members. Students, however, stated or inferred that the STEM women faculty members were incompetent or were "ignorant" of information about their field. Here Dr. Ryan, a professor who also identifies as a Middle Eastern woman of color, shared her experience with students. She says:

> In a classroom setting, I've come to realize the male figure is what they expect to see. They are always willing to accept whatever mistakes the [male] teacher makes in terms of... like if he was late in giving back the reports or said something students don't like. But with women, at least with me, it wasn't accepted. It always ended up on my teaching evaluation in some mean or devastating way.

Through this statement, Dr. Ryan's status and rank as a STEM professor was not given the same respect as she believed was given to her male colleagues. Male STEM students also questioned the educational background and openly challenged STEM women faculty on various topics. Male students were more likely than female students to not believe, respect, or recognize the qualifications or station of the female professors in whose courses they were enrolled. Dr. Ryan makes this point when she says:

It's a passive-aggressive kind of thing. I would say something and they [male students] wouldn't do it. And then they wouldn't believe the results. And its just more the integrity and their work ethics- they would leave early, come late. It was the work ethic and that they didn't acknowledge my authority as a woman in the lab, the PI. So it was both scientific and personal.

Disrespecting of women STEM faculty was also voiced by Dr. Cheng who reports that she was subjected to objectification by male students in her classroom. This came in the form of male students ogling at her in a lecherous manner. The research team coined the term clothing microaggression to classify what Dr. Cheng describes. She told us: "When I was younger, I used to dress in short skirts. I distinctly remember male students telling me 'Oh you can't be in engineering' because of my short skirt. And at some point I stopped doing that. Now I hardly ever wear skirts."

Four other participants shared an experience about someone making a comment about their wardrobe or their physical appearance in the course evaluations. This was obviously not part of the course content, yet students would anonymously feel free to make snide and hurtful comments about how women STEM faculty dressed or their mannerisms. Dr. Garcia tells us about a colleague in her department. She explains:

My favorite story about this comes from a colleague who would ride her bike to school every day. She had a pair of shoes in her office to wear with her nice clothes. And on her class evaluation from students someone wrote "why do you wear the same shoes every day?" And its like...I don't think I have ever noticed who is wearing what shoes. But it is just interesting... I know if a guy had worn the same sweater ten times...I don't know if anyone would have written that on his evaluation. So, it is just interesting.

Microaggressions, whether they occurred in department meetings or in the classroom, were daily reminders to women faculty that they were different from their male colleagues. Another way in which women and men in academia are different is that they live in a social world in which they have different relationships with families. While attitudes are changing, women are still expected to take primary responsibility for caretaking in their domestic lives. Universities have not paid enough attention to this reality (Kornberg, 2008).

A LACK OF SUPPORTIVE WORKPLACE POLICIES FOR WORK–LIFE BALANCE

Women faculty report having to contend with the reality that many of the so-called "family friendly" university initiated policies do not take into consideration the hidden hegemonic requirements for success in the STEM fields. For example, FMLA policies do allow women to take up to 12 weeks off following the birth of a child (unpaid unless they have accumulated enough sick/vacation to cover the leave). However, STEM women faculty are well aware of the competitive nature of labs/fieldwork and are sensitive to the ways that departments stigmatize scientists who take time from work for family matters. This means that women, who by societal standards are expected to take care of the children, find themselves caught between their career aspirations and what the dominant cultural norms expect them to do. Lateral pressure to be a full-time stay-at-home mother also came from relatives or biological mothers who often do not know about the hidden pressures on the "mommy track" in academia (Kornberg, 2008).

Dr. Scott, a professor who has worked at OSU for five years, shared her experience as she examined her options for having a baby while on the tenure track. Dr. Scott noted that this issue is perplexing for women because research-based universities continue to be based on a male trajectory for success. Women have not been part of the institutional imagination of what accommodations are needed to create a more equitable and socially just environment for STEM women faculty. There is a culture of performance, competitiveness, and total dedication to one's job and lab that is nearly impossible for women to maintain when caring for young children. Dr. Scott tells us:

> It's an issue for women because men don't get pregnant. They do have children but they don't get pregnant. Men don't have to worry about taking time from work when their child comes along. Its assumed that men will not have his career trajectory disrupted by having a baby. Spouses take over the brunt of domestic chores.

Dr. Scott went on to tell us a great deal more about her experience preparing for the tenure and promotion process while pregnant. Her assertive attitude toward having a child and also announcing it to the world was not common among our interviewees. Seven of the 13 STEM women did not take this approach. The women in this study were mostly timid and reserved about the fact they got pregnant or that they had a child. Most kept it a secret that they might have temporarily stepped off of the academic treadmill in order to be at home with their young children. Here, Dr. Scott tells us her feelings about tenure and promotion policies:

> I think that having a child should be welcomed, it should be encouraged, it should be embraced, and it should not be penalized. And being told not to talk about it in my tenure statement, made it seem like it was this deep dark secret. But it wasn't. And so I put it in my tenure letter. Actually it was the very first statement I had, I said, I've gotten a lot out of the last six and a half years, including a baby boy. And it just doesn't seem like the life history of women are incorporated into the tenure package. It's just a very male system, and I'm sorry, women are very different. I've seen data on this where, a women's productivity is very bimodal over the course of a lifetime. And in terms of productivity at work, a lot of energy goes into reproduction, in that center year, and a little less goes toward writing papers. And, you know that's not what tenure is. Tenure is, you know as they say, balls to the wall. Which is VERY MALE.

Dr. Cheng, a STEM faculty member, had a similar experience:

> When I had kids, it…people didn't talk about the fact that faculty had kids. It took one or two of us saying "You know scheduling a meeting for 7:30 in the morning is really bad because we are taking our kids to school right then and we won't be here until 8:30 in the morning" and that was uncommon— you just didn't say that. You just didn't say "I am sorry I am not here at 4 pm because I come in at 7:00 and leave at 3:00 because I have to take care of my kids after school."

Dr. Cheng goes on to say that she believes this attitude is slowly changing for younger female faculty who are coming into a workplace where the men have become more accustomed to working closely with female STEM faculty (Ecklund & Lincoln, 2016). These younger and more progressive men may have attended a graduate school that was a little more diverse and so after many years of this exposure to competent and capable female STEM colleagues, the "men's club" has softened up for the newest cohort of STEM women faculty. Dr. Cheng tells us:

I think it's different now. I really do. We have young faculty now and they have kids and they are like, "I am not around—I have to go and take care of my kids." So I think that there's much more acceptance now than there was ten or fifteen years ago.

As women who joined the STEM fields in the academy in larger numbers after the 1980s, a question that was heard was the difficulty they had in trying to find a balance between having a successful academic career with the realities of their own family clock. For the women in this ADVANCE study, the question of finding a work–life balance, raising a family, and being a partner loomed heavily on women's minds. This question existed for 9 of the 13 women in this sample from the time they were contemplating going beyond an undergraduate degree and pursuing a master's or doctoral degree. For men in a similar circumstance, the question of children and taking time from work to raise them was rarely considered as a factor that would affect their career trajectory. The socialization of women in our culture suggests that there is an added cultural pressure for women compared to men to feel guilty about having children and then neglecting them by going off to a paid labor position outside the home. The most damaging form of gender bias seems to be triggered by motherhood. A maternal bias includes descriptive stereotyping that results in strong assumptions in STEM disciplines that is part of the DNA which assumes that women scientist will lose their work commitment and competence after they have children (Correll, Benard, & Paik, 2007; Cuddy, Fiske, & Glick, 2004), as well as prescriptive stereotyping that penalizes mothers who remain indisputably committed (Benard & Correll, 2010).

SERVICE QUEENS AND PROVIDING EMOTIONAL LABOR

A variety of studies show that tenure track and tenured male faculty members focus more on research than do female faculty (Fox & Colatrella, 2006). While men are not necessarily more productive than women, they are more protective of their research time (Fox & Colatrella, 2006). Tenured women faculty, on the other hand, tend to devote more time to teaching, mentoring, and service, and particularly to activities that may be seen as building bridges around the university (Fox & Colatrella, 2006). Women are more likely to be doing unrecognized emotional labor for colleagues, staff, and/or students. Emotional labor includes managing relationships and can be a time-consuming activity in increasingly diverse classrooms. Women note they are asked to "help" when their colleagues are working with students different from themselves. Yet, these pursuits hold less value in promotion cases in many institutions, especially at tier-one research universities (Guarino & Borden, 2017). Women in most STEM disciplines are also more likely to be called upon to do the "domestic labor" of a college (taking meeting notes or organizing events, for example). Faculty of color are also more likely to be tapped to do the service work that requires that they go outside of the unit and act as the diverse public face for the department or college thereby demonstrating how inclusive the program is for students and potential alumni donors.

A study of tenured and nontenured faculty at more than 140 institutions (Guarino & Borden, 2017) found strong evidence that on average, women faculty perform more service than male faculty, and that the service differential is driven particularly by the expectation for women to participate in internal (campus committees) rather than external (professional associations) service. This is important because service loads are likely to also have an indirect impact on productivity in other areas of faculty effort, such as research and teaching, and these latter activities can lead to promotion and salary differentials as they are tied to merit pay and salary increases (Guarino & Borden, 2017).

We found considerable evidence of these trends taking place at OSU in the STEM fields. Women consistently reported that they were asked to do more service than their male counterparts. Dr. Walker, an associate professor, reflected on this:

> In our college, the group that manages and implements the events is always the women. The White males never step-up. These individual knew exactly what they needed to do in order to be successful and rise up in the ranks. The women in contrast often struggled to get credit and praise for the valuable contributions they make to help with the other team building or social events with students. And people defend that by saying women are the sex who naturally work well with students due to their "maternal insticts."

Others like Dr. Paul, who has been in her department for 15 years, had a different take on women in her unit volunteering for service. She felt that women come forward to do service jobs in their unit because it is part of gender socialization that starts at an early age. Mentoring of faculty, students, and staff is preferable among women faculty because many receive a psychological sense of mattering and belonging for doing this service work. Despite this, Dr. Paul also recognized the importance of publications, international reputation, and research as the key to future promotion, prestige, and higher salary. Dr. Paul was clear in her description of the circumstance she has observed:

> I am going to use a generalization that women volunteer to do stuff for the group, and it is certainly the case in my unit. I have a woman associate professor in my department and she has taken on a lot of responsibility and she internalizes that service... So she's in a position where she probably can't get promoted higher because we don't have promotion and tenure guidelines that reward her for service sufficiently. At the end of the day, for a professor it comes down to international reputation, publications, and research, and she's sacrificed that on behalf of the group. We should be promoting her, not somebody who goes off- like this other person who brings in tons of money and does nothing for the unit our students. So I think that's a huge problem.

INSTITUTIONAL BETRAYAL HARMS WOMEN FACULTY

"Institutional Betrayal" as defined by Smith and Freyd (2014) involves those "situations when an institution causes harm to an individual who trusts or depends upon that institution." This perspective includes the features of a university that can condone, hide, or normalize experiences of harm. The betrayal is most often felt in the tenure and promotion decision-making process. This is particularly so when the university is not giving clear guidance as to what options are available for an individual to stop their tenure clock. It is also apparent when an individual is either encouraged to take on a great a service burden for the university, or at least receives no mentoring to discourage too much service. The betrayal can also come when an individual is told one thing about their tenure requirements and contributions to the program and then later realizes during the preparation of their tenure dossier that a new set of expectations will be used to access their tenure case. In situations where verbal agreements were made, it is very easy for the individual to feel betrayed down the road when a new department head shows up and all previous agreements are not recognized. When a faculty member does not have a position description that clearly articulates her/his job responsibilities, or if there are different understandings of how to judge the work assigned, faculty can feel betrayed by the institution.

Harassment or bullying by colleagues in departments is yet another form of institutional betrayal particularly if the university does not have a formal reporting mechanism in place or a specific neutral "Ombuds" office to help mediate grievances between the leadership and faculty. Furthermore, there may be no recourse in the university to call unfair practices into question. These are all potential examples of institutional betrayal for faculty.

Throughout our interviews, we heard how institutional betrayal was experienced by STEM women faculty. The growing body of research from ADVANCE and elsewhere is showing that incidences are not always isolated; rather, there are some patterns that continue to repeat themselves. Allen et al. (2000) and Gardner (2012) found in their research that STEM women faculty tend to be overburdened with service roles of mentoring and advising students on campus and serving on committees that focus on diversity, race, and gender-related issues and initiatives compared to their male counterparts. Observing these incidences at OSU gives us a chance to identify the systemic barriers that STEM women faculty experience on a regular basis. In the examples below our participants reveal how they experienced a sense of betrayal when their service to the university and or students was expected, but not recognized by the tenure and promotion rules and regulations at the institution.

The first example comes from Dr. Ryan, a professor who has been at OSU for over a decade. She tells us about a horrible department culture she endured for years before OSU had an office on campus to advocate or protect her from colleagues who relentlessly bullied and harassed her. Dr. Ryan tells us:

> I'm in a department right now that's not the department that is closest to my expertise. I had to move because the department I was hired to work in was toxic, it contained a group of men who regularly bullied me. I got tired of fighting with this small group of entitled men year after year.... Even though I had seniority as department chair this group of men bullied me relentlessly. The university had no office during those days that I could go to get help dealing with gender related harassment issues... I even had

a colleague grab my butt and not get into any trouble for doing that. At that time the university did not do anything about bullying for the victim. The perpetrator could do as he pleased without much fear of being fired for the psychological or physical abuse of a colleague. Doing something to a student however would have been a different matter!

Dr. Sage tells us about the way White male STEM faculty shirk their institutional responsibility to mentor or supervise students on a regular basis. This has the effect of leaving students "high and dry" in their pursuit of their graduate degree. The women STEM faculty in the same department will often come to rescue abandoned graduate students while at the same time jeopardizing their own careers. This self-sacrificing act of kindness is rarely recognized by the institution's tenure and promotion process. As a result, some STEM women faculty and faculty of color can find themselves unable to accrue the requested number of publications or international presentations to justify achieving the next level of promotion. Dr. Sage, a professor, says:

> There are some White male faculty who really have not lived up to their responsibility with master's or doctoral students finishing, and so the students are left kind of stranded. The male faculty are not fulfilling their roles as mentors or supervisors. The male faculty rarely provide any emotional support for their students. So the students go looking for someone to help them because they're in this program. This is where they find women like me ready to help them out....I have a colleague who has something like 15 graduate students that she's working with, and quite a few of them are because the student fled their White male chair of their committee because he wasn't living up to his responsibility. And so there really becomes this imbalance in work where some of the White males around here can just not do the work they were hired for, and no one ever holds them accountable and asks, "Why aren't you actually attending to these students?" I suppose we could say no, but I feel an obligation to our students, so we get way too many students to work with and our research publications suffer as well as our chances for promotion to higher ranks. The institution just seems to turn its back on us.

Conclusion

The academy in general and the STEM fields in particular at research institutions continue to be bastions of male-normed behaviors and practices. Women often find themselves walking a tightrope between being seen as too feminine to be competent—or too masculine to be likable. The tightrope reflects prescriptive stereotyping, and stems from the fact that science is seen as requiring masculine qualities—but women are expected to be feminine. Thus women often find themselves pressured to take on dead-end roles in STEM departments. Women often face a backlash for behaving in stereotypically masculine ways, such as being assertive, angry, or self-promoting and confident.

The labs and other STEM research areas are a "boys club" space where the cultural rules of patriarchy, sexism, and cisgenderism are naturalized and part of the "DNA" of everyday department life. This chapter has highlighted the issues for women STEM faculty at one research university that included their credentials being questioned regularly by students, women experiencing sexism on a daily basis, microaggressions, institutional betrayal, invisible labor and having to give emotional labor to colleagues and students.

STEM women faculty at OSU are subject to different degrees of cultural rules, and as a result they are required to deal with these issues in order to be successful in their day-to-day activities. Male faculty on the other hand can focus on their research and worry less about being subjected to academic cultural expectations while they are on campus. This male-dominated STEM space leaves women exposed to a hostile environment that requires women to navigate many systemic and institutionalized barriers in the academy that make it more difficult for them to become world-class scientist with an international reputation.

Despite their best intentions to be respected scientists, STEM women faculty can feel betrayed by the tenure and promotion processes that often do not recognize or acknowledge the invisible labor or department service work in which women disproportionately engage. The academy also does not recognize the barrage of microaggressions STEM women and faculty of color often endure from colleagues, students and administrators. The academy further lacks progressive and supportive policies and resources for child and elder care which women are often required to take on. These examples represent different forms of institutional betrayal.

What seems clear from our ongoing research through the ADVANCE grant at OSU is that the issues women faced entering a male-dominated field 30 years ago remain. Not all units are not putting into place proven models in order to alleviate the disadvantages STEM women might face.

What we see often are Band-Aid solutions that are often implemented on an ad hoc basis. Glacial-paced changes in the workplace hurt both male and female faculty over the long term (Ecklund & Lincoln, 2016).

The lack of changes in the culture means that faculty are not working at optimal strength—at the university or at home. Some faculty can feel so traumatized by these circumstances that coming to work is an onerous affair for them. Many talented STEM scientists just silently leave and look for employment away from the academy.

While these experiences exist at OSU, our ADVANCE project is one way to challenge the systems of oppression in STEM. As noted above, we are giving dozens of senior faculty and administrators a deep dive into the study of systems of oppression, and a way to bring their awareness to action. Each seminar graduate is expected to leave with an Action Plan that will address barriers in their spheres of influence. Some of these actions include: embedding seminar material into graduate student and faculty orientations; revising search practices; including a commitment to equity and inclusion in *all* position descriptions and annually evaluating those commitments, among other initiatives (advance.oregonstate.edu). As we interview our seminar graduates one year post seminar and follow their Action Plans for several years, we hope that we will hear different narratives from faculty in STEM.

Acknowledgements We acknowledge the support provided by the National Science Foundation through grant HRD 1409171. Any opinions, findings, and conclusions or recommendations expressed in this material are those of the authors and do not necessarily reflect the views of the National Science Foundation.

NOTES

1. Throughout this chapter we will use direct quotes from interviews with our participants. The names used are pseudonyms for the women featured in this chapter. We use professional labels (e.g., Dr. Jones) as we heard from many that referring to women by their first names in the classroom was different from their men colleagues and felt belittling.
2. Founded in 1868, OSU is a Land Grant University. OSU is one of only two universities in the United States to have Sea Grant, Space Grant, and Sun Grant designations. OSU also holds the Carnegie Foundation's top designation for research institutions and its Community Engagement classification. The university has nearly 30,000 students and offers more

than 200 undergraduate and 80 graduate degree programs. It has nearly 3500 faculty members in its 11 colleges. OSU in Corvallis, OR, is located in the traditional territory of the Chepenefa ("Mary's River") band of the Kalapuya. After the Kalapuya Treaty (Treaty of Dayton) in 1855, Kalapuya people were forcibly removed to what are now the Grand Ronde and Siletz reservations, and are now members of Confederated Tribes of the Grand Ronde Community of Oregon (https://www.grandronde.org) and the Confederated Tribes of Siletz Indians (http://ctsi.nsn.us).

3. Gareth Morgan (1998) defined the corporate DNA metaphor as the "visions, values, and sense of purpose that bind an organization together" to enable individuals to "understand and absorb the mission and challenge of the whole enterprise." When we use the term DNA in this chapter, we imply a culture where the norms and practices that benefit men in STEM are so pervasive that they are entrenched in the day to day operation, invisible and rarely questioned.

4. Since 2001, the NSF has invested over $270M to support ADVANCE projects at more than one hundred institutions of higher education. The goal of the ADVANCE program is to increase the representation and advancement of women in academic science and engineering careers. ADVANCE encourages institutions of higher education to address various aspects of STEM academic culture and institutional structure that may differentially affect women faculty and academic administrators.

References

Aguirre, A., Jr. (2000). Women and minority faculty in the academic workplace: Recruitment, retention, and academic culture. *ASHE-ERIC Higher Education Report, 27*(6). Jossey-Bass Higher and Adult Education Series: ERIC.

Allen, T. D., Herst, D. E., Bruck, C. S., & Sutton, M. (2000). Consequences associated with work-to-family conflict: A review and agenda for future research. *Journal of Occupational Health Psychology, 5*(2), 278.

Augoustinos, M., & Every, D. (2007). The language of "race" and prejudice: A discourse of denial, reason, and liberal-practical politics. *Journal of Language and Social Psychology, 26*(2), 123–141.

August, L., & Waltman, J. (2004). Culture, climate, and contribution: Career satisfaction among female faculty. *Research in Higher Education, 45*(2), 177–192.

Austin, A. E., & Gamson, Z. F. (1983). *Academic Workplace: New Demands, Heightened Tensions*. ASHE-ERIC Higher Education Research Report (Vol. 10). Washington, DC: Association for the Study of Higher Education.

Barnes, A. S. (2000). *Everyday Racism: A Book for All Americans*. Chicago, IL: Sourcebooks, Inc.

Benard, S., & Correll, S. J. (2010). Normative discrimination and the mother-hood penalty. *Gender & Society, 24*(5), 616–646.

Clark, S. M., & Corcoran, M. (1986). Perspectives on the professional sociali-zation of women faculty: A case of accumulative disadvantage? *The Journal of Higher Education, 57*(1), 20–43.

Collins, P. H. (2002). *Black Feminist Thought: Knowledge, Consciousness, and the Politics of Empowerment*. New York: Routledge.

Constantine, M. G., Smith, L., Redington, R. M., & Owens, D. (2008). Racial microaggressions against Black counseling and counseling psychology fac-ulty: A central challenge in the multicultural counseling movement. *Journal of Counseling & Development, 86*(3), 348–355.

Correll, S. J., Benard, S., & Paik, I. (2007). Getting a job: Is there a mother-hood penalty? *American Journal of Sociology, 112*(5), 1297–1338.

Cuddy, A. J., Fiske, S. T., & Glick, P. (2004). When professionals become moth-ers, warmth doesn't cut the ice. *Journal of Social Issues, 60*(4), 701–718.

Ecklund, E., & Lincoln, A. E. (2016). *Failing Families, Failing Science: Work-Family Conflict in Academic Science*. New York: NYU Press.

Essed, P. (1991). *Understanding Everyday Racism: An Interdisciplinary Theory* (Vol. 2). Newbury Park: Sage Publications.

Etzkowitz, H., Kemelgor, C., & Uzzi, B. (2000). *Athena Unbound: The Advancement of Women in Science and Technology*. Cambridge, New York: Cambridge University Press.

Fleras, A. (2016). Theorizing Micro-aggressions as Racism 3.0: Shifting the dis-course. *Canadian Ethnic Studies, 48*(2), 1–19.

Fox, M. F. (2001). Women, science, and academia: Graduate education and careers. *Gender & Society, 15*(5), 654–666.

Fox, M. F., & Colatrella, C. (2006). Participation, performance, and advance-ment of women in academic science and engineering: What is at issue and why. *The Journal of Technology Transfer, 31*(3), 377–386.

Frazier, K. N. (2011). Academic bullying: A barrier to tenure and promotion for African-American faculty. *Florida Journal of Educational Administration & Policy, 5*(1), 1–13.

Gardner, S. K. (2012). "I couldn't wait to leave the toxic environment": A mixed methods study of women faculty satisfaction and departure from one research institution. *NASPA Journal About Women in Higher Education, 5*(1), 71–95.

Grant, L., Kennelly, I., & Ward, K. B. (2000). Revisiting the gender, marriage, and parenthood puzzle in scientific careers. *Women's Studies Quarterly, 28*(1/2), 62–85.

Guarino, C. M., & Borden, V. M. (2017). Faculty service loads and gender: Are women taking care of the academic family? *Research in Higher Education, 58*(6), 672–694.

Hagedorn, L. S. (2000). Conceptualizing faculty job satisfaction: Components, theories, and outcomes. *New Directions for Institutional Research, 2000*(105), 5–20.

Hill, J. H. (2009). *The Everyday Language of White Racism*. Oxford, UK: Wiley.

Jayakumar, U. M., Howard, T. C., Allen, W. R., & Han, J. C. (2009). Racial privilege in the professoriate: An exploration of campus climate, retention, and satisfaction. *The Journal of Higher Education, 80*(5), 538–563.

Johnsrud, L. K., & Heck, R. H. (1994). A university's faculty: Identifying who will leave and who will stay. *Journal for Higher Education Management, 10*(1), 71–84.

Johnsrud, L. K., & Wunsch, M. (1991). Junior and senior faculty women: Commonalities and differences in perceptions of academic life. *Psychological Reports, 69*(3), 879–886.

Kornberg, J. C. (2008). Jumping on the mommy track: A tax for working mothers. *UCLA Women's LJ, 17*, 187.

Kubota, R. (2015). Race and language learning in multicultural Canada: Towards critical antiracism. *Journal of Multilingual and Multicultural Development, 36*(1), 3–12.

Morgan, G. (1998). *Images of Organization* (The Executive Edition). California: Berrett-Koehler Publishers Inc. and Sage Publications.

National Science Foundation. (2006). *ADVANCE: Increasing the Participation and Advancement of Women in Academic Science and Engineering Careers*. Retrieved from http://www.nsf.gov/funding/pgm_summ.jsp?pims_id=5383.

Ong, M. (2005). Body projects of young women of color in physics: Intersections of gender, race, and science. *Social Problems, 52*(4), 593–617.

Patton, M., & Westby, C. (1992). Ethnography and research: A qualitative review. *Topics in Language Disorders, 12*(3), 1–14.

Pérez Huber, L., & Solorzano, D. G. (2015). Visualizing everyday racism: Critical race theory, visual microaggressions, and the historical image of Mexican banditry. *Qualitative Inquiry, 21*(3), 223–238.

Pittman, C. T. (2010). Race and gender oppression in the classroom: The experiences of women faculty of color with white male students. *Teaching Sociology, 38*(3), 183–196.

Rosser, V. J. (2004). Faculty members' intentions to leave: A national study on their worklife and satisfaction. *Research in Higher Education, 45*(3), 285–309.

Rothblum, E. D. (1988). Leaving the ivory tower: Factors contributing to women's voluntary resignation from academia. *Frontiers: A Journal of Women Studies*, 14–17.

Shin, H. (2015). Everyday racism in Canadian schools: Ideologies of language and culture among Korean transnational students in Toronto. *Journal of Multilingual and Multicultural Development, 36*(1), 67–79.

Shoshana, A. (2016). The language of everyday racism and microaggression in the workplace: Palestinian professionals in Israel. *Ethnic and Racial Studies, 39*(6), 1052–1069.

Smart, J. C. (1990). A causal model of faculty turnover intentions. *Research in Higher Education, 31*(5), 405–424.

Smith, C. P., & Freyd, J. J. (2014). Institutional betrayal. *American Psychologist, 69*(6), 575.

Strauss, A., & Corbin, J. (1998). *Basics of Qualitative Research: Procedures and Techniques for Developing Grounded Theory.* Thousand Oaks, CA: Sage.

Turner, C. S. V. (2002). Women of color in academe: Living with multiple marginality. *The Journal of Higher Education, 73*(1), 74–93.

Turner, C. S. V., & González, J. C. (2011). Faculty women of color: The critical nexus of race and gender. *Journal of Diversity in Higher Education, 4*(4), 199.

Umbach, P. D. (2006). The contribution of faculty of color to undergraduate education. *Research in Higher Education, 47*(3), 317–345.

Ward, K., & Wolf-Wendel, L. (2004). Academic motherhood: Managing complex roles in research universities. *The Review of Higher Education, 27*(2), 233–257.

Wolf-Wendel, L., & Ward, K. (2013). Work and family integration for faculty: Recommendations for chairs. *Department Chair, 23*, 1–3.

Xu, Y. J. (2008). Gender disparity in STEM disciplines: A study of faculty attrition and turnover intentions. *Research in Higher Education, 49*(7), 607–624.

Zhou, Y., & Volkwein, J. F. (2004). Examining the influences on faculty departure intentions: A comparison of tenured versus nontenured faculty at research universities using NSOPF-99. *Research in Higher Education, 45*(2), 139–176.

PART II

Hierarchical Layers and Practices

Teacher Incivility in Toxic School Climates: Its Consequences and What Could Be Done

Thomas G. Reio Jr. and Stephanie M. Reio

Incivility and its related behaviors are an escalating issue in workplaces across the world (Fevre, Robinson, Lewis, & Jones, 2013). Organizational researchers have examined its nature, prevalence, antecedents, and outcomes in a broad array of organizational settings ranging from hospitals and manufacturing plants (e.g., Trudel & Reio, 2011) to government agencies (e.g., Cortina, Magley, Williams, & Langhout, 2001) and universities (e.g., Hunt & Marini, 2012). To date, however, little research has touched upon public K-12 teachers, despite the onslaught of the overwhelming difficulties facing the teaching profession (Fox & Stallworth, 2010). For example, because more and more students are being channeled to charter schools in the United States, public schools are receiving less financial support, yet strident calls from legislators for accountability remain (Fox & Stallworth, 2010). This relentless accountability pressure (e.g., through school district mandates, societal

T. G. Reio Jr. (✉)
School of Education and Human Development, Miami, FL, USA

S. M. Reio
University of Louisville, Louisville, KY, USA

© The Author(s) 2018   153
C. L. Cho et al. (eds.), *Exploring the Toxicity of Lateral Violence and Microaggressions*, https://doi.org/10.1007/978-3-319-74760-6_8

expectations) is in light of issues associated with unfunded mandates to deliver better academic performance for ethnic and cultural minorities, immigrants, and students with disabilities, with no respite in sight (Steffgen & Ewen, 2007). Educational policy makers and superintendents, and in-school instructional and administrative (e.g., principals) leaders need to be more mindful that these stressful conditions can produce toxic school workplace contexts unfavorable for optimal teacher well-being and performance. Toxic school settings are associated with poorer teacher efficaciousness and performance, which negatively impact student learning and development (Reio & Reio, 2011). In these challenging conditions, teachers become disillusioned, less motivated, and on the verge of leaving the profession, the opposite of what the school mandates and societal demands had intended (Fox & Stallworth, 2010). Toxic school workplaces seem to be the ideal setting for fostering teachers' uncivil behaviors (Sulea, Filipescu, Horga, Ortan, & Fischmann, 2012; Waggoner, 2003).

Workplace incivility is defined as "low intensity deviant behavior with ambiguous intent to harm the target, in violation of workplace norms for mutual respect. Uncivil behaviors are characteristically rude, discourteous, displaying a lack of respect for others" (Andersson & Pearson, 1999, p. 457). Incivility depends on one's perception as an instigator, target or onlooker as to what constitutes being uncivil (Porath & Pearson, 2010). This perception can vary by setting and the norms associated with that setting. For example, shouting at a fellow teacher in a meeting might fit within the norms of mutual respect at one school, but not at another. At the first school, one might perceive the behavior as being perfectly acceptable "passion"; on the other hand, it might be perceived as "crossing the line" and uncivil at the other. Incivility in the form of passive-aggressive behavior like stubbornness, refusing to cooperate with colleagues, dragging out completion of work assignments, and ignoring co-workers and supervisors can become "the norm" at schools where there is an authoritarian principal (Bennett & Robinson, 2000). The trouble is that this normed behavior, perceived as being acceptable by the teachers as a means to deal with a problematic principal, may not be perceived as acceptable by the principal in question or a new principal sent to lead the school, despite the challenging workplace climate that remains. Organizational researchers have distinguished several antecedents to uncivil behavior such as conflict management style (Trudel & Reio, 2011), situational constraints (Reio, 2011), personality traits (e.g., neuroticism), negative affect (e.g., frustration), and a host of demographic (e.g., age, gender, ethnicity) and background variables (e.g., being an immigrant, having a disability, hierarchical status within the organization) as some of the best predictors of uncivil behavior in the workplace (Fevre et al., 2013; Pearson, Andersson, & Porath, 2000; Reio & Trudel, 2013). Incivility labels associated with uncivil behavior include being callous, insensitive, biting, supercilious, boorish, and abusive, among others (Andersson & Pearson, 1999). Workplace incivility has also been linked with organizational outcomes like reduced employee engagement, job performance, physical health, organizational commitment and job satisfaction (Reio & Ghosh, 2009), and increased turnover intentions (Laschinger, Leiter, Day, & Gilin, 2009).

Acknowledging that incivility has been understudied among K-12 teachers, the aim of this chapter is to examine teacher incivility and its associated outcomes. We stress here that we are not looking into teacher–student nor teacher–parent incivility; rather, we focus upon being the target of teacher–teacher and principal–teacher incivility. Thus, these two areas (coworker and supervisory incivility) have been identified in prior research in other helping professions (e.g., nursing) as the most vexing and powerful predictors of poor individual and organization outcomes (Laschinger et al., 2009; Trudel & Reio, 2011). Further, we will discuss the frequency of teacher incivility, how it might turn into more intentional patterns of behavior like bullying and physical violence, and present recent empirical studies that link such behavior to important individual and organizational outcomes. We will follow with recommendations for research and practice.

Review of the Background Literature

In this section, workplace incivility is linked to intentional acts of aggression in the form of bullying and physical violence (Fox & Stallworth, 2010; Porath & Pearson, 2010). Second, we review two recent empirical studies examining teacher incivility.

The incivility spiral: Incivility, bullying, and physical violence. Andersson and Pearson (1999) theorized that incivility was a relatively mild form of deviance or aggression, ambiguous as to intent and harm, that can initiate a spiraling process of "tit for tat" exchanges between the instigator and target. These seemingly innocuous, isolated behaviors can spiral into the intentional form of uncivil behavior or aggression called bullying. From there, bullying can spiral into physical violence. Ostracizing, giving negative eye contact, neglecting, ignoring, and cursing are all forms of disrespectful workplace behaviors that can spiral into more serious forms of aggression and physical violence (Andersson & Pearson, 1999; Fox & Stallworth, 2010). Thus, leaders and managers should be made aware about the seriousness of workplace incivility because it can lead to more aggressive forms of behavior (Fox & Stallworth, 2010). While every instance of workplace aggression may not be the result of being treated uncivilly by coworkers or supervisors, instances of uncivil behavior leading to actual physical violence in workplaces like K-12 schools are real and of therefore great concern (Fox & Stallworth, 2010; Waggoner, 2003). If only measures had been taken earlier to prevent the incivilities in the first place, the likelihood of bullying and physical violence could have been greatly reduced.

School change (e.g., an unpopular school district mandate) and the nature of the work environment are situational factors that might impact the frequency of uncivil behaviors. Schools where there is little control over one's job, high intensity and interpersonal conflict set the stage for more uncivil behavior and aggression (Neuman & Baron, 1998; Steffgen & Ewen, 2007). Social factors might include being treated poorly by one's principal or district personnel and a school climate that supports uncivil and aggressive behavior (Fox & Stallworth, 2010; Waggoner, 2003). Individual difference factors can be personality traits; that is, certain traits are linked to more aggressive tendencies, and becoming more physically violent than others (e.g., extraversion, neuroticism, anger). Consequently, the combination of social and situational factors may affect individuals differently depending on their interaction with personal factors.

Empirical teacher incivility studies. We highlight two empirical studies of teacher incivility in this section. The first will be Reio and Reio's (2011) research conducted in the US Midwest and the second will be a western Romanian investigation (Sulea et al., 2012).

In the only study of both coworker and supervisory incivility among US public school teachers, Reio and Reio (2011) examined the two constructs and their hypothesized linkages to school commitment and teacher turnover intent in a sample of 94 urban middle-school teachers in the US Midwest. Employing a cross-sectional design, the data were collected via paper-and-pencil surveys in the four middle schools participating in this research. The two incivility measures were modified versions of the 7-item Cortina et al. (2001) Workplace Incivility Scale of target incivility. The two new coworker and supervisory incivility measures were now 12-item Likert-type surveys demonstrating high internal consistency (αs $\geq$ .94). The items were identical for the two scales, but the instructions differed; one asked the questions related to coworkers and the other asked the questions related to supervisors. Sample items included asking whether coworkers or supervisors "Addressed you in unprofessional terms, either publicly or privately?" and "Made demeaning or derogatory remarks about you?" The Cronbach's alpha coefficients for the 15-item commitment (Mowday, Steers, & Porter, 1979; "I really care about the fate of this organization") and 3-item turnover intent (Singh, Verbeke, & Rhoads, 1996; "I often think about quitting") scales were .90 and .78, respectively. All teachers participated under the condition of anonymity. The surveys were distributed by a school officer to the teachers' mailboxes; the response rate was 33.9%. The majority of the participants was female (60.6%) and Caucasian (54.8%). The mean teaching experience was approximately 6 years at the school where they were currently working and nine years overall. The teachers worked a mean of 40.5 hours per week.

First, the researchers examined the frequency of being the target of both coworker and supervisor incivility where they found that roughly 85% of the teachers reported being the target of some form of coworker incivility in the past year. Similarly, 71% indicated they were the target of supervisor incivility as well. Over 50% experienced coworker incivility at the "from time to time" to "always" levels; 33% experienced supervisor incivility from time to time to always. Thus, the majority of the participants experienced coworker and supervisory incivility over the past year. These results mirror other helping professions such as nursing (Laschinger et al., 2009), government (Federal Court employees; Cortina et al., 2001), and international studies involving teachers (European Foundation for the Improvement of Living and Working Conditions, 2010).

Second, in contrast to prior research (e.g., Trudel & Reio, 2011), the MANOVA findings did not reveal gender or ethnic differences in experiencing coworker or supervisory incivility. The correlational results indicated that coworker and supervisory incivility were negatively related to organizational commitment, but positively associated with turnover intent. In the moderated hierarchical regression results, after controlling for gender, years teaching at school and hours worked per week, the results demonstrated that supervisor, but not coworker incivility was a significant, strong predictor of both commitment and turnover intent. The effect sizes were relatively large. The interactions did not contribute unique incremental variance in any of the analyses.

What these findings suggest is that being the target of uncivil behavior significantly predicted negative organizational outcomes. A standard deviation increase in experiencing supervisor incivility would "cause" a $-.68$ standard deviation decrease in commitment to the school. Likewise, a standard deviation increase in experiencing supervisor incivility would "cause" a .39 standard deviation increase in turnover intent. These findings are important to note because this is one of the only teacher incivility studies and they support much prior research that incivility occurs all-too-frequently, not just from coworkers but also supervisors. Many of the participants experienced incivility at least "from time to time" and 12% reported experiencing these incivilities "always," which moves from being seemingly discrete, ambiguous-as-to-harm acts to a distinct pattern of behavior; that is bullying (Andersson & Pearson, 1999). The upshot of this research is that supervisor incivility matters in that it is linked to less teacher commitment to the school and greater intent to turnover from the profession. Although these were preliminary nonexperimental findings, human resource interventions designed to foster more sensitive and respectful communication among teachers and principals would seem prudent in light of the results.

The Sulea et al. (2012) workplace mistreatment and burnout study was conducted with Western Romanian secondary and high school teachers. There were 193 teachers, with 88% being female; mean age of 40.63 years. The mean length time employed at the school was almost 15 years and they reported working 29.40 hours per week. Like Reio and Reio (2011), the authors used a cross-sectional design where they collected the data at the respective schools via paper-and-pencil surveys; they also collected data on both coworker and supervisor incivility. Confidentiality was assured and the response rate was 74.0%. A number of measures were used: personality (Mowen, 2000), abusive supervision (Tepper, 2000), undermining (Duffy, Ganster, & Pagon, 2002), ostracism (Ferris, Brown, Berry, & Lian, 2008), unwanted sexual advances (Fitzgerald, Gelfand, & Drasgow, 1995), workplace incivility (Cortina, Kabat-Farr, Leskinen, Huerta, & Magley, 2013), and employee burnout (Schaufeli, Leiter, Maslach, & Jackson, 1996). All the scales employed Likert-type items and the internal consistencies were acceptable (.75–.90).

It was not clear whether the survey battery was administered in English or Romanian. Sample items included: personality (e.g., organized), abusive supervision (e.g., puts me down in front of others), undermining (e.g., How often has a coworker intentionally spread rumors about you?), ostracism (e.g., others ignore you at work), unwanted sexual attention (e.g., touched you in a way that made you feel uncomfortable?), workplace incivility (e.g., In the past, have you been in a situation where peers or coworkers addressed you unprofessionally?), and burnout (not reported). Demographic data were also collected.

Sulea et al. (2012) measured what they called "workplace mistreatment" as it was associated with burnout. Thus, burnout was examined as a function of abusive leadership, ostracism, undermining, unwanted sexual attraction, and incivility. The researchers also measured personality as a statistical control variable. We will focus upon undermining, ostracism, abusive leadership and incivility as these fit most closely with Andersson and Pearson's (1999) original definition of incivility. Unwanted sexual attraction is illegal in many countries, so that is beyond the incivility definition.

The authors unfortunately did not report frequency data regarding the uncivil behaviors. However, they reported extensive correlational and hierarchical regression results. The strength and the magnitude of the zero-order correlations were as predicted by the authors in that each of the mistreatment variables was related significantly to the three burnout dimensions. Conscientiousness was negatively related to emotional exhaustion, cynicism, and professional inefficacy. Neuroticism, on the other hand, was positively related to cynicism and professional efficacy, but not emotional exhaustion. Agreeableness was negatively related to cynicism and professional inefficacy, but again not emotional exhaustion. The multiple regression results were much more revealing. After controlling for the demographic (step 1), and personality trait variables (step 2), the workplace mistreatment variables accounted for significant, unique variance in the burnout variables. The mistreatment variables in all but one case were positive and significant predictors of the three burnout dimensions. Surprisingly, undermining was negatively linked through to emotional exhaustion.

What the Sulea et al. (2012) result demonstrate is that experiencing workplace mistreatment in the form of abusive leadership, undermining, ostracism, and incivility are significant predictors of teacher burnout. This is the only study with which we are familiar that examines this combination of variables concurrently. Further, it goes beyond the US setting to Romania with results that mirror organizational study findings with similar variables in many parts of the world. As with Reio and Reio (2011), incivility was a strong predictor of a negative organizational outcome. Interestingly, ostracism was the most powerful predictor by a large margin, indicating that making principals and coworkers aware that experienced ostracism can be very costly to targets in the form of emotional exhaustion, cynicism, and professional inefficacy. Because each has been shown to be strong predictors of voluntary turnover in prior research, it is incumbent upon district administrators and principals to do something to relieve the strain brought about by the insensitive and cutting nature of being ostracized. Notably, incivility was the second most powerful predictor of the three dependent variables and suggests that just as with being ostracized, the other forms of incivility, albeit to a lesser extent, also contribute to teacher burnout.

Together, the Reio and Reio (2011) and Sulea et al. (2012) empirical studies provide preliminary evidence that experiencing incivility, even after statistically controlling for demographic and personality (Sulea et al.) variables, was a powerful negative predictor of commitment to the school and a positive predictor of turnover intent (Reio & Reio) and each of the three dimensions of teacher burnout (Sulea et al.). We must caution, however, that these are but two exploratory, cross-sectional studies. The nonexperimental nature of the studies precludes making causal claims and we must be clear that roughly 70% of the variance in the dependent variables remains unexplained; therefore, there are exciting possibilities of new moderator and mediator variables that might explain meaningful incremental variance. Discrete emotions like anxiety, anger, ambivalence, and shame might be interesting variables to explore as they interact with demographic and incivility variables to predict other organizational outcomes.

Research could be carried out in online settings as well because rude, uncivil behavior are very common (Lim & Teo, 2009). Lim and Teo (2009) reckoned that rude emails generated roughly $5 billion in health-related costs to organizations due to targets' stress-related illnesses. In the Hong Kong banking and financial service sector, they found that experiencing cyber incivility predicted reduced job satisfaction and organizational commitment. Intriguingly, females engaged more in passive forms of incivility like not replying to emails; males used more active forms of cyber incivility like saying hurtful things through email.

This is merely the beginning of the research that could be done to refine what we know about online incivility behaviors and their possible outcomes related to learning, socialization practices, coaching and mentoring, and employee well-being.

Phenomenological research could be designed to get at how teachers actually experience types of incivility like ostracism and undermining to gather additional insights into experiencing incivility and how it is associated with their teaching behavior and subsequent student learning. We must also remember that instigating and being an onlooker of uncivil behavior may also impact teacher behavior. Reio and Ghosh (2009), for instance, found that high incivility instigators tended to be less satisfied with their jobs and perceived lower perceived physical health.

IMPLICATIONS FOR PRACTICE

If educational leaders and researchers hope to increase teacher commitment to their school and job satisfaction and decrease turnover intent, they need to find creative ways to reduce the likelihood of being the target of uncivil behaviors from coworkers and supervisors.

Based on Pearson et al. (2000), we propose ten strategies for identifying, tackling, and thwarting incivility among teachers at schools:

Taking an honest look in the mirror (Pearson et al., 2000). Principals should systematically examine not only how they behave toward subordinates but also how teachers behave among themselves. Peer feedback, videotaping and evaluating meetings or working with consultants would be a means toward this end. Essential to creating and supporting a civil work environment would be modeling behaviors that demonstrate trust in and value for teachers in all their diversity. Valuing diversity is a way to recognize and celebrate differences and understanding and utilizing unique perspectives for the benefit of the school.

Setting expectations (Pearson et al., 2000). Clear expectations for civil interpersonal interactions are necessary to guide day-to-day interactions and conduct at the school. Individuals should be treated respectfully regardless of their position or tenure. Moreover, ideas should be valued, no matter who originated them. Good, healthy relationships between coworkers should be encouraged to improve communication and understanding and reduce the likelihood of incivility. For example, regular team-building activities could be designed to create bonding among teachers and school leadership that would open new avenues of communication/understanding. The team-building activities may help colleagues work through the issues they might be having in an honest and straightforward or civil manner. This team-building approach would seem especially important with teachers because so much of what they do requires teamwork, particularly in elementary school settings.

Setting zero tolerance expectations (Pearson et al., 2000). A school might create a healthy school climate by establishing policies and procedures against uncivil behavior. The organizational setting plays an important role in either encouraging or preventing workplace incivility. Policies and procedures communicate boundaries within which employees of the organization can operate. Incivility thrives in school environments where input from teachers is not acted upon and the teacher perceives that by speaking up he or she might increase the risk of repercussion from the instigator. Thus, policies that encourage feedback about uncivil behavior should be developed so that teachers can report uncivil acts without any hesitation (Pearson et al., 2000). This policy should outline a disciplinary procedure for the violators of the policy. The instigator of incivility should be given a time frame to improve his or her behavior or face the consequences of their behavior.

A model anti-civility/bullying policy include the following elements: (a) an informal yet confidential complaint procedure that includes an ombudsperson knowledgeable about workplace incivility and bullying, (b) a timely investigation that protects the anonymity of both the target and alleged instigator(s), (c) protection against retaliation for both the target and the instigator(s), (d) the implementation of corrective action where warranted, (e) awareness training for all, and (f) regular monitoring and evaluation of the overall policy as well as its components. By communicating the standards of behavior through such policies and by opening channels of communication for reporting a formal complaint against workplace incivility or bullying, uncivil acts at school can be reduced. Additionally, school leaders can also include a conduct statement with examples of acceptable behavior in the teacher handbook, discuss appropriate workplace conduct in orientation/induction classes, and highlight the school's position of zero tolerance for offensive or uncivil behavior in school newsletters (Reio & Ghosh, 2009).

Weeding out trouble before it enters your organization (Pearson et al., 2000). Although one of the major ways to prevent uncivil behavior is through team-building exercises designed to facilitate communication and awareness, another effective way of reducing incivility is to stop the instigators from entering the school in the first place. Human resource professionals can identify applicants who have a greater likelihood of engaging in uncivil behaviors at school thorough background checks on applicants' work history (Pearson et al., 2000). Individuals associated with screening and selecting applicants should be informed of the likely profiles of teachers who engage in uncivil behaviors at work. However, it is often difficult to identify problematic applicants through background checks as many organizations might not provide information about a past employee due to the fear of being litigated against on the grounds of defamation of the personal character (Reio & Ghosh, 2009). Moreover, as applicants mostly provide socially desirable information in interviews, it becomes difficult for the interviewers to identify the true character of an applicant in interviews. This dilemma might be solved by including role plays in interviewing techniques. Role plays provide information about the applicant through actions and conversations by asking the applicant to do or act instead of just talking about a topic. It is a simulation where participants act out typical attitudes and behaviors of individuals in a given situation. Such role plays might help to identify disturbing traits such as lack of patience, bad temper, and assertiveness in applicants.

Providing orientation/inducting and training (Pearson et al., 2000); *teaching civility* (Reio & Reio, 2011). School expectations about interpersonal behaviors should be carefully communicated to new teachers in orientation/induction activities. Written policies and procedures about civility and related topics should be discussed. Training for civility is skills-based and can include competencies such as conflict resolution, negotiation, handling difficult people, managing stress, listening, and coaching. Professional development activities at school can include topics of diversity, mutual respect and civility, eradicating passive-aggressive behavior (e.g., cooperating more with coworkers and principals), and coaching and mentoring activities.

Human resource practitioners can help prevent uncivil workplace acts by training school leaders and teachers on observing warning signs of deviant behaviors in the school (Reio & Ghosh, 2009). In many instances, the instigator exhibits the likelihood of indulging in uncivil acts at school and early identification and counseling might prevent the instigating employee from being uncivil to his or her coworkers. If principals and assistant principals are trained to identify disturbing behavioral cues, they can help to prevent a teacher from being uncivil. Moreover, as the school workforce is increasingly becoming diverse, differences in cultural norms might foster miscommunication which can imply rudeness at times (Pearson et al., 2000). Thus, diversity training can prepare employees to understand each other better and therefore communicate in a more productive manner. Additionally, improving individual competencies such as conflict resolution, negotiation, stress management, listening skills, and etiquette can help to prevent workplace incivility.

Heeding warning signals (Pearson et al., 2000). Feedback should be gathered throughout the employment cycle, from principals, peers, and subordinates, to curtail and correct uncivil behavior. Open channels for reporting possible violations should be maintained.

Hammering incivility when it occurs (Pearson et al., 2000). Address incidents of incivility; do not ignore or risk otherwise condoning them. Although a teacher might behave uncivilly, consider it is possible that he or she may not be aware that they are doing so. Although addressing and documenting incidents of incivility are important, educating the instigator about his or her actions and providing tools for changing ideas, beliefs, and behaviors could be more effective for the teachers and the school. Such education and training might be provided by human resource professionals, off-site providers, or even a counselor secured through an Employee Assistance Program or insurance plan. Additionally, a policy against retaliation should be included.

Dealing with the instigator (Pearson et al., 2000); *not making excuses for powerful instigators* (Reio & Reio, 2011). Do not transfer or promote an instigator to get rid of the problem that she or he creates; such shuffling might spread the incivility instead of ending it. Confront and hold accountable all instigators, regardless of talents, clout, or experience.

Counseling. One way of preventing instances of deviant behavior at work is to provide access to counseling services (Reio & Ghosh, 2009). Such counseling services might help teachers cope better with personal and professional pressures or stress. Employee Assistance Programs (EAPS) can assist the teachers who have been victims of incivility. EAPS is an assessment, referral, and a counseling program which is voluntary, confidential, and aimed at employees. It usually involves professional counselors who can effectively counsel a troubled employee and offer healthy means of venting out resentment. Moreover, peer counseling can also be effective because there is a trust factor involved when teachers take advice and help from peers who understand their situation.

Invest in post-departure interviews (Pearson et al., 2000). After previous teachers have distanced themselves from the school and are stable in new work environments, request feedback regarding their experiences in your organization.

Collect valuable information from exit interviews of teachers who leave due to incivility. However, it is often difficult to ascertain the actual reason of departure because the teachers hesitate to identify incivility as the reason for leaving. Many of those who leave because of incivility do not report the real reason for their exiting because: (1) they think that the school does not care; (2) they feel they might sound weak if they complain; and (3) they believe that in their school, the potential for negative repercussions outweighs the hope of any corrective action (Reio & Reio, 2011). Thus, post-departure interviews with former teachers who have distanced themselves from the school and have secured positions in their new jobs can sometimes retrieve more candid disclosures about previous experiences of uncivil behavior in the school. Such post-departure interviews can provide frank disclosures about accounts of incivility at the school and help human resource practitioners identify the instigators of the uncivil behavior.

CONCLUSIONS

Educational leaders need to know, in the presence of daunting daily workplace pressures, that teachers are too often the target of frequent uncivil behavior from coworkers and principals. Although the frequency of incivility found was consistent with prior empirical research in the helping professions, we should be concerned with the knowledge that uncivil behavior, unimpeded, can escalate into bullying forms of intentional aggression and physical violence. These uncivil behaviors, albeit seemingly harmless, have been found to be strong positive predictors of turnover intent and teacher burnout, and negative predictors of school commitment and job satisfaction. Teachers work daily with our children; more must be done to reduce its likelihood in schools.

REFERENCES

Andersson, L. M., & Pearson, C. M. (1999). Tit for tat? The spiraling effect of incivility in the workplace. *Academy of Management Review, 24,* 452–471.
Bennett, R. J., & Robinson, S. L. (2000). Development of a measure of workplace deviance. *Journal of Applied Psychology, 85,* 349–360.

Cortina, L. M., Kabat-Farr, D., Leskinen, E., Huerta, M., & Magley, V. J. (2013). Selective incivility as modern discrimination in organizations: Evidence and impact. *Journal of Management, 39,* 1579–1605.

Cortina, L. M., Magley, V. J., Williams, J. H., & Langhout, R. D. (2001). Incivility in the workplace: Incidence and impact. *Journal of Occupational Health Psychology, 6,* 64–80.

Duffy, M. K., Ganster, D. C., & Pagon, M. (2002). Social undermining in the workplace. *Academy of Management Journal, 45,* 331–351.

European Foundation for the Improvement of Living and Working Conditions. (2010, April). *Physical and Psychological Violence at the Workplace.* Dublin, IE: Eurofound.

Ferris, D. L., Brown, D. J., Berry, J. W., & Lian, H. (2008). The development and validation of the Workplace Ostracism Scale. *Journal of Applied Psychology, 93,* 1348–1366.

Fevre, R., Robinson, A., Lewis, D., & Jones, T. (2013). The ill-treatment of employees with disabilities in British workplaces. *Work, Employment & Society, 27,* 288–307.

Fitzgerald, L. F., Gelfand, M., & Drasgow, F. (1995). Measuring sexual harassment: Theoretical and psychometric advances. *Basic and Applied Social Psychology, 17,* 425–445.

Fox, S., & Stallworth, L. E. (2010). The battered apple: An application of stress-emotion-control/support theory to teachers' experience of violence and bullying. *Human Relations, 63,* 927–954.

Hunt, C., & Marini, Z. A. (2012). Incivility in the practice environment: A perspective from clinical nursing teachers. *Nurse Education in Practice, 12,* 366–370.

Laschinger, H. K., Leiter, M., Day, A., & Gilin, D. (2009). Workplace empowerment, incivility, and burnout: Impact on staff nurse recruitment and retention outcomes. *Journal of Nursing Management, 17,* 309–311.

Lim, V. K., & Teo, T. S. H. (2009). Mind your e-manners: Impact of cyber incivility on employees' work attitude and behavior. *Information & Management, 46,* 419–425.

Mowday, R. T., Steers, R. M., & Porter, L. W. (1979). The measurement of organizational commitment. *Journal of Vocational Behavior, 14,* 224–247.

Mowen, J. C. (2000). *The 3M Model of Motivation and Personality: Theory and Empirical Applications to Consumer Behavior.* Boston, MA: Kluwer Academic.

Neuman, J. H., & Baron, R. A. (1998). Workplace violence and aggression: Evidence concerning specific forms, potential causes, and preferred targets. *Journal of Management, 24,* 391–419.

Pearson, C. M., Andersson, L. M., & Porath, C. L. (2000). Assessing and attacking workplace incivility. *Organizational Dynamics, 29,* 123–137.

Porath, C. L., & Pearson, C. M. (2010). The cost of bad behavior. *Organizational Dynamics, 39,* 64–71.

Reio, T. G., Jr. (2011). Supervisor and coworker incivility: Testing the work frustration-aggression model. *Advances in Developing Human Resources, 13,* 54–68.

Reio, T. G., Jr., & Ghosh, R. (2009). Antecedents and outcomes of workplace incivility: Implications for human resource development and practice. *Human Resource Development Quarterly, 20,* 237–264.

Reio, T. G., Jr., & Reio, S. M. (2011). Workplace incivility in schools. *International Journal of Adult Vocational Education and Technology, 2,* 23–35.

Reio, T. G., Jr., & Trudel, J. (2013). Workplace incivility and conflict management style: Predicting job performance, organizational commitment, and turnover intent. *International Journal of Adult Vocational Education and Technology, 4,* 15–37.

Schaufeli, W. B., Leiter, M. P., Maslach, C., & Jackson, S. E. (1996). Maslach burnout inventory—General survey. In C. Maslach, S. E. Jackson, & M. P. Leiter (Eds.), *The Maslach Burnout Inventory—Test Manual* (3rd ed.). Palo Alto, CA: Consulting Psychologists Press.

Singh, J., Verbeke, W., & Rhoads, G. K. (1996). Do organizational practices matter in role stress processes? A study of direct and moderating effects for marketing oriented boundary spanners. *Journal of Marketing, 60,* 69–86.

Steffgen, G., & Ewen, N. (2007). Teachers as victims of school violence—The influence of strain and school culture. *International Journal of Violence and Schools, 3,* 81–93.

Sulea, C., Filipescu, R., Horga, A., Ortan, C., & Fischmann, G. (2012). Interpersonal mistreatment at work and burnout among teachers. *Cognition, Brain, and Behavior, 16,* 553–570.

Tepper, B. J. (2000). Consequences of abusive supervision. *Academy of Management Journal, 43,* 178–190.

Trudel, J., & Reio, T. G., Jr. (2011). Managing workplace incivility: The role of conflict management styles—Antecedent or antidote? *Human Resource Development Quarterly, 22,* 395–423.

Waggoner, C. (2003). Teachers behaving badly. *The American School Board Journal, 90*(8), 29–31.

CHAPTER 9

Rites of Passage in Practice Teaching Experiences: A Necessary Evil?

Yvette Daniel and John Antoniw

The motivation for our collaboration in the writing of this piece arises from our passion and commitment to opening up crucial conversations (Patterson, Grenny, & McMillan, 2011) about the field placement experiences of teacher candidates (pre-service teacher training) which is an integral part of their preparation to enter the teaching profession. Throughout this chapter, we use the term "teacher candidates," although we acknowledge that the term "student teachers" is often used in the literature on this topic. We wish to share some key insights, based on our experiences, into the acts of microaggressions and injustices that are not discussed candidly and are not addressed in many cases. By and large, most practice teaching experiences are fulfilling and rewarding both for mentor/associate teachers and for the teacher candidates under their tutelage. However, in a community of practice (Lave & Wenger, 1991) we should be able to dialogue, critique, and open up the lines of communication in order to innovate, change, and remain current in our quest for quality teaching and learning for the students in our care. The purpose of this paper is to critically interrogate the manner in which

Y. Daniel (✉) · J. Antoniw
Educational Administration and Policy Studies, Faculty of Education,
University of Windsor, Windsor, ON, Canada

© The Author(s) 2018   169
C. L. Cho et al. (eds.), *Exploring the Toxicity of Lateral Violence and Microaggressions*, https://doi.org/10.1007/978-3-319-74760-6_9

teacher candidates are initiated into a community of practice through legitimate peripheral participation and the so-called unwritten *rites of passage* through which teacher candidates as "sojourners" are required to negotiate. These issues are of particular significance to teacher candidates in general, and especially to those from immigrant and ethnically diverse backgrounds who face special challenges related to linguistic and cultural dissonance and a lack of intercultural competence at the school level. Powers and Duffy (2016) argue that although there has been much progress "there is still a great need for reflexive work on intersectionality and cultural competence" (p. 61). It is a matter of professional integrity and responsibility for all those involved in teacher education in any capacity (whether as associate/mentor teachers, university professors, university and school administrators, or other stakeholders) to address the injustices, expressed mainly through microaggressions, encountered by some teacher candidates in their initiation into the teaching profession. The argument commonly made is: "If you (meaning the teacher candidate) cannot handle the pressures, then it is not the profession for you." We know that in every profession there is a period in which novices struggle to *learn the ropes* and the apprenticeship model places them in a power differential where they have to stay quiet and *suck it up* if they wish to be successful in their field placement (the practicum). Such a discourse nurtures a culture of fear, creates spaces for microaggressions to occur, and further bolsters the idea that everyone has to do it and suffer these injustices in silence thus stifling the potential for teacher candidates to experience authentic learning in a supportive and nonthreatening environment.

This is a reflective and interrogative piece on the state of the practicum, in which we glean from our own experiences and also from various informal discussions with teacher candidates (from whom we obtained informed consent) about their perceptions of the field experience component. This is not a study of all teacher candidates in our program and elsewhere. The fact that the voices of associate teachers are not being heard is another limitation of this chapter (and something we wish to pursue in another paper). We do not wish to make generalizations of the entire practice. Despite these caveats, we bring to the forefront some troubling issues about the practicum that are talked about privately, but are rarely discussed in the open with all those who are involved in these practicum experiences. We ought to conduct a serious investigation into existing structures and power dynamics in the field experience component of teacher education in order to engage in an open and honest dialogue with a sense of fearlessness for a common purpose; namely to improve the practice teaching experience.

The first author, a professor at a faculty of education in Ontario, has extensive experience in education across various levels, and also in teacher education at different universities in Ontario; the second author was a teacher candidate in Ontario a few years ago. We have purposely come together (one with many years of experience and the other with fresh perspectives from the field) so that we can use different lenses to view these issues and arrive at a synthesis of ideas. We believe it is time to deconstruct current unwritten practices and the taken-for-granted way of conducting business so that we can transform teacher education to bene-fit the profession, and in particular the students we are entrusted to edu-cate in the best manner possible. We ask pertinent questions and offer testimonials from teacher candidates; however, our intention in under-taking this task is not to malign associate teachers/mentors and their service to the profession, but to propose ways to open up the dialogue on current practices that are inadequate in many aspects in meeting the needs of teacher candidates who will be teaching twenty-first century skills. Sometimes, teacher candidates are not being given authentic learn-ing and mentorship experiences. In a world filled with rapid changes, new challenges and ambiguities, inauthentic approaches are not con-ducive to teacher education and to professional development. Current practices continue to propagate the status quo in terms of teaching and learning as opposed to having a new discourse infused with fresh ideas and perspectives. When innovation and different ways of thinking are suppressed, it not only hurts the teacher candidates and their mentors, but ultimately the students who could benefit from thinking differently. It is dangerous rhetoric to harbor a mentality that everyone has to "bear the cross" during practice teaching. We have to increase awareness of the role of institutionalization which "occurs when there is a reciprocal typi-fication of habitualized action by types of actors" (Berger & Luckmann, 2002, p. 42). When we "get stuck" in habitualized actions, we per-petuate the idea that oppression is acceptable just because it is familiar (Adams, Bell, & Griffin, 1997) and we become socialized into accepting this way of doing things as a *rite of passage*.

This paper begins with a brief overview of some of the main concepts that define the parameters within which the field experience compo-nent of teacher education takes place. Next, we provide voices from the field to provide powerful illustrations of the issues and problems, with a specific focus on microaggressions and injustices that occur for some teacher candidates during the practice teaching phase of their teacher education program. In the concluding section, we provide suggestions for opening up the dialogue for crucial conversations (Patterson et al., 2011) to occur so that we continue to engage in authentic learning in a community of practice.

CONCEPTUAL FRAMEWORKS

We frame our discussion of the complexity of the field experience by elaborating on the context and content of the notion of a *rite of passage* and the role it plays in a community of practice—namely the community of practice of the teaching profession. Under the umbrella of practice teaching as a rite of passage lurks the potential for microaggressions and lateral violence that must be discussed as we deconstruct the complex relationship between teacher candidates and associate teachers during the practicum.

A Rite of Passage

Practice teaching/field experience is considered a rite of passage for novices'[1] entry into the teaching profession. In the field experience segment, teacher candidates are assigned to particular schools and classrooms for a period of time. The Ontario Ministry of Education mandates a minimum of 80 days of practice teaching over the course of a two-year teacher education program. During the practice teaching period, also called the practicum, teacher candidates are mentored by associate teachers who usually are teachers with considerable classroom experience, and further, school principals recommend these teachers to serve as associate/mentor teachers to teacher candidates.

Interestingly, as we headed into the final edits for this chapter we were directed to a recent issue of the *Journal of Education for Teaching* (2017) devoted to the topic of the rite of passage for teacher candidates as they train to become master teachers. Previously, Head (1992) and White (1989) built upon research done in anthropology on initiation rites/rites of passage in order to draw analogies to student teaching/practice teaching. Almost three decades ago White (1989) wrote about student teaching as a rite of passage, and therefore, inherently fraught with problems and tensions. She argues that "initiation rituals are powerful tools for the social organization of people, ideologies, and social practices" (p. 178). White investigated previous studies on rites of passage to show that the induction of novices into the profession followed a classic rites of passage format: separation (where they leave the confines of the university classroom); transition (where they learn the strategies of the classroom, teacher, students, cultural frames, and other aspects); and incorporation (when they are successful at the end of the program they can enter the teaching profession). For the purpose of this paper, we focus on the first two stages: separation and transition. Head (1992) also wrote about practice teaching as an initiation into the teaching profession using the term *liminality*[2] to underscore the threshold stage of ambiguity and uncertainty for teacher candidates/student teachers where they are neither here (students) nor there (teachers)— rather, in an in-between stage. Petersen (2017) quotes Turner (1969, p. 359) to describe liminality as "betwixt and between." Hence, as teacher candidates encounter both the first two stages of the cultural compression stage and liminality, they experience a lack of a sense of belonging, identity confusion, and disappointment as their expectations are not met (Petersen, 2017). They begin to conceptualize their experiences with the system and with their associate teacher as a rite of passage. They may see it as something that has to be done in order to cross over that proverbial bridge to becoming a teacher. Therefore, even when teacher candidates do not agree with the associate teacher's directives (for example, being assigned to do "busy work" as opposed to attending to skills and strategies), they often perceive such directives as a necessary evil, a rite of passage that everyone has to endure in the process of becoming a professional teacher.

Head further points to five important elements in what she terms the *cultural compression stage* that are congruent with the separation and transition stages described by White (1989). In the cultural compression stage (Head, 1992), as teacher candidates enter a community of practice, they experience: (1) isolation and separation when teacher candidates are removed from the university classroom and separated from their peers; (2) an emphasis on giving and receiving, but often not knowing how much support they will receive and to what extent they can take an initiative while being careful not to disrupt the associate teacher's routines and practices; (3) a sacred atmosphere that could be equated to an intimidating atmosphere as they are not sure how the associate teacher is going to treat and assess them; (4) the use of strangers as instructor/mentors as they do not know the associate teacher and his/her temperament, style and expectations; and (5) rigid rules of conduct where they are fearsome about what they can and cannot do under the tutelage of the associate teacher. These five domains of experiences in the practicum become a slippery slope for microaggressions (slights, insults, disrespect, devaluation) (Beaulieu, 2016) to flourish due to the power differential between the associate teacher and the teacher candidate.

Correa, Martiniez-Arbelaiz, and Aberasturi-Apraiz (2015) frame beginning teachers as "sojourners" and the teacher candidates in this paper fit that description. As sojourners, they are pressured into aligning themselves with the status quo that is a state of compliance (also mentioned by Leshem, 2012). Further, Correa et al. (2015) argue that as sojourners they are viewed from a deficit perspective by their schools and associate teachers coupled often with an unrealistic expectation "that a teacher education program can produce what might be termed the finished product straight off their assembly line" (Gilroy, 2017, p. 129). However, it is important to underscore that during the rite of passage, perceived as the liminal stage between the university and the classroom, the teacher candidates are at the periphery of legitimate participation in the profession, and as such, they often cannot explore the numerous theories, concepts, and ideas discussed and debated in the university classroom. Oberski, Ford, Higgins, and Fisher (1999) provide an argument that furthers the idea that teacher candidates may feel pressured into doing what they are told as they attempt to jump through the proverbial "hoops" of the practicum/field experience component of a teaching program. Oberski et al. found that teacher candidates often hesitated to be open and honest with senior members of the school staff, specifically with regard to areas that could be viewed as problematic for their practice teaching experiences. Hobson (2002) also provides an example of a student who was afraid of her mentor and was deemed to be "quiet" because she was reluctant to speak up. In fact, the student was quiet because she was treading carefully and wanted to ensure that she would have a successful experience and get a favorable final report. In teacher education, as in many other professional degree programs, the internship/practicum inherently has a power imbalance as associate teachers have the power to pass/fail teacher candidates, thus becoming gate-keepers to the profession.

Microaggressions and Lateral Violence

The hierarchical nature of the relationship between associate/mentor teachers and teacher candidates by its very nature could, sometimes, lead to an abuse of power manifested in microaggressive behaviors. The concepts of microaggression and lateral violence are relevant and important to the field of teaching and learning. Sue et al. (2007) provide a definition from Piece from the 1970s that defines microaggressions as being automatic and subtle nonverbal exchanges that are used as put-downs. For example, one teacher candidate could not enter the assigned classroom until the associate unlocked the classroom door for her. This might not appear problematic on the surface. However, it was important for this teacher candidate to have access to the classroom to prepare and set up before classes commenced and her associate unlocked the classroom only 5–10 minutes prior to the first bell. This act implies that the teacher candidate is not worthy of having access to this space and that their time and needs are not being respected. Another example of such behavior was manifested when an associate teacher abruptly interrupted the teacher candidate and took over the lesson (thereby sending a message to students that the teacher candidate was not capable of teaching). Such acts undermine the teacher candidate's status in the classroom and further erodes his/her self-confidence. Such instances are so ingrained through different interactions in daily life that they are dismissed or accepted as part of the rite of passage. Teacher candidates who experience such microaggressions will often accept such behaviors as their lot to bear in order to succeed.

Lateral violence (or horizontal violence/hostility) refers to intergroup conflict and aggression, with examples being nonverbal innuendo, withholding information, sabotage, scapegoating, backstabbing, not respecting privacy, etc. (Stanley, Martin, Michel, Welton, & Nemeth, 2007). Lateral violence is identified as a workplace stressor that has both personal and organizational consequences by leading to a decrease in job satisfaction and commitment. It is important to raise awareness and understanding of lateral violence in order to create a genuinely friendly and supportive work environment and to reduce attrition rates (Ceravolo, Schwartz, Foltz-Ramos, & Castner, 2012). An interesting parallel to this finding is prevalent in our testimonials. One teacher candidate mentioned how acts of microaggression/lateral violence against her accumulated over the course of the three-week practicum leading to an emotional breakdown and a short hospitalization for stress. Despite the poisonous environment she endured, she persisted and completed the practicum. She shared with us her feelings of dread and trepidation and the visceral reaction she had every time she even drove by a school, leading her to consider quitting the profession.

In our paper, we demonstrate how some teacher candidates face microaggressive behaviors from their associate teachers/mentors during their practice teaching experiences in schools. Some of these attitudes have been identified as being influenced by biases and stereotypes about certain groups of people. The dynamics of power and privilege often play a role for some associate teachers/mentors to demonstrate their rank and to ensure teacher candidates are in compliance. Some teacher candidates face innuendos and also outright comments regarding their age, experience level, creative choices, race, and background; perceived by teacher candidates as attempts by some associate teachers to exert their dominance over teacher candidates assigned to their care. Andersson and Pearson (1999) identify how acts of microaggression, lateral violence, and workplace incivility could pose a larger problem if not addressed in a timely manner. Such behaviors can escalate quickly, spiral out of control toward a tipping point where coercion, conflict, and threats develop. One aim of this chapter is to open the dialogue to recognize the moral implications of such acts in order to strategize ways for change to create a community of practice (Lave & Wenger, 1991) so that we can foster more productive and positive experiences during this rite of passage into the teaching profession.

Lave and Wenger's: A Community of Practice

The process of learning to teach is about "becoming a member of a sustained community of practice" (Lave, 1991, p. 65); the process does not exist in a vacuum or in the abstract but is a product of negotiation and consensus in a learning community. In this paper, we employ Lave and Wenger's (1991) conceptual framework that embodies interrelated ideas of a *community of practice* in which *situated learning* through *legitimate peripheral participation* guides the learning of a novice and their initiation into a profession. Lave and Wenger's framework underscores the notion of reciprocity in learning as teacher candidates move from legitimate participation at the periphery in their role as novices to the center of a community of practice, in the situated learning context of their field placements. In the sphere of apprenticeship-expert learning, Lave and Wenger's work is internationally respected and referenced, and although they do not speak specifically to teacher candidates' practices in the field experience component of education, we find important parallels that we employ to anchor our discussion in this paper.

We examine each of the aforementioned interrelated concepts in a linear fashion with a qualifier that, in reality, these are iterative activities. We further wish to declare that Lave and Wenger's work is complex with multiple definitions and interpretations. In this short paper, it is not feasible to explain these complex terms in detail that is required to do them full justice. Therefore, we draw upon the salient features of the concept of a community of practice with the explicit purpose of using key understandings as they relate to the messiness of the novice-expert relationship that is the subject of this paper.

We begin by explicating the key elements of a community of practice. What is a community of practice according to Lave and Wenger, and what are its implications for teacher candidates in their field placements? A learning situation where newcomers and experts engage with each other in a collective enterprise (in our case that of learning to teach) is a community of practice. Wenger (2006) as quoted in Woodgate-Jones (2012) states that "communities of practice are groups of people who share a concern or a passion for something they do and learn how to do it better as they interact regularly" (p. 148). Lave and Wenger identify three dimensions of a community of practice: *mutual engagement, joint enterprise,* and a *shared repertoire.* Mutual engagement is understood to be when two or more people engage in learning as a social activity in a community in which there is enabling engagement or a sense of belonging and diversity (i.e., diversity of ideas, opinions, experiences, and skills). Mutual engagement is also characterized by a community in which disagreements and differences are perceived as integral to learning:

> A community of practice is neither a haven of togetherness nor an island of intimacy insulated from political and social relations. Disagreements, challenges, and competition can all be forms of participation. As a form of participation, rebellion often reveals a greater commitment than does passive conformity. A shared practice thus connects participants to each other in ways that are diverse and complex. (Wenger, 2006, p. 76)

The second characteristic of a community of practice is a joint enterprise, which does not mean that the beliefs and practices of all members of this community are aligned, but that disagreements and differences are viewed as part of the process/enterprise and are "communally negotiated" (p. 78). The third characteristic of a community of practice is a shared repertoire that includes mutually agreed upon roles, rituals, tools, ways of doing things, symbols, gestures, and other aspects that comprise a repertoire in a community:

> The repertoire combines both the reificative and participative aspects. It includes the discourse by which members create meaningful statements about the world, as well as the styles by which they express their forms of membership and their identities as members. (p. 83)

Situated learning (or situated social practice) and legitimate peripheral participation in a community of practice are most relevant to the dynamics between the teacher candidate and mentor/associate teacher. Situated learning is synonymous with experiential learning where learners are actively involved in learning through real-life experiences. This description fits well with the practice teaching requirements in most teacher education and teacher training programs. The field experience (or practicum) provides teacher candidates opportunities to engage in real life teaching experiences, to learn from their challenges, successes, and failures in a safe and supportive environment so that they can build upon the ideas, concepts, and theories discussed in their university classrooms.

Hobson's (2002) study further investigated the practicum experience through interview data from teacher trainees about their school-based mentoring experiences. Some of the limitations they mentioned included: mentors not making time for them, lack of feedback or constructive criticism, lack of support from mentors, personality clashes, and mentors being out of date with changing theories and practices. Surprisingly, Hobson identified that 12 of the 16 participants reported some problems with at least one of their associate teachers (p. 14). Hobson delineated some of the ways that associate teachers utilized their power dynamic in order to get teacher candidates to comply with their directives. One participant mentioned that at the direction of the associate teacher, he had to teach classes not allocated to him. Hobson argued that teacher candidates needed supports and a safe learning environment to grow as future educators. The teacher candidates in Hobson's study stated that learning to teach is often a stressful and threatening experience and the lack of support might lead to teacher candidates dropping out of their program of study. We must explore these issues in order to deconstruct dysfunctional and unproductive mentorship relationships that are being perpetuated due to the institutionalization (Berger & Luckmann, 2002) of such a rite of passage. We ought to interrogate the effects these experiences have on teacher candidates, school culture, students, and ultimately the teaching profession in general. Such unproductive practices have far-reaching and long-lasting effects on all actors involved in this socialization process.

Sharing Their Stories, Hearing Their Voices

In this section, we present selected testimonials and provide analyses using the lens of rites of passage through legitimate peripheral participation in a community of practice. We have removed all identifying markers to protect the confidentiality and to preserve the anonymity of participants. As these participants are recent graduates who are seeking employment in the field, we have taken great care to ensure that we do not jeopardize their futures. These precautions are an indictment of the field where there is a danger in speaking out boldly against the current state of affairs. Further, it is important to note that participants have agreed to allow us to present their voices so that readers get a glimpse into the dilemmas and the subtleties of microaggressions that novices face in their rite of passage into a community of practice. In fact, some expressed an eagerness to have their voices heard in the hope that changes could take place to benefit others who will follow in their path in future years. Below are two poignant excerpts from testimonials provided by one teacher candidate who was in an intermediate/senior cohort three years ago.

Testimonial #1:
I was very fortunate to have wonderful practicum experiences. However, as a sociologist by training, I intently observe and reflect on human behaviour. I found it interesting in some of my practicum experiences to see the dynamics of interaction between myself and my associate when trying to engage with different methods. I am very interested in educational technologies and integrating them to benefit student learning. I tried to make aspects of a dry unit/lesson plan into something fun and exciting for students through technology enhanced engaging projects. I remember being told by my associate that I should not use so much technology and instead should utilize his method as students apparently liked it better.

The mentality and motto of "why reinvent the wheel" was frequently discussed and I recall an associate passing me their book of notes and telling me to just follow along.

Testimonial #2:
I recall an instance when I had a whole lesson planned and I had it paired with a very specific video. However, when I was about to start my lesson, my associate teacher interrupted me and took over by asking the class if they wanted to watch the film that I had specifically selected and aligned to the curriculum, or if they wanted to watch another totally unrelated film that he had selected. The class immediately turned on me and wanted to watch this other film, scrapping my lesson to the side.

In the testimonials stated above we see that the mentors/associate teachers involved were generally well-intentioned, but oftentimes the assessor role took over, nullifying the need to move teacher candidates from the periphery into the mainstream of action. These narratives that further align with Correa et al. (2015) claim that teacher candidates, as sojourners, might feel pressured into compliance, and therefore, be unable to explore the different concepts taught in the university classroom. The compliance with the mentor/associate when they veered off the lesson demonstrated the inauthentic experience that sometimes occurs for the teacher candidate as a sojourner in a community of practice. Furthermore, when the teacher candidate attempted to introduce new ideas, these lessons were viewed as potentially threatening. While teacher candidates have much to learn from an experienced teacher and mentor, they also bring fresh ideas and unique perspectives that they should feel safe discussing and sharing in a community of practice. Teaching is messy, and teacher candidates should have opportunities to try and also to fail as they learn from their experiences. Teaching should not always be about fail-safe practices.

The following anecdote from another recent graduate demonstrates the sense of insecurity that mentor/associate teachers might experience when their own students favor a younger and more energetic person who establishes a better rapport with students.

Testimonial #3:
I recall at the end of one of my practicum experiences, I asked for anonymous feedback from students so I could see what they liked, what they didn't like, etc. and one student said they had learned more with me than they did with their time before with the associate teacher.

Obviously, one could argue that this is the voice of a single student and there are other factors to consider, but we should be asking whether teacher candidates, even as novices, have something to bring to the table, and if their ideas could potentially enhance the learning experience for students and the experienced associate teacher. There are ways to harness the novice's potential for creativity if we wish to create a community of practice in which reciprocity (manifested in the exchange of ideas and learning experiences) benefits everyone involved.

The climate of the school plays a decisive role in the teacher candidates' practicum and lunch-time rituals are especially informative. We have heard narratives about lunch-time and staff-room experiences repeatedly over the years and in different settings, and therefore, we chose one testimonial that represents a concern expressed by several teacher candidates. In some schools, teacher candidates were explicitly directed to stay away from the staff room at lunchtime claiming that seating space was an issue. In other instances, the cold reception they encountered (through lack of a warm word or hostile glances in their direction) conveyed that they were not welcome into the staff room as they were not "real" teachers. Therefore, throughout the day these teacher candidates did not have a place they could go to for a break, and to connect with other teachers, discuss ideas and strategies in a community of practice. Furthermore, due to security issues in some schools, teachers also locked their classrooms, so alternative venues for breaks, and to prepare for the afternoon, were taken away from teacher candidates.

Testimonial #4:
I went to various schools during my practicum experience, and the lunch hour rituals were interesting to observe. At all of my schools, the associate/mentor teacher would go on their own at lunch. At one school, I entered the lunch room to a hostile environment where the teachers were gossiping, and in general I sensed some negative energy. I was oftentimes the only teacher candidate in this lunch room and I would sit in the corner and not be acknowledged. There was a very clear mentality that I was subordinate to these "real" teachers. I even noticed that the only time someone really would talk to me in this lunch room was when they were an occasional teacher for the day. This was also because they were categorized as being subordinate in this hierarchy of power. At another school, the lunch room was similar, however I had other teacher candidates to eat lunch and discuss things with. However, the few of us were crammed into a corner and were left to talk to each other as opposed to the teachers in that school.

The example in the testimonial above is reminiscent of what Head (1992) argued was a result of liminality—a stage of ambiguity and uncertainty for teacher candidates as they were neither here (students at the university), nor there (teachers), rather they were in an awkward in-between stage. Since teacher candidates do not have clearly defined identities (i.e., they experience liminality), they do not fit into the power structure or hierarchy of a full-fledged teacher, and therefore, they are seen as not deserving of time or respect from peers in the lunchroom. Furthermore, the above testimonial demonstrates the lack of mutual engagement, specifically in regard to a sense of belonging, that is a necessary component in order to engage in a community of practice.

Some teacher candidates have discussed troubling issues of racial and cultural biases that teacher candidates from immigrant backgrounds, specifically from Asian or Middle-Eastern backgrounds encounter during the practicum, thus adding an additional level of complexity to the debate:

Testimonial #5:
I still recall one of my fellow peers, also belonging to an ethnic minority, telling us of her unsettling experience with an associate teacher. A substitute teacher, filling in for an associate, told this teacher candidate about how surprised she was with the proficiency of her English because she was under the impression that there might be communication and language problems associated with her accent. My peer was shocked at this remark and wondered how an educator could pass this kind of uninformed judgment based on race and ethnicity. No one should have to question their ability as teachers just because they are from a different country or different from other teacher candidates. Unfortunately, this is a common occurrence.

In placing teachers in schools, the field experience office at our university (most faculties of education have office staff dedicated to organizing and placing teacher candidates in schools for their practicum) will try to ensure that placements are as compatible as possible by asking schools for their preferences in terms of available mentors and classrooms and then the office staff will attempt to match teacher candidate and school accordingly. One of the authors who work in an advisory capacity was shocked the first time she heard comments from a couple of schools such as: "Please don't send me teacher candidates with funny sounding names." The following testimonials are taken from one teacher candidate who came from a South Asian background and had a distinct name such that even before she arrived at the school, certain stereotypical assumptions were already in place

Testimonial #6:
The attitudes of many of my fellow minority teacher candidates can be summed up in the opinion expressed by one of my classmates. He said that he appreciated the efforts of the faculty of education in recruiting and retaining ethnic minority teacher candidates, however, he was concerned about the selection process of associate teachers and the acts of subtle racism occurring during placements.

The prevalence of disrespect, and the perpetuation of microaggressions expressed in the testimonials above "communicate hostile, derogatory, or negative messages" (Beaulieu, 2016). We had considerable challenges in picking just a few voices for this paper from the plethora of narratives we gathered about teacher candidates' field experiences. Most teacher candidates stated that they have had positive experiences and learned a lot about teaching by being in the field and gaining pedagogical skills. Unfortunately, too often, we also heard narratives such as the ones shared in this paper. The teaching profession is grounded in a moral imperative of justice and fairness, but both were missing in the accounts given here. We refer back to Head (1992) who delineated the cultural compression stage in which individuals were in an intimidating atmosphere with the uncertainty of how they were going to be treated. The testimonials above demonstrate the manner in which the cultural compression stage was experienced by these particular teacher candidates: They encountered an atmosphere that was hostile and intimidating with an undercurrent of racism.

Teacher candidates provided examples, and reflected on subtle aggressions they experienced:

Testimonial #7:
In my own experience, I can recount many occasions where certain restrictions were unfoundedly imposed upon me. For example, some of my associates did not give me the freedom to photocopy materials, or in some cases, they withheld the list of my students' names from me for many days. Similarly, associate teachers refused to provide me with any resources and took a long time to respond to my e-mails.

Testimonial #8:
I was given feedback right in front of the students. My associate never hesitated to belittle me for insignificant and trivial things. This kind of uncooperative demeanor undermined my confidence as an aspiring educator, it was even more demeaning to my sense of worth even though I worked very hard to please my associate and did everything I was told to do. I was very hurt that my associate teacher failed to acknowledge and respect my dignity and intrinsic value as a human being.

Testimonial #8, in which a teacher candidate describes being belittled and insulted in front of students, is a clear example of microaggressive behavior under the guise of mentoring. The teacher candidate became anxious about what she could or could not do under the rule of the associate teacher. Testimonial #7 brings to mind Head's cultural compression stages, specifically stage five which addresses rigid rules of conduct. In both testimonials above, we can sense fear and ambiguity, as both teacher candidates were filled with doubts of what they could accomplish based on their associate teacher's use of power. In the first example, the denial of access to resources demonstrated a denial of Lave and Wegner's dimensions of a community of practice, i.e., the third characteristic as a shared repertoire (e.g., mutually agreed roles, rituals, tools, ways of doing things) (p. 78). However, this particular associate teacher was not sharing resources, thus, the associate teacher was not contributing toward a community of practice built upon mutual engagement, joint enterprise, and shared repertoire.

We need to understand the ramifications the microaggressions in the above testimonials have on teacher candidates and their future as educators and human beings:

Testimonial #9:
While all of this was hard to handle, I took the turmoil of these experiences positively and instead of losing heart, I tried to incorporate them into my own teaching. I pledged to become more compassionate towards all my students, including the ethnic minority students in my class, who sometimes face inequities on a daily basis

The thoughtful reflection noted above from a teacher candidate from a minority background (and with a considerable teaching experience in other settings outside of Canada) provides a glimmer of hope and remarkable resiliency from someone who had to endure a rite of passage fraught with microaggressive behaviors. Because we know the details of the unjust treatment that this teacher candidate experienced, we were amazed at her strength in articulating hope and compassion. However, the question that we ask repeatedly is "Why does it have to be this way?". Does this rite of passage have to be manifested in an attack on the teacher candidate's sense of self and efficacy or is there potentials for it to be supportive and nurturing?

Testimonial #10:
These practicums produce the next generation of teachers who have low self-esteem and a low level of conviction and confidence in their teaching. Furthermore, hostility and an unappreciative attitude can act as catalysts for the dissipation of passion for teaching. After dealing with discouraging experiences at the hands of associate teachers, many teacher candidates become dispassionate about an aspect of their lives that they were once hopeful and enthusiastic about—educating our future generations. The harsh and high stress environment of the practicums sometimes even forces teacher candidates to rethink their choice of this noble profession.

Testiminal #11:
Look at me. I loved teaching all of my life, from tutoring kids when I was just a teenager, to my actual teaching in schools on two different continents. Now I don't even want to look at schools when I pass them while driving. How can these placements create such a phobia in someone?

The powerful message provided by both testimonials #10 and #11 underscores the urgency to open the conversation between the school/ school boards and the faculties of education. The teacher candidate in the above testimonial barely survived the last month of the practicum due to the stress and the unwelcoming environment that she had to endure throughout her placement. The potential for a wonderful and symbiotic relationship to benefit all parties involved, and in particular, the students in that classroom turned into something more dark and threatening. We feel a sense of urgency to discuss these matters, not for the purpose of maligning individuals, but to take a proactive stance so that such experiences could be avoided or eliminated.

Suggestions Moving Forward

There are many eager, passionate and committed teacher candidates ready to take on the challenge of the teaching profession and there are many outstanding and supportive mentor/associate teachers. Most teacher candidates have positive and rewarding practicum experiences in their rite of passage into becoming fully qualified teachers. However, in this chapter, we have focused on those teacher candidates who experienced microaggressions, as we wanted their voices to be heard and also to underscore the complexity of the undertaking that is the practicum. Even when such cases of microaggression are few, they have to be addressed. We contend that if the practice teaching experiences of even a few teacher candidates are fraught with microaggression leading to great anxiety and stress, then we cannot dismiss these cases merely as a rite of passage.

It is often said that it is easy to critique, but it is more challenging to propose constructive solutions. We again reiterate that the social construction of institutional practices permits certain ways of doing things to be taken for granted. In order "to make the familiar strange", bold and forward-looking steps must be taken. We believe that enhanced training in mentorship for associate teachers would be helpful. Therefore, universities, the Ontario College of Teachers, Ministries of Education and school boards should make a serious commitment and investment in pre-service teacher education that would include intensive training for associate teachers in preparing them for this very pivotal mentorship role. In this training, the elements of a community of practice (as outlined earlier in the paper) must be interrogated through a reflective and reflexive process so that we create a genuine learning community among teacher candidates, associate teachers/mentors, schools and university personnel. In such a community of practice, ambiguity and complexity are embraced so that a safe environment free from aggression and injustice is nurtured. Although power dynamics between novice and veteran cannot be totally eradicated (nor is it advisable to do so), the dynamic, although hierarchical to some extent, must allow for nonthreatening spaces for crucial conversations to occur as part of this repertoire of education and training.

The concept of the "art of crucial conversations" (Patterson et al., 2011) has been used extensively in business and leadership training programs. What does it mean and how could we employ it in practice? Patterson et al. (2011) state that a crucial conversation is a "discussion between two or more people where (1) stakes are high, (2) opinions vary, and (3) emotions run strong" (p. 3) and the outcome greatly impacts their lives. The authors offer insights into strategies for successful dialogue among people and underscore the importance of mastering the art of crucial conversations through understanding and practicing the skills and strategies needed to have a high-risk conversation.

Further, they state that fear kills dialogue—an important assertion especially in the case of a power differential between the associate teacher and the teacher candidate. We have to train our teacher candidates to overcome fear by providing them with supports needed in order to have a free flow of ideas and suggestions while engaging in a high stakes conversation (as required) with their associate teachers. We believe that both associate teachers and teacher candidates should be provided with the necessary skills and strategies (emotional resilience, ways to address injustices, standing up for oneself in a nonconfrontational manner and other such strategies) to deal with emotionally and professionally risky dialogues. An investment in training, although cost prohibitive in an era of belt-tightening and cut-backs, should be given high priority as there are potential long-term benefits for all.

Of course, these ideas sound easy on paper but they require guidance and practice, and most importantly the will to make a difference. None of the ideas suggested in this paper will come to fruition if stakeholders lack the will to think differently. We wish to conclude this paper with one more testimonial from a recent graduate of our program.

> Testimonial #12:
> I believe that the associate teacher should be responsible for creating a safe, affirming and positive learning environment not only for their students but also for their teacher candidates. Teacher candidates should feel safe and secure under the wings of their associates so that they can practice that freedom to express and implement their ideas during practicum. I believe that it is imperative that teacher candidates are allowed this freedom and are not made to feel insecure and unworthy.

The aforementioned testimonial is a powerful insight from a teacher candidate as to what they believe an associate teacher should provide. When we consider this narrative, it becomes apparent that they are asking for basic dignity and respect. They are essentially asking the associate teachers to provide the same type of learning environment to them as they are supposed to be extending and modeling to their own students in the classroom.

We understand that a community of practice is a complex and messy entity. However, we need to learn to be open to and embrace the messiness that comes from these interactions. In the words of the beloved cartoon educator Ms. Frizzle (from the series *The Magic Schoolbus*):

"take chances, make mistakes, get messy!" Ms. Frizzle's quote teaches us that in order to have authentic learning experiences, we need to embrace a level of uncertainty. We need to have skills to deal with tough experiences that include disagreements, challenges, and difficult conversations. As previously outlined, these are all valid forms of participation in a community of practice that will allow for authentic learning, rather than passive conformity. However, in order for teacher candidates to feel confident and comfortable disagreeing, challenging, and proposing difficult discourses, they need to feel supported and respected. If there are rigid power dynamics and structures in place that build barriers against teacher candidates, there will never be a chance for educators to take that leap into a community of practice. Pailliotet's (1997) study (from two decades earlier) of teacher candidates found cases of disempowerment, with unauthentic learning and lack of communication; it is unnerving that such narratives, although not rampant, still persist.

Teacher candidates are at a fork in the road. They are neither here (university students), nor there (teachers); they are in a liminal stage. They fall into an awkward in-between stage, many feeling stuck, helpless, and without a sense of identity. They lack a formal place and space in their professional milieu. Associate teachers, as members of a profession dedicated to learning, collaboration, and social justice, should be working toward a community of practice that fosters inclusive and safe environments for teacher candidates to learn, experiment, and grow. Given the number of years, teacher education in North America has required a practice teaching component it is fair to assume that most, if not all teachers, have once been in the shoes in which teacher candidates currently stand. While it is easy to get caught up in power dynamics, it is important for the associate teacher to pursue reflective practice to understand and deconstruct their own professional journey, starting from the time when they were the inexperienced novice.

Acknowledgements We are grateful to all participants who have given consent to have their testimonials included in this chapter.

NOTES

1. Note that not all teacher candidates are novices in the true sense of the word. Some teacher candidates who may be certified and experienced in other countries take this program to gain certification to teach in Ontario. Further,

we need to consider the group of teacher candidates who might have come to teacher education after having had previous careers (Gilroy, 2017).

2. Petersen's (2017) article further explores this liminal stage faced by novice teachers. Based on a research study she conducted in South Africa, she argues that novices often encounter numerous challenges at this stage and that their expectations are often unrealistic.

REFERENCES

Adams, M., Bell, L., & Griffin, P. (1997). *Teaching for Diversity and Social Justice: A Sourcebook*. New York and London: Routledge.

Andersson, L. M., & Pearson, C. M. (1999). Tit for tat? The spiraling effect of incivility in the workplace? *Academy of Management Review, 24*(3), 452–471.

Beaulieu, R. (2016). A critical discourse analysis of teacher-student relationships in an third-grade literacy classroom: Dynamics of microaggression. *Cogent Education, 3*(1), 1–20.

Berger, P., & Luckmann, T. (2002). The social construction of reality. In C. Calhoun, J. Gerteis, J. Moody, S. Pfaff, & I. Virk (Eds.), *Contemporary Sociological Theory* (pp. 42–50). Malden, MA: Blackwell.

Ceravolo, D. J., Schwartz, D. G., Foltz-Ramos, K. M., & Castner, J. (2012). Strengthening communication to overcome lateral violence. *Journal of Nursing Management, 20*, 599–605.

Correa, J. M., Martinez-Arbelaiz, A., & Aberasturi-Apraiz, E. (2015). Postmodern reality shock: Beginning teachers are sojourners in communities of practice. *Teaching and Teacher Education, 48*, 66–74.

Gilroy, P. (2017). Pre-service student teachers and their programmes: The rite of passage from student to master teacher. *Journal of Education for Teaching, 43*(2), 129–131.

Head, F. (1992). Student teaching as initiation into the teaching profession. *Anthropology & Education Quarterly, 23*(2), 89–107.

Hobson, A. J. (2002). Student teachers' perceptions of school-based mentoring in initial teacher training (ITT). *Mentoring and Tutoring, 10*(1), 5–20.

Lave, J. (1991). Situation learning in communities of practice. In L. Resnick, J. Levine, & S. Teasley (Eds.), *Perspectives on Socially Shared Cognition* (pp. 63–82). Washington, DC: APA.

Lave, J., & Wenger, E. (1991). *Situated Learning: Legitimate Peripheral Participations*. Cambridge: Cambridge University Press.

Leshem, S. (2012). The many faces of mentor-mentee relationships in a pre-service teacher education programme. *Creative Education, 3*(4), 413–421.

Oberski, I., Ford, K., Higgins, S., & Fisher, P. (1999). The importance of relationships in teacher education. *Journal of Education for Teaching, 25*(2), 135–150.

Pailliotet, A. (1997). "I'm really quiet": A case study of an Asian language minority preservice teacher's experience. *Teaching and Teacher Education, 13*(7), 675–690.

Patterson, K., Grenny, J., & McMillan, R. (2011). *Crucial Conversations: Tools for Talking When the Stakes Are High.* New York: McGraw-Hill Education.

Petersen, N. (2017). The liminality of new foundation phase teachers: Transitioning from university into the teaching profession. *South African Journal of Education, 37*(2), 1–9.

Powers, B., & Duffy, P. (2016). Making invisible intersectionality through theatre of the oppressed in teacher education. *Journal of Teacher Education, 67*(1), 61–73.

Stanley, K. M., Martin, M. M., Michel, Y., Welton, J. M., & Nemeth, L. S. (2007). Examining lateral violence in the nursing workforce. *Issues in Mental Health Nursing, 28,* 1247–1265.

Sue, D. W., Capodilupo, C. M., Torino, G. C., Bucceri, J. M., Holder, A. M. B., Nadal, K. L., & Esquilin, M. (2007). Racial microaggressions in everyday life. *Implications for Clinical Practice, 62*(4), 271–286.

Turner, V. (1969). *The Ritual Process: Structure and Anti-structure.* Chicago, IL: Aldine Transaction.

Wenger, E. (2006). *Communities of Practice: Learning, Memory and Identity.* New York: Cambridge University Press.

White, J. (1989). Student teaching as a rite of passage. *Anthropology & Education Quarterly, 20*(3), 177–195.

Woodgate-Jones, A. (2012). The student teacher and the school community of practice: An exploration of the contribution of the legitimate peripheral participant. *Educational Review, 64*(2), 145–160.

CHAPTER 10

Horizontal Violence in Early Childhood Education and Care: Implications for Leadership Enactment

Louise Hard

The notion of leadership has been defined by numerous authors and there has been considerable work in this area over the past century, yet the picture remains incomplete. Terms related to leadership include individual traits, influence over people, role relationships and situational characteristics. Other related factors include meeting people's needs, mobilising power, negotiating agreements and political actions. According to Macbeath (2004), the term is 'full of ambiguity and has a range of interpretations. It is a "humpty-dumpty" word that can

---

This chapter has been reprinted with permission of the publisher *Early Childhood Australia*. It originally appeared as Hard, L. (2006). Horizontal violence in early childhood education and care: Implications for leadership enactment. *Australian Journal of Early Childhood, 31*(3), 40–49. www.earlychildhoodaustralia.org.au/australasian-journal-early-childhood/.

L. Hard (✉)
Murray School of Education, Charles Sturt University,
Albury, Australia

         191
C. L. Cho et al. (eds.), *Exploring the Toxicity of Lateral Violence and Microaggressions*, https://doi.org/10.1007/978-3-319-74760-6_10

mean "just what we want it to be"' (from Humpty Dumpty, in Alice in Wonderland) (p. 4). Management and leadership are interrelated concepts and a clear separation is not necessarily possible or desirable, particularly in early childhood education and care (ECEC). According to Jorde Bloom (2003), management involves systems to attain a vision, while leadership goes beyond to create ideas and motivate people. Management positions often do incorporate some leadership, and most often leadership involves management duties. Perhaps the essence of the term leadership revolves around the notion of creating positive changes in organisations. This paper explores the relationship between the notion of leadership in ECEC and factors identified as internal to the field which inhibit leadership enactment.

LITERATURE REVIEW

Three schools of thought have traditionally dominated leadership literature; and these include individual traits, behaviours of leaders and the context of the leadership. Individual traits have often been characterised as self-confidence, dominating, achievement-orientated and social agreeableness. Trait theories see leaders as concerned with the big picture rather than process, and this approach is often associated with the 'great person' notion of leadership (Northcraft & Neale, 1994). According to Hill and Ragland (1995), leadership understandings have not progressed far from 'assuming that the tallest man would naturally be the best leader' (p. 9). Current literature suggests that consideration of traits should not be dismissed entirely, since the personality of the leader does make a difference (Lingard, Hayes, Mills, & Christie, 2003). Leadership behaviours often polarise into either task- or production-orientated leaders or socio-emotional leadership. It seems that effective leaders demonstrate moderate levels of both behaviours, with subordinates more satisfied by leaders with high socio-emotional behaviours (Black & Porter, 2000). Leadership in context, and particularly the work by Fiedler (1967), suggests that flexibility in leadership behaviour from autocratic to participative depends on the context. For Fiedler (1967) there needed to be a match between the individual traits and their situation.

Contemporary leadership approaches have defined concepts of transformational and transactional leadership. Transformational leaders often exhibit a charismatic style, have vision, are risk-takers, and usually see themselves as agents of major change. According to Robbins, Millett and

Waters-Marsh (2004) these leaders are able to arouse, excite and inspire their followers to achieve group goals. This approach has resonance with the 'great person' or 'great man' trait approach and has been influential in social perceptions of what defines leadership. Transactional leadership rewards workers for their achievements and is concerned about improving working conditions and benefits and providing more engaging working conditions. These leaders engage in shared decision-making and develop teams. Their success is somewhat dependent upon the followers' perceptions of the leader's ability (Schultz & Schultz, 1998). This style is more pragmatic than that of the transformational leader but not exclusive, and both approaches make a contribution to leadership understandings.

The terms visionary leadership and charismatic leadership are now also part of contemporary leadership discussions. According to Nanus (1992), the visionary leader sees what is possible and desirable, is able to communicate their vision and persuade others to commit to make the vision a reality. The charismatic leader inspires and influences others and communicates high expectations.

More recently, feminist perspectives are focusing on leadership and questions are being asked about traditional concepts. According to authors such as Collinson and Hearn (2003) and Hill and Ragland (1995), these traditional concepts have been defined in male terms. Sinclair's (1998) work suggests that leadership has been linked to male traits and consequently marginalises many females. In discussing leadership in the corporate world, Sinclair (1998, p. 320) states that:

> These archetypes of corporate leadership derive from embedded cultural stories and icons; they continue to pervade the supposedly objective assessment of leadership potential in our organisations. And threaded through these archetypes are emblems of masculinity ... rites of passage, in the language of combat and sport, in-jokes and assertions and demonstration of sexual and physical prowess.

The stoic, hardworking and heroic image of the leader is, according to Collinson and Hearn (2003) and Wajcman (1999), associated with authoritarian, competitive and independent notions of leadership. The dominance of such images has marginalised many females from leadership and made it problematic when women do enact leadership. In its enactment, women need to contest the perception that females do not possess characteristics such as logic and toughness, while also suggesting that these are not the only qualities valuable for effective leadership.

According to Horner (2003), leadership is moving towards a team-based environment where there is less focus on the leader and the follower and more on the process of leadership. These authors cite the work of Drath and Palus (1994), who 'suggest studying the social process that happens with groups of people who are engaged in an activity together' (p. 35). Here leadership involves coordinating the efforts of the group in moving together, with all participants playing an active role. In such a leadership landscape, the process of supporting the team demands collaboration and openness in order to achieve a shared meaning that elicits commitment from group members. Hersey, Blanchard and Johnson (2001) discuss group and team leadership and highlight the need for goals which are understood by all participants. 'Common or at least harmonious goals or purposes are, therefore, not criteria of groups, but of effective groups' (p. 318). Blake, Mouton and Allen (1987) discuss the potential for team synergy when the interaction in a team transcends the contribution possible by individuals creating 'spectacular teamwork' (p. 6). However, these authors acknowledge the need for vision, and the consequence of its absence for a team can mean 'it will drift from day to day in a survival mode' (p. 5). This approach has implications for later discussion of leadership understandings in ECEC. Discontinuities emerge between the team-based leadership literature and the interpretation of this notion by participants in this study.

Leadership in education has focused in the main on notions of context and leadership beyond those of positions such as principal. Spillane, Halverson and Diamond (2001) suggest that distributed leadership views teachers as potential leaders, however; York-Barr and Duke (2004) refer to a number of studies which indicate that reality reflects more traditional forms of one-person leadership, suggesting that traditional models of leadership continue to have currency in school settings.

Until recently, leadership in the Australian field of early childhood education and care had not been widely researched. Leadership research revolved mainly around the work of Rodd (1998), Stonehouse (1994) and Hayden (1996), although recently Boardman (2003), Boyd (2001), Geoghegan, Petriwskyj, Bower, and Geoghegan (2003), Nupponen (2001), Stamopoulos (2003) and Waniganayake, Morda, and Kapsalakis (2000) have examined leadership in various ECEC contexts. Such research has elucidated issues around leadership in ECEC which include incongruence between the rhetoric of democratic governance with the reality of traditional line management approaches. There is recognition of ECEC personnel drawing on an eclectic mix of traits and behaviours in their enactment of leadership. Carter and Curtis (1998) provide an ECEC interpretation of visionary leadership with a model that includes attention to three areas. These are leadership involving managing and overseeing; coaching and mentoring and building and supporting community. Literature in ECEC leadership has in the main focused on specific contexts, while this present study sought to explore broader understandings of leadership from multiple ECEC contexts and variously trained professionals to understand their interpretations of leadership.

METHODOLOGY

The principal research question in this study focused on how ECEC personnel understand leadership and its enactment within the field. Specific interview questions afforded participants the opportunity to explore their own understandings of leadership and to reflect and comment on how they see leadership enacted within their field, well beyond their own service context. This provided the potential to understand what informs leadership ideas and if these are factors external and/or internal to the field. I was interested to see how influential traditional notions of leadership are informing ECEC personnel in their definitions of leadership. I was also interested to understand how these participants see leadership enacted within and for the ECEC field. How do the understandings of leadership align or contradict with the enactment of leadership as understood by these ECEC personnel? Are there tensions and discontinuities or is leadership a clearly defined and coherent notion within the field? Given the highly feminised nature of the ECEC field, how is a notion of leadership so heavily imbued with traditional heroic male dominant constructs of leadership interpreted by these participants?

In seeking a research design which would afford the exploration of these issues I identified a qualitative approach and, in particular, the use of symbolic interactionism as a methodological tool. Symbolic interactionism involves the study of individuals in society and what impacts on their own subjective insights and feelings. Importantly, symbolic interactionism maintains that individuals structure their external world by their perceptions and interpretations of what they conceive that world to be (Benzies & Allen, 2001). George Herbert Mead is considered the father of symbolic interactionism and his work was later developed by Blumer (1969), who provided a conceptual frame around which a significant amount of interpretative/ethnographic research has been conducted over the past century. According to Blumer (1969), symbolic interactionism involves interpretation of the actions or remarks of another person and how one is to act. It is through this process that participants fit their own acts to the ongoing acts of one another and guide others in doing so. Mead (1934) asserted that individuals develop socially by entering into their community and coming to recognise the conditions that determine thought and practice. It is the individual who modifies the social influences through their interpretation of the particular context. Consequently, this methodological tool affords the opportunity to view how ECEC personnel interprets leadership influenced by social factors and cultural aspects in the ECEC field. The individual is an active agent, not passively responding to social forces but undergoing the experience, and also being aware of the experience.

Appreciation of feminist theory was pertinent to this study, given the highly feminised nature of the ECEC field. Feminist theory assists in unpacking some of the taken-for-granted aspects of the ECEC field as well as the heroic, male dominance of the leadership literature. Feminist authors make problematic leadership as being historically and culturally associated with men. According to Wajcman (1999), leadership 'is seen as intrinsically masculine, something that only men do. The very language of management is resolutely masculine' (p. 7). This study sought to ask questions about these notions through exploring how leadership is understood and enacted in a highly feminised field. What role do traditional notions of leadership play in the enactment of leadership?

Data Collection

To address the research question in a way that is consistent with symbolic interactionist data collection methods, interviews and focus groups were used as the main means to gather data. In addition, during the interviews I asked the participants if there were any materials they accessed and used to inform their understandings of leadership. These artefacts were accessed or acquired in some cases and their relevance to participants' understandings of leadership explored in the analysis. In total, I conducted 26 semi-structured interviews with participants from a range of ECEC services. Of the 26 interviews, 16 participants were from a regional area and the remaining 10 were from New South Wales, Queensland, Victoria and Tasmania. Participants included long day care directors, family day care coordinators, early childhood undergraduate students, early childhood academics, preschool directors and people working in organisations associated with the provision of services for children and families. The interviews and focus groups were audio-taped and later transcribed. Emerging themes were coded, and categories emerged related to the research questions. The interviews were also saved as audio-text on the computer.

The Findings

Analysis of the data revealed two interrelated categories, the first being Interpreted Professional Identity and the second Interpreted Leadership Capacity, and I propose that the interpretation of one's professional identity is linked to one's interpreted leadership capacity. In other words, I am suggesting that this data and analysis indicates that the capacity of participants to enact leadership is influenced by their own interpretation of their professional identity (Fig. 10.1).

Interpreted professional identity emerged from the participants' accounts of the ECEC field and the wider community. It involves how individuals interpret the expectations of these cultures in terms of their individual sense of self. It became apparent that, for many participants, their own professional sense of self is informed by multiple factors, some of which they recognise as external to the ECEC field and others as evident within the field itself. In addition, participants recognise incongruence between leadership beyond ECEC and leadership within the field, and this made apparent tensions about how leadership is understood and enacted. The interpretation of social expectations which require nurturance and care in ECEC personnel appeared as somewhat incompatible

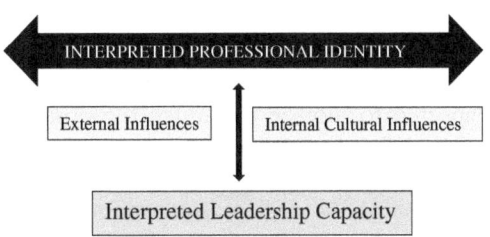

Fig. 10.1 Diagrammatical representation of data analysis

with the requirements for leadership as understood by many participants. The interpretation of others' views creates uncertainties for some participants about their own professional identity. The discourse of niceness continues to pervade images of what is required of ECEC personnel, and for participants this was a leadership inhibitor. For participants there were limited images of how to be an ECEC leader, and, for the early childhood student participants, this was a notable absence since they had few images with which to inform their own emerging professional identity.

For participants in this study, their interpretation of the ECEC culture impacts significantly on their ability to enact leadership. They articulated this for themselves and recounted how they saw this happen for others. I will elaborate on this in more depth by providing some rich data to illustrate the power of such interpretations and its inhibiting effect on ECEC leadership.

Interpreted Professional Identity is influenced by factors external to the ECEC field as well as by internal or cultural aspects of the field. Participants identified numerous factors external to the field as significant to their professional identity. These comments, by others, were recounted by participants and, while they themselves held an intrinsic belief in the value of their work in ECEC, these external values played a powerful role in influencing participants' understandings of themselves as professionals. In many cases, participants' interpretations of their sense of self (and their professional identity) were strongly influenced by the views of others. This did not manifest into a robust image of themselves as professionals. A relationship between the interpretation of factors external to the ECEC field (such as remuneration levels and low social kudos) and aspects of horizontal violence will be explored later in this paper.

One of the most notable factors internal to the ECEC field was the expectation that leadership be enacted in a non-hierarchical manner. Participants' understandings of leadership in ECEC were strongly articulated along the lines of a team-based leadership approach. Participants interpret their field as requiring an approach to leadership that is more dispersed amongst numerous workers, and those in positional leadership roles are expected to 'not be too much the boss'. One early childhood academic stated that 'in early childhood ... we want to be seen as one of the team a little bit more than the all-powerful one that makes all the ultimate decisions'. According to the director of a long day care centre, 'I think as a leader you have to be part of the team as well.' For a preschool teacher leadership meant that you 'don't have to be the

"top dog"' and 'you don't want to be too much of the person in charge'
... in case 'it puts the staff off.' One early childhood academic recounted
a personal experience when she stated:

> What I probably see as the biggest problem for good leadership or effec-
> tive leadership is that people ... like if there's a director of a centre or
> they're in a leadership role, they like to be seen as one of the team players
> or one of the gang and if there are any privileges or anything that stands
> them out separately they quickly adjust and pretend they are one of the
> team again.

For this participant, being part of the team can be problematic. She
sees it demanding a conformity that prevents notoriety often associated with leadership. Leadership enactment emerges as non-positional
in many respects, and this is congruent with what participants describe
as a pervading culture of niceness. Niceness surfaces as an ironic category with links to compliance and other behaviours. Although Not Just
Nice Ladies by Anne Stonehouse was published in 1994, the discourse
of niceness continues as a powerful expectation. Participants illustrated
this when they made the following comments. 'We're the soft option for
being a teacher ... I still think we're those nice ladies in pearls'. In addition, there were other specific references to the notion of niceness when
another participant noted, 'There's niceness there indirectly, directly, it's
there and in a way you're swayed into being you know nice, nice, nice.
I reckon it's at odds with us as a profession.' Work by Griffin (1995, as
cited by York-Barr & Duke, 2004) on leadership inactivity in school contexts identified a similar behaviour or what he terms 'politesse', where
teachers were reluctant to draw attention to the shortcomings of other
teachers lest such attention would be generalised to the whole group.

So what are the implications of this team-based leadership expectation and the lingering discourse of niceness? For participants, this cultural expectation of niceness demands a degree of compliance. This is
evident in the following comment by an early childhood academic: 'I
see that they [EC services] are little environments of conformity and
of course like minded ideas group together.' Similarly, a comment
from a participant working in a support organisation elaborates this
point: 'If someone is getting a little too confident, there is this "you
get back in your box," because that's not your position, that's not your
role ... we can't have that happening.' Again from another participant,

the comment that 'I think it is your peers that ... hold you back the most' illustrates a need to comply with expectations in the ECEC field. For the director of a long day care centre, her concern was for a pre-school teacher and how she was received within the staff team: '...some people were quite nasty to her ... [they] have got particular points of view and get together and create their own little culture and they expect everyone else to be the same—it's worrying isn't it?'. It seems ironic that, within a culture of niceness and an understanding of leadership as somewhat team-based or focused, such behaviours are possible or toler-able. These interpretations suggest a relationship to the notion of hori-zontal violence identified in nursing literature (Farrell, 2001; McKenna, Smith, Poole, & Coverdale, 2003) as well as a relationship to the 'crab bucket mentality' articulated by Duke (1994). This has similarities to the work of York-Barr and Duke (2004), who suggest that '...one of the most prevailing norms in the teaching profession is egalitarianism which fosters the view that teachers who step up to leadership roles are stepping out of line' (p. 272). Consequently, there emerges a relation-ship between cultural behaviours and the potential for individuals to enact leadership.

Horizontal Violence

Horizontal violence is explored extensively in nursing literature as an attempt to explain staff conflict (Farrell, 2001). Specifically, it is defined as 'psychological harassment, which creates hostility, as opposed to physical aggression. This harassment involves verbal abuse, threats, intimidation, humiliation, excessive criticism, innuendo, exclusion, denial of access to opportunity, disinterest, discouragement and the withholding of information' (McKenna et al., 2003, p. 92). Horizontal violence is related to self-concept development and in particular self-confidence and self-esteem. Randle (2003), in the nursing litera-ture, links the construction of different selves to the social interaction people undertake and the feedback they receive. Are participants rec-ognising a culture that is constrained by expectations of niceness but which manifests into aspects of horizontal violence as a result of low professional status?

A poignant account of a personal experience of horizontal violence is provided by an early childhood academic reflecting on her teaching career:

I did enter a childcare centre years ago and had a lot of confidence knocked out of me. If there was anything that was a bit different, which I did have some different practices, people would sort of, not tall poppy syndrome but—people would try and pull you apart because I wasn't part of the normal culture. For example, you know, taking inside toys like dinosaurs outside got to be the big issue and I really basically I resigned over that. I worked for a city council not really very far from here and, um, the collective were very different to me and if the director of the centre was a little bit more visionary she could actually see where I was coming from and that differences are a good thing, you know. She could have helped me out but she didn't; she was a lousy leader—she basically humiliated someone like myself who wanted to do things a bit differently—like simple things like bring all the drawing and all the painting materials and everything to the children's level, just really basic things—every little thing was a big issue.

The director of a long day care centre provided a detailed account of an experience she witnessed:

I actually think I saw that kind of thing happening in our centre when I first got there with our new preschool teacher. Now she's an outsider in a sense because she's got different training to everyone else and there was a lot of things that other staff did, in, you know, quite subtle ways that, you know, made her uncomfortable and kind of kept her from expressing things or even attempting new things the way that she wanted to ... Some people were quite nasty to her, which, I found out later but, you know, just in like derogatory comments or not including her in any social thing that was being organised for all the staff or, you know, just those things really. Some of them were quite overt but some of them were quite subtle things or just ignoring what she might have had to say or even just saying something about her program—and it is really where people don't want someone to be a bit different.

And from an academic near retirement:

It's often now older women because they're people like me where we're at the point where we are saying, 'I don't care now—I'm going to say it because this is important and, whether people like it or not, I'm going to say it, because we need to say these things for the profession.

Somewhat similar to the notion of horizontal violence, Duke (1994) defined the term 'crab bucket mentality' This was in the context of leadership in education, and he made use of this as a metaphor to explain what he identified as the prevailing norms of the culture of teaching that constrain leadership behaviour.

> Anyone who has gone crabbing knows that it is unnecessary to cap a crab bucket because as soon as one crab tries to scuttle out, the others drag it back down. Some faculties function in the same way, actively resisting the efforts of any member to press beyond normal practice. Teacher leadership can hardly thrive in such circumstances. (Duke, 1994, pp. 269–270)

This powerful metaphor by Duke (1994) correlates with the notion of horizontal violence. It suggests that, in education, cultures exist to constrain leadership by requirements for personnel to conform to accepted expectations. One participant in the present study referred to state organisations where people do a lot of 'watching the person next to you to make sure they're not getting too up themselves you know'. Another participant, on the subject of ECEC workers, suggested, 'If someone is getting a little too confident, um, there is this you get back in your box because that's not your position, that's not your role;' and facetiously added, 'We can't have that happening.' These are examples of the crab bucket mentality and horizontal violence in action. An abdication of one's place can apparently marginalise individuals, making leadership enactment problematic and potentially unattractive.

WHY HORIZONTAL VIOLENCE AND A CRAB BUCKET MENTALITY?

In the present study, there is resonance between the ECEC participants and nursing literature in terms of horizontal violence and ways this affects the culture of the field. This appears relevant to the formation of an individual's interpreted professional identity based on expectations prevalent within the field. McKenna et al. (2003) investigated neophyte nurses' experiences of horizontal violence and reported that, in the main, interpersonal conflict involved being undervalued by peers, having learning opportunities blocked, and feeling neglected and distressed by the conflict between others. Randle (2003) makes a link between the effects of horizontal violence and self-esteem. Randle's study linked the construction of different 'selves' to the social interaction people undertake and the feedback they receive. While Randle (2003) does not refer here to symbolic interactionism, there is a connection with the present study. The nursing literature supports a relationship between workplace culture, self-concept and confidence, and this is relevant to the suggestion that professional identity has links to ECEC leadership capacity. In addition, the notion suggested by Randle (2003), that self-esteem is a major predictor of behaviour, provides support for the concept that cultural aspects of the field can influence self-concept and consequently constrain an individual's interpreted leadership capacity.

Do ECEC personnel demonstrate horizontal violence and the crab bucket mentality as the result of low self-esteem and confidence? Goffman's work with restaurant personnel elicited the notion of '"front" and "back" regions' (1959, p. 107) to explore how the persona adopted by waiters, as they serve the public, contrasted with their attitude while back of house. This work illustrated that the performance the waiters provided for the client reflected an attitude not actually held by the staff. 'The staff, then, mount a collaborative performance to project themselves as the capable and committed deliverers of that service; they play back the clients' own self-conceptions as the well-regarded, gratefully and gracefully serviced clients' (Cuff, Sharrock, & Francis, 1998, p. 141). In 'back of house', staffs are able to express their alternative persona, reversing the relationship of servility and reinforcing their sense of self. This example illustrates symbolic interactionist concerns about how people involved in work which has a low or negative social esteem maintain their sense of self-worth 'in a society which told them they were worthless individuals' (Cuff et al., 1998, p. 140).

What this suggests is that waiting staff express their own value behind the scenes by behaving in ways that demean the clients in order to assert themselves. It is possible that the horizontal violence acknowledged by many participants in this study is a demonstration of the frustration felt by ECEC personnel when they are required to conform to a discourse of niceness and its constraining expectations.

Those investigating horizontal violence link such behaviour to oppressed groups who lack power and consequently 'attack one another in order to vent their frustration and anger with the system they find themselves in' (Randle, 2003, p. 399). This behaviour is particularly relevant given Goffman's assertion that the back-of-house behaviour is a means to reinforce a sense of self in a profession that has a low social standing (Cuff et al., 1998). Other aspects of the present study (reported in Hard, 2005) suggest that participants interpret factors external to the field as strong influences on their professional identity. The interpretation of low social kudos for ECEC was demonstrated in comments such as the following:

I mean, I can give an example. My daughter, years ago, commented at 15 that she went and looked after a child after school each night because his mother [was] a school teacher, an educated person, and when they went away she looked after the dog each night and they paid her more to feed the dog. What is this telling us?

The implication is that a perceived low social standing can contribute to a limited professional identity which can result in behaviours such as horizontal violence and the crab bucket mentality. These actions demand that others comply or risk marginalisation, and such a culture is not one in which leadership activity is encouraged or supported.

IMPLICATIONS FOR ECEC LEADERSHIP

The discourse of niceness continues to pervade participants' interpretations of the ECEC culture, yet the emergence of its antithesis in horizontal violence demands debate and discussion. Aspects of horizontal violence and crab bucket mentality manifest in behaviours which covertly and overtly marginalise others through demanding compliance with certain ways of being and acting. If such elements are part of the ECEC culture, as these participants suggest, then the outcome is likely to be limited leadership activity. Participants felt constrained in their activities in case they draw undue attention to themselves as individuals. The interpretation of a team-based leadership approach appears superficially to suggest a progressive and innovative leadership style which other spheres of leadership literature have explored only recently. However, this remains contentious given team-focused leadership literature discussed earlier which describes such leadership as involving an articulation of a vision or shared goals. The interpretation of team-based leadership by participants in this study was not couched in terms which involved specific vision or common articulated goals but, rather, may be an expectation of similarity and a lack of potential to challenge expected norms.

Rather than an egalitarian rationale, this team-based approach suggests an expectation of certain behaviours and aspirations which avoid individual notoriety. In itself, this may be laudable. However, when it demands compliance to certain ways of acting and thinking it is constraining. The initial definition of leadership in this paper involved change in organisations, and this is difficult to achieve in a culture which does not support varied ideas and discussions. In a climate where effective leadership is increasingly a measure of an organisation's or a profession's success, ECEC personnel might well consider alternative ways of acting. Discussions with undergraduate students showed that they too have already witnessed, if not directly experienced, horizontal violence on placements. Incorporating discussions of how the culture of ECEC can demand compliance and its implications for leadership could be an important element of undergraduate courses. Without conversations around such issues, leadership is unlikely to prosper, and strategic leadership for the field will not be supported. The pervading nature of this discourse is such that, without overt and deep exploration of how this activity occurs, the ECEC field will continue to crave leadership but be unable to provide the culture in which it can be fostered and flourish.

CONCLUSION

This study explored how leadership is understood and enacted within the field of ECEC. What emerges is a complex interplay of factors that interact in people's understandings of leadership. In addition, the use of symbolic interactionism as a methodological tool helps to illustrate that individuals interpret their professional identity through their engagements with others, both within and beyond their field. These engagements have a powerful influence in assisting or constraining leadership aspirations and enactment. What emerges as a significant cultural factor is horizontal violence, which plays out in behaviours that exclude or marginalise those who do not conform to expected norms. In conjunction with Duke's (1994) metaphor of the crab bucket mentality, horizontal violence illustrates a powerful constraint interpreted by participants. The challenge is to openly discuss this cultural expectation and the ways it is evident in behaviours in the field. Further, it is important to consider this as a non-productive and potentially destructive aspect which requires overt attention to avoid the ongoing constraints it puts upon leadership behaviour.

REFERENCES

Benzies, K. M., & Allen, M. (2001). Symbolic interactionism as a theoretical perspective for multiple method research. *Journal of Advanced Nursing, 33*(4), 541–547.

Black, J. S., & Porter, L. W. (2000). *Management: Meeting New Challenges.* Upper Saddle River, NJ: Prentice Hall.

Blake, R., Mouton, J., & Allen, R. (1987). *Spectacular Teamwork: How to Develop your Talented People into High-Performance Teams.* London: Sidgwick and Jackson.

Blumer, H. (1969). *Symbolic Interactionism.* Englewood Cliffs, NJ: Prentice-Hall.

Boardman, M. (2003). Recognition? Trust? Support? Presence? What really counts in early childhood leadership? *Australian Research in Early Childhood Education, 10*(1), 1–11.

Boyd, G. (2001). *Early Childhood Teachers' Perceptions of Their Leadership Roles.* Unpublished doctoral dissertation, Edith Cowan University.

Carter, M., & Curtis, D. (1998). *The Visionary Director: A Handbook for Dreaming, Organising, and Improvising in your Centre.* St Paul, MN: Redleaf Press.

Collinson, D., & Hearn, J. (2003). Critical studies on men, masculinities and management. In N. Bennett, M. Crawford, & M. Cartwright (Eds.), *Effective Educational Leadership* (pp. 201–215). London: The Open University.

Cuff, E. C., Sharrock, W. W., & Francis, D. W. (1998). *Perspectives in Sociology* (4th ed.). New York: Routledge.

Drath, W. H., & Palus, C. J. (1994). *Making Common Sense: Leadership as Meaning-Making in a Community of Practice.* Greensboro, NC: Centre for Creative Leadership.

Duke, D. (1994). Teacher leadership: A failure to conceptualize. In D. Walling (Ed.), *Teachers as Leaders: Perspectives on the Professional Development of Teachers* (pp. 255–273). Bloomington, IN: Phi Delta Kappa Educational Foundation.

Farrell, G. A. (2001). From tall poppies to squashed weeds: Why don't nurses pull together more? *Journal of Advanced Nursing, 35*(1), 26–33.

Fiedler, F. (1967). *A Theory of Leadership Effectiveness.* New York: McGraw-Hill.

Geoghegan, N., Petriwskyj, A., Bower, L., & Geoghegan, D. (2003). Eliciting dimensions of educational leadership in early childhood education. *Journal of Australian Research in Early Childhood Education, 10*(1), 12–22.

Goffman, E. (1959). *The Presentation of Self in Everyday Life.* New York: Anchor Books.

Griffin, G. A. (1995). Influences of shared decision making on school and classroom activity: Conversations with five teachers. *Planning and Changing, 32,* 164–183.

Hard, L. (2005). Would the leaders in early childhood education and care please step forward? *Journal of Australian Research in Early Childhood Education, 12*(2), 51–61.

Hayden, J. (1996). *Management of Early Childhood Services: An Australian Perspective.* Sydney: Social Science Press.

Hersey, P., Blanchard, K., & Johnson, D. (2001). *Management of Organisational Behaviour: Leading Human Resources.* Upper Saddle River, NJ: Prentice Hall.

Hill, M. S., & Ragland, J. (1995). *Women as Educational Leaders: Opening Windows, Pushing Ceilings*. Thousand Oaks, CA: Corwin Press.

Horner, M. (2003). Leadership theory revisited. In N. Bennett, M. Crawford, & M. Cartwright (Eds.), *Effective Educational Leadership* (pp. 27–43). London: The Open University.

Jorde Bloom, P. (2003). *Leadership in Action: How Effective Directors Get Things Done*. Lake Forest, IL: New Horizons.

Lingard, B., Hayes, D., Mills, M., & Christie, P. (2003). *Leading Learning*. Maidenhead, UK: Open University Press.

MacBeath, J. (2004). *The Leadership File: Twenty-Five Definitions of Leadership with Activities to Help You Recognise Their Relevance to School Practice*. Melbourne: Hawker Brownlow Education.

McKenna, B., Smith, N., Poole, S., & Coverdale, J. (2003). Horizontal violence: Experiences of registered nurses in their first year of teaching. *Journal of Advanced Nursing, 42*(1), 90–96.

Mead, G. H. (1934). *Works of George Herbert Mead. Volume 1: Mind, Self and Society from the Standpoint of a Social Behaviourist*. Chicago: University of Chicago Press.

Nanus, B. (1992). *Visionary Leadership*. San Francisco: Jossey-Bass.

Northcraft, G., & Neale, M. (1994). *Organizational Behavior: A Management Challenge* (2nd ed.). Orlando: Dryden Press.

Nupponen, H. (2001). Leadership and management in child care services: Contextual factors and their impact on practice. In *Proceedings of the QUT Postgraduate Conference*. Brisbane.

Randle, J. (2003). Bullying in the nursing profession. *Journal of Advanced Nursing, 43*(4), 395–401.

Robbins, S., Millett, B., & Waters-Marsh, T. (2004). *Organisational Behaviour*. Sydney: Pearson Education.

Rodd, J. (1998). *Leadership in Early Childhood Education* (2nd ed.). Sydney: Allen & Unwin.

Schultz, D., & Schultz, S. (1998). *Psychology and Work Today: An Introduction to Industrial and Organizational Psychology* (7th ed.). Upper Saddle River, NJ: Prentice Hall.

Sinclair, A. (1998). *Doing Leadership Differently: Gender, Power and Sexuality in a Changing Business Culture*. Melbourne: Melbourne University Press.

Spillane, J., Halverson, R., & Diamond, J. (2001). Investigating school leadership practice: A distributed perspective. *Educational Researcher, 30*(3), 23–28.

Stamopoulos, E. (2003). *Leadership and change management in early childhood*. Paper presented at the Early Childhood Australia Conference, Children—The Core of Society, Hobart.

Stonehouse, A. (1994). *Not Just Nice Ladies*. Castle Hill: Pademelon Press.

Wajcman, J. (1999). *Managing Like a Man: Women and Men in Corporate Management.* Sydney: Allen & Unwin.

Waniganayake, M., Morda, R., & Kapsalakis, A. (2000). Leadership in child care centres: Is it just another job? *Australian Journal of Early Childhood*, 25(1), 13–19.

York-Barr, J., & Duke, D. (2004). What do we know about teacher leadership? Findings from two decades of scholarship. *Review of Educational Research*, 74(3), 255–316.

CHAPTER 11

The Transition of Women to Leadership in Post-secondary Institutions in Canada: An Examination of the Literature and the Lived DIM Experiences of Two Female Leaders

Lorraine M. Carter and Diane P. Janes

An Introduction to Women in Leadership in Post-secondary Education

Historically, professional women have tended to work in the 'helping professions' with elementary and secondary School teaching, nursing, and social work among their top choices, and it is within these areas that they have held leadership positions. While the value of women's leadership in these fields cannot be underestimated, it would be an untruth to

L. M. Carter (✉)
Centre for Continuing Education, McMaster University,
Hamilton, ON, Canada

D. P. Janes
Learning Engagement Office (LEO), Faculty of Extension,
University of Alberta, Edmonton, AB, Canada

© The Author(s) 2018   209
C. L. Cho et al. (eds.), *Exploring the Toxicity of Lateral Violence and Microaggressions*, https://doi.org/10.1007/978-3-319-74760-6_11

say that their experiences have been anything but hard-won. As an example, the nursing literature is full of instances of incivility not only among nurses in practice but also aggression toward female colleagues in senior roles (Laschinger, Wong, Cummings, & Grau, 2014). Social work and teaching are noted for similar patterns.

Despite certain less than glamorous experiences in the helping professions, women are now finding their way into senior leadership roles in domains where they did not go previously and where there is more proportional gender representation: business, the technology sector, medicine, and academe are four such areas. It is the last environment—post-secondary education—that serves as the setting for this chapter. Given the public's understanding that universities and Colleges are places where tolerance, inclusion, and equity are declared cornerstones, one might extrapolate that women are well received and respected as academic and administrative leaders. Regrettably, women have a long way to go in these milieus. Women, as they transition from practice to leadership in their mid-to-late careers in academe, often encounter difficult and demoralizing circumstances. These outcomes are especially the case when the female leader is committed to authentic leadership and acts as a change maker. Her role as leader can be characterized by considerable dissonance as well as subtle and not so subtle acts of incivility and aggression.

Thinking About Contemporary Leadership

For many years, the leadership literature pertained principally to the world of business. Today, this is changing. With increasing complexities and unprecedented pressures in large organizations such as post-secondary institutions and healthcare organizations, there are new ways of thinking about and practicing leadership. The move is from 'command and control' hierarchies to 'next generation' models that use employee empowerment to leverage dramatic improvement in organizational performance. According to McKimm and O'Sullivan (2012), today's leaders need 'to practice in very different ways, responding to increased complexity, demographic change, technological advances, global economic trends and increased… involvement [by stakeholders] and accountability' (p. 485). A defining characteristic of contemporary leadership is that it should be shared, 'The notion that a few extraordinary people at the top can provide all the leadership needed today is ridiculous and it's a recipe for failure' (Kotter, 2013, para. 9). With leadership evolving to include shared models built on ideas of empowerment and collaboration, leaders are those who can motivate others, generate enthusiasm, and harness the collective to achieve intended results (Cameron & Green, 2012; Graban, 2012; Rose & Bergman, 2016).

What do these ideas about leadership mean for women in Colleges and universities? As a starting point, while women have long been recognized for their collaborative skills, most senior leadership positions in post-secondary settings in Canada and other jurisdictions continue to be held by men (Jones, 2013; Bilen-Green, Froelich, & Jacobson, 2008). Moreover, universities are places where there are distinct hierarchies in all aspects of the organizational structure. Tradition and its trappings sit at the heart of academic life with its Senates, Secretariats, and Deaneries. Finally, like many religious organizations, universities are grounded in a history of knowledge control and dissemination, with male persons acting as the primary gatekeepers of the academy (Bilen-Green et al., 2008; Morley, 2014).

In all, even in 2018, the transition of a female person to a senior leadership role in higher education can be rocky.

Differences Between Male and Female Leaders in Universities

One might think that the differences between men and women as leaders in post-secondary education could not be that substantive. After all, to work at a senior level in a university means that the person, regardless of gender, aspires to the vision, mission, and values of the university. He or she has either come up through the ranks or been selected after a careful recruiting process for a specific role: the person 'fits' with the organization and has something others see as important to the role.

As further insight into senior leadership roles at universities, Bruner (2017) suggests that temperament and readiness are critical to transitioning to a leadership position. Regarding temperament, he suggests that the person needs to have solid self-confidence, resilience, and humility in equal measure, and an inclination to action. As for readiness, Bruner recommends leadership experience acquired over time, awareness of the ways of the world, and skill in getting things done.

So, what distinguishes the female temperament and level of readiness for leadership from the male person's temperament and level of readiness?

The differences, to some extent, tie to socialization and other realities of nature. While today's children and adolescents are often socialized differently than their parents were, persons presently in or considering leadership roles were likely socialized based on their gender (Little & McGivern, 2014). As an outcome, it is often suggested that female leaders may be more nurturing than male leaders (Sherwin, 2014; Zenger & Folkman, 2012). In some contexts, this tendency may be regarded to be a weakness, or perceived as inability to be firm and direct. Current research even suggests that girls as young as six perceive boys to be smarter based on their responses to the question 'who is smarter – boys or girls?' (Bian, Leslie, & Cimpian, 2017a, 2017b).

Female leaders may also carry heavier loads at home than their male counterparts do. When a female leader takes time to care for an ill child or elderly parent, this decision may be seen as detracting from the role of leader (Bilen-Green et al., 2008). By contrast, when a female chooses to be a leader who is 'self-aware and genuine; mission driven and results focused; [who leads with the] heart and focus[es] on the long term' (Kruse, 2013, p. 1), she faces another conundrum. Rather than being perceived as strong and capable, she may be labeled aggressive (Oakley, 2000, pp. 324–325).

A DIM Experience: Dissonance, Incivility, and Microaggression

All too often, female leaders experience the unfortunate realities of dissonance, incivility, and microaggression—namely, DIM. In some instances, DIM derives from the woman herself such as when she questions her abilities in relation to those of her male colleagues and/or other female colleagues. Alternately, she may wonder if she has had adequate preparation for leadership given career interruptions including maternity and family care leaves (Bilen-Green et al., 2008). More often, DIM comes from persons in the women's professional circle and variables over which she has little control including entrenched beliefs about leadership (Caplan, 1992).

Dissonance for the female leader in the university can present in several guises: incongruence with personal expectations; conflicting expectations involving faculty and staff; contrary expectations held by supervisors; and environmental factors including the history of the unit and ingrained behavior patterns by faculty and staff. By comparison, experiences of incivility and microaggression are grounded in attitudes that convey hostility or jealousy toward the female leader and manifest in inappropriate behaviors. Such behaviors can range from gossip to subtle opposition to overt sabotage of the position of the female leader.

Female leaders who move from academic practice to academic leadership are subject to several constructs that appear in the literature: Among others, these constructs include the invisibility of men relative to the visibility of women in leadership contexts; language; and preconceived ideas about what constitutes academic management. While expectations are changing, the academy remains a place where leadership is often male and support staff is often female. Women continue to be underrepresented at higher levels of leadership and to receive lower salaries (Fisher & Fisher, 2007). Although new management models in academe seem to promote '...new more women friendly environments' (Fisher & Fisher, 2007, p. 508), 'micro-level analysis of the effects of the audit and evaluative seem to suggest that hegemonic masculinities and gendered power are being reinforced by the emphasis on competition, targets, and performance' (Fisher & Fisher, 2007, p. 508; Morley, 2003). These ideas are reflected in the understanding that 'men lead and women manage,' an understanding in which leadership is associated with power and management with oversight of tasks (Langland, 2012, p. 1). Langland (2012) remarks on how this belief is deeply rooted in long-standing cultural narratives that are difficult to change:

> I hate to end on a sarcastic note, but it does reflect the difficulty of changing cultural narratives, especially when they are grounded in deeply held convictions about human nature and essence and informed by a Renaissance leadership text titled *The Prince*. (Langland, p. 9)

An Up-Close Look at the Experiences of Two Female Leaders in Post-secondary Settings

In this section, the experiences of two women in leadership positions in post-secondary education are recounted. In addition to descriptions of the cultures and historical practices the women found, considerations of their experiences through the DIM lens are provided.

Meet Mary

At the time of her leadership experience, Mary had acquired her Ph.D. in education with a focus on online education for nurses. She had extensive expertise in health and nursing education; health education research; and administration at two universities. She further had a broad network of colleagues in the healthcare sector. Mary came to the university discussed in this chapter to lead a center dedicated to faculty support and online course development. She was also provided a faculty position in the School of Nursing.

Two years into Mary's time at the university, she was approached by the Dean to assume the role of Director in the School of Nursing. While Mary did not have a Bachelor of Science in Nursing (BScN), the Dean expressed confidence in her skills, and Mary agreed to take the position. Notably, Mary had taught nonclinical undergraduate and graduate level courses in nursing and carried out various administrative responsibilities in a School of Nursing at her former university.

Environmental context. The environment of the School of Nursing in which Mary assumed the role of Director was complex. Although there were no graduate programs to support, its undergraduate nursing programs were distinguished by different philosophies and teaching pedagogies.

During the time Mary was at the University, the School offered a large face-to-face collaborative BScN program with the local community College; a large online learning program for diploma-prepared nurses wishing to acquire BScN status; and a BScN program grounded in the principles of narrative inquiry and delivered in another city. The School was under-resourced from both a staff and a faculty perspective. Given the northern location of the University, it has always been difficult to recruit appropriately credentialed faculty.

In the first program described above, there was considerable negative history between the College and university faculty which tended to manifest in acrimonious meetings, gossip, general distrust, and overall ineffectiveness.

In the second program, the environment was positive but precarious: The faculty and staff responsible for the program were exceptional persons deeply committed to the success of students. The program, however, had continued to grow every semester, and there were inadequate resources to support such growth. Still, the University continued to pressure the School to accept new students. At the same time, due to other fiscal problems experienced by the University, it was not willing to hire new full-time faculty. Thus, faculty on short-term contracts or employed on a sessional basis taught the program. The supports for the online and clinical requirements of this program were similarly limited. Quality online education is a complex undertaking and requires dedicated experts who understand how to adapt curriculum for meaningful delivery and who recognize the criticality of instructor training and supports. Finding and organizing appropriate clinical placements for more than 800 nurse-students across the province requires a team rather than the two persons presently charged with this work. Additionally, some faculty in the collaborative program questioned how it was possible to have a quality online nursing program.

In the third program, there were, prior to Mary's leadership, difficulties associated with its development and accreditation status. Innovative in its approach to nursing education, the program was misunderstood by non-participating faculty and was, thus, a target for criticism. Like the online program, it was inappropriately resourced and involved extensive partnerships. Because it was delivered in a city located four hours away by driving from the University, there were additional variables affecting close connections with the program and the development of relationships with the faculty on the main campus.

DIM experiences. Mary's experiences as Director reflect the DIM phenomenon on many levels. As outlined above, the dissonance factor existed in the School before Mary's arrival. However, the fact that Mary was not a nurse seemed to intensify the agitation of those in the collaborative program. The prevailing sentiment was that it was simply not possible for Mary as a non-nurse to lead a School of Nursing despite her long-standing work in the nursing field and her successful leadership of a complex national accreditation process in the School. The national accrediting body had no concerns about Mary's non-nurse status and was impressed with her leadership skills and scholarly accomplishments.

In contrast with the faculty in the collaborative program, the faculty in the other two programs were supportive of Mary. Mary understood the realities of online programming and what is involved in bringing new programs to life. The support of these faculty members meant a great deal to Mary. Perhaps Mary's identification with the challenges of the online program and the new innovative program fueled the negativity of some of the nurses in the collaborative program.

The evidence of Mary's DIM realities is varied in nature. On the one hand, Mary regularly experienced the scrutiny by a member of the nursing leadership team who demanded to participate in meetings to which she was uninvited. Mary's sense was that this person did not believe that a female colleague who was a non-nurse could make appropriate decisions for the department. Not surprisingly, for Mary, repeated instances of this kind of experience culminated in internal dissonance and questioning of whether she should have taken the position in the first place.

Mary's recommendations at meetings with the faculty in the collaborative program were tensely received. Not lost to Mary was the reality that the nurses in the collaborative program tended to be older and more set in their thinking about nursing education and leadership than their colleagues in the other programs. They comprised, however, the dominant voice in the School and set a negative tone. Mary experienced the incivility of negative statements about her capabilities in formal and informal settings as well as the microaggression of omission. On various occasions, she found herself not invited to discussions in which she should have been included.

Mary approached the Dean at different times about the realities of School life and faculty behaviors. While there was general support, no action was taken to address the macro- and micro-elements of negative play in the School and in relation to Mary.

Outcomes. After a year in this role, Mary chose to resign. Her personal health and professional reputation were more important than a leadership role at this university.

Mary's perspective on her experiences as leader. Since the above experience, Mary has engaged in considerable reflection and tried to situate it in context and in relation to the literature. She was aware of the challenges that existed in the School before she took on the role; she was aware too of the hefty scholarly literature dealing with incivility among nursing as a profession. This literature includes accounts of nurses' poor treatment of each other and student-nurses and their difficult relationships with physicians and hospital administration (Roche, Diers, Duffield, & Catling-Paull, 2010; Vessey, DeMarco, Gaffney, & Budin, 2009).

At the same time, Mary had believed that a School of Nursing that needed leadership would be pleased to get it even if she was a non-nurse. She had wrongly assumed that a School of Nursing would be different from what she knew about nursing practice through her work as a researcher.

For Mary, the ironies are that nursing educators declare themselves to be part of a caring profession that values inter-professionalism and pride themselves in fostering leadership knowledge and skills in their students. In Mary's case, acceptance of her inter-professional and leadership skills did not seem possible.

Mary has further reflected on the idea that women aspiring to academic leadership should seek the mentorship of other female leaders. While this inherently makes sense, it begs the larger question of leadership of programs offered by the academy where the faculty are principally female: nursing, social work, the rehabilitation sciences, education, and perhaps some disciplines in the humanities and social sciences. In Mary's estimation, there is still a long road ahead if female leadership in these fields is to become something that women can carry out with support, respect, and integrity.

Based on her hypothesizing about what might have been the experiences of a new male director, Mary holds two minds. The literature emphasizes that both men and women are more accustomed to accepting male leaders than female leaders due to their socialization experiences (Little & McGivern, 2014). There is other literature that suggests that, in the caring professions including nursing, social work, and education, females possess the best blend of traits to provide caring and effective leadership (Dickson & Tholl, 2014). In all, Mary was unable to fully discern a clear picture of how gender played out in her experience; she was, however, certain that it played a primary role.

The role of the Dean in supporting a new leader has also been an area of reflection for Mary. Her observations are that a Dean needs to mentor a new leader for at least a year as she or he learns the operational patterns and general dynamics of the unit. Moreover, when there are complex dynamics, the leader needs to have an open line of communication with the Dean and experience guidance during the navigation of difficult issues. If there is a troubled history in the leader's unit, the Dean's support is especially important. In Mary's case, her non-identity as a nurse might have been addressed by the Dean with the faculty prior to her assuming the role and, thus, lessened her DIM experience.

Meet Susan

At the time of the leadership experience discussed here, Susan who already held a Master's degree in Education and a Ph.D. in Higher Education was completing a Master of Business Administration with a focus on community economic development. She had worked in several educational institutions, mostly universities, in diverse capacities: Her various roles included work as a laboratory instructor and instructional designer early in her career, as a consultant, and as a project manager. Susan had also held two tenured faculty positions and been promoted early during her first appointment.

Over her 20 plus year career, Susan had chaired academic committees, represented faculty in Senate, led strategic initiatives, and undertaken the creation of new courses and programs in team settings and working as an individual. She had also been Chair of a new Education Department for two years and served a two-year term as Chair of a School of Professional Studies.

At the point in her career described here, Susan was offered the position of Associate Dean (AD) in a School of Business in a mid-sized community College. The community College was located in part of the country that Susan knew and aspired to return to in her mid-career. Susan's contract did not include an option to join the faculty if the position did not 'work out.' She was advised that the College was not prepared to offer such a provision to her contract; while she asked for this limitation to be reconsidered, the terms of the contract were firm. Because she was keenly interested in exploring leadership at the level of Dean, she accepted a one-year contract with this College. She anticipated that she would be successful and that the contract would be converted to a full-time continuing position.

Environmental context. When Susan arrived at the College, it had been experimenting with reorganization in anticipation of becoming a university-level degree-granting institution. Susan was the first Associate Dean to be hired during the reorganization efforts. Her expertise in transitioning new departments and change management, her innovative use of technology to develop contemporary curricula, and her experience in university governance were seen as strengths. These areas of expertise were important since the history of the School of Business had been fraught with change in the years before Susan's arrival.

As context, three years earlier, the long-term Dean had been 'let go' with the arrival of a new President and administration; this person had been the Dean for more than seven years and had provided oversight for the transition of the then Business Department to a new downtown campus. After the departure of this Dean, the faculty found themselves led by a temporary Dean from the main campus for almost a year. During this time, the College engaged in a search for a new Dean.

The new Dean was a volunteer member of the College's community fundraising team and an employee of a local financial institution. While this person had an undergraduate degree in business and was well connected in the community, he had no experience as a senior leader in a post-secondary education institution. As part of his early work, the Dean sought the designation of School for the former Business Department and undertook the search and hire of the Associate Dean for the School.

As the successful candidate of the search, Susan arrived at the College in the middle of this change. Having consulted with Associate Dean colleagues at other institutions, Susan conjectured that she needed a three-year window to establish a steady foundation for the School to go forward: year one to get the 'lay of the land'; year two to build processes; and year three to finesse changes started in years one and two. Her Dean, however, wanted all of this work accomplished in year one.

DIM experiences. The expectations that the Dean had for Susan were numerous and demanding. As an example, before Susan came aboard, the Dean had decided that the College's 'chair model' of administration, in the form of three faculty chairs responsible for the operations of seven programs, was to be eliminated. While the existing chairs had tried to dissuade the Dean from this structure before and after Susan's arrival, within three months of arriving, the work of the three chairs fell her way. Her role, as characterized by the Dean on several occasions, was to be that of an 'Uber [or Ultimate] Chair.' Susan was also responsible for the well-being and monitoring of students, the hiring and mentoring of full- and part-time faculty, professional development, evaluation and teaching assignments, curriculum development, and taking the lead on School negotiations with external partners.

The Dean's involvement with the community, his political aspirations, and his personal need to support senior management before his staff and faculty complicated the situation. Within six months, he had withdrawn most of his formal support for Susan and refused to have meetings longer than one hour a week with her. Although often absent from the School, he continued to maintain control over decision making, limited the purview of the Associate Dean, and impeded a smooth transition from Dean-led to Associate Dean-led decision making. The Dean was very preoccupied with Susan supplying him reports to pass forward to senior management and minimally concerned about the faculty and the mundane operations of the School.

In addition to the Dean, there was an external force that created conflict for Susan in her work as Associate Dean. Before her arrival, the Dean had contracted a private consultant to assist him with transitioning from his previous work to the position of Dean of a School of Business. This consultant had no relationship with the College; however, he seemed to have considerable influence over the Dean, as exemplified in the following remarks.

After his arrival, the Dean experienced several confrontations with faculty and believed that they were not 'engaged' with his vision for the School. About midway through Susan's initial one-year contract, the consultant was asked to conduct a survey of the faculty and of the Dean's office staff, with the aim of assessing the Dean's and Susan's ability to engage faculty. Susan agreed to the survey, believing that it would be used to improve and focus her work and assist the School in the process of becoming more like a university. Additionally, she had been working with the Dean toward a more conciliatory position with respect to the faculty, and felt that the faculty, in general, were engaged. Before the faculty left for their summer holidays, the survey was administered. The results were to be analyzed by the consultant, and a report to be supplied to the Dean and Susan at the end of the summer.

When the report was ready, the Dean was on vacation, and he instructed Susan to meet with the consultant privately. She agreed to meet the consultant off campus at a local golf course. The location seemed to be an odd choice, but she chose to be accommodating. At the meeting, the consultant proceeded to deconstruct the survey data, informing Susan that the survey revealed her 'inability to continue as AD,' 'her inability to engage,' 'the catastrophic choice of the hiring committee in choosing her as AD,' and 'her need to consider a career change.' Susan was stunned by this information as well as the fact that it was being delivered by someone unaffiliated with the College with no authority to convey such information. The consultant refused to provide his comments in writing, despite Susan's request personally and then later by email. She left the meeting with a copy of the report. Neither Human Resources nor the Dean made any attempt to support Susan when she spoke to them after the meeting with the consultant.

Outcomes. A week later, Susan chose not to renew her contract. However, just before leaving her appointment, she was invited to a meeting with the President and several new Associate Deans from the main campus. Susan's Dean did not attend the meeting; the Deans of all the other Associate Deans were present. Susan's work in advancing the Associate Dean structure and doing so from the 'distance' of the downtown campus was positively recognized. Several members of other Schools had observed what had unfolded in the School of Business and thus kept some or all of their chairs during the hire of an Associate Dean. Additionally, by the time Susan left the College, senior administration had revisited the idea of an Associate Dean returning to or joining a faculty after an appointment. Further review of the consultant's report identified that his analysis of the data was incorrect and should not have been the basis of any decision by the Dean.

Susan's perspective on her experiences as leader. What was most frustrating for Susan was the isolation she experienced and the lack of support by a Dean who took guidance from a third party. Susan had expected that her Dean would know the College's systems and understand the relationships important to her work. By contrast, Susan worked with a novice Dean more interested in politics than academic administration and with a faculty group reeling from change. Given these circumstances, Susan was not set up for success. This lack of support contrasted sharply with an amazing team of male and female staff, faculty, students, and main campus colleagues. While such support is extremely valuable, without mentorship from one's supervisor—in this case, the Dean—a person can only go so far. It is unknown if this situation would have developed differently had Susan been male. What is clear is that her replacement, a male Associate Dean, has held the position since Susan left.

Several concerns continue to stand out for Susan regarding the survey experience described earlier: use of a survey on engagement never used in an academic leadership setting as evidence of her leadership skills; the Dean's reliance on an external party to convey the apparent findings; and his decision to use these findings as a performance measure. Contrary to the verbal debrief on the survey Susan received from the consultant at the golf course, the raw data revealed that, in one year, Susan had been rated as 'engaging' by over 50% of the faculty and that she was in the process of engaging with another 25% at the time of the survey. Given a period of less than one year in a new and complex position involving a faculty in turmoil, these are hardly poor outcomes.

Upon reflection, Susan believes that, if the School of Business had not tried to be political by 'going it alone' in establishing itself as the College's first School, the additional support of the other Associate Deans on main campus would have mitigated many of Susan's frustrations, given that adequate support was not likely from her Dean. Colleagues could have worked together on processes, thus creating some consistency across the academic landscape of the main and downtown campuses. The instances of incivility and microaggression (e.g., the Dean's refusal to meet weekly for more than a half hour on School business; the lack of transfer of authority for operations; and the external consultant engaging with Susan outside of the College administration) experienced by Susan during her time with the College would have also been diminished if she had had colleagues to consult with and form relationships. These relationships/mentors would have given her access to the history and culture of the College that was new to her, giving her the opportunity to make adjustments—to know where the boundaries might have been. This would have benefited any new Associate Dean, male or female. Her ability to collaborate with faculty simply needed time to flourish. Unfortunately, the Dean's perception of leadership was markedly different. In an ironic turn, many of the strengths Susan was hired for (her curriculum expertise, her ability to manage change in institutions wanting to be a university, her higher education knowledge) became many of the reasons for her departure.

From Surviving to Thriving

While the experiences of Mary and Susan are only two instances of women in leadership in Canadian post-secondary institutions, they provide insight into a cross-section of issues reported by other female leaders and reflected in the literature. Each of the issues noted here and recommendations for responding to them are discussed in the following paragraphs: failure by other leaders to set people up for success; institutional failure; the inexperience of new leaders and those supporting them; unrealistic expectations; and the issue of gender. Although gender is discussed last, by no means should this suggest that it is less significant than the other elements. In fact, based on the experiences of Mary and Susan, gender was a primary factor in their experiences as leaders.

The task of setting a new leader up for success is no small undertaking. Foremost, the leader's supervisor wants to believe that he or she has selected wisely and that, after what seems to be a reasonable time period, the initial supports can be withdrawn. What constitutes a reasonable time period can be difficult to discern. Is it six months? A year? The supervisor may choose to meet with the staff in the unit that the leader is joining to provide insight into changes that may be forthcoming when the new person arrives. This way, the new leader is spared the task of communicating all changes for the first time: The staff has had the proverbial 'heads up.'

In the cases of Mary and Susan, such pre-work was not carried out to a helpful extent. As Mary indicated, she inherited a raucous faculty with a difficult past. The same occurred for Susan: Her faculty and staff would have benefited from clarity about the road ahead for them from the Dean. As Morley (2013) suggests, 'It is pertinent to ask why women should desire or aspire to enter HE leadership at all. This often involves taking on a completely new job – sometimes without any socialisation, training or support' (p. 118). The question 'why' touches on various other issues including support, experience, vision, and change.

In addition to the support of individuals, leaders require supports at the institutional level (Katsinas, 1996; Rose & Bergman, 2016; Striffolino & Saunders, 1989). Assuming a position where there may be a change of institution, a relocation, and a new career focus is a significant life event. If, upon arrival, the person discovers gaps in what is available to do the job well, she is markedly disadvantaged.

In Mary's case, she was dealing with under-resourcing in relation to faculty, and the supports required to deliver two innovative and complex programs. Budgets did not permit new hires either in the School or the University. Susan, by contrast, was confronted with the perplexing task of starting to bring faculty and staff forward from a College identity to a university identity in a unit physically separated from the rest of the institution. Regrettably, the road map for doing so was being created as she forged ahead. Having a Dean with no academic leadership experience was another substantive obstacle. While one might argue that different support strategies may need to be in place for female leaders, Mary and Susan have wondered if the supports they needed were not put in place because they are women. Hypothesizing, given that the two Deans were male, it may be possible that, if Mary and Susan had been male persons, their Deans might have responded in more proactive and supportive ways; in fact, Susan was replaced by a male Associate Dean who remains in the role three years later.

While newness can mean freshness and alternate ways of thinking about and doing things, too much newness is problematic. Indeed, there is much in the leadership literature about persons who move through organizational structures to positions of greater responsibility until they are in positions for which they have received no formal training (Dickson & Tholl, 2014). Certainly, many new leaders can be successful without leadership development training, but preparation will enhance that success. Additionally, achieving success without institutional support is a daunting proposition. Reflecting specifically on female leader, Morley (2014) calls for 'more investment ... to be made in mentorship and leadership development programmes for women ... [while] gender needs to be included in existing leadership development programmes' (p. 124). When such guidance is not provided, such as in Susan's case, the risk of not being successful increases. The best scenario occurs when the female leader has a strong mentor (or group of mentors) who will inform her of institutional strengths and shortcomings and provide guidance as she experiences difficult and delicate situations. This way, the leader is less likely to experience career landmines and not only survive but thrive.

An obvious but often underestimated element of new leadership is the time it takes to enable change and roll out the new leader's vision. In Mary's situation, to go forward, some undoing of historical practices and attitudes was necessary. While the literature tells us that skills can be acquired in fairly straightforward ways and according to predetermined timelines, change of dispositions is another matter (Carter, 2008). Simply put, the building of healthy culture is an incremental process with few shortcuts. In Susan's setting, the expectation that a new person could incite will and energy to transform institutional identity from that of College to that of university in one year was simply unrealistic.

In both Mary's and Susan's situations, gender played an important role, albeit in different ways. Susan found herself in a School of Business, a professional School historically dominated by males. While her Dean may have thought that he was supporting Susan, it was from a male person's perspective: conscious and unconscious bias was prevalent in a number of ways including failure to understand and use Susan's expertise. Instead, her collaborative, problem-solving model of engagement ran counter to the Dean's views. His ideas about leadership and engagement were clearly different from Susan's and resulted in a 'lack of fit' (Jaffe, 2014, para. 8), the reason for Susan's leaving. In Mary's case, she, too, was mentored by a male person but in the context of working with a team of women. Perhaps this situation was a contributor to the dissonance Mary experienced. In all, Mary's day-to-day experiences were complicated by the gender composition of the group.

The gender factor is one that requires careful consideration. There are issues of men (and women) who cannot or will not accept women in positions of senior leadership. Perhaps this will change given the call for equity and inclusion across this country and beyond (Rochon, Davidoff, & Levinson, 2016). Still, historical patterns are difficult to amend, and change rarely happens as quickly as it should. Alternately, are women hard on women who assume leadership roles because they are jealous or because they are unable to take direction from a colleague of the same gender? Or, have women been affected by long-standing mores and values about leadership grounded in male thinking? Another perspective is that 'acknowledging that women experience working with other women as difficult or that they may preference male leadership becomes an uneasy confession' (Vongalis-Macrow, 2016, p. 96). Either way, the twenty-first-century movement that encourages women to mentor women is not as straightforward as it first might seem, just as the realities of present-day higher education remain distinctly complex. For higher education to remain relevant, 'new forms of leadership and new leaders (will be) called upon to navigate through these turbulent times' (Hannum, Muhly, Schockley-Zalaback, & White, 2015, p. 65). Block and Tietjen-Smith (2016) 'believe that the lack of purposeful mentoring by same-gender role models is contributing to this shortage' (p. 306) of women leaders. Mentors can take many roles, with 'influential mentors ...[acting as] sponsors first, then counselors, coaches, and teachers' (Block & Tietjen-Smith, 2016, p. 312).

Ely and Meyerson (2000) have discussed the importance of values and approaches that reflect awareness of gender including valuing feminine leadership skills, creating equal opportunities, and revising the work culture. They have also suggested that the first two have no or limited impact on women as leaders; the last item though is critical to ensuring the success of female leadership. According to Morley (2014), gender is not simply a demographical variable, it is in continual production via sociocultural and organizational practices. Additionally, women in Morley's (2014) study reported how they are not, or are rarely, identified, supported, and developed for leadership. Nor do they achieve the most senior leadership positions in prestigious, national coeducational universities.

So how do we proceed? According to Morley (2013),

> a goal should be to make the academy gender-free. Leadership roles appear to be so over-extended that they represent a type of virility test. We need to ask how leadership practices can become more sustainable, with concerns about health and well-being as well as competitive performance in the global arena. In other words, we need new rules for a very different game. (p. 126)

FINAL THOUGHTS

As this chapter has revealed, the experience of women in leadership in universities remains difficult. For historic, gender-based, and diverse institutional reasons, many women do not sit at leadership tables without the company of dissonance, incivility, and microaggressions. It is, as Morley (2013) suggests, time to change the game.

Strong and capable women need to continue to aspire to leadership since women bring perspectives that their male counterparts cannot. The qualities that can make a woman's experience of leadership prickly are often the same qualities that universities need in order to evolve as places distinguished by a sense of community and social accountability. Concurrently, women are as capable as men in being clear thinkers and strong decision makers, particularly when perspectives about gender do not cloud the leadership experience.

Within the academy, the thriving of women as leaders is predicated on resolving a number of issues, some of which are not gender specific and which will support both men and women who actively seek leadership roles.

First, we need to change the self-narrative. We need to shout out our accomplishments and focus on our skills; in the case of women, this strategy disrupts the narrative that we are just supports and family-focused individuals. How we tell our stories impacts our 'placement' in the academy; how we view our experiences and strengths increases our viability and shows our right to leadership.

Women in leadership need to focus on their skills of speaking up and eliciting, integrating, and learning from feedback while also supporting younger women who aspire to be the next generation of leaders.

Extending support and providing mentorship to others are important signs of leadership. And, when women experience negativity toward their female colleagues who have gone on to leadership, it is important to take time to reflect on the motivations and drivers behind such situations.

Finally, women in leadership need to focus on what constitutes leadership today and how this understanding informs their shorter- and longer-term goals. Sollman (2012) suggests the following:

> The definition of leadership is changing for everyone and the news is good for women. As our economy continues to globalize, as the world gets "flatter" and as technology continues to change how we work, leadership is evolving into a relational rather than a hierarchical activity. We're transitioning from command and control to facilitative and collaborative leadership that works across teams, time zones, cultures and disciplines. What we think of as "soft skills" are becoming critical to leadership – and early career women, generally speaking, are comfortable and adept leading with these kinds of skills and abilities. (para 4)

Extending Sollman's ideas, women's capacity for relational, facilitative, and collaborative leadership foreshadows an important place for women in the twenty-first-century university. The academy, however, will need to work deliberately and strategically to oust vestiges of DIM thinking and practice. Although doing so will take time, through dispositional change and strategic effort, the university will be a stronger, more equitable, and more inclusive place for its female leaders.

References

Bian, L., Leslie, S.-J., & Cimpian, A. (2017a). Why young girls don't think they are smart enough. *The New York Times*. Retrieved January 26, from https://www.nytimes.com/2017/01/26/well/family/why-young-girls-dont-think-they-are-smart-enough.html?_r=1.

Bian, L., Leslie, S.-J., & Cimpian, A. (2017b). Gender stereotypes about intellectual ability emerge early and influence children's interests. *Science, 355*(6323), 389–391. https://doi.org/10.1126/science.aah6524.

Bilen-Green, C., Froelich, K. A., & Jacobson, S. W. (2008). *The Prevalence of Women in Academic Leadership Positions, and Potential Impact on Prevalence of Women in the Professorial Ranks*. 2008 WEPAN Conference Proceedings. Retrieved from https://www.ndsu.edu/fileadmin/forward/documents/WEPAN2.pdf.

Bruner, R. (2017). The three qualities that make a good dean. *The Chronicle of Higher Education*. Retrieved January 15, from http://www.chronicle.com/article/The-3-Qualities-that-Make-a/238883?cid=trend_right_h.

Block, B. A., & Tietjen-Smith, T. (2016). The case for women mentoring women. *Quest, 68*(3), 306–315. https://doi.org/10.1080/00336297.2016.1190285.

Cameron, E., & Green, M. (2012). *Making Sense of Change Management* (3rd ed.). Philadelphia: Kogan Page.

Caplan, P. J. (1992). *Lifting a Ton of Feathers: A Woman's Guide to Surviving in the Academic World*. Toronto: University of Toronto Press.

Carter, L. (2008). Perceptions of writing confidence, critical thinking, and writing competence among registered nurse-learners studying online. *Canadian Journal of University Continuing Education, 34*(2), 63–87.

Dickson, G., & Tholl, B. (2014). *Bringing Leadership to Life in Health: LEADS in a Caring Environment*. London: Springer.

Ely, R. J., & Meyerson, D. E. (2000). Theories of gender in organizations: A new approach to organizational analysis and change. *Research in Organizational Behavior, 22*, 103–151. Retrieved from http://dx.doi.org/10.1016/S0191-3085(00)22004-2.

Fisher, V., & Fisher, G. (2007). 'You need tits to get on around here': Gender and sexuality in the entrepreneurial university in the 21st century [Special issue]. *Ethnography, 8*(4), 503–517. Retrieved from http://www.jstor.org/stable/24048095.

Graban, M. (2012). *Lean Hospitals: Improving Quality, Patient Safety, and Employee Engagement* (2nd ed.). New York: CRC Press.

Hannum, K. M., Muhly, S. M., Shockley-Zalabak, P. S., & White, J. S. (2015). Women leaders within higher education in the United States: Supports, barriers, and experiences of being a senior leader. *Advancing Women in Leadership, 35*, 65–75. Retrieved from http://awljournal.org/Vol35_2015/Hannum_Women_Leaders_within_Higher_Education2.pdf.

Jaffe, E. (2014). The new subtle sexism toward women in the workplace. *Fast Company*. Retrieved from https://www.fastcompany.com/3031101/the-new-subtle-sexism-toward-women-in-the-workplace.

Jones, S. (2013). The 'star' academics are so often white and male. *The Guardian*. Retrieved from https://www.theguardian.com/education/2013/apr/22/university-jobs-not-being-advertised.

Katsinas, S. G. (1996). Preparing leaders for diverse institutional settings. *New Directions for Community Colleges*, 15–25. https://doi.org/10.1002/cc.36819969504.

Kotter, J. (2013). Management is (still) not leadership. *HHR Blog*. Retrieved from http://blogs.hbr.org/2013/01/management-is-still-not-leadership/.

Kruse, K. (2013). What is authentic leadership? *Forbes.* Retrieved from https://www.forbes.com/sites/kevinkruse/2013/05/12/what-is-authentic-leadership/#5ddf732bdef7.

Langland, E. (2012). Cultural narratives of academic leadership at the dawn of the 21st century. *Forum on Public Policy,* 1–9. Retrieved from http://forumonpublicpolicy.com/vol2012.no2/archive/langland.pdf.

Laschinger, H. K., Wong, C. A., Cummings, G. G., & Grau, A. L. (2014). Resonant leadership and workplace empowerment: The value of positive organizational cultures in reducing workplace incivility. *Nursing Economics,* *32*(1), 5–15.

Little, W., & McGivern, R. (2014). Chapter 5. In *Introduction to Sociology* (1st Canadian ed.). Rice University (CC international license 4.1). Retrieved from https://opentextbc.ca/introductiontosociology/chapter/chapter5-socialization/.

McKimm, J., & O'Sullivan, H. (2012). Developing and accessing medical leadership. *British Journal of Hospital Medicine, 73*(9), 484–485.

Morley, L. (2003). *Quality and Power in Higher Education.* The Society for Research into Higher Education. Maidenhead: Open University Press.

Morley, L. (2013). The rules of the game: Women and the leaderist turn in higher education. *Gender and Education, 25*(1), 116–131. https://doi.org/10.1080/09540253.2012.740888.

Morley, L. (2014). Lost leaders: Women in the global academy. *Higher Education Research & Development, 33*(1), 114–128. https://doi.org/10.1080/07294360.2013.864611.

Oakley, J. G. (2000). Gender-based barriers to senior management positions: Understanding the scarcity of female CEOs. *Journal of Business Ethics, 27,* 321–334. Retrieved from https://link.springer.com/content/pdf/10.1023%2FA%3A1006226129868.pdf.

Roche, M., Diers, D., Duffield, C., & Catling-Paull, C. (2010). Violence toward nurses, the work environment, and patient outcomes. *Journal of Nursing Scholarship, 42*(1), 13–22.

Rochon, P. A., Davidoff, F., & Levinson, W. (2016). Women in academic medicine leadership: Has anything changed in 25 years? *Academic Medicine, 91,* 1053–1056. https://doi.org/10.1097/ACM.0000000000001281.

Rose, K. J., & Bergman, M. (2016). Reaction to leadership misplacement: How can this affect institutions of higher education? *New Horizons in Adult Education and Human Resource Development, 28,* 26–29. https://doi.org/10.1002/nha3.20149.

Sherwin, B. (2014). Why women are more effective leaders then men. *Business Insider.* Retrieved from http://www.businessinsider.com/study-women-are-better-leaders-2014-1.

Sollman, K. (2012). How the definition of leadership is changing for women. *Forbes*. Retrieved from https://www.forbes.com/sites/85broads/2012/09/20/how-the-definition-of-leadership-is-changing-for-women/#64190c5a27a1.

Striffolino, P., & Saunders, S. A. (1989). Emerging leaders: Students in need of development. *NASPA Journal, 27*(1), 51–58.

Vessey, J. A., DeMarco, R. F., Gaffney, D. A., & Budin, W. C. (2009). Bullying of staff registered nurses in the workplace: A preliminary study for developing personal and organizational strategies for the transformation of hostile to healthy workplace environments. *Journal of Professional Nursing, 25*(5), 299–306.

Vongalis-Macrow, A. (2016). It's about the leadership: The importance of women leaders doing leadership for women. *NASPA Journal About Women in Higher Education, 9*(1), 90–103. https://doi.org/10.1080/19407882.2015.1114953.

Zenger, J., & Folkman, J. (2012). Are women better leaders than men? *Harvard Business Review*. Retrieved from https://hbr.org/2012/03/a-study-in-leadership-women-do.

CHAPTER 12

Breaking Out: The Institutionalized Practices of Youth Prison Guards and the Inmates Who Set Them Free

Natalie Davey

My research on the educational experiences of youth in detention has brought forward unanticipated findings around incivilities that were lived out between 2002–2007 amongst staff of what was a youth detention centre in Toronto, Ontario. The qualitative narrative findings come from a place-based educational study of the youth prison that asked "What is 'educational' in education?" A re-reading of the interviews with former staff and residents of the facility brings forward unanticipated threads that tie into the study of workplace incivilities and lateral violence. Specifically, there is a sewing together of the detention facility's hierarchical layers and practices as further narrative analysis of the interviewee transcripts reveals various examples of lateral aggressions and incivilities between the institution's staff. The interview transcripts from guards and staff who participated in the project repeatedly reference the word *institutionalized* to describe common staff-to-staff interactions. And yet, with hope, that narrative analysis also points to the role of education as a way to de(colonize) such an institution as those same guards and staff shared

N. Davey (✉)
Toronto District School Board, Toronto, Canada

© The Author(s) 2018
C. L. Cho et al. (eds.), *Exploring the Toxicity of Lateral Violence and Microaggressions*, https://doi.org/10.1007/978-3-319-74760-6_12

memories of youth inmates who acted for them as models of conflict resolution. Such stories point to an unanticipated hierarchical flip that occurred as inmates became teachers of positive *micro-messaging* (Young, 2007). Extended from the detention centre's narrative data is the consideration that hierarchical disruptions are key to making space for conflict resolution in such a place of enclosure.

The chapter is prefaced with an introduction to the original research project and the participant-interviewees. I then contextualize the narrative analysis by parsing vocabulary from literature pulled from the fields of microaggressions, lateral violence and incivility. The rest of the chapter uses narrative material mined from the interview transcripts, divided into three sections. I consider *hierarchical layers and practices, the role of silence in micro/lateral aggressions and incivility* and *de(colonizing) institutions* as each of these themes played out in the participants' stories of the now-closed York Detention Centre (YDC). Based on my close reading of their stories I conclude with some future projections for how the former prison's narrative data can be extended. Specifically, I suggest that further analysis of hierarchical disruption is key to making space for educational conflict resolution in such a place of enclosure.

THE WHO AND HOW: PARTICIPANT-INTERVIEWEES AND TRANSCRIPT ANALYSIS

To contextualize the original research project, I began my teaching career as a literacy teacher for one of the largest schools boards in Canada. I was placed in an alternative classroom that was located in what was Ontario's central booking facility for youth awaiting trial. The former youth prison—YDC—was closed in 2009 but the building remains standing in downtown Toronto, and the experience of teaching there has continued to shape my life as an educator to this day. Over the two years that I taught at YDC I met various students and staff who maintained positive relationships with each other and the detention centre even after its closure. My doctoral research brought me back to some of those relationships in 2013 when I decided to return to YDC to investigate why this long-closed facility has continued to impact my educational journey. I wondered if memories of time spent in the centre had a similar educational impact on others who had passed time within its walls. The study adopted narrative analysis as its methodological approach, an approach that looks to various forms of storytelling and narration as forms of authentic knowledge dissemination.[1] My ethics-approved study was comprised of document analysis, pulling forward remnants of old YDC student assignments that were salvaged before the closure. A secondary component of the research emerged from participant interviews where I spoke with two former residents and two different staff members. Those interviews were designed to help diversify the educational stories I hoped would be shared of YDC. This approach situated and helped to validate my connection to YDC as a former teacher, and thus informed both the interview questions and the conversations that followed.

The process for mining and coding the interview transcripts was influenced by McCormack's (2000) strategy of adopting "lenses" for the work of narrative analysis. To view the interview transcript through multiple lenses means:

> Immersing oneself in the transcript through a process of *active listening*; identifying the narrative *processes* used by the storyteller; paying attention to the *language* of the text; acknowledging the *context* in which the text was produced; and identifying *moments* in the text where the unexpected [occurs]. (p. 285)

Because the data involves already marginalized voices of incarcerated youth, joined in story with those whose job was to enact certain systems of power over them, J. Arendt (2011) writes about the importance of adding "layers of significance in the narrative process" (p. 265). Thus, in this project interpretive layers were added with every new lens I adopted throughout my analysis. I give this contextual snapshot to set the scene for what were highly charged, memory-based interviews with four individuals who had passed time together at YDC: Mila, Dee, Alex and Naomi.[2]

Mila was a former YDC Child and Youth Worker (CYW) who spent four years on the detention centre's staff roster. As a full-time employee Mila was the primary caseworker for youth assigned to her care whilst they were incarcerated. One such former youth was Dee. The two have remained in contact as unofficial mentor and mentee in the years since the centre's closure. Because of her various arrests, Dee was a regular at YDC, and as she grew older was incarcerated in the youth superjail that replaced YDC in 2009. In our conversation, Dee informed me that she had also spent a two-month stint in an adult prison facility. Alex, the other former youth participant, was not in and out like Dee, but spent two straight years inside YDC due to the severity of his charges. Alex and Dee crossed paths during his two-year stay but neither have been in contact with the other in the years since their release. Finally, Naomi was hired first as a CYW when YDC was still operated by Ontario's Ministry of Child and Youth Services. She stayed on with the centre, through privatization, to become a part of the detention centre's management as School Coordinator. Naomi was with YDC for 11 years in total. My own personal reflections on my own role as a former teacher at YDC weave their way through the mining of these interviews.

In their interviews Naomi, Mila, Alex and Dee each told stories from their past experiences at YDC, sharing *missed* moments of "educational becoming" that I worked to tease out in my original research (Davey, 2016, Dissertation, p. 6). Each interviewee described very personal feelings attached to the former detention centre and how those memories informed their interactions with, and movements in, the place that was YDC. The crux of my original research was that meaning-making (Till, 2005) in and of such a space was relationally based, symptomatic of the set-up that was YDC's environment as a whole. With my research, I desired to shine a light on what was missed in the closure of that facility. The interviews showed in story after remembered story that almost in spite of itself, the institutional and environmental makeup of YDC facilitated educational moments that positively fostered who those on the inside were to become over time. A commonly shared experience was that inmates, guards and teacher all lived out incarcerated experiences of doing time in some fashion. The notion of *doing time* became more nuanced and educationally imbued, for it was noted by all five of us that in our various roles each was impacted by having entered the space at an age of great influence. Our connected narrative showed that the time spent inside the prison walls affected not only our developing sense of selves but also the world around us.

And yet, even with this hopeful light shone on the memory of what could have been a very dark place, a narrative analysis of the original transcripts that is read with an alternative lens (McCormack, 2000) points to an issue that is not new to the original research project, but has remained in the shadowed periphery of the study until now. This chapter obligates a closer look at the dysfunctional realities that were lived out in the YDC staff-to-staff incivilities. I believe that they must be attended to for the former prison to truly be deemed as having ongoing educational potential.

MICROAGGRESSIONS, LATERAL VIOLENCE AND INCIVILITY

To help me analyze the participant narratives, looking specifically at staff conflict, the lexicon from which I am drawing coheres various studies done on microaggressions, lateral violence and incivility.

Brennan (2014) describes microaggressions as "subtle verbal and non-verbal insults directed toward [people of colour], often done automatically and unconsciously. They are layered insults based on one's race, gender, class, sexuality, language, immigration status, phenotype, accent, or surname" (p. 1). Microaggression is a term coined by psychiatrist Chester Pierce in the 1970s to describe acts of racism so subtle that neither the perpetrator nor the victim is even fully conscious of what is happening. Though there is work being done (Brennan, 2014) to dissect and categorize vocabulary for literature in the larger field, the language used in the study of microaggressions, lateral violence and incivility exists with some interchangeable fluidity. The literature around lateral violence has grown predominantly from studies in hospitals that have examined nurse-to-nurse aggression. According to Roberts (2015) the most commonly cited theoretical explanation for lateral violence "is based on the oppressed group behaviour theory of Freire (1971), who theorized that members of powerless, oppressed groups develop distain for members of their own group" (Roberts, 2015, p. 37). Freire's theory suggests that the oppressed group's belief in their own inferiority is a result of "feeling devalued in a culture where the power resides in another more dominant group" (p. 37). In the traditionally gendered environment of the healthcare industry where the power of nurses is subject to the more dominant power of doctors, studies note that the ten most common forms of lateral violence in nursing are: non-verbal innuendo, verbal affront, undermining activities, withholding information, sabotage, infighting, scapegoating, backstabbing, failure to respect privacy and broken confidences (Griffin, 2004). Such descriptors connect with what has also been determined to be incivility in the workplace (Andersson & Pearson, 1999), that which is defined as "low intensity deviant behaviour with ambiguous intent to harm the target, in violation of workplace norms for mutual respect" (p. 457). Authors of criminology literature have defined incivilities as "low-level breaches of community standards that signal an erosion of conventionally accepted norms and values" (LaGrange, Ferraro, & Supancic, 1992, pp. 311–312 as cited in Andersson & Pearson, 1999). Each of these definitions are differently nuanced but are still commonly linked by a focus on relational power dynamics that are lived out in the workplace.

Versions of these descriptions for microaggression, lateral violence and incivility all connect to what Mila and Naomi describe in their interviews regarding their past working conditions in the prison setting. The incivility spiral—the movement from incivility to acts of aggression or intent to harm—is similar if one were to read Roberts (2015) interrogation of the hospital environment and my analysis of the youth detention setting side by side. Both spaces are constructed around built-in requirements of caregiving and hierarchy so that their impact may not be noticed or effectively addressed. Of such spaces, Andersson and Pearson (1999) writes that,

> Our social interactionist perspective emphasizes the interpersonal and situational factors involved in the exchange of incivilities and coercive actions...the situation can sometimes cause instigators to perceive their own incivilities as legitimate or moralistic, potentially perpetuating the exchange of negative behaviours. (p. 453)

Essentially, both nurses and CYWs work in environments where they are charged with the care of powerless and often traumatized clients, and have to do that challenging work under the cloud of systemic and workplace hierarchies that render them powerless as well. For example, there is limited power for a CYW in the face of a legal system that presents, at a policy level, to work for the benefit of the children it houses, but proves itself otherwise as young people become caught in its wake (Alvi, 2012). As overworked caregivers feel both powerless and devalued negative behaviours such as incivilities between colleagues are brought to the fore. As energies are focused on the client's ladder of needs, incivilities occur within the ranks, not from above or below.

Thus, even as the nuanced differences between these various delineations are worth noting, in light of the prison setting being analyzed in this chapter, the term *incivility* will be used to describe the harms lived out between staff in the detention centre, contrasted at the end of the piece with Young's (2007) positive counterpoint of *micro-messaging* observed in resident-to-staff interactions.[3]

SETTING THE BAR: HIERARCHICAL LAYERS AND PRACTICES WITHIN YDC

The not so subtle play on words that makes up this section's subtitle gestures to the hierarchical set-up lived out in the prison setting—bars define such a space, keeping inmates contained and keeping staff in control. The physical environment dominates in such a setting as every action and movement is determined according to constraints. Students were physically searched with a metal detector when moving between the unit where they slept and the rest of the detention centre, including the school. One of my interview questions asked the participants to describe their feelings around this daily search experience:

> *Davey:* What about the routine of literally going to class—like the wanding routine? I remember that we actually stood quite close together in those moments...
>
> *Alex:* There was some bonding experience there because we'd have to be in a tight line going up and down the stairs...one of the reasons I wasn't a big fan of it was that when I hurt my leg it hurt going up and down the stairs...but you did get to learn a little bit about people as we joked around...though some of the staff took it very seriously...[4]

Alex's memory of his injured leg signifies much about the space that was YDC. The injury dominates his response to a question that asked specifically about the experience of having been wanded, a physical statement and daily reminder to the residents of their incarceration. I am struck by Alex's focus on his injury because as he makes mention of bonding with his fellow residents "going up and down the stairs" he punctuated his awareness of "staff who took [such routines] very seriously" with references to shared jokes in tight spaces. Because the stairwells had to be climbed many times a day, to and fro the unit to school and mealtimes in the cafeteria, his reframing of the stairwell as a space that in fact facilitated the forming of relationships, points to complicated hierarchical constructs lived out between guards and inmates in the former detention centre.

Dee's response to the same question started with a description of the superjail facility that she was sent to upon her arrest at the age of 16. She described life in both facilities as very different, specifically speaking to the hierarchical set-up between staff and the residents. Dee said of the superjail: "It was just different [from YDC]. Just different...They tried to treat it like adult jail." When I asked her to tell me in more detail about how they were different she said:

> At YDC you guys were in your own clothes but at [the superjail] they were wearing like the actual correctional outfits – ya – so they would actually treat us like prisoners – they would act like they were real cops and at YDC you guys were like teachers or Youth Workers. Uniform meant their chest was too high so they would talk to you like this or like that – and at YDC they actually talk to you...like a person.

Dee's awareness of each site's hierarchical dynamic informs her response differently than Alex, even though both refer to a relational atmosphere that defined for them the space that was YDC. Alex was in one very enclosed place for two years whereas Dee had the experience of moving around, thus exposing her to two very different realities. Both facilities were detention centres, thus prison-based hierarchical patterns of behaviour underscored relational encounters in both settings. Of note is how different the resident responses to YDC's environment are from the memories shared with me by former staff, Mila and Naomi. The residents tell stories that mitigate hierarchical layers and practices within the space through relationships—the staff tell a very different story.

Mila, for example, gestures to institutional rules and regulations that she felt opposed to when thinking back on her time at YDC. She balked at the instructions given to her by her superiors regarding what was considered appropriate staff-to-student conversation. She says,

> I felt the way we were supposed to talk to them wasn't realistic. It was a lot about "You know that thing you did was dumb right?"

I pushed further with questions of educational impact and place-based relationships to which she responded:

> I never thought of myself as impacting them...I guess they thought I wasn't supposed to be that real with them and they were surprised [that I was]. So then they would talk to me about problems with their girlfriends. What they should do. No, that wasn't teaching them life lessons for like careers...but that was the "in the moment" person I was. I think I went into YDC thinking I'd be working with a bunch of criminals...thinking "what am I going to do with them?" But when I was leaving I felt I'd miss the kids more than the staff. I engaged with them. They taught me as much as I taught them.

Thus, for Mila, relationships with the residents were more important than those developed with her colleagues. I wanted to investigate why this was so, and as I spent time with Naomi the picture started to come into focus. Naomi's response to YDC's hierarchical practices was affected by her managerial role within the prison. As the school coordinator, she was tasked with the responsibility of directing fellow staff, encouraging them to participate in the school setting as much as on the unit. She was not their boss but the dynamic was impacted by a power differential. She said of her superiors:

> I've been blessed on my journey to have bosses who have trusted me to do what I do. I just wanted it to be a learning environment. Not just for the students but for the staff too! ...The staff would fight about who would have to come to school.

I went on to ask about her opinions of fellow staff in the school setting and her response took on a philosophical tone.

Davey: What was that about? I had one interviewee, a staff, who said she felt more freedom to do one-to-one "teaching" upstairs on the unit whereas in school they felt disengaged from the classroom space.

Naomi: But that's up to the individual. If you're going to be engaged and interactive...I mean anyone can sit back and hold a chair. It's on you to assist the teacher, be part of the learning...

Davey: Do you think some of their negative experiences at YDC came from their own schooling experiences?

Naomi: Ya...I mean maybe that whole environment was...

Davey: Loaded.

Naomi: Could be...and similar to a lot of the youth who'd attend. A lot of the time the youth are forced to go but when they're in their community school they're not...to be put in the classroom, in that school environment, similar to the staff needing to be engaged and involved, it was the same with the youth.

Naomi's analysis of her co-workers was not collegial; Naomi's managerial position informed her tone as she remembered the detention centre's I/They dichotomy. Her tone is important to my overall narrative reading of YDC's staff story since it sets the scene, especially when read side by side with Mila's account of her impactful relationships with residents. Narrative analysis demands of the researcher that the words of the interviewee be considered, but a nuanced attentiveness to tone is equally important in discerning and making meaning of the story being shared and shaped by the teller (McCormack, 2000). Both Naomi and Mila highlight relationships that were impactful and very much defined by power differentials.

"We Were Institutionalized!"—The Role of Silence in Micro/Lateral Aggressions and Incivility

The staff-to-staff power differential was remembered most explicitly by Mila in her interview. She said,

> My experiences waking up at YDC were not always good…it was me having come from going out [partying]. The kids were very respectful of my having been out and thought I was hung over…and because I struggled trying to fit in or…um…[was] trying to figure it out…I used them seeing me as human as a way to be human with them. I never told them what we did or where we went but it gave me an opportunity to sit and talk to them. I used every chance I could get to talk with them. I didn't do a lot of night shifts…but leaving and coming out of the buildings started to change for me when dynamics with the staff changed…because we all became institutionalized. When in Walmart I'd hear them call for assistance it would actually give me a jolt because it was like hearing "assistance needed in south unit."

Mila's use of the term *institutionalized* jolts me as much as hearing the Walmart "call for assistance" did for her. My original research question looked at the impact of physical space on one's relationships to it and within it. Mila's personal reflection on such a loaded term speaks to how trapped she felt, and how contained the inmates truly were for her to make such a comparison. I am reminded of Legault's (2012) essay on *King Lear* when he refers to all of the wounded characters as mental health patients who are obligated to take care of each other; the sick taking care of the sick. When analyzing YDC from Mila's perspective, one turns the pages on a comparable story. As a CYW she would spend hours with the inmates in the school setting of YDC and even more time with them on the unit. That time spent together in close quarters created space for blurred boundaries, specifically regarding who was the caregiver and who might be receiving care in that place. She remembers,

> There was one guy, P_____, who said he'd take care of me outside. So when there were problems male staff would send me down the hall to calm him down…I remember being really uncomfortable with it…using strategies that were instinctive – or just me being me. He could see what the male staff were doing. I could see what they were doing.

Mila names being uncomfortable with her fellow staff members' response to the resident, and all the more their reliance on her to keep the peace for them but not with them. She recognized that her being female was something her colleagues used as a tool to calm this resident down for he had shown himself to struggle with male authority within the YDC facility. Her summary of that time:

> It was in the mess moments – that I figured out after, in the midst of a lot of other mess – right? We were all institutionalized. There was a lot of ugliness.

Naomi had a very different relationship with YDC by virtue of her having been in the position of school supervisor, a position that was not quite management and not quite staff. She remembers having enjoyed a sense of independence and personal mission that was less instinctive than Mila's dedication to the residents, more definitively built around her role and title:

> *Naomi*: Being the school coordinator it was school that I woke up for. Having the brief [meeting] every morning with the teachers—and then upstairs again with the staff—gave me a sense of mission...What [conflict] was from upstairs would come down and our [school] team had to deal with that. It all fell on us. Ready to work, ready to teach.
>
> *Davey*: So did you feel more team with one side or the other?
>
> *Naomi*: I was already pegged as management because of my supervisorial role in that school space, so I always felt divided. I might have seen behaviours in the day that I would record differently on the page than the staff who would be like "No, no, no, why are they getting a 5?"[5]...but I might have put down that they had a great day [in school]...so it was about that measure of success based on relationship, where we might see small successes even if someone else doesn't [based on the space in which it happened?]. Measures of success could be so static because across an eight-hour staff day how do you sum it up? But my job was to be in charge of that small chunk of time. And I would ask [the kids]—how do you think your day went?

This section of Naomi's interview is rich because evidence of conflict is not necessarily overt but, read through a different lens, incivilities lived out in that setting start to come into focus. On a first reading, I saw Naomi's attention placed heavily on her relationship with students, valuing interactions with the residents much like Mila. But upon a second and third reading, where I focused on tone and diction, I read Naomi's power struggle with staff as having impacted her day-to-day duties with those residents in the workplace. What presents most clearly when reading Naomi and Mila's interviews side by side, is that differences in opinion regarding inmate behaviour served to divide the people who were hired as a team to supposedly guard and guide them towards rehabilitated behaviours.

DE(COLONIZING) INSTITUTIONS—DETAINED YOUTH IN(ACTION) THROUGH POSITIVE MICRO-MESSAGING

There is a striking contrast between the marred staff relationships that Mila and Naomi remembered during their interviews with me, and the positive stories of resident/staff relationships shared by all four of the participant-interviewees. That contrast has necessitated a term to help me describe what I believe to be an unusual or unanticipated hierarchical shift in power. What Young (2007) calls *micro-messaging* Brennan (2014) calls *micro-affirmations*. She says,

> [M]icro-affirmations [are] a way of reaching out to those who suffer from micro-inequities [in the workplace]. Micro-affirmations may take the shape of deliberately reaching out to a student, colleague or co-worker who is isolated. One might make a special point of recognizing this person's contribution in the workplace. The idea is the positive micro-messaging can redress and rebalance the harms caused by micro-inequities. (p. 16)

What emerged in my re-reading of their shared stories has been a surprisingly consistent narrative thread; the ways in which the residents practiced positive micro-messaging or micro-affirmations with staff like Mila and Naomi worked to positively affect the space for all of the individuals who spent significant time within the former detention centre. Said another way, a re-storying of YDC shows student-residents, even from their incarcerated position of weakness, to have been active powerbrokers in establishing an inherently educational ethos for their caregivers.

For example, Alex shared with me an insight made of the former detention centre, reframing it as a space of learning:

> Like in the resident area you could learn some things from the staff...or other residents...ummm...by just like hanging out and like playing different kinds of little board games or just even talking...you would learn something either about them or...umm...I don't kind'ov know how to put it...you'd learn about them. It was like you were always learning something new about ummmm... people.

I said in response "That makes a lot of sense to me. Because education for me is about learning, not just about what we kind of construct as school." Alex then hit on the heart of what is educational in education when he replied, "Ya. Not just about what's in a book." And putting words into action, Alex went on to share with me a story that occurred after his release from YDC:

> *Alex*: One thing I was pretty glad about was that while I was at YDC I accumulated money doing chores and stuff like that...and... When I was found not guilty all of that extra money I had saved up I was like just get them something like pizza or something like that...something nice for people who were like...there...
>
> *Davey*: Why'd you do that?
>
> *Alex*: Just thought do something nice for all of the kids and staff...so it would get used up...like it was almost $60. I mean I said it...I don't know that they did it...but I hope they did.

Ritske (2012) writes "There are many views of decolonization, often contrasting and competing, but one thing is common: the belief that through action, change can occur." Alex's decision to share his earnings with his place-mates gestures to the change that can occur. The colonial power dynamics that imbue the construction and running of both prisons and educational systems are part of the present-day discourse (Alvi, 2012; Bhatti, 2010; Gooch, 2013). Yet Alex and Dee, who remains in a mentoring relationship with Mila to this day, proffer narratives in which action, and therefore change, are in fact occurring at both the personal and systemic levels inside prison walls.

The positive micro-messaging delivered by residents to staff provided momentary respite for people like Mila who expressed feeling great unhappiness with her colleagues near the end of her tenure at YDC.

She described feeling constantly judged before even entering the building for a shift saying, "They stared at me as I walked across the street from them, arms crossed and staring." Such silent acts of incivility had the potential to wound—and obviously did—but I am struck by the mitigating effects of residents' positive micro-messaging to the staff. Through positive micro-messaging, Alex and Dee had the power to redress and rebalance the harms caused by staff-to-staff.

So it is with hope that I suggest there be further study on such topics so as to add into the limited discourse and literature available around education and youth in detention. My own narrative analysis points to the role of education as a way to de(colonize) school and prison-based institutions as youth inmates are reframed to be mentors and educators who acted for staff as caregivers and models of conflict resolution. These stories point to the benefits of positive micro-messaging in spaces of containment, a potentially powerful tool to disrupt incivilities experienced by those who work on the inside. Thus, extended from the detention centre's narrative data is the consideration that hierarchical disruptions are key to making space for conflict resolution in such places of enclosure.

NOTES

1. See Denzin (1994) and Polkinghorne (2007) for more detailed descriptions of Narrative Analysis.
2. The names of the participant-interviewees have been changed to protect their privacy.
3. An example of one researcher who is working to interrogate the vocabulary in this wide field is Brennan (2014) who "worries about the language of 'micro-aggression' [as different from micro-inequity for] wrong-doing and culpability … seem built into the idea of aggression and aggressive behaviour and that is not the case for micro-inequities. Indeed, the question of wrong-doing and micro-inequities is part of what is at issue here" (p. 3). Her dissection of these terms points to the necessity for specificity and clarity as more literature in these intersecting fields is disseminated.
4. The quotations for this chapter have been mined from the original research interviews, completed in July, 2014.
5. Inmates were given a daily rating of one to five based on their interactions with fellow residents and staff. Those ratings were used to reward inmates with extra privileges or to have certain privileges removed as punishment.

REFERENCES

Alvi, S. (2012). *Youth Criminal Justice Policy in Canada: A Critical Introduction*. New York: Springer.

Andersson, L. M., & Pearson, C. M. (1999, July). Tit for tat: The spiraling effect of incivility in the workplace. *The Academy of Management Review, 24*(3), 452–471.

Arendt, J. (2011). [In]Subordination: Inmate photography and narrative elicitation in a youth incarceration facility. *Cultural Studies Critical Methodologies, 11*(3), 265–273. https://doi.org/10.1177/1532708611409543.

Bhatti, G. (2010). Learning behind bars: Education in prisons. *Teaching and Teacher Education, 26*(1), 31–36. https://doi.org/10.1016/j.tate.2009.06.020.

Brennan, S. (2014). The moral status of micro-inequities: In favour of institutional solutions. Retrieved from https://works.bepress.com/samanthabrennan/.

Davey, N. (2016). A [Re]membered place: Missed opportunities of the "educational" for incarcerated youth and the ongoing effects of York Detention Centre's closure (Doctoral dissertation). Retrieved fromhttps://yorkspace.library.yorku.ca/xmlui/bitstream/handle/10315/32748/Davey_Natalie_J_2016_PhD.pdf?sequence=2.

Denzin, N. K. (1994). The art and politics of interpretation. In N. K. Denzin & Y. S. Lincoln (Eds.), *Handbook of Qualitative Research* (pp. 500–515). Thousand Oaks, CA: Sage.

Freire, P. (1971). *Pedagogy of the Oppressed*. New York: Seabury Press.

Gooch, K. E. (2013). *Boys to Men: Growing Up and Doing Time in an English Young Offender Institution*. Retrieved from http://etheses.bham.ac.uk/4170/1/Gooch13PhD.pdf.

Griffin, M. (2004). Teaching cognitive rehearsal as a shield for lateral violence: An intervention for newly licensed nurses. *Journal of Continuing Education in Nursing, 35*, 257–263.

McCormack, C. (2000). From interview transcript to interpretive story. *Field Methods, 12*(4), 282–297. Retrieved from http://www.utsc.utoronto.ca/~kmacd/IDSC10/Readings/interviews/analysis.pdf.

Polkinghorne, D. E. (2007). Validity issues in narrative research. *Qualitative Inquiry, 13*(4), 471–486. https://doi.org/10.1177/1077800406297670.

Ritske, E. (2012). What is decolonization and why does it matter? *Intercontinental Cry*. Retrieved from https://intercontinentalcry.org/what-is-decolonization-and-why-does-it-matter.

Roberts, S. J. (2015). Violence in nursing: A review of the past three decades. *Nursing Science Quarterly, 28*(1), 36–41. https://doi.org/10.1177/0894318414558614.

Till, K. E. (2005). *The New Berlin: Memory, Politics, Place*. Minneapolis.

Young, S. (2007). *Micro Messaging: Why Great Leadership is Beyond Words*. Columbus, OH: McGraw-Hill.

PART III

Towards Systemic Change

CHAPTER 13

Locating Racial Microaggressions Within Critical Race Theory and an Inclusive Critical Discourse Analysis

Anver Saloojee and Zubeida Saloojee

This chapter builds upon work by Saloojee and Stewart (2016) as we argue that the concept of racial microaggression in the contemporary era has great utility for an analysis of race, racism and the everyday experiences of people of colour in our society and on our campuses. In particular, an understanding of racial microaggression allows for greater awareness of the often subtle, barely discernible and barely detectable manifestations of racism that can emerge on campuses in classrooms and in everyday conversations and interactions between people of colour and White people. Microaggressions as modes of interaction between members of historically marginalized communities and members of the dominant society reveal how the ideology of racism is secreted in these interactions and reveal the ways in which power and privilege are taken

A. Saloojee (✉)
Department of Politics and Public Administration,
Ryerson University, Toronto, ON, Canada

Z. Saloojee
Child and Youth Program, School of Social and Community Services,
George Brown College, Toronto, ON, Canada

© The Author(s) 2018   249
C. L. Cho et al. (eds.), *Exploring the Toxicity of Lateral Violence
and Microaggressions*, https://doi.org/10.1007/978-3-319-74760-6_13

for granted in everyday actions and interactions. And within the university environment, this can take many forms including interactions between students, faculty and students, faculty and faculty, and the classroom and university climate and environment.

Much of the literature on racial microaggression is from the USA, and it situates racial microaggression in the context of Critical Race Theory (CRT). This understanding speaks directly to the importance of naming racial microaggressions as covert racism and not allowing it to elide into the vapours of nothingness.

There is little substantial Canadian research and literature on microaggressions, the uniquely Canadian contribution to the study of microaggression is to extend the analysis of racial microaggression from a critical race perspective to locating it with a broader inclusive critical discourse analysis (CDA) or what others have called a Critical Race Feminism and Anti-Colonialism perspective.

RACISM, MICROAGGRESSION AND RACIAL MICROAGGRESSION: THEORIZING MICROAGGRESSION IN AN INCLUSIVE DISCOURSE ANALYSIS

In 1969, Dr. Chester Pierce, an African American psychiatrist, medical doctor and scholar, introduced the notion of "offensive mechanisms" when he said, "To be black in the United States today means to be socially minimized. For each day blacks are victims of white 'offensive mechanisms' which are designed to reduce, dilute, atomize, and encase the hapless into his 'place.' The incessant lesson the black must hear is that he is insignificant and irrelevant" (p. 303). In 1970 in a chapter "Offensive Mechanisms," Pierce extends this concept and first introduces the term microaggression to explain what he called the "subtle and stunning" forms of offensive actions,

> Most offensive actions are not gross and crippling. They are subtle and stunning. The enormity of the complications they cause can be appreciated only when one considers that these subtle blows are delivered incessantly. Even though any single negotiation of offense can in justice be considered of itself to be relatively innocuous, the cumulative effect to the victim and to the victimizer is of an unimaginable magnitude. Hence, the therapist is obliged to pose the idea that offensive mechanisms are usually a microaggression. (pp. 265–266)

A decade later, he distinguished between microaggressions and racial microaggressions when he wrote of the everyday racism encountered by

Black people in the USA and used the term "racial microaggression" to refer to: "The subtle, stunning, repetitive event that many whites initiate and control in their dealings with blacks can be termed a racial microaggression. Any single microaggression from an offender to a defender (or victimizer to victim) in itself is minor and inconsequential. However, the relentless omnipresence of these noxious stimuli is the fabric of black–white relations in America" (1980, p. 251). In 1995, Pierce speaks to microaggressions and its impacts on the victims of racism and sexism,

> the most grievous of offensive mechanisms spewed at victims of racism and sexism are microaggressions. These are subtle, innocuous, preconscious, or unconscious degradations, and putdowns, often kinetic but capable of being verbal and/or kinetic. In and of itself a microaggression may seem harmless, but the cumulative burden of a lifetime of microaggression can theoretically contribute to diminished mortality, augmented morbidity, and flattened confidence. (Pierce, 1995, p. 281)

Pierce's rich and incredibly textured research and theorizing on microaggression and on racial microaggression forms the basis for the emergence of CRT and in turn is firmly situated by scholars on the terrain of CRT (Pérez Huber & Solórzano, 2014). His pioneering work also forms the basis for the work by Sue and others in the early twenty-first century.

Racial microaggression needs to be understood in the context of a critical analysis of racism and racial discrimination but it needs to simultaneously transcend the limits of CRT. The United Nations has provided a well thought out, all-encompassing definition of racial discrimination:

> 1. In this Convention, the term "racial discrimination" shall mean any distinction, exclusion, restriction or preference based on race, colour, descent, or national or ethnic origin which has the purpose or effect of nullifying or impairing the recognition, enjoyment or exercise, on an equal footing, of human rights and fundamental freedoms in the political, economic, social, cultural or any other field of public life. (United Nations, *International Convention on the Elimination of all Forms of Racial Discrimination* 1965, Article 1)

Racial discrimination as a form of social exclusion that has race as a social construct, at the heart of exclusion is unequal access to rights, it is unequal assess to the valued goods and services in society, it is about unequal access to the labour market, and it extends to all fields of public life. It is about incomplete citizenship, undervalued rights, undervalued recognition and undervalued participation. The study of structured racial inequality, discrimination, rights and privileges recognizes that Indigenous people and people of colour who enter the labour market, enter the educational system and seek goods and services (among other things) will face a structure of opportunities that are mediated by their race, gender, disability, etc.

Racism manifests itself in a number of forms—as individual, institutional, structural and systemic forms of racial discrimination. The analysis of systemic racial discrimination allows us to focus not on the intentionality but on the effect of racism in general and racial microaggression in particular. For Saloojee (2003), the study of racial inequality and racial discrimination is a study of racialization—how human differences are structured, imbued with meaning, continually reproduced and used to deny people access to the valued goods and services in society.

> Structured racial exclusion is the process by which individuals from the dominant white racialized group in society are better positioned (than are individuals from subordinate racialized and marginalized minority groups) to secure a greater share of society's valued goods, services, rewards and privileges and to use these benefits to reinforce their control over rights, opportunities and privileges in society. Through this process, racial inequality and unequal access to the valued goods and services in society are structured and continually reproduced. (p. 4)

Racial inequality and discrimination are historically derived, have persisted over the centuries and are constantly reproduced in old and new ways; hence, the argument that in the contemporary era, racial microaggressions are the latest manifestations of racism. The persistence of racial inequality and racial discrimination and the patterns of inequality and discrimination generally have proved to be highly resistant to change because of the powerful socio-economic, political and ideological forces which maintain and reproduce the patterns. The analysis of racial microaggression has to be located within an inclusive CDA—an analysis that begins with CRT as the essential analytical framework. Locating racial microaggression in the context of CRT is an explicit recognition of the centrality of covert forms of racism in the everyday experiences of people of colour, and it allows for an understanding that racial microaggressions are intimately linked to institutional, structural and systemic racial discriminations and oppression.

In the 1990s, the anti-oppression perspective was initially seen as challenging the dominant discourses in social theory. While throwing the limitations of the dominant discourse into sharp relief, the anti-oppression framework was unable to deal with the specificity of racism. It was unable to deal specifically with anti-Indigenous, anti-Black racism and Islamophobia.

An anti-racism discourse uses race as the lens through which to understand multiple interlocking systems of oppression (Dei, 1996). For anti-racism scholars and practitioners, intersectionality is vitally important. Within an anti-racism discourse, "race" is the lens through which we understand power differentials and how multiple sources of oppression and discrimination including inequality, poverty, gender, ability and heterosexism interact. Racism is about power and privilege, and it about how one group believes itself to be superior to others and exercises power and privilege over others based solely on phenotypic characteristics. Mari Matsuda (1991) has defined CRT as: "... the work of progressive legal scholars of color who are attempting to develop a jurisprudence that accounts for the role of racism in American law and that works toward the elimination of racism as part of a larger goal of eliminating all forms of subordination" (p. 1331). Along with others, Matsuda (Matsuda, Lawrence, Delgado, & Crenshaw, 1993) identifies the following five themes which define interdisciplinary CRT:

1. A recognition that racism is pervasive in American society;
2. A scepticism towards dominant discourse that focuses on neutrality, meritocracy and colour-blindness;
3. Understanding the relationship between racism and the advantages and privileges that accrue to White people in a racially stratified society;
4. Validating the experiential knowledge of people of colour; and
5. Social change—ending racial domination and oppression as part of the goal of eliminating all forms of discrimination, oppression and injustice.

The discourse of anti-racism posited by CRT scholars, however, has been critiqued by Lawrence and Dua (2005) on a number of important grounds (i) ignoring the complicity of people of colour in the historic project of settler colonialism and the oppression of the Indigenous peoples of Canada; (ii) not understanding that people of colour have power and privileges and access that Indigenous people simply do not have; and (iii) misunderstanding the roots of modernity—as not beginning with slavery but beginning with colonialism and settler colonialism and the genocide against the Indigenous people of the world. In addition, the anti-racism discourse has been critiqued for its reductionism—focusing on race as the entry point to analysing systems and structures of oppression. In so doing, a progressive discourse contributes to the creation of a hierarchy of oppressions (Williams, 1999). As Williams (1999) notes: "Single standpoint politics have the potential to create hierarchies of oppressions in which groups eschew their points of commonality for open competition and thus become unproductive to the achievement of equality" (p. 214).

There is therefore a need for an inclusive critical discourse framework that allows the scholar, the teacher and the practitioner to understand the complexity of interconnected oppressions faced by people of colour, women and LGBTQ2S, while at the same time allowing them to focus on the specific and dominant form of oppression. According to Lê, Le and Short (2009), CDA "aims at unearthing the intricate relationship between power, dominance and social inequality in different social groups" (Lê et al., 2009, p. 9). Critical discourse is concerned with how discourse produces inequality and is transformative (Lê et al., 2009). It is important to distinguish an inclusive CDA from an anti-oppression framework because the latter subsumes what needs to be highlighted— for example, anti-Indigenous racism or Islamophobia. We argue an inclusive CDA is based on a CRT foundation; however, we distinguish an inclusive CDA from a CRT framework because the latter does not specifically address Islamophobia, anti-Semitism, discrimination and oppression of Indigenous people and the oppression and discrimination faced by members of the LGBTQ2S community.

In a similar vein, Pon, Gosine and Phillips have called for a Critical Race Feminism and Anti-Colonialism arguing "Due to its increasingly mainstream status, we propose jettisoning anti-oppression perspectives in favour of critical race feminism and anti-colonialism. We assert that these emergent perspectives more effectively theorize white supremacy, anti-Black and anti-Native racism, and how the nation's exalted subject is inseparable from the welfare state" (Pon et al., 2011, p. 402).

Whether one calls it "inclusive critical discourse analysis" or "Critical Race Feminism and Anti-Colonialism," what is important is to focus on the central tenets of an inclusive CDA which includes notions of human agency and power-sharing, reflexivity, understanding the individual and the family in a sociopolitical, historical and cultural context and understanding the relationship between a dominant identity and form of oppression and multiple and interlocking identities and oppressions. Racial microaggressions can best be understood in the context of an inclusive CDA because it allows for a nuanced understanding of the many different forms of microaggressions that are manifest and that are directed at people of colour, at LGBTQ colleagues, at Muslims, etc.

WHITENESS, RACISM AND RACIAL MICROAGGRESSION

An inclusive CDA (firmly rooted in an anti-racist, feminist, anti-colonial framework) is one that allows for an analysis of the specificity of anti-Black racism, anti-Indigenous racism, anti-Asian racism, sexism, Islamophobia, homophobia and ableism while at the same time understanding interlocking systems and structures of oppression. It allows for an analysis of the subtle distinctions in the forms that anti-Muslim, anti-Black, anti-Asian, anti-Latino, anti-LGBTQ2S, anti-women and other forms of microaggressions take.

Building on the seminal research of Pierce (1970, 1980, 1995), Solórzano, Ceja, and Yosso (2000) undertook research on racial microaggression on post-secondary campuses by utilizing CRT. Pierce's work undoubtedly opened new vistas of research and there emerged a huge body of influential work on microaggression as an expression of racism. Sue et al. (2007), in their work on racial microaggression and the Asian American experience, define microaggression as "brief and commonplace daily verbal, behavioral, and environmental indignities, whether intentional or unintentional, that communicate hostile, derogatory or negative racial slights and insults to the target person or group" (p. 273). They provide a very useful taxonomy of microaggression when they break it down into microaggressions as verbal, behavioural and environmental and note the various forms they take as microassault, microinsult and microinvalidation.

Microassaults, closely linked to blatant overt racism, are "explicit racial derogation(s) characterized primarily by a verbal or nonverbal attack meant to hurt the intended victim through name-calling, avoidant behavior, or purposeful discriminatory actions" (Sue, Capodilupo, et al., 2007, p. 274). Microassaults are often intentional. *Microinsults* are deliberate negative, humiliating put-downs that "convey rudeness and insensitivity and demean a person's racial heritage or identity" (Sue, Capodilupo, et al., 2007, p. 274).

And *microinvalidations* "exclude, negate, or nullify the psychological thoughts, feelings, or experiential reality of a person of color" (Sue, Capodilupo, et al., 2007, p. 274). Since Sue, Capodilupo, Torino, Bucceri, Holder, Nadal and Esquilin posited this taxonomy, there has been a surge in the literature and research on racial microaggression as well as on the forms and manifestations of racial microaggression on campuses in the USA (see Wong, Derthick, David, Saw, & Okazaki, 2014). This taxonomy is a very useful starting point, but as researchers have pointed out not all racial micro-aggression identified by participants in their respective studies fall neatly into the taxonomy (see, e.g., Cho, 2010; Houshmand, Spanierman, & Tafarodi, 2014; Poolokasingham, Spanierman, Kleiman, & Houshmand, 2014; Rollock, 2012; Wong et al., 2014).

Minikel-Lacocque (2013) reflecting on the vast CRT literature specifically in higher education notes that "… taken as a whole, CRT research in higher education has highlighted the microaggressions and racial harassment that faculty of colour often face as well as hostile racial climates and racial profiling that students of color encounter" (p. 437). Minikel-Lacocque points to an important function of CRT to challenge "the experiences of White European Americans as the normative standard" (p. 437). Pérez Huber and Solórzano (2014) speak of the importance of CRT is highlighting how structural and systemic racism get played out in the forms of everyday racial microaggression. CRT stresses the vital importance of understanding racism through the experiences of people of colour. It is this latter notion that Pérez Huber and Solórzano speak of when they say,

> Racial microaggressions are a form of systemic, everyday racism used to keep those at the racial margins in their place. They are: (1) verbal and non-verbal assaults directed toward People of Color, often carried out in subtle, automatic or unconscious forms; (2) layered assaults, based on race and its intersections with gender, class, sexuality, language, immigration status, phenotype, accent, or surname; and (3) cumulative assaults that take a psychological, physiological, and academic toll on People of Color. Microaggressions allow us to 'see' those tangible ways racism emerges in everyday interactions. At the same time, they have a purpose. For instance, whether conscious or not, microaggressions perpetuate a larger system of racism. Microaggressions are the layered, cumulative and often subtle and unconscious forms of racism that target People of Color. They are the everyday reflections of larger racist structures and ideological beliefs that impact People of Color's lives. (p. 302)

For them, racial microaggressions are inextricability linked to and bound with institutional, structural and systemic racism.

Pierce's work (1970, 1980 and 1995), that of Solórzano et al. (2000) and the pioneering work by Sue and his colleagues (including 2007; 2008), has opened new avenues for research on the different manifestations and impacts of microaggression in higher education on students, faculty and staff. In particular, research has focused on microaggression and gender, microaggression and the experiences of Asian Americans, microaggression and Latino students, faculty and staff and microaggression and LGBTQ2S students.

There is a growing body of research on racial microaggressions research particularly in the USA, where the concentration of empirical research has been on African Americans (Constantine, 2007; Pérez Huber & Solórzano, 2014; Solórzano et al., 2000; Sue et al., 2008; Yosso, Smith, Ceja, & Solórzano, 2009), Asian Americans (Lin, 2010; Sue, Bucceri, et al., 2007), Latina/o Americans (Rivera, Forquer, & Rangel, 2010) and the Indigenous population (Clark, Spanierman, Reed, Soble, & Cabana, 2011). Very little research has been done in Canada on racial microaggression (see Cho, 2010, 2014; Clark, Kleiman, Spanierman, Isaac, & Poolokasingham, 2014; Hernandez, Carranza, & Almeida, 2010; Houshmand & Spanierman, 2014).

For Solórzano et al. (2000), CRT for education is different from other CRT frameworks because (i) it foregrounds race as the lens through which to understand the experiences of people of colour; (ii) it takes an intersectional approach and seeks to unearth how discourses on race intersect with those on gender, disability and class; and (iii) it looks at how education, the curriculum, the textbooks, the classroom dynamics, etc., all impact students of colour to create a hostile campus environment. They extend Pierce's work to focus on the campus climate and explore this through four interrelated questions: (1) How do African American college students experience racial microaggressions? (2) What impact do these microaggressions have on African American students? (3) How do African American students respond to racial microaggressions? (4) How do racial microaggressions affect the collegiate racial climate?

African American students spoke to Solórzano et al. (2000), of their marginalization inside and outside the classroom and on campuses—they pointed to their invisibility and singular visibility; being singled out to represent all African Americans; being ignored; having to deal with distorted stereotypes of African Americans; faculty expectations of them;

creeping self-doubt; segregation in group work; nonverbal microaggression where White faculty, students and staff impute assumptions about Black students and assumptions about their academic qualifications and how they got into university; and their individual success is not generalized to all African American students but their deficiencies are generalized (Solórzano et al., 2000). Solórzano, Ceja, and Yosso, speak of the detrimental impacts these microaggressions have on African American students—including feelings of doubt; lowering of self-esteem; frustration, isolation the pressure to negotiate these microaggressions on a daily basis while still being striving to maintain high academic standards. "The sense of discouragement, frustration, and exhaustion resulting from racial microaggressions left some African American students in our study despondent and made them feel that they could not perform well academically" (p. 69). The participants were unanimous in saying education is not a level playing field for African American students and that racism was prevalent and was detrimental to their academic success.

Sue, Bucceri, et al. (2007) undertook research on microaggression and the Asian American experience, and their participants identified the numerous ways in which microaggressions manifested in society and on campuses—including participants feeling like foreigners in their own land; assumptions about "intelligence"; assumptions about academic preferences; pathologizing cultural values and colour-blindness; denial of their racial identity; "exoticization" of the Asian woman; invalidation of interethnic differences; unequal (second class) citizenship; and communication styles, invisibility and being overlooked. With respect to the impact of these microaggressions, they concluded,

> [o]ur study provides strong support that microaggressions are not minimally harmful and possess detrimental consequences for the recipients. Most participants described strong lasting negative reactions to the constant racial microaggressions they experienced from well intentioned friends, neighbours, teachers, co-workers and colleagues. They described feelings of belittlement, anger, rage, frustration, alienation, and of constantly being invalidated. (p. 77)

Faculty, staff and students of colour all experience microaggressions differently, and this is equally true for persons with disabilities, women, LGBTQ2S and Indigenous faculty, students and staff. While there are some similarities in the forms of microaggressions and in the impacts of microaggressions, it is important to understand the nuances and complexities which is why the Canadian contribution can be to address microaggression in the context of the multiple overlapping and intersecting forms of oppression, discrimination and power differentials. The literature of microaggression identifies a number of effects on microaggression—including feelings of isolation and alienation (Sue, Capodilupo, & Holder, 2008; Solórzano et al., 2000); a hostile campus climate (Solórzano et al., 2000); health and stress of the recipients of microaggression; self-worth and self-esteem; stereotyping (which is different for different groups of ethno-racial minorities); academic expectations (again different for different groups); power differentials; unequal citizenship; the daily struggle to continually deal with microaggressions; and second guessing whether a microaggression actually occurred. Wong et al. (2014) address the relationship between microaggression and health and well-being,

> When minorities perceive discrimination they also exhibit poorer health and mental health outcomes. Reviews of existing research ... suggests that perceived stigmatization pertaining to gender, race, and sexual orientation is associated with depression, and anxiety symptoms, decreased psychological well being, lower self regard and physical health issues. (p. 193)

Their research on the impact of the insidious and subtle forms of microaggression which are becoming more common found similar results; however, they only found one study that "explicitly explored the long-term effects of experiencing racial microaggressions" (p. 193). More research and certainly more research in Canada on the ways in which different racialized minority groups experience racial microaggression is needed. And in the Canadian context, this needs to be extended to immigrant communities as well.

Sue et al. (2008) argue that "[a]lthough any group can potentially be guilty of delivering racial microaggressions, the most painful and harmful ones are likely to occur between those who hold power and those who are most disempowered" (p. 183). For Sue and his colleagues (2007, 2008), racial microaggressions reflect the conscious and unconscious world view of exclusion, White superiority and White privilege that is advertently and inadvertently imposed on ethno-racial minorities.

There is need for a nuanced concept and understanding of microaggressions, and racist and sexist microaggressions need to be understood in the context of the multiple forms of structural and systemic discrimination and in the context of power relations in the workplace and in society (see, e.g., Sue & Constantine, 2007).

Critical race theorists and feminist scholars have used the concept of microaggressions to address the sociocultural and verbal cues directed at them that make them feel unwelcome in institutions and in the dominant society. These cues are subtle insults which are often done automatically and unconsciously and unintentionally. Similarly, Solórzano et al. (2000) described racial microaggressions as "subtle insults (verbal, nonverbal, and/or visual) directed toward racial minorities, often automatically or unconsciously" (p. 60). Mahmud (2005) considers them, "affronts to human dignity and self-respect; they are behaviors that impact not only the social existence of the victims but also potentially leave scars on their psyche" (pp. 58–59).

Central to an understanding of microaggression within an inclusive CDA are the concepts of Whiteness and White privilege. McIntosh (1990) sees Whiteness as being about the invisibility of power and privilege. Whiteness normalizes everyday racism by allowing those with power and privilege to go about their everyday lives without being conscious of their social location, their unearned privileges and what society confers on them by virtue of the colour of their skin. It also allows them to take these for granted and it makes them defensive when confronted by what the historic and contemporary legacy of racism has bequeathed them. For Gillborn (2008), "white privilege" is only one component of a larger complex of power and domination that is integral to Whiteness. Whiteness as "a way of being in the world that is used to maintain White Supremacy" (Gillborn, 2008, p. 198). Picower (2009) reflects on the tools her White students use to maintain their positions of power and dominance "...[the] tools of Whiteness facilitate in the job of maintaining and supporting hegemonic stories and dominant ideologies of race, which in turn, uphold structures of White Supremacy. In an attempt to preserve their hegemonic understandings, participants used these tools to deny, evade, subvert, or avoid the issues raised" (2009, p. 205).

Rollock (2012) notes that much of the power of Whiteness "...lies in the fact that it is often disguised and *mis*recognised, to borrow from Bourdieu ... as the morally acceptable, as normal, as natural" (p. 518). Microaggression as a manifestation of Whiteness is racial microaggression which intentionally or unintentionally expresses the power and dominance of Whites over people of colour. It finds expression in the most subtle and barely discernible ways, and in what is said, how it is said, in gestures and tones and what is conveyed are notions of superiority and inferiority, forms of exclusions and modes of othering.

As noted above, the very subtlety of racial and gender microaggression leaves the victim wondering what actually occurred. And on the other side, there is the issue of intentionality. Here, a number of questions related to deeply embedded White privilege need to be posed and these can guide future research on racial microaggressions and on the perspective of the perpetrator:

1. Did the perpetrator of the racial microaggression intend to be racist?
2. Did it occur to them they were racist?
3. Did they simply take it for granted (their unearned privilege) that they can say what they please regardless of the impact on the other?
4. Whose responsibility is it to call them on their racism?
5. What would their reaction be to being called out—especially if they see themselves as allies?

White privilege puts the victims of racial microaggressions in situations with multiple difficult points—did the microaggression actually occur? Should they name it and engage in a difficult discussion? And if they did raise it, the perpetrator could well deny it or say the victim is making a mountain out of a molehill. And last if nothing is said, the victim is left simultaneously enraged and debilitated, while the perpetrator remains blissful in their privilege. Conversely, White privilege puts perpetrators in advantageous situations where they can engage in the microaggressions and feign ignorance or go on the offensive by suggesting the victim is overly sensitive. Interestingly, a 2017 study by Kanter et al., of 33 Black and 118 non-Hispanic White undergraduate students, done at a large public university in the Southern/Midwest US students found that overt acts of racism were on the wane; however, racial microaggression was on the increase especially among those who believed minorities were too sensitive about race issues.

The White students who were more likely to be microaggressive were also more likely to support colour-blind, symbolic and modern racist attitudes. They were less favourably disposed towards Black people. This was particularly the case for White students who thought that minorities are too sensitive to issues related to racial prejudice. The overwhelming majority of Black students experienced being called "too sensitive".

For Kanter et al. (2017), "[t]hese findings provide empirical support that microaggressive acts are rooted in racist beliefs and feelings of deliverers, and may not be dismissed as simply subjective perceptions of the target" (p. 4). Acts of racial microaggressions go beyond the realm of perception because "The delivery of microaggressions by white students is not simply innocuous behavior and may be indicative of broad, complex, and negative racial attitudes and explicit underlying hostility and negative feelings toward black students" (Kanter et al., 2017, p. 1).

The persistence and prevalence of both racial microaggression and the willingness to blame the victims and label them as too sensitive are key indicators of the power of White privilege to continually reproduce itself in new ways over generations. Both speak voluminously to power and privilege in the educational system and in society at large. And the effect on the victims is to denigrate them, deny them their lived experience, alienate, reinforce their subordinate status and attempt to silence them. This is the exercise of White power and privilege.

Rollock (2012) calls these the "rules of racial engagement," where White privilege gets played out in multiple forms of denial—denial of intentionality, denial of what was said or how it was said, and denial of being racist. Rollock suggests that too often, racial microaggressions are missed not only because of their subtlety but because one assumes "good people" and allies cannot be racist (p. 18). Ladson-Billing speaks of the reproduction of racism in new and ever-changing ways "… our conception of race, even in a postmodern world and/or postcolonial world, are more embedded and fixed than in a previous age. However this embeddedness or 'fixed-ness' has required new language and construction of race so that denotations are submerged and hidden in ways that are offensive though without identification" (cited by Rollock, 2012, p. 519). It is up to students of colour, faculty and staff of colour and people of colour generally to manage these subtle persistent and pernicious expressions of racial microaggressions as they go about their daily lives.

It is up to the researcher to uncover these subtle forms of microaggressions that are gendered, racist, homophobic, Islamophobic and anti-Indigenous. Researchers have the responsibility of connecting the intricate dots between and among Whiteness, White privilege, denial, microaggressions in all its subtle and not so subtle forms and their effects on historically marginalized populations. On the one hand, we have critical race theorists and feminist scholars who explore and bring to the fore the concept and the expressions of microaggressions. On the other hand, there has emerged a counter-narrative that sees any attempt to speak, for example, of racial microaggressions as "political correctness" and question why their speech has to be curtailed or at least moderated to account for the sensitivities of others. What could actually be a productive dialogue is shutdown and positions become polarized. What is clear is that microaggressions are perceived very differently by the perpetrator and the victim (and more broadly if one identifies with the perpetrator or the victim). And this becomes highly problematic particularly in a workplace when the microaggression relates to race or gender. Microaggressions have a cumulative effect. This is what Pierce was referring to when he talked of the "subtle, stunning, repetitive event that many whites initiate and control in their dealings with blacks" (1980, p. 251).

New Avenues for Research in Canada

In Canada, there is not a great deal of literature on microaggression and its effects on victims. A 2016 study by Bailey on the experiences of Indigenous students at one Canadian University found they faced a number of institutional, structural and personal barriers, including interpersonal discrimination, frustration with the university system and feelings of isolation. Indigenous students spoke of the lack of interaction with non-Indigenous students, a lack of awareness of the Indigenous history, culture, identity and a general lack of awareness of the specific issues faced by Indigenous students. As Bailey notes, the findings are consistent with those by Clark et al. (2014),

> In Clark et al.'s (2014) study, salient themes included unconstrained voyeurism, jealous accusations, cultural elimination/misrepresentation, expectations of primitiveness and isolation. Participants in the current study provided support for these themes while also emphasizing the following: interaction levels; perceptions of the university environment and the forms of racism therein; audience effects; in-class and social experiences; the university 'system'; and the persistence of racism. (p. 1266)

Poolokasingham et al. in their (2014) study identified eight racial microaggression themes targeting South Asian Canadian undergraduate students: perceived as fresh off the boat (FOB); excluded from social life; a notion that being Brown is a liability; assumption of ties to terrorism; compulsion to be a cultural expert; ascription of intelligence in stereotypical domains; invalidation of interethnic and racial differences; and treated as invisible. Some of the findings were consistent with the literature on Asian Americans (experienced ascription of intelligence, invisibility and invalidation of interethnic differences). Five forms of microaggressions, however, "were novel to the literature on racial microaggressions in North America" (p. 200).

One study by Houshmand et al. (2014) looked at the experiences of East Asian international students on one university campus in Canada. They identified six racial microaggression themes which the students experienced: (a) excluded and avoided; (b) ridiculed for accent; (c) rendered invisible; (d) disregarded international values and needs; (e) ascription of intelligence; and (f) environmental microaggressions (structural barriers on campus). These themes are consistent with the taxonomy developed by Sue et al. However, they noted that the themes being avoided and excluded actually were experienced by international students as microinsults, microassaults and microinvalidations. The Houshmand et al. (2014) study also added to the research on microaggressions by (i) signalling the importance of "ridiculed for accent" and (ii) linking to ascription of intelligence (the notion that a student's intelligence is ascribed by ethno-racial and cultural stereotypes). Research participants spoke of an interesting duality—on the one hand, they were ridiculed for their accent (and even excluded from social groups on campus); on the other hand, in class their accent was perceived as having increased intelligence in maths and science—closer to the myth of the "Model Minority student". In addition, like other researchers noted above, they found forms of microaggression that did not fit neatly into the taxonomy—for example, ascriptions of intelligence based on accents.

Cho (2010), in her article on the experiences of self-identified immigrant teacher candidates (ITCs), debunks the myth of meritocracy and points to other important structural factors which inhibit success in entering the teaching profession. She addresses "the cultural capital that is and is not valued by schools and the ways in which the linguistic capital of ITCs is contested in schools" (p. 4). Her research points to the ways in which racial microaggressions have detrimental impacts on the employment opportunities of aspiring teachers from immigrant backgrounds.

Cho contends that the "… narratives of immigrant teacher candidates are being silenced. Their stories trouble the myth of meritocracy in education and challenge privileged ways of knowing" (p. 10). Without using the Sue, Bucceri, et al. (2007) taxonomy, an important point of research for Cho is how the teacher candidates attempt to negotiate their way through these microassaults, the microinsults and the microinvalidations. She found that they take numerous forms including the myth of meritocracy, perceptions of capabilities, ascriptions of intelligence based on the accents and because of linguicism, being othered because of accent, skin colour, modes of dress and being benchmarked against " ...the prototypical image of the Canadian teacher" (p. 10). Cho's research, while consistent with the Sue et al. taxonomy, extends it by identifying forms of racial microaggression not identified in the taxonomy. In giving voice to the narratives of the ITCs, Cho not only identified the structural and systemic barriers they faced but also identified their resilience and their agency to deal proactively with their barriers. Far from being passive victims of racial microaggressions, the narratives "illuminate the ways in which ITCs have successfully navigated the system and infused their cultural capital in their teaching and learning" (Cho, 2010, p. 18).

The research on racial microaggression in the USA has opened new avenues for research in Canada—including research on how microaggressions are experienced by different historically marginalized groups in Canada. There is scope for Canadian research to both build on the CRT framework and enhance the taxonomy of racial microaggressions developed by Sue et al. With respect to the latter, some of the areas of research could focus on:

1. How members of Indigenous nations experience microaggressions in society and on university and college campuses?
2. How South Asian, East Indian, Black Canadians, Muslim Canadians, Haitian Canadians and other Canadians of minority backgrounds experience microaggressions?
3. How linguistic and religious minorities experience microaggressions— in particular, how are microaggressions in the forms of Islamophobia and anti-Semitism expressed and how, for example, do Muslim and Jewish students, faculty and staff experience microaggressions on college and university?
4. How trans and LGBTQ2S members of our society experience microaggressions?
5. How Indigenous students, students of colour and students from other historically marginalized communities on our campuses experience microaggressions?

6. How Indigenous faculty, faculty of colour and faculty from other historically marginalized communities on our campuses experience microaggressions?
7. How Indigenous staff, staff of colour and staff from other historically marginalized communities on our campuses experience microaggressions?
8. How international students from racialized minority backgrounds experience microaggressions?

CONCLUSION

What the vast and increasing literature from the USA points to is that the nuanced and subtle racism as racial microaggression is deeply embedded in the everyday and is more embedded than is realized in public discourses. Too often the racist and sexist dimensions of the microaggression are not visible to those who are not affected but have detrimental impacts on the victims. In order to address microaggressions, Saloojee and Stewart (2016) found post-secondary institutions are increasingly relying on civility codes and respectful working environment policies. Existing anti-harassment and anti-discrimination codes also incorporate notions of civility and employ a regulatory framework designed to deal with formal complaints of harassment. This approach utilizes a single instrument to deal with a variety of behaviour from rudeness to discrimination and "… more importantly it poses real problems as it elides threatening comments that could be hate speech with more or less subtle expressions of derision or intimidation" (Saloojee & Stewart, 2016, n.p.).

If we argue that racist and sexist microaggressions are to be understood in the context of the multiple forms of systemic and structural discrimination, then it is important to separate anti-discrimination policies and procedures from civility policies. In post-secondary workplaces, marginalized groups who are the usual targets of microaggressions are vastly underrepresented on the academic staff, despite long-standing employment equity policies. Effectively addressing the context that gives rise to microaggressions requires systemic change.

Racial microaggressions are real and are part of the lived experiences of people of colour in society. And on our campuses, it is the often daily lived experiences of students, staff and faculty, of colour. In this chapter, it has been suggested that the uniquely Canadian contribution to the theoretical and conceptual underpinning of racial microaggressions can be located within CRT and can go beyond to locating the various forms of microaggressions with an inclusive CDA—this needs greater theorizing. There is much to be learnt from the global research on racial and other forms of microaggressions. It is time for Canadian researchers and academics to make their contributions—the public good, the common good depends on critical engagement with this under-researched area.

REFERENCES

Cho, C. L. (2010). "Qualifying" as teacher: Immigrant teacher candidates' counter-stories [Special Issue Educational Policy and Internationally Educated Teachers (IETs)]. *Canadian Journal of Educational Administration and Policy, 100*. Available on-line http://www.umanitoba.ca/publications/cjeap/.

Cho, C. L. (2014). "Why don't you Canadians stop lying to us immigrants?": Immigrant teacher candidates' experiences with pre-service education and Canada's multicultural act. *The International Journal of Diverse Identities, 13*(1), 14–25.

Clark, D. A., Kleiman, S., Spanierman, L. B., Isaac, P., & Poolokasingham, G. (2014). "Do you live in a Teepee?" Aboriginal students' experiences with racial microaggressions in Canada. *Journal of Diversity in Higher Education, 7*(2), 112–125.

Clark, D. A., Spanierman, L. B., Reed, T. D., Soble, J. R., & Cabana, S. (2011). Documenting Weblog expressions of racial microaggressions that target American Indians. *Journal of Diversity in Higher Education, 4*, 39–50.

Constantine, M. G. (2007). Racial microaggressions against African American clients in cross-racial counseling relationships. *Journal of Counseling Psychology, 54*, 1–16.

Dei, G. S. (1996). *Anti-racism Education: Theory and Practice*. Halifax, NS: Fernwood.

Gillborn, D. (2008). *Racism and Education: Coincidence or Conspiracy?* London: Routledge.

Hernandez, P., Carranza, M., & Almeida, R. (2010). Mental health professionals' adaptive responses to racial microaggressions: An exploratory study. *Professional Psychology: Research and Practice, 41*, 202–209.

Houshmand, S. L., & Spanierman, L. B., & Tafarodi, R. W. (2014). Excluded and avoided: Racial microaggressions targeting Asian international students in Canada. *Cultural Diversity and Ethnic Minority Psychology, 20*(3), 377–388.

Kanter, J. W., Williams, M. T., Kuczynski, A. M., Manbeck, K. E., Debreaux, M., & Rosen, D. C. (2017). A preliminary report on the relationship between microaggressions against black people and racism among white college students. *Race and Social Problems, 9*(4), 291–299. https://doi.org/10.1007/s12552-017-9214-0.

Lawrence, B., & Dua, E. (2005). Decolonizing anti-racism. *Social Justice: A Journal of Crime, Conflict and World Order, 32*(4), 120–143.

Lê, T., Le, Q., & Short, M. (2009). *Critical Discourse Analysis: An Interdisciplinary Perspective*. New York: Nova Science Publishers.

Lin, A. I. (2010). Racial microaggressions directed at Asian Americans: Modern forms of prejudice and discrimination. In D. W. Sue (Ed.), *Microaggressions and Marginality: Manifestation, Dynamics, and Impact* (pp. 85–103). Hoboken, NJ: Wiley.

Mahmud, T. (2005). Citizen and citizenship within and beyond the nation. *Cleveland State Law Review, 52*(1/4), 51–61.

Matsuda, M. (1991). Voices of America: Accent, antidiscrimination law, and a jurisprudence for the last reconstruction. *Yale Law Journal, 100,* 1329–1407.

Matsuda, M., Lawrence, C., Delgado, R., & Crenshaw, K. (Eds.). (1993). *Words that Wound: Critical Race Theory, Assaultive Speech, and the First Amendment*. Boulder, CO: Westview Press.

McIntosh, P. (1990). White privilege: Unpacking the invisible backpack. *Independent School, Winter,* 31–36. Retrieved September 26, 2017, from http://code.ucsd.edu/pcosman/Backpack.pdf.

Minikel-Lacocque, J. (2013). Racism, college and the power of words. *American Education Research Journal, 50*(3), 432–465. https://doi.org/10.3102/0002831212468048.

Pérez Huber, L., & Solorzano, D. G. (2014). Racial microaggressions as a tool for critical race research. *Race Ethnicity and Education, 18*(3), 297–320. https://doi.org/10.1080/13613324.2014.994173.

Picower, B. (2009). The unexamined Whiteness of teaching: How White teachers maintain and enact dominant racial ideologies. *Race Ethnicity & Education, 12*(2), 197–215.

Pierce, C. (1970). Offensive mechanisms. In F. Barbour (Ed.), *The Black Seventies* (pp. 265–282). Boston, MA: Porter Sargent.

Pierce, C. (1980). Social trace contaminants: Subtle indicators of racism in TV. In S. Withey & R. Abeles (Eds.), *Television and Social Behavior: Beyond Violence and Children* (pp. 249–257). Hillsdale, NJ: Lawrence Erlbaum.

Pierce, C. (1995). Stress analogs of racism and sexism: Terrorism, torture, and disaster. In C. Willie, P. Rieker, B. Kramer, & B. Brown (Eds.), *Mental Health, Racism and Sexism* (pp. 277–293). Pittsburgh: University of Pittsburg Press.

Pon, G., Gosine, K., & Phillips, D. (2011). Immediate response: Addressing anti-native and anti-black racism in child welfare. *International Journal of Child, Youth and Family Studies, 2*(3/4), 385–409.

Poolokasingham, G., Spanierman, L. B., Kleiman, S., & Houshmand, S. (2014). "Fresh off the boat?" racial microaggressions that target South Asian Canadian students. *Journal of Diversity in Higher Education, 7*(3), 194.

Rivera, D. P., Forquer, E. E., & Rangel, R. (2010). Microaggressions and the life experience of Latina/o Americans. In D. W. Sue (Ed.), *Microaggressions and Marginality: Manifestations, Dynamics, and Impact* (pp. 59–83). Hoboken, NJ: Wiley.

Rollock, N. (2012). Unspoken rules of engagement: Navigating racial microaggressions in the academic terrain. *International Journal of Qualitative Studies in Education, 25*(5), 517–532.

Saloojee, A. (2003). *Social Inclusion, Anti-racism and Democratic Citizenship.* Toronto: Laidlaw Foundation.

Saloojee, A., & Stewart, P. (2016, December). Commentary/Intense scrutiny over microaggressions. *CAUT Bulletin.* Retrieved September 17, 2017, from https://bulletin-archives.caut.ca/bulletin/articles/2016/12/commentary-intense-scrutiny-over-microaggressions.

Solórzano, D., Ceja, M., & Yosso, T. (2000). Critical race theory, racial microaggressions, and campus racial climate: The experiences of African American college students. *Journal of Negro Education, 69,* 60–73.

Sue, D. W., Bucceri, J., Lin, A. I., Nadal, K. L., & Torino, G. C. (2007). Racial microaggressions and the Asian American experience. *Cultural Diversity and Ethnic Minority Psychology, 13*(1), 72.

Sue, D. W., Capodilupo, C. M., Torino, G. C., Bucceri, J. M., Holder, A., Nadal, K. L., & Esquilin, M. (2007). Racial microaggressions in everyday life: Implications for clinical practice. *American Psychologist, 62,* 271–286.

Sue, D. W., Capodilupo, C. M., & Holder, A. (2008). Racial microaggressions in the life experience of Black Americans. *Professional Psychology: Research and Practice, 39*(3), 329.

Sue, D. W., & Constantine, M. G. (2007). Racial microaggressions as instigators of difficult dialogues on race: Implications for student affairs educators and students. *College Student Affairs Journal, 26*(2), 136.

United Nations. (1965). *International Convention on the Elimination of All Forms of Racial Discrimination.* New York: United Nations.

Williams, C. (1999). Connecting anti-racist and anti-oppressive theory and practice. Retrenchment or reappraisal? *British Journal of Social Work, 29*(2), 211–230.

Wong, G., Derthick, A. O., David, E. J. R., Saw, A., & Okazaki, S. (2014). The what, the why, and the how: A review of racial microaggressions research in psychology. *Race and Social Problems, 6*(2), 181–200.

Yosso, T., Smith, W., Ceja, M., & Solórzano, D. (2009). Critical race theory, racial microaggressions, and campus racial climate for Latina/o undergraduates. *Harvard Educational Review, 79*(4), 659–691.

CHAPTER 14

Building Resilience in Graduates: Addressing Horizontal Violence in the Profession of Nursing

Laurie Peachey and Karey D. McCullough

RESILIENCE AND MICROAGGRESSION

The complex nature of the Canadian healthcare environment requires effective communication, collaboration, critical thinking, and leadership to competently provide care to patients and their families, and the newly graduated nurse has acquired many of those essential skills to safely advocate for the patient, and to positively influence health outcomes (Pines et al., 2014). However, resilience, broadly explored by disciplines in the social sciences and humanities, is also gaining attention in nursing science. There is a growing need for nursing graduates to develop resilience as they transition to becoming nurses; unfortunately, they face the

L. Peachey (✉)
Collaborative Nursing Program, School of Nursing, Nipissing University, North Bay, ON, Canada

K. D. McCullough
Collaborative Nursing Program, Associate Graduate Faculty, Graduate Studies and Research, Nipissing University, North Bay, ON, Canada

© The Author(s) 2018   271
C. L. Cho et al. (eds.), *Exploring the Toxicity of Lateral Violence and Microaggressions*, https://doi.org/10.1007/978-3-319-74760-6_14

likelihood of microaggression within the nursing profession, causing workplace adversity in their nursing practice.

In this chapter, resilience is presented from a critical perspective as a way to empower nurses in their entry into professional practice. In the first section, the need to prepare nurses for resilience in their entry-to-practice is identified as an important safeguard against the traditional hierarchy of healthcare institutions. Workplace violence, enacted as microaggression within the clinical practicum setting, is a form of horizontal violence pervasive in the student clinical practicum experience. In the second section, practice education in nursing is outlined to highlight to gain an understanding of the practicum setting and the policies that exist in identifying and responding to workplace violence. While the aggressions originating from outside of the profession are also depicted, the image of the nurse in the media is described as an important part of building resilience against lateral violence. In the third section, nursing preceptorship is presented as an important educational strategy to build resilience, to strive toward readiness for practice, and to prepare the nursing graduate to enter the profession.

Resilience in Nursing

Resilience is an important element of nursing practice. As nursing students graduate from Canadian Schools of Nursing, resilience leads to the adjustment to a new workplace while assuming the role of the registered nurse (RN). This section provides a description of the microaggression and lateral violence in the nurse's workplace, and the horizontal violence that occurs in enacting the scope of practice in nursing.

THE RESILIENT PERSON

According to Garmezy (1993), the core element of resilience "lies in the power of recovery and in the ability to return once again to those patterns of adaptation and competence that characterized the individual prior to the pre-stress period" (p. 129). Tusaie and Dyer (2004) describe the resilient person as being able to integrate the characteristics in day-to-day encounters that lead to bouncing back from life's setbacks, stress, and adversity. A resilient person adjusts in moments of adversity to find their sense of balance, control, and ability to move forward

(Moran, 2012). In the context of health care, the resilient practitioner responds to the rapid pace of events to find balance in the current context, and to explore ways to move ahead. Resilience is developed over time with a multitude of experiences. Fine (1991) distinguishes a two-tiered process: During the acute phase, the person's attention is directed to diminishing the impact of the aggression, while the second phase consists of a reorganization of ideas to confront a new reality.

THE RESILIENT NURSE

Acquiring personal resilience has the potential to empower nurses toward job satisfaction, health, and well-being (McDonald, Jackson, Wilkes, & Vickers, 2012). The resilient health professional has personal attributes that balance their self-image, their social environment, and their learning (McAllister & McKinnon, 2009). Being a resilient nurse leads to building positive social relationships and the necessary supportive environment when confronting adversity in health care. According to McDonald et al. (2012), personal resilience "intersects with the tacit knowledge and practical skills requisite for a long, and rewarding career in nursing" (p. 378). Resiliency enables nurses to connect with their social context, their physical environment, their past and present lived experiences, their spirituality, their personal values, and their worldview (McAllister & McKinnon, 2009).

ADVERSITY AND THE TRADITIONAL HIERARCHY OF THE NURSE'S WORKPLACE

In terms of lateral violence within the profession, nurses are vulnerable to workplace adversity as a result of the challenging workplace conditions in health care that create an unsupported heavy workload and a lack of understanding of the nurse's role within the interprofessional team (McDonald et al., 2012). McAllister and McKinnon (2009) reveal the adversity faced by new graduates as they "experience the negative effects of hierarchy, top-down decision-making, inter- and intra-professional hostility, limited autonomy, public stereotyping and invalidation" (p. 372). Today's learner perceives hospitals, the traditional workplace of nurses, as institutions offering unattractive professional opportunities with expectations to work under stressful conditions and limited autonomy created by rigid management styles, financial instability, rapid turnover, and unpaid extra hours (McAllister & McKinnon, 2009). As educators in nursing, it is essential to accord importance to that perspective. Upon graduation of a baccalaureate degree in Canada, the nurse is required to demonstrate entry-to-practice competency through an initial licensure process combined with continued competence in a self-regulated profession. As the scope of practice of the nurse expands, a shift in responsibility is also occurring rapidly, creating added pressure on nursing students. Increasingly, nurses work in a variety of advanced nursing settings that necessitate postgraduate certification and graduate studies in university. The scope of practice of the nurse practitioner and the clinical nurse specialist provides examples of roles requiring additional preparation at the graduate level (Canadian Nurses Association [CNA], 2008). The advancement of scope of practice for the RN in response to the aging population and the increased complexity of care creates a need for mentoring of new nurses. However, the RN workforce is also aging, and while RN retirement results in employment opportunities for the new graduate nurse, nurses are seeing a gap in the expertise needed to mentor new nurses through the challenges of increasingly acute and complex care. The upcoming retirement of seasoned nurses from our aging workforce in health care creates opportunities for the new graduate nurse to select roles traditionally requiring seniority and postgraduate certification in specialized settings such as neonatology, pediatrics, perinatal nursing, emergency nursing, critical care nursing, and gerontology.

Despite the nature of the workload demands, the complexity of health challenges, and the obvious need for collaboration between healthcare professionals, professional relationships in health care remain hierarchical. Alarmingly, the profession is presented in this context to nursing students and new graduates. For instance, the nurse's decision-making remains largely dependent on traditional physician orders; this in turn influences the structure and direction of interprofessional collaboration, and the overall design of safe delivery of health care (Benner, Sutphen, Leonard, & Day, 2010). Incidentally, nurses currently entering the profession challenge those traditional practices to benefit patient care by expanding the scope of nursing and by stepping into advanced nursing practice roles. In Ontario, Canada, as a way to respond to the needs of an aging population through advancements in the scope of nursing practice, public policy changes are underway to move forward legislative changes for medical assistance in dying (MAID) and independent RN prescribing of medication. Expanding the scope of nursing requires building resilience in the new graduate nurse who is quickly immersed in advanced nursing role practices. Nursing curriculum needs to constantly reflect change in health care.

Professional Socialization of Student Nurses

In fast-paced and profound interactions, a nurse cares for people in a time of delicate need and potentially life-altering crises (McAllister & McKinnon, 2009). A caring nursing practice involves self-giving where the student nurse must sincerely want to care for people and their loved ones. While the nursing student learns about the ethics of caring, the compassion required in their practice also represents an emotional risk for them as a learner and as a professional. Nurses often perceive that they are caring for too many patients for safe practice, and they lack the time for meaningful patient–nurse interactions, resulting in difficulty with the clinical decision-making required in life-changing situations (McAllister & McKinnon, 2009). The novice nurse works to mitigate the risks for the patient by identifying a culture of patient safety which prevents falls, injuries, and other adverse events such as medication errors. Interpersonal conflicts too often exist between healthcare professionals, further burdening the self-confidence of student nurses. Thus, the combined tensions in health care result in high levels of reported compassion fatigue, burnout, absenteeism, rapid turnover, and ultimate exit from the nursing profession (Pines et al., 2014). Nurses report high levels of displeasure with their limited role and a low sense of self-efficacy in helping others (McAllister & McKinnon, 2009). In nursing education, the experience of the nursing students entails a journey toward understanding the meaning of being a nurse, moving away from treating disease under a hierarchy where the physician is often placed at the top, toward profession practice guided by entry-level competencies based on professional responsibility and accountability, knowledge-based practice, ethical practice, service to the public, and self-regulation (College of Nurses of Ontario [CNO], 2014).

In their undergraduate degree, nursing students reflect on the meaning of their interactions with patients to shape their own assumptions and to develop the salience to respond to the nursing profession with an increasing familiarity to clinical situations (Benner et al., 2010; Registered Nurses Association of Ontario [RNAO], 2016). The twenty-first-century learner requires a multitude of experiences to develop the competencies for entry-level nursing practice (CNO, 2014).

Image of Nursing in the Twenty-First Century

Today's nurse enters the profession in an age of postmodern technology, trying to understand the profound scope of the nurse in a world saturated with media messages (Heilemann, 2012) that often influence the public perception of nurses. For decades, nurses have been depicted negatively in the media; for example, the image of the nurse is falsely enacted in recent medical dramas such as "Hawthorne," "Nurse Jackie," "House," and "Grey's Anatomy" and in previous productions such as "ER," "MASH," and "One Flew over the Cuckoo's Nest" (McHugh, 2012). In these dramatizations, the media narrative misrepresents the nurse as incompetent, naughty, sexy, bold, nasty, and risk-taking. Also noteworthy is that conversely, the image of the angelic, subservient, mindless nurse following a physician for rounds creates an ineffective and inaccurate image (McHugh, 2012). The negative image prevalent in the media leads to a lack of understanding of the demanding, skilled work performed by nurses. As nursing associations represent nurses in profound topics of workplace violence and inadequate nurse-to-patient ratios, the media often leaves out the clinical judgment and the refined skills nurses bring to provision of care as central to the argument that nurses are at the center of quality health care (Cabaniss, 2011; McHugh, 2012). In a joint position paper, the CNA and the Canadian Federation of Nurses Unions (CFNU) affirm that workplace violence is a serious issue in nursing in the form of both horizontal violence and aggression by clients (2008). Workplace violence, threatening effective patient care, has an impact on morale, productivity, absenteeism, psychological functioning, recruitment, and retention. According to the CNA and CFNU (2008), a new graduate is most vulnerable to leave the profession because of workplace violence in their first six months of practice than any other time in their profession. Nursing associations like CNA work to highlight issues from a nursing perspective at a national level, believing it is essential to provide the public with an accurate image of nursing and a truthful account of the nurse's story.

Finding and Sharing Wisdom Through Story

Buresh and Gordon (2000) urge nurses to consider sharing narrative accounts of their daily work to dispel the misguided image of the nursing profession. By taking charge of the image of the professional nurse, nurses heighten an understanding of their role in the public.

A distinct aspect of nursing practice poorly understood by the media is the nurse's role beyond the medical needs of the patient; specifically, the nurse's role also encompasses caring, decision-making, advocating, educating, and comforting (CNO, 2017). Canadian journalist and health reporter Picard (2017) features stories highlighting the demand for nurse practitioners, the need for health policies in end of life and palliative care, MAID legislative changes, mental health and addiction as a public health crisis, and the overall inefficiencies in Canadian health care. Similarly, nurses need to take a narrative approach to explain the gentle acts of kindness and the lived experience that define them as nurses.

The unrealistic images portrayed by entertainment corporations leave the public with narrow visions of the role of nurses, leaving behind prospective learners from entering the profession to choose other healthcare professions (Baltodano, Darder, & Torres, 2008). Nursing educators need to counter such inaccuracies by including a comprehensive historical overview of the nursing profession in undergraduate nursing curriculum to consequently explore the future of the nursing profession.

There are lessons to be learned from other disciplines regarding the need for a strong professional identity as a way to build resilience. Other health professions and their heroic dispositions are often depicted in the media. For example, tragic world disasters such as the terrorist attacks in New York City, in France, most recently in London, and Manchester in the UK appropriately and rightfully highlight emergency responders in a positive manner with stories and illustration of their service work in our society. Through various environmental disasters created by tsunamis, hurricanes, and tornadoes, the world has seen paramedics, police service, and firefighters covered in the media as heroes in those tragedies (Baltodano et al., 2008; McHugh, 2012). Most recently, the emergency preparedness covered in the media during Hurricane Harvey and Irma reveals the extended shifts of several days to an entire week by medical teams to ensure access to health care during the storm. While American schools continue to strategize against issues of gun violence, the public recalls the news media highlighting one beautiful, heroic teacher huddling in the closet with the children in her class during a tragic school attack at the Sandy Hook Elementary School (Baltodano et al., 2008). As highly trusted health professionals, nurses also deserve the recognition among other respected skilled professions who carry out careful and intelligent responses in times of public crisis. In recent nursing history, first responders and nurses caring for the victims of the horrific Boston marathon bombing, the mass shootings in an Orlando night club, and a Las Vegas concert are portrayed as heroic by the public. In the media, nurses also bring forward the professional ethical dilemma of caring for the assailant of the Boston marathon attacks in their expected response to global disasters (McHugh, 2012). Nurses' stories are also now more common in the world of entertainment. In his monologue, late night talk show host Jimmy Kimmel publicly acknowledges the nurses who cared for his newborn, calling attention to the skilled knowledge required for a nurse to first detect the symptoms of tetralogy of Fallot in his son's first days of life (Canadian Broadcasting Corporation, 2017). Nurses, like teachers, need to be spoken of openly and eloquently regarding their intelligent acts of kindness in their practice (Buresh & Gordon, 2000).

RECRUITMENT OF THOUGHTFUL, COMPETENT LEARNERS

A positive image is important to the recruitment of nurses in the profession. To attract thoughtful, competent, and caring learners, the professional image of the nurse needs to embody the advanced knowledge of health promotion, health protection, and an in-depth understanding of disease and the current complexities of health care (McHugh, 2012). Since 2005, the Bachelor of Science in nursing is an entry-level requirement to practice in Ontario (CNO, 2014). According to the Council of Ontario Universities (2010), the change in educational requirement is in response to "the greater levels of critical thinking and nursing knowledge that were required in a healthcare system with advanced technology and higher levels of complexity of patients and environments" (p. 1). It is important to provide opportunities to nursing students to shape their professional image and to consider the issues relating to critical media literacy (Buresh & Gordon, 2000).

CURRICULA AND TEACHING APPROACHES OF THE TWENTY-FIRST CENTURY

As emphasized by McAllister and McKinnon (2009), "the concepts of transformative education have their foundations in critical social theory, a theory that explores and develops concepts and practices to promote social justice and equality" (p. 375). It is essential that topics such as marginalization, injustice, power imbalances, and ethical dilemmas be considered for the new graduate nurse to acquire the constructive thinking required for problem-solving and reflective practice. A commitment to resiliency within health education curriculum is imperative to build capacity in the twenty-first-century learner. The Canadian Association of Schools of Nursing (CASN) (2011) outlines quality education for the twenty-first-century learner as an environment which,

> focuses on students' development of clinical reasoning and judgment, exposure to Canadian health issues, and the honing of critical analysis and communication skills. Such high-level skills require an education that is based on real practice situations that may be supported by the use of simulation. (p. 3)

Nurses devote their work to compassionate practice, which includes listening, comforting, advocating, empowering, and educating patients about their health. Across Canada, the nursing curriculum is predominantly based on theoretical foundations of caring (CASN, 2011). The relational practice which often distinguishes nursing from other health professions fosters critical thinking and clinical judgment (Tanner, 2010). The medicalized image conveyed poses a problem for nurses as it places the caring science that defines them as a less important aspect of health care. Thus, nurses miss the opportunity to articulate the lived experience of compassionate practice, to speak about their role, their actions, and the impact of their relational practice on the health of the Canadian population. Nurses are urged to review the provision of care in today's health care from a critical perspective and to recognize the importance of the determinants of health at the macro-level to increase involvement in political action, in leadership, and in research (Buresh & Gordon, 2000). Raising the level of public knowledge of their scope of practice may lead nurses to become more resilient in their nursing careers and to have the resources to effectively practice with new graduate funding initiatives, funded professional development opportunities, full-time, and stable employment (RNAO, 2016).

Practice Education in Nursing

In this second section, the nursing student experience in clinical practicum is explored to understand the professional context embodied as learners. Nursing students embrace the culture of Canadian health care environments in which they are called upon to identify salient information from their studies toward the safe, competent provision of care for patients and their family (McAllister & McKinnon, 2009). The mentoring process varies in each discipline. A practicum consists of a teaching–learning relationship between faculty, a mentor, and a learner collaborating on the process of summative and formative evaluation of performance in the practical component in professional education (Ralph, Walker, & Wimmer, 2009). The clinical practicum, commonly beginning in the first year of most nursing programs, is where the nursing student gains practical insight into the landscape of health care (RNAO, 2016). To become a new graduate nurse, the nursing student requires the ability to rapidly respond to a patient's deteriorating condition and to recognize the possible mortality of any clinical situation while encompassing all aspects of nursing as a science and as an art. Although a practicum is scheduled in each year of study, in reality, nursing students experience brief experiences where they find it difficult to feel a sense of comfort needed for salient response to practical situations. In a large multi-site, national study, Benner et al. (2010), use narrative strategies to understand the student experience in placement. One participant in that study describes the chaos of placement by stating, "we are constantly being rotated through different units. As soon as we have been on the unit long enough to get the hang of things, we rotate to a new unit or hospital" (p. 61). Another student interviewed by Benner et al. (2010) expresses a disconnect between the classroom and the practicum setting and claimed that when nurses working on the units are asked about nursing theories, "it's frustrating, it's a lot of paperwork, and they laugh at me. They say, 'Nobody uses that'" (p. 88). On the night before each clinical practicum experience, nursing students are expected to complete extensive preparation for effective delivery of care. The preparatory homework normally includes a review of the illness, pharmacological, and non-pharmacological treatments, and nursing actions relevant to the clinical case. In health care, the healthcare team glorifies the acts that save lives, leaving out the tenets of nursing as important components of caring for a person in a holistic approach. As students report a gap between the classroom and the placement setting, it also noteworthy to add that much of the students' learning engagement emphasizes the practical aspect in providing care producing an educational curriculum highly based on a biomedical model, a model centered on the biological aspect of treating an illness. As a result, the ethic of caring that defines nursing is undervalued in the biomedical model of care. In their assignments, the nursing student often overlooks the rich opportunity to describe the lived experience of a person during illness. To propose a radical transformation in nursing education, Benner et al. (2010) suggest "narrative pedagogies, such as experience-based narratives of practice situations, journals, or debriefing and reflection on practice, are also effective ways to uncover and articulate everyday ethical comportment and notions of good central to nursing practice" (p. 222). This means a shift in thinking; it is a call for educators to prepare nursing students to deeply understand their professional identity and to explore the ways that nurses provide compassionate care. Resilient nurses need an integrated approach to theory and practice that brings the classroom, the practical laboratory, the simulation laboratory, and the practicum closer together.

INTERPROFESSIONAL COLLABORATION

Although nurses work within a team of healthcare professionals, they are educated in classrooms, laboratories, simulation activities, and clinical practicum groups with other nursing students; there are very few situated learning encounters with students from other health disciplines during their studies outside of the clinical practicum courses. In practicum, nursing students are exposed to the issues that exist in the workplace by seeing firsthand the effects of a heavy nursing workload and low nurse-to-patient ratio as they observe nurses lack the time and resources to provide quality care, and see firsthand a devaluing of the time required to provide care by members of the interprofessional care team. Since understanding roles and functions is deemed an essential skill in interprofessional education (IPE), the clinical experience offered in the IPE context allows students from various health professions to establish and maintain a climate of respect while utilizing effective communication strategies (Pines et al., 2014). As nursing students are at risk as new graduates to face workplace violence, their practicum should include education on creating healthy and safe workplaces with an ability to identify policies on violence and bullying.

As highlighted by Pines et al. (2014), nursing students need to adopt strategies that "include building positive nurturing professional relationships and networks, maintaining positivity, developing emotional insight, achieving life balance and spirituality, and becoming more reflective" (p. 86). The refinement of these skills is to become a resilience nurse who has a positive influence on health outcomes while incorporating the lived experience of caring.

Preceptorship in Nursing

In this third section, preceptorship is identified as one of the most beneficial arenas for students to develop skills related to resilience to address lateral violence in the profession. Preceptorship affords undergraduate nursing students the opportunity to develop a professional identity and autonomy in practice (McCullough, 2016). In this final section of this chapter, preceptorship is defined and its benefits as a teaching/learning tool are highlighted as they relate to the development of resiliency in nursing students.

Today's learning needs in clinical education are complex. Educating nurses for the future in areas such as resiliency, critical thinking, handling lateral violence, and practical wisdom is achievable in a practicum setting. In addition to the practical skills and knowledge that are a requisite for safe patient care, students must learn to apply theory in the clinical practice context, the term coined as the "practice-theory link" (Benner et al., 2010). Nursing students are required to understand the importance of ethical reasoning, reflective practice, institutional culture, organizational semantics, and systems thinking, especially as these impact the development of resiliency skills. Resilience in thinking is developed through direct experiential and situational contact with the patient (Tanner, 2010). Attributes of relational practice are best learned in the clinical practicum (RNAO, 2016). Preceptorship is one such clinical arena; it is an approach to clinical teaching and learning during which students, through immersion in the work of nursing, come to directly understand their professional role. Students are acculturated into that role through the guidance, facilitation, and direction of the practicing RN.

PRECEPTORSHIP DEFINED

Preceptorship is a teaching/learning approach employed by many undergraduate nursing programs in Canada (Altmann, 2006), providing "a perfect medium in which clinical practice and education can combine to achieve a common goal: the preparation of present and future practitioners and leaders" (Myrick & Yonge, 2005, p. 5). Preceptorship is well defined in the literature (Andrews & Wallis, 1999; Billay & Myrick, 2007; Kaviani & Stillwell, 2000; Lockwood-Rayermann, 2003; Nehls, Rather, & Guyette, 1997). For the purpose of this chapter, preceptorship is viewed as a one-to-one teaching/learning approach in which the expertise of the

RN is drawn on by the student for a predetermined period of time in the clinical setting and which offers them the relevant knowledge and skills to become socialized into the profession of nursing. The essence of preceptorship involves a triad of individuals: the student, referred to as the preceptee; the preceptor, an experienced RN who guides the learning of the preceptee in the clinical setting; and the faculty advisor, who oversees the overall preceptorship placement. The preceptee assumes the learner role in this triad. The preceptor is a RN who, above and beyond their regular responsibilities as a working professional, assumes the role of the clinical teacher (Kaviani & Stillwell, 2000; Lennox, Skinner, & Foureur, 2008). The preceptor teaches, counsels, and inspires the preceptee by acting as a role model, guide, and facilitator. The preceptor supports the growth and development of the student for a predetermined period of time. The faculty advisor acts as teaching/learning resource by providing teaching strategies, guided learning, and facilitation of communication. The preceptorship placement offers a period of support throughout the transition of the student into the professional practice setting (Bain, 1996; Chickerella & Lutz, 1981; Nehls et al., 1997).

BENEFITS OF PRECEPTORSHIP

There are numerous observed advantages of preceptorship, the most discernible being the acquisition of clinical experience and a more "solid knowledge base" in clinical practice (Altmann, 2006, p. 11). Preceptorship "promotes effective learning and transfer of knowledge" on the part of the student (Udlis, 2008, p. 28). Most notable in the preceptorship approach is the opportunity that instruction is delivered to meet the needs of the nursing student. This tailored learning approach is individualized to address specific types of student learners. In the clinical practicum, the learner actively engages in the learning process by utilizing the hands-on learning approach. The practical, experiential learning approach moves them from nursing student to new nurse graduate. During the preceptorship, students experience the role of the RN through a variety of learning styles which, in turn, optimizes the learning process.

There are many benefits of preceptorship placements, both locally and internationally, that extend beyond the scholastic achievements of the student. For example, a preceptee is socialized into the nursing profession through a period of support as he/she transitions into the professional practice setting (Bain, 1996; Nehls et al., 1997), which could in turn decrease lateral violence for the student/new hire. In addition, networking occurs more easily and is possibly the reason that those who are preceptored tend to do well in organizations and are more likely to remain in the nursing profession (Chickerella & Lutz, 1981; RNAO, 2016). Further, introducing students to professional practice and the realities of clinical nursing during the preceptorship placement has been recognized as a retention factor for nurses in the profession (Lockwood-Rayermann, 2003). The preceptor–preceptee relationship provides much substance for career growth, benefitting both the preceptor and the preceptee. This relationship may result in less horizontal violence in the workplace as preceptees become welcomed into the profession by experienced nurses. The preceptee can network, become integrated into the work environment more easily, and attain experience and advice throughout the process. If the preceptee obtains employment in the institution, the organization acquires an employee who is already familiar with the organization's culture and function, as a result of directly with a preceptor who is an experienced member of the organization and accepted by their peers (Norris & Gillespie, 2009).

International Preceptorship in the Twenty-First Century

International placements may also have a positive effect on microaggression in the workplace in the profession of nursing. As students seek international educational opportunities and employers continue to seek a global employee, international preceptorship placements are becoming a reality in nursing education (Rubin, 2009). In the late 1990s, Canadian nursing faculties reported international undertakings with 81 countries (Ogilvie, Paul, & Burgess-Pinto, 2007). Since that time, that number has escalated; international education in the twenty-first century is evermore present and emerging. An international educational placement affords students the opportunity to prepare for the realities of an interdependent world, including the building of an internationally competitive workforce (Smedley, Morey, & Race, 2010). Larson and Allen (2006) point out that there is now an emerging awareness of a "global neighbourhood, which recognizes that social crises are not constrained by traditional political boundaries and that there is significant impact of economic globalization for marginalized groups" (p. 507). International preceptorship placements serve to broaden nursing education, nursing practice, and nursing theory, to explore concepts and contexts that include nurses from all nations. International preceptorship also allows students to increase their understanding of their own and other cultural and political systems. Taken together, these additional skills, brought to the nursing workplace, may add resiliency, patience, understanding, and a culturally sensitive lens.

In today's world, societal perspectives in Canada have come to embrace global citizenship, which in turn have direct impact on the educational system. In the current context of professional nursing, and with the emergence of global perspectives in nursing education, international preceptorship placements can offer unique opportunities for students to participate in a variety of key learning experiences early in their nursing career. International preceptorship placements are becoming particularly important as students, academic institutions, and the profession of nursing request a more globally minded practitioner. An international preceptorship can provide students with a holistic and global view of the world, as well as provide them with the knowledge and skills necessary to make informed and prudent judgments about contemporary world issues (Hanson & Meyerson, 1995; Kushigian, 1998). While borderless learning increases as a result of increasing online resources, ease of travel, and heightened global awareness, international nursing exchanges and placements have also become more prevalent. It is, therefore, prudent to address appropriately the processes or pedagogical theories that support a heightened prevalence of international preceptorships, as these processes are a key underpinning of successful placements. A fundamental goal for all nursing students is to be globally savvy, and to achieve this goal, there is a need for nurse educators to create international placement opportunities (Mill, Astle, Ogilvie, & Gastaldo, 2010). It is important that nurse educators develop specific strategies and design innovative curricula that will provide opportunities for students to become engaged in global citizenship and to learn about the role nurses can play in the global context (Mill, Yonge, & Cameron, 2005).

THE NEW GRADUATE NURSE EXPERIENCE

The new nurse graduate needs to prepare for entry-to-practice by meeting requirements for licensure: passing a jurisprudence examination, passing the National Council Licensure Examination for the RN (NCLEX-RN), submitting a criminal record verification, and payment of registration fees with their provincial legislative body. The process of licensure takes several weeks for nursing graduates. Many work as temporary RNs for up to six months while undergoing the licensure requirements, while other new graduate nurses focus on the licensure requirement prior to taking employment. In the early months of transition, being a new graduate nurse is often recalled as a stressful, challenging time in a nurse's career (Dyess & Sherman, 2009; Parker, Giles, Lantry, & McMillan, 2014). The new routine, the teamwork, and the workload may cause anxiety for the new nurse graduates who also put high expectations on themselves to perform as they did as students (Casey, Fink, Krugman, & Propst, 2004; Parker et al., 2014). Having a greater understanding of their professional identity as nurses, combined with an ability to identify workplace adversity, eases the transition into practice beyond their preceptorship. The experiences in preceptorship and in the first months of practice provide new graduate nurses with the resilience to respond effectively to the lateral violence in the profession.

Nursing students flourish under mentoring relationships, especially in their final year prior to licensure in which most programs include a large component of clinical placement hours. Those hours in placement are rich in reflective practice opportunities while building interpersonal skills within the healthcare team. In terms of transitioning into practice, Benner et al. (2010) recommend a year-long new graduate nurse residency to build resilience and to foster professional formation. Establishing nurturing relationships with their preceptor and the health professionals on the collaborative team fosters a positive transition into their role in health care.

Summary and Conclusion

In the first section, workplace violence is outlined as a serious issue in nursing. Nursing students are at risk of horizontal violence, bullying, and aggression by patients. Workplace violence has a serious impact on patient care, morale, productivity, absenteeism, psychological functioning, recruitment, and retention of nurses. A new graduate nurse is most vulnerable to leave the profession because of workplace violence in their first six months of practice than any other time in their profession (CNA, 2008).

In the second section, practice education in nursing is presented as playing an important role in developing resiliency in the undergraduate nursing student. Resilience is examined from a critical perspective to create learning environments that develop and strengthen nursing graduates. Building resilience in nursing education empowers the new nurse graduate in their journey into health care through a multitude of new practicum experiences in the Canadian context.

In the third section, the preceptorship model highlights the preparation for the nursing student to enter the role of the new graduate nurse. The nursing student's need for resilience is an important consideration in nursing education, especially in preceptorship where they learn to face the complexity of the Canadian health care and the workplace adversity. Working effectively in a collaborative interprofessional team requires a resilient healthcare professional. The twenty-first-century learner has the potential to build resilience and to create important changes in the current healthcare context to make interprofessional collaboration a priority.

References

Altmann, T. K. (2006). Preceptor selection, orientation, and evaluation in baccalaureate nursing education. *International Journal of Nursing Education Scholarship, 3*(1), Article 19, 1–15.

Andrews, M., & Wallis, M. (1999). Mentorship in nursing: A literature review. *Journal of Advanced Nursing, 29,* 201–207.

Bain, L. (1996). Preceptorship: A review of the literature. *Journal of Advanced Nursing, 24,* 104–107.

Baltodano, M. P., Darder, A., & Torres, R. D. (2008). *The Critical Pedagogy Reader* (2nd ed.). New York: Routledge.

Benner, P., Sutphen, M., Leonard, V., & Day, L. (2010). *Educating Nurses: A Call for Radical Transformation.* San Francisco, CA: Jossey-Bass.

Billay, D., & Myrick, F. (2007). Preceptorship: An integrative review of the literature. *Nurse Education in Practice, 8,* 258–266.

Buresh, B., & Gordon, S. (2000). *From Silence to Voice: What Nurses Know and Must Communicate to the Public.* Ottawa, ON: Canadian Nurses Association.

Cabaniss, R. (2011). Educating nurses to impact change in nursing's image. *Teaching & Learning in Nursing, 6*(11), 112–118. https://doi.org/10.1016/j.teln.2011.01.003.

Canadian Association of Schools of Nursing. (2011). *Position Statement on the Education of Registered Nurses in Canada.* Ottawa, ON. Retrieved from https://www.casn.ca/vm/newvisual/attachments/856/Media/EducationofRNsinCanadaEng.

Canadian Broadcasting Corporation. (2017). *Jimmy Kimmel Tearfully Recounts Newborn Son's Heart Surgery.* Toronto, ON: CBC/Radio Canada News. Retrieved from http://www.cbc.ca/news/entertainment/jimmy-kimmel-baby-surgery-1.4095059.

Canadian Nurses Association. (2008). *Advanced Nursing Practice: A National Framework*. Ottawa, ON. Retrieved from https://www.cna-aiic.ca/~/media/cna/page-content/pdf-en/anp_national_framework_e.pdf.

Canadian Nurses Association & Canadian Federation of Nurses Unions. (2008). *Joint Position Statement—Workplace Violence and Bullying*. Ottawa, ON. Retrieved from https://cna-aiic.ca/~/media/cna/page-content/pdf-en/Workplace-Violence-and-Bullying_joint-position-statement.pdf.

Casey, K., Fink, R., Krugman, M., & Propst, J. (2004). The graduate nurse experience. *The Journal of Nursing Administration, 34*(6), 303–311.

Chickerella, B. G., & Lutz, W. J. (1981). Professional nurturance preceptorship for undergraduate nurses. *American Journal of Nursing, 81*(1), 107–109.

College of Nurses of Ontario. (2014). *Competencies for Entry Level Registered Nurse Practice*. Toronto, ON. Retrieved from http://www.cno.org/Global/docs/reg/41037_EntryToPracitic_final.pdf.

College of Nurses of Ontario. (2017). *Practice Standard, Therapeutic Nurse-Client Relationship*. Toronto, ON. Retrieved from https://www.cno.org/globalassets/docs/prac/41033_therapeutic.pdf.

Council of Ontario Universities. (2010). *Council of Ontario Universities Position Paper on Collaborative Nursing Programs in Ontario*. Toronto, ON. Retrieved from http://cou.on.ca/publications/reports/pdfs/cou-position-paper-on-collaborative-nursing-progra.

Dyess, S. M., & Sherman, R. O. (2009). The first year of practice: New graduate nurses' transition and learning needs. *Journal of Continuing Education in Nursing, 40*(9), 403–410. https://doi.org/10.3928/00220124-20090824-03.

Fine, S. B. (1991). Resilience and human adaptability: Who rises above adversity? *The American Journal of Occupational Therapy, 45*(6), 493–503. https://doi.org/10.5014/ajot.45.6.493.

Garmezy, N. (1993). Children in poverty: Resilience despite risk. *Psychiatry, 56*(1), 127–136.

Hanson, K., & Meyerson, J. (1995). *International challenges to American colleges and universities: Looking ahead. American Council on Education Series on Higher Education*. Phoenix, AZ: Oryx Press.

Heilemann, M. V. (2012). Media images and screen representations of nurses. *Nursing Outlook, 60*(5), 1–3. https://doi.org/10.1016/j.outlook.2012.04.003.

Kaviani, N., & Stillwell, Y. (2000). An evaluated study of clinical preceptorship. *Nurse Education Today, 20*, 218–226.

Kushigian, J. A. (1998). *International Studies in the Next Millennium: Meeting the Challenges of Globalization*. Westport, CT: Praeger.

Larson, G., & Allen, H. (2006). Conscientization—The experience of canadian social work students in Mexico. *International Social Work, 49*(4), 507–518.

Lennox, S. M., Skinner, J., & Foureur, M. (2008). Mentorship, preceptorship, and clinical supervision: Three key processes for supporting midwives. *New Zealand College of Midwives Journal, 39,* 7–12.

Lockwood-Rayermann, S. (2003). Preceptor leadership style and the nursing practicum. *Journal of Professional Nursing, 19*(1), 32–37.

McAllister, M., & McKinnon, J. (2009). The importance of teaching and learning resilience in the health disciplines: A critical review of the literature. *Nurse Education Today, 29*(4), 371–379. https://doi.org/10.1016/j.nedt.2008.10.011.

McCullough, K. (2016). *The Process Involved in International Preceptorship in Undergraduate Nursing Education.* Unpublished doctoral dissertation, University of Alberta, Edmonton, AB.

McDonald, G., Jackson, D., Wilkes, L., & Vickers, M. H. (2012). A work-based educational intervention to support the development of personal resilience in nurses and midwives. *Nurse Education Today, 32*(4), 378–384. https://doi.org/10.1016/j.nedt.2011.04.012.

McHugh, K. (2012). Nurse Jackie and the politics of care. *Nursing Outlook, 60*(5), 12–18. https://doi.org/10.1016/j.outlook.2012.06.003.

Mill, J. E., Astle, B., Ogilvie, L., & Gastaldo, D. (2010). Linking global citizenship, undergraduate nursing education and professional nursing: Curricular innovation in the 21st century. *Advances in Nursing Science, 33*(3), E1–E11.

Mill, J. E., Yonge, O., & Cameron, B. S. (2005). Challenges and opportunities of international clinical practica. *International Journal of Nursing Education Scholarship, 2,* 1–13.

Moran, R. (2012). Retention of new graduate nurses: The literature informs staff educators. *Journal for Nurses in Staff Development: JNSD: Official Journal of the National Nursing Staff Development Organization, 28*(6), 270–273. https://doi.org/10.1097/NND.0b013e318272584a.

Myrick, F., & Yonge, O. (2005). *Nursing Preceptorship: Connecting Practice and Education.* Philadelphia, PA: Lippincott, Williams & Wilkins.

Nehls, N., Rather, M., & Guyette, M. (1997). The preceptor model of clinical instruction: The lived experiences of students, preceptors, and faculty-of-record. *Journal of Nursing Education, 36,* 220–227.

Norris, E. M., & Gillespie, J. (2009). How study abroad shapes global careers: Evidence from the United States. *Journal of Studies in International Education, 13*(3), 382–397.

Ogilvie, L., Paul, P., & Burgess-Pinto, E. (2007). International dimensions of higher education in nursing in Canada: Tapping the wisdom of the 20th century while embracing the possibilities for the 21st century. *International Journal of Nursing Education Scholarship, 4*(1), Article 7, 1–22.

Parker, V., Giles, M., Lantry, G., & McMillan, M. (2014). New graduate nurses' experiences in their first year of practice. *Nurse Education Today, 34*(1), 150–156. https://doi.org/10.1016/j.nedt.2012.07.003.

Picard, A. (2017). *Matters of Life and Death: Public Health Issues in Canada.* Toronto, ON: Douglas & McIntyre.

Pines, E. W., Rauschhuber, M. L., Cook, J. D., Norgan, G. H., Canchola, L., Richardson, C., & Jones, M. E. (2014). Enhancing resilience, empowerment, and conflict management among baccalaureate students: Outcomes of a pilot study. *Nurse Educator, 39*(2), 85–90. https://doi.org/10.1097/NNE.0000000000000023.

Ralph, E. G., Walker, K., & Wimmer, R. (2009). Practicum and clinical experiences: Postpracticum students' views. *Journal of Nursing Education, 48*(8), 434–440. https://doi.org/10.3928/01484834-20090518-02.

Registered Nurses Association of Ontario. (2016). *Practice Education in Nursing.* Toronto, ON. Retrieved from http://rnao.ca/sites/rnao-ca/files/SHWE_Quick_Reference_Guide_-_WEB_0.pdf.

Rubin, J. (2009). *Why Your World is About to Get A Whole Lot Smaller: Oil and the End of Globalization.* Toronto, ON: Random House.

Smedley, A., Morey, P., & Race, P. (2010). Enhancing the knowledge, attitudes, and skills of preceptors: An Australian perspective. *Journal of Continuing Education in Nursing, 41*(10), 451–461.

Tanner, C. A. (2010). Connecting the dots: What's all the buzz about integrative teaching? *Journal of Nursing Education, 46*(12), 531–532.

Tusaie, K., & Dyer, J. (2004). Resilience: A historical review of the construct. *Holistic Nurse Practice, 18*(1), 3–10.

Udlis, K. A. (2008). Preceptorship in undergraduate nursing education: An integrative review. *Journal of Nursing Education, 47*(1), 20–29.

CHAPTER 15

Leading and Working with Millennials in Universities: A Case of Delicate Dancing or "You're Not the Boss of Me!"

Lorna E. Rourke and Lorraine M. Carter

INTRODUCING DELICATE DUETS

Universities are wonderful places, or so it would seem: From the public's perspective, they are places where academic and professional civility abounds and where actions are grounded in practices reflecting social betterment and personal value. While beautiful buildings and green spaces have an undeniably positive impact on visitors to university campuses, those who have worked in them may have some different stories.

Those who have worked in the academy are familiar with tales of professors being obstructed from tenure and promotion because of infighting and academic jealousy; environments such as medical schools which rely heavily on the administrative skills of women who, in turn, may not be adequately recognized or compensated; and TAs and sessional instructors who are expected to teach large classes for inadequate pay and no

L. E. Rourke (✉)
St. Jerome's University, Waterloo, ON, Canada

L. M. Carter
McMaster University, Hamilton, ON, Canada

© The Author(s) 2018
C. L. Cho et al. (eds.), *Exploring the Toxicity of Lateral Violence and Microaggressions*, https://doi.org/10.1007/978-3-319-74760-6_15

job security. Those with lived experience in the university also know about elitism and entitlement—the respect for research output over passion and excellence in teaching, and the politics around leadership appointments.

Recently, another challenge has found its way into our universities. While a positive work environment for faculty, administrators, and staff is a goal in all universities, achievement of this goal has, in some contexts, become complicated by the different values and ideas about work held by senior university leaders and by staff who belong to the millennial generation. The outcomes can be situations of frustration for both millennial employees and their supervisors. There can also be a disconnect between what the baby boomer leader perceives as microaggression by the millennial and the perceptions of their actions by the millennials themselves. In many cases, middle to senior leaders who belong to early Generation X and the baby boomer generation find themselves dancing delicate duets with millennial employees and having their toes stepped on. While there are two partners in most dances, the overriding perspective offered in this chapter is that of the partner with more life and work experience. This noted, evidence-informed insights into the millennial employee are also provided since they are critical to this discussion.

The crux of this situation of delicate dancing lies in how millennials "espouse work values and have career expectations that are markedly different from those of Gen Xers and baby boomers" (Ng & McGinnis Johnson, 2015, p. 129). While many baby boomers "say they have a strong sense of pride in their work, only a quarter of millennial(s)... agree, highlighting a striking disconnect in attitudes about work...across generations" (Prudential, 2017, para. 1). Maier, Tavanti, Bombard, Gentile, and Bradford (2015) have found millennials "likely to challenge workplace norms such as... the standard workday and employee/supervisor relations" (p. 388). Because younger staff members often understand leadership differently from those who hold leadership positions at universities, the outcome has been, in some instances, situations of microaggression and dissonance such as disrespectful comments and disruptive behaviors. The leader may experience a lack of support from those early in their careers and be routinely challenged for his or her decisions. Given the ideal of freedom of ideas and speech, university leaders can likewise find themselves in situations of professional strife involving millennial staff.

Through a thoughtful examination of the literature and examples of various "delicate dances," this chapter provides a description of millennials in the work setting; ideas held about leadership by millennials juxtaposed with ideas held about leadership by those to whom millennials report; and the subtle and sometimes not so subtle tensions between millennial staff and their supervisors in universities. Examples of micro-aggressions and dissonance are provided based on the experiences of university administrators who have worked with millennials. Attention is also paid to the role of unions and human resources experts in navigating the different perspectives of millennials and baby boomers. Recommendations for working through differences, effectively leading millennials, and establishing productive and respectful teams in universities close the chapter.

Who Are the Millennials?

Fry (2016) remarks that "generations are analytical constructs, and developing a popular and expert consensus on what marks the boundaries between one generation and the next takes time" (para. 3). Hence, there are variations in the ages and date ranges attributed to various generations, although, in 2017, millennials are generally regarded to be around 20–36 years old. They are variously considered to have been born between 1980 and 1990 (Howe & Strauss, 2000); between 1982 and 2004 (Ellin, 2014); and between 1981 and 1997 (Fry, 2016). By comparison, persons belonging to Generation X are reported to have been born between 1965 and 1980, thus making them approximately 37–52. The baby boomers born between 1946 and 1964 are, at present, between 53 and 69 years of age (Fry, 2016).

Described as determined and narcissistic (Allen, Allen, Karl, & White, 2015), millennials are reported to be tech savvy and to see technology as a necessity rather than a convenience in their lives. Vincent (2012) notes that "technology is a way of life, not just a handy tool...Millennials...are highly tech savvy and prefer communicating quickly via text or instant message" (p. 144). They are often dependent on their parents who are often more involved in their lives than parents from earlier times were in the lives of their adult children (Coomes & DeBard, 2004). Millennials are further reported to dislike tasks requiring a sustained effort and to need immediate feedback (Pinzaru et al., 2016). While some generational researchers claim that millennials are more tolerant of diversity and socially minded in their visions of life and society (Oblinger & Oblinger, 2013) than earlier generations, others disagree, indicating that there is no credible evidence to support this claim (Twenge, 2012).

Many researchers have contributed to the literature on how different generations learn and work (Coomes & DeBard, 2004; Dede, 2005). The position that generational exposures, trends, and common life events are the primary influences on how a generation interacts with the world and performs in the workplace is common in this literature. At work, "the events in members' [members of a generation] lives and how they are perceived mold unique work attitudes" (McNamara, 2005, p. 1149).

So how do millennials perform in the workplace? And what are the events in their lives that have shaped their values and behaviors at work?

The short answer to the first question is that, in the workplace, the values of millennials often collide with those of their older colleagues and, almost certainly, with the values of their supervisors from Generation X and the baby boom generation. Additionally, those in leadership roles from Generation X may be resentful of millennials since, as Street (2016), a member of Generation X, points out "we [members of Generation X] are forgotten, caught between our parents' generation angrily shaking their fists at the natural passage of time, and the digital natives in our offices who know how Snapchat works" (para. 11). By comparison, in today's popular press, millennials have received a great deal of attention. Millennials' relationships with their baby boomer colleagues who adhere to long-established rules of behavior and have radically different ways of conducting business are, at best, challenging; at worst, adversarial (Howe & Strauss, 2000). Reeves and Oh (2008) in their early work on millennials and baby boomers characterize baby boomers as being responsible and having a strong work ethic while their experiences of their younger colleagues can be markedly different.

Of the shaping influences on millennials' approaches to life and work, three stand out: changing economies and uncertain employment opportunities, technology, and globalization. Each of these realities has dramatically affected the lives of millennials and the knowledge, skills, and attitudes they bring to the work environment (Goldman Sachs, 2016; Hutt, 2016; Jenkins, 2017).

Millennials live in times when their economic futures are unknown and, by extension, their ability to purchase homes, start families, and pursue some of the goals that defined their parents' lives are next to impossible. Routinely, they find themselves either underemployed or unemployed. How often do we hear about university graduates working at Starbucks, going overseas because there are no jobs here, and jumping from one short-term contract to the next? Both the academic literature and the public press are rife with examples of these circumstances, as well as evidence that many millennials are basement dwellers in their parents' homes for extended periods of time, a fact that baffles the baby boomers who moved directly from school to work and a first apartment (Bleemer, Brown, Lee, & Van der Klaauw, 2014).

The millennial generation is the first generation to have grown up with technology from toddlerhood and, perhaps, even earlier. Given this level of exposure to technology, millennials have adopted the many strengths and weaknesses that come with living in a wired world. Their experience of the world has been described by some as e-living (Brocade, 2011). They know how to bank, communicate, socialize, and find where and what they want to eat, all through an insatiable appetite for information acquired through their mobile phones. What they may not know how to do are to unplug, deal with ideas beyond information bites, write in standard English, and stay on task for more than a short period of time (Bebell, 2015; Nour, 2017; Sinek, 2017). Similarly, while they may be able to converse with Facebook friends around the world, they may be awkward in their interactions with peers closer to home unless there is a mobile phone involved. McWilliams (2016) remarks that "texting or chatting online, or even exchanging emails, enables users to avoid the edgy ambiguity of a face-to-face exchange.... Digital natives in particular have embraced online ersatz friendships as the genuine article" (p. 22).

Globalization, for the baby boomers, was no more than an idea. In Canada, the baby boomer from Ontario who headed to Alberta for a summer job was worldly and adventurous. By contrast, for millennials, globalization is a daily reality. They travel the world and remain connected to friends they have met and connect with those they aspire to meet through all forms of social media. Even without travel, millennials live and breathe the global village. In a single day, a millennial can connect with her brother and his family in China via WeChat with text messages, audio messages, and videos; send pictures to her parents through a text message, Snapchat, or e-mail; and interact with friends in Canada and Europe via Facebook. Millennials are aware of and even involved in political happenings around the world in ways that were hitherto not possible. Every day, the millennial is immersed in a world that is far bigger and more complex than that of their parents and grandparents. While there are advantages to this connectivity, there is also potential for an overload of information and negative emotions given the direness of today's world events and the graphic nature of much of the news.

Working with and Leading Millennial Staff: Echoes from Academic Corridors

To illustrate some of the challenges that university leaders may experience working with and leading millennials, the experiences of two university leaders from the baby boomer generation who are responsible for millennial staff are provided below. Each leader provides several examples of interactions with millennials as evidence of the different and delicate aspects of working with millennials in a university context.

Meet Genevieve

As noted above, Genevieve is a baby boomer. She is also the director of a mid-sized educational development unit at a Canadian university. Accomplished in her field, she has served as an academic administrator at three universities and as the education manager of a large provincial health network. She is a well-published researcher and presenter and has served as president of two national educational associations with direct relevance to her field of practice.

Workplace context. In the workplace, Genevieve provides oversight to a staff of 35 including baby boomers, persons from Generation X, and millennials. Although Genevieve's reputation and experience as a leader is extensive and positive, these elements are not always acknowledged by the staff. The staff is distinguished by what Genevieve refers to as "millennial character" which can sometimes manifest in difficult attitudes and behaviors.

Millennial moments. For the most part, staff do not interact directly with Genevieve but with their direct supervisors. On the rare occasions when Genevieve has approached millennial staff for some item of work, she has heard responses such as "I can't do that," "I am too busy," or "I don't have the time." Similarly, while there is some flexibility in work hours in the unit, this same flexibility is not always extended to the leadership team when it needs a millennial staff member to stay longer to complete a task. Importantly, the instances when Genevieve or some other member of the leadership team might ask a millennial staff member to stay a little longer to finish a task are rare. Thus, the millennial's unwillingness to accommodate is confusing. Moreover, it contrasts sharply with how the baby boomers in the office might say, "Sure. I can spend another twenty minutes and get that task completed."

When the leadership team makes a decision about work assignments and informs the team, millennial staff members may push back with comments including "Well, I'm doing my Master's. I know about X and should be allowed to do that work." Additionally, work days can be punctuated with queries of "why?". Despite efforts by the leadership team to present decisions thoughtfully, the millennials often challenge new directions and actions even before they have been tried and assessed. Considered together, these responses seem to suggest a lack of respect for the leadership team and the experience and expertise it has acquired over time. While the leadership group is happy to be held to a high standard, it is difficult to conceptualize how the millennial staff have adequate knowledge and experience to make a negative judgement before a new strategy is tested.

There can be a sense of entitlement among some of the millennial staff. While opinion is valued in meetings, the ways in which opinions are expressed by the millennials are not always respectful. In face-to-face meetings, opinions are expressed strongly and sometimes couched in thinking that organization-wide practices should be tailored to accommodate individual interests and preferences.

Although social media usage is acceptable in this unit because of the nature of its work, it appears that staff are using social media for more than their work and that this is affecting productivity. A recent budget planning exercise revealed that the work productivity ratio for the staff is lower than it was five years ago. While there may be a multiplicity of reasons for this, time lost to personal use of social media may be one of them.

Perhaps the most interesting outcome of the above dispositions and behaviors by the millennials is their impact on those in the office from Generation X. Some literature suggests that persons from Generation X may resent millennials: Having come of age in a poor job market, members of Generation X have been reported to feel threatened by the entry of this generation of creative, tech-savvy youngsters—namely the millennial generation—into the workplace (Erickson, 2010). In this specific workplace, however, the millennials seem to influence their Generation X colleagues. Thus, this staff acts more like a millennial entity than the generationally diverse group it is.

For Genevieve and the broader leadership team, this millennial effect has led to situations of some tension and unbalance. Dealing with a staff where 50% are millennials is one thing; dealing with a staff where closer to 75 or 80% are millennial-like in how they work and think about leadership is another. Leading those who don't want to be led, or who want to be their own bosses, or who see themselves as entrepreneurs within the same unit is, in Genevieve's words, the "hardest and most perplexing leadership task I have ever assumed." As a baby boomer who values hard work and believes in respect for all, Genevieve reports frustration with trying to get the "dance of it all right."

Meet Elizabeth

Elizabeth is the manager of an academic unit in a small university. She is a seasoned academic administrator, having worked in a larger university before coming to her present institution. She is respected by her peers, has won a number of awards, has served as president of her professional association, and, like Genevieve, is a baby boomer. The examples Elizabeth has provided about millennials are based either on her direct experiences with millennials or on the experiences of her university colleagues.

Workplace context. Because the university is small, the staff members know each other well. The team is composed of millennials, members of Generation X, and baby boomers. In addition to working with each other, they work closely with undergraduate students, faculty, and other university staff.

Millennial moments. A recurring problem related to millennial staff members involves the inappropriate use of social media and lack of adherence to standard work hours and protocols. An example of the former occurred when the manager assigned a specific task to a millennial to work on for the afternoon. An hour later, the manager discovered the staff member texting a friend while there was no evidence that the employee had even started the task. When questioned, the employee did not apologize but rather explained why she needed to text her friend. Similarly, employees in this place of work openly text and post to Instagram during discussions and team meetings. They neither apologize nor change their behaviors when they are asked to stop. A further lack of accountability occurs when millennial staff are scheduled to be at specific service points at specific times and are not. Instead, there have been times when staff members have left the area unattended and even gone home without asking or telling anyone, thus leaving patrons without persons to assist them.

On a different but related note, the staff have been asked at meetings, in one-on-one conversations, by e-mail, and even during performance reviews not to use their phones or laptops at the service desk. This practice has been shown to be off-putting for patrons who require assistance and are hesitant to interrupt the staff. Despite this rule, millennial staff continue to use their devices at the desk.

To further demonstrate the lack of adherence to rules by some millennial staff, staff in the department have always used a message board to post absences from the office for reasons such as meetings, lunch, and conferences. If a staff person is noted to be "in," the person is expected to be at his or her desk. In the case of one millennial employee, she marks herself as "in" all day on most days, even when she is gone for hours at a stretch. Sometimes when she returns to the office, she has been away for a massage or a yoga class; often, colleagues have been looking for her.

The millennials in the unit do not always display respect for their baby boomer colleagues. On the first day that a baby boomer manager and a millennial staff person worked together, the millennial told the manager that her idea was "twenty years out of date." Likewise, when a baby boomer manager asked to speak to a millennial staff member for a few minutes, the staff person agreed but kept typing on her laptop. When the manager asked the employee to stop typing for a few minutes, the employee refused and continued to send materials to the office printer making it obvious and audible what she was doing. When the manager became frustrated, the staff person indicated that she did not understand why: In her opinion, she was capable of multitasking and listening even when, to the baby boomer, it did not appear that the employee was paying any attention. The outcome was that the manager did not feel listened to or respected.

Another example of disrespect occurred when a millennial staff person interrupted a baby boomer professor who was in the middle of teaching a class to tell her that she was not using technology properly. The staff person then proceeded to walk into the classroom, uninvited and unauthorized, to make adjustments to the computer settings in front of the students. While the professor was embarrassed and angered by this intrusion, the staff person felt that he was simply being helpful.

As the above examples offered by Genevieve and Elizabeth suggest, at times, the baby boomer leader may require the help of others to ensure a positive and effective work environment when there are millennials on staff. Sometimes this may mean soliciting guidance from the human resources unit. In the unionized environment, it always requires working within the directives of the collective agreement under which the millennial may work. This next section offers insights into the intersection of collective agreements, human resources, and leadership when the university leader is responsible for millennial staff.

Dancing with Other Players

Ideally, labor unions ensure fairness and protect the rights and benefits of members. Further, they provide clarity for managers and employees regarding appropriate workplace practices. Black and Silver (2011) comment that a collective agreement "places limits on the potentially arbitrary exercise of power by employers, and empowers union members to defend themselves against abuses in the workplace" (para. 3). Certainly, university leaders aspire to the comprehensive goals of a well-conceptualized collective agreement. In the case of some of the millennial behaviors described earlier in this chapter, however, university leaders—even with an exceptionally well-crafted collective agreement—can find themselves in situations of uncertainty. Areas of uncertainty may include the use of social media at work and conformity to workplace standards.

Regarding practices such as social media use, it is helpful when agreements clarify employer requirements and employee rights, since philosophies and tolerances pertaining to social media, privacy, and freedom of speech often vary between different employee levels and between generations. Lam (2016) suggests that "unions can...be proactive in providing constructive suggestions to employers in shaping the social media policy" (p. 434) and in constructing and enforcing standards and employment practices that are fair and appropriate for everyone. When such guidance is not provided in the agreement, the leader can experience precariousness. In the case of social media, which is a key element in the lives of almost all millennials, the leader needs the clarity of an agreement to navigate fairly.

The right to academic freedom, one of the most important values in the academy, is enshrined in all collective agreements and thus affects all university employees: "A good higher education union contract protects the freedom of choice and expression we value in members of a university community.... A well-written union contract helps... members become the individuals they want to be" (Nelson, 2011, para. 12).

Unfortunately, in some cases, these freedoms can be abused, and collective agreements may actually provide protection for staff when their performance and workplace behaviors do not meet expectations. Simply put, some of the challenges that leaders face working with millennials may be exacerbated by the safeguards afforded in their collective agreements. As an example, an administrator at a Canadian university recently reported that a millennial staff person justified a department-funded purchase of obscure and costly materials as an exercise of her academic freedom: She insisted that the purchase had value to her and that she was exercising her individual rights. The union agreed and threatened a grievance if the employer took disciplinary action.

Similarly, comments that may be interpreted as microaggressions, including ageist comments made by millennials to and about their baby boomer managers, may be justified as staff expressing their individuality and exercising the freedoms enshrined in their contracts. Given this kind of thinking, it becomes very difficult to prove any kind of harassment against a manager by a millennial staff member. The strong protection afforded by unions and the forthrightness of many millennial employees can generate a potent situation for the leader.

When situations such as those described above arise, a relationship with human resources is important. Human resources staff members work on behalf of all employees and, ideally, have the expertise to guide all parties to situations of mutual understanding and effective work strategies. Because the values and behaviors of millennials are new in many workplaces, leaders need to be able to call upon those with enhanced expertise in human interactions in the work setting in order to dance successfully.

RECOMMENDATIONS FOR BETTER DANCING IN THE ACADEMY

While this chapter has focused on how some university leaders are experiencing their millennial staff members, it would be shortsighted to suggest that the attitudes and behaviors described are not found in other generational cohorts. Similarly, within a single sample of millennials, there will be much diversity in how they view and experience life and work. Not all millennials hold the same values or perceptions of work. Many ascribe to values and beliefs similar to those who belong to Generation X and, at times, even the baby boomer generation. As well, there is much that is authentically positive about the millennial employee: alternate ways of thinking about and accomplishing work, capability with technology, an understanding of globalization that their generational predecessors could not have, and the courage to challenge previously held values and viewpoints are powerful elements in the workplace. Because a workplace has generally functioned one way for many years should not mean that it will continue to operate the same way for years to come. Based on the increasing use of technology in almost all aspects of work and millennials' significant competence with technology, they have much to offer to the evolution of work and places of work. Not to tap into the tremendous expertise of millennials in this area would be incredibly shortsighted.

So, what does successful leadership of millennials involve? Returning to the dance metaphor that has informed this chapter, a first and critical step is to "know thy partner." While too much information from the peer-reviewed literature and popular press about any generational group may engender bias in the leader, the risks of not enough information are substantive. It has been well established that the millennial generation holds ideas about work and leadership that are substantively different from those before them. Thus, not learning about, acknowledging, and respecting these differences can lead to discord.

In addition to the wealth of information about millennials and how they perform in the workplace in the human resources domain, there is valuable information about how millennials think and work in the education and training sectors. Not insignificantly, university teachers have found themselves challenged to know how to engage millennials and enable learning in generationally diverse classrooms (Kasworm, 2009). Many of the insights that educators have regarding millennials are transferable to the workplace.

An important way to establish and maintain a positive working relationship with a millennial employee is to make all expectations clear in job postings and interviews. Millennials need to know exactly what is expected of them through detailed information. When they are fully informed about a position, they may even choose not to apply for the position or to decline it if they know it will not hold their interest. Once a person has been hired, expectations, job requirements, and even the steps toward promotion should continue to be clarified (Harvey & Clark, 2016).

Connecting with the millennial on the personal level is highly encouraged. If a millennial staff member experiences willingness in the leader to understand the stressors of an uncertain economic future, some of the benefits of 24/7 connectivity, and the value that millennials place on work-life balance, the leader stands a much better chance of being accepted and respected than otherwise. Knowing what a leader can and cannot change is likewise critical. The views and values of the millennial generation may be very different from those of older colleagues and particularly those of baby boomers.

Changes in the physical setup of the workplace may enhance the interactions between younger and older learners. While baby boomers and Generation X staff tend to value personal space, private offices, and defined schedules, millennial staff tend to be "as portable as their mobile devices and as informal as [university] students" (O'Neill, 2013, p. 11). One of the authors of this chapter recently visited a high-tech, ultra-modern workplace in Toronto, Ontario, which has embraced the workplace trend that Letchford (2017) calls "agile working." At this office, each staff person, including each manager, has a locker but no permanent workspace. Such flexibility offers choices to all generations of staff. Each workday, employees can decide to work at any available spot in the office. Some staff, mostly millennials, tend to choose a different spot each day, while baby boomers select their familiar spots most of the time. While some private offices are available in this workplace, many remain unoccupied as the millennial staff tend to work at long tables adjacent to their colleagues. Accommodating the space needs of all staff can help produce a more harmonious and productive working environment for everyone.

The ideas of acceptance and respect in the workplace require special consideration. In days past, these realities came automatically with the position of leader. There was no question about it: Staff members in academic units respected the dean or other academic leader while their colleagues in administrative units afforded their managers the courtesies of acceptance and respect. By contrast, in the case of some millennials, acceptance and respect may not be given until the leader has earned them, and possibly not even then. While good leaders know that they need to be able to sustain the respect of staff members, it also follows that the leader should be able to assume a level of acceptance and respect given his or her years of experience, overall expertise, and other relevant variables. Although some leaders may not be effective in their roles, most do good work and should be granted the cooperation and respect of their staff. If a university leader is not experiencing acceptance by millennial staff, he or she may wish to consider reaching out to human resources for guidance.

Hodge (2016) notes that organizations must work to understand their "mixed" workforces. He remarks:

> With millennials gaining employment alongside generation X and baby boomers, understanding the very different expectations of each group is crucial for keeping dissatisfaction at bay...What works for a millennial might not work for a baby boomer nearing retirement. Recognizing these differences will ensure your whole team is satisfied in their roles. Be flexible and trust your team members to work in a way that suits them. (para. 16)

Intergenerational workplace relationships can, of course, result in improvements to the workplace for all generations and levels of staff, and symbiotic relationships between generations can provide many advantages. Bennett, Pitt, and Price (2012) note that newer (and often younger) employees want clear directions and guidance, and react positively when these are provided by experienced and capable managers. At the same time, McKay, Arnold, Fratze, and Thomas (2008) acknowledge that providing regular feedback may be challenging given the "limited amount of time the baby boomer has to provide the unique one-to-one attention the millennial seeks" (p. 95). Nonetheless, aspiring to provide such feedback so that working relationships are enhanced and staff productivity is increased is an excellent goal.

Just as millennials desire feedback from their supervisors and leaders, baby boomers may need assistance from their millennial colleagues. Having faced unprecedented technological change "from typewriter to the iPhone, PCs, Internet, email, mobiles and Blackberries, in little more than twenty years...," baby boomers can learn much from the support and mentoring of their millennial employees (Bennett et al., 2012, p. 282). Support and mentoring can bring great advantages to all staff and to the workplace more generally. The university leader may also benefit from a small group of peers who can offer support and insight to the leader during periods of delicate dances. A group of respected colleagues will help the leader determine when it is appropriate to choose the path of lesser resistance and when it is best to stand firm.

FINAL THOUGHTS

While it would be inaccurate to suggest that all members of a generational group share the same values and characteristics, there is little question that employees from different generational groups often hold diverse values and workplace attitudes and behaviors. In the case of baby boomer leaders and millennial staff, these disparities can create unique challenges for both groups.

In addition to providing relevant literature from the academic literature and the popular press, this chapter has provided numerous examples of generational differences and the challenges that can arise from them in the academic workplace. The experiential authenticity of the chapter derives from the willingness of two baby boomer leaders from two universities to share their experiences of leading and working with millennials. Suggestions for how boomers can exist more harmoniously with millennial staff have also been provided. When all participants in the intergenerational workplace can work together toward common goals and with understanding of each other, the dance can move from delicate to life affirming and productive.

REFERENCES

Allen, R. S., Allen, D. E., Karl, K., & White, C. S. (2015). Are millennials really an entitled generation? An investigation into generational equity sensitivity differences. *The Journal of Business Diversity, 15*(2), 14–26. Retrieved from http://search.proquest.com.proxy.lib.uwaterloo.ca/docview/1766244151.

Bebell, B. (2015). Stop pressuring millennials to unplug. *Time.* Retrieved from http://time.com/money/3993202/millennials-wont-unplug/.

Bennett, J., Pitt, M., & Price, S. (2012). Understanding the impact of generational issues in the workplace. *Facilities, 30*(7), 278–288. Retrieved from http://dx.doi.org/10.1108/02632771211220086.

Black, E., & Silver, J. (2011, June 10). *Fast Facts: How Unions Protect Our Human Rights.* Retrieved from https://www.policyalternatives.ca/.

Bleemer, Z., Brown, M., Lee, D., & Van der Klaauw, W. (2014). *Debt, Jobs, or Housing: What's Keeping Millennials at Home?* (FRB of New York Staff Report, Rep. No. 700). New York: Federal Reserve Bank of New York. Retrieved from http://dx.doi.org/10.2139/ssrn.2530691.

Brocade. (2011). *Enterprise and Mobility: What E-living Is Teaching About E-learning.* San Jose, CA: Brocade Communication System. Retrieved from http://www.brocade.com/downloads/documents/technical_briefs/mobility-e-living-teaching-e-learning-tb.pdf.

Coomes, M. D., & DeBard, R. (2004). A generational approach to understanding students. *New Directions for Student Services, 2004*(106), 5–16.

Dede, C. (2005). Planning for neomillennial learning styles. *EDUCAUSE Quarterly, 28*(1), 7–12.

Ellin, A. (2014, March). The beat (up) generation. *Psychology Today, 47*(2), 56–62. Retrieved from https://www.psychologytoday.com/articles/201403/the-beat-generation.

Erickson, T. (2010). *What's Next, Gen X? Keeping Up, Moving Ahead, and Getting the Career You Want.* Boston, MA: Harvard Business Press.

Fry, R. (2016, April 25). *Millennials Overtake Baby Boomers as America's Largest Generation.* Retrieved from http://www.pewresearch.org/fact-tank/.

Goldman Sachs. (2016). *Millennials Coming of Age.* Retrieved from http://www.goldmansachs.com/our-thinking/pages/millennials/.

Harvey, E., & Clark, S. (2016). *Millennials vs. Boomers: Listen, Learn, and Succeed Together.* Naperville, IL: Simple Truths.

Hodge, N. (2016). The enemy within: How employee loyalty-or lack there-of-creates risk for employers. *Risk Management, 63*(9), 26–29. Retrieved from http://www.rmmagazine.com.

Howe, N., & Strauss, W. (2000). *Millennials: The Next Great Generation.* New York: Vintage.

Hutt, R. (2016, January). *What Do Young People Value?* Retrieved from the World Economic Forum website: https://www.weforum.org/.

Jenkins, R. (2017, January 23). *Who Are Millennials and Five Monumental Reasons Why They Matter.* Retrieved from http://www.ryan-jenkins.com/.

Kasworm, C. (2009). Adult learners in a research university: Negotiating undergraduate student identity. *Adult Education Quarterly, 60*(2), 143–160. Retrieved from https://doi.org/10.1177/0741713609336110.

Lam, H. (2016). Social media dilemmas in the employment context. *Employee Relations, 38*(3), 420–437. Retrieved from https://doi.org/10.1108/er-04-2015-0072.

Letchford, J. (2017). The agile movement. *The Estates Gazette,* 62–64. Retrieved from http://search.proquest.com.proxy.lib.uwaterloo.ca/docview/1862641448.

Maier, T., Tavanti, M., Bombard, P., Gentile, M., & Bradford, B. (2015). Millennial generation perceptions of value-centred leadership principles. *Journal of Human Resources in Hospitality and Tourism, 14*(4), 382–397. Retrieved from https://doi.org/10.1080/15332845.2015.1008386.

McKay, R., Arnold, D., Fratzl, J., & Thomas, R. (2008). Workplace bullying in academia: A Canadian study. *Employee Rights and Responsibilities Journal, 20*(2), 77–100. Retrieved from https://doi.org/10.1007/s10672-008-9073-3.

McNamara, S. (2005, June). Incorporating generational diversity. *AORN Journal, 81*(6), 1149–1152. Retrieved from http://dx.doi.org/10.1016/S0001-2092(06)60377-3.

McWilliams, J. (2016). Saving the self in the age of the selfie: We must learn to humanize digital life as actively as we've digitized human life—Here's how. *The American Scholar, 85*(2), 22. Retrieved from https://theamericanscholar.org.

Nelson, C. (2011). *What Faculty Unions Do*. The James G. Martin Center for Academic Renewal. Retrieved from https://www.jamesgmartin.center.

Ng, E., & McGinnis Johnson, J. (2015). Millennials: Who are they, how are they different, and why should we care? *The Multi-Generational and Aging Workforce: Challenges and Opportunities* (pp. 121–137). Cheltenham: Edward Elgar.

Nour, D. (2017). *Five Essential Facts for Marketing to Millennials*. Retrieved from http://www.huffingtonpost.com/david-nour/5-essential-facts-for-mar_b_9677220.html.

Oblinger, D., & Oblinger, J. (2013). *Is It Age or IT: First Steps Toward Understanding the Net Generation*. Retrieved from http://www.educause.edu/research-and-publications/books/educating-net-generation/it-age-or-it-first-steps-toward-understanding-net-generation.

O'Neill, M. (2013). Limitless learning: Creating adaptable environments to support a changing campus. *Planning for Higher Education, 42*(1), 11–27.

Pînzaru, F., Vatamanescu, E., Mitan, A., Savulescu, R., Vitelar, A., Noaghea, C., Balan, M. (2016). Millennials at work: Investigating the specificity of generation Y versus other generations. *Management Dynamics in the Knowledge Economy, 4*(2), 173–192.

Prudential: Union attitudes changing for millennials, survey finds. (2017, February 15). *New York Times*. Retrieved from http://markets.on.nytimes.com.

Reeves, T., & Oh, E. (2008). Generational differences. In *Handbook of Research on Educational Communications and Technology* (3rd ed., pp. 295–303). New York: Routledge.

Sinek, S. (2017). *Leaders Eat Last: Why Some Teams Pull Together and Others Don't*. New York: Penguin.

Street, A. (2016, October 19). Why are Generation X left out of the stupid boomer vs. millennials blame fest? *Stuff: Business Day*. Retrieved from http://www.stuff.co.nz/business.

Twenge, J. (2012). Teaching generation me. *Teaching of Psychology, 40*(1), 66–69.

Vincent, E. (2012, September). Generation gaps in the workplace: Making friends with technology and millennials. *American Medical Writers Association Journal, 27*(3), 144.

CHAPTER 16

Social Infrastructure: Designing for Online Civility

Ramona Pringle

In our hyper-connected world, for many the term microaggressions conjures images of digital infractions: the racist rant of an angry Twitter troll, the toxic rhetoric left behind by a user in the comments section of a newspaper, or the sexist banter in an online forum that is unwelcoming to anyone new or different. When we speak of microaggressions, "brief and commonplace daily verbal, behavioral, or environmental indignities, whether intentional or unintentional, that communicate hostile, derogatory, or negative racial slights and insults toward people of colour" (Sue et al., 2007, p. 273), it is hard not to immediately think of a Twitter timeline, full of hostile remarks and hateful rhetoric from angry "eggs" out to cause controversy and incite uproar.

It would appear that nowhere are microaggressions more common-place, or more inherent, than across the Internet, where platform design seems to foster, if not fuel, toxic behavior. From Twitter, to online games such as *League of Legends*, to the comments section of Canada's public broadcaster, the *CBC*, few corners of the online world are free from the mounting toxicity that has become all too common in these digital spaces. The list of news outlets that have gotten rid of commenting

R. Pringle (✉)
RTA School of Media, Ryerson University, Toronto, Canada

© The Author(s) 2018   309
C. L. Cho et al. (eds.), *Exploring the Toxicity of Lateral Violence and Microaggressions*, https://doi.org/10.1007/978-3-319-74760-6_16

features altogether includes the *Toronto Star, NPR, Reuters, Popular Science, The Telegraph,* and *Recode.* Canada's broadcaster closed down commenting on all articles related to the Indigenous population, because they were consistently filled with bigotry and hateful rhetoric instead of the intended helpful dialogue (Pringle, 2017). While some of these outlets claim to have closed down commenting in order to better focus their limited resources on social media channels, others, like Popular Science admit that "trolls and spam-bots" have overwhelmed their ability to provide intellectual debate, saying "even a fractious minority wields enough power to skew a reader's perception of a story" (Labarre, 2013).

Colloquial words of wisdom such as "don't read the comments" and "don't feed the trolls"—troll being slang for someone who seeks out discord by posting inflammatory remarks online—have become widely adopted strategies for managing online incivility; unfortunately, they do little to remedy the issue. As a result, online public spaces—the digital equivalents of the town square where ideas are shared and ideologies are discussed—have become hijacked by the toxic minority, whose loud and angry presence often overwhelms any attempt at civil dialogue or debate. While communal online environments have the potential to be valuable collaborative spaces, the opportunity to learn from each other is negated when civil discussion is prohibited by a dominant aggressive culture. In fact, in the context of news platforms, studies show that comments can actually taint how content is perceived; once the comments section associated with a piece of media has been overtaken by venomous or discordant posts, those who might have previously been interested in a meaningful discussion will stop engaging. Maria Konnikova calls this "the nasty effect," whereby the nastier the comments, the more polarized readers become about the contents of the article in question (Konnikova, 2013). Users who are exposed to polite comments do not change their view of the contents of the article, but those who read nastier comments tend to have a more negative take on the topic at hand.

The challenge of how to make the commenting that takes place within online communities less aggressive spaces spans beyond news outlets, into other Internet domains such as gaming and social media, and left unresolved, can have negative implications for businesses, as users opt to disengage rather than face unnecessary hostility. Just as *CBC* closed down commenting on articles about Canada's Indigenous population, other platforms are plagued by the vile treatment of women, people of color, and minorities. The harassment of female players is notorious in online games, and social network Twitter is plagued by its reputation for being a hotbed of verbal abuse. While strategies including user registration, the prohibition of anonymity, and pre- and post-moderation, whereby posts are reviewed by a moderator before being made visible to the public or reviewed by a moderator shortly after being submitted, are already being implemented by different organizations (Ksiazek, 2015), fixing the toxicity of online culture is a time-, money- and labor-intensive undertaking, all of which can be prohibitive factors for organizations seeking to increase the civility of their communities.

Across sectors and disciplines, aggression and toxicity have become commonplace online, and need to be addressed. After all, these spaces, though digital, are where we spend a great deal of our time, attention, and energy, and despite being pixels and data, the impact of harmful online comments can be very real. As Marshall McLuhan stated, "we shape our tools, and then our tools shape us" (McLuhan, 1994, p. xxi). In this sense, it can be argued that offline microaggressions can be fueled by the rampant toxicity online (Johnson, 1997)—especially when there are little to no repercussions for this kind of behavior.

Given that the design of these platforms seems to foster rampant toxicity, there is a strong argument to be made that it is by design, too, that these issues can be combatted. This chapter will examine how design solutions and social infrastructure can be developed for the online world, with examples from several digital platforms, including gaming environments, news portals, online forums, and other collaborative spaces, in order to provide a framework by which we can start to mitigate microaggressions online.

THE SOCIAL AND COMMERCIAL VALUE OF ONLINE COMMENTING AND SOCIAL SPACES

On the one hand, it is understandable that so many outlets and organizations have made the decision to remove commenting, the communal conversation around a given topic, and close down comment sections, the destinations where these digital exchanges take place, because it can feel like an unwieldy issue. But for all the trolling that occurs online, it is vital to not forget how powerful the Internet can be as a tool that connects us to information, people, and ideas. This is the central premise of Clay Shirky's *Cognitive Surplus* (Shirky, 2010), in which he discusses the immense potential for creative and intellectual output that can result from the collaborative efforts of people's online hobbies and pastimes.

But the problem of poisonous online rhetoric cannot be solved by avoidance, or by simply closing down forums. Where some organizations, such as those in journalism and media, might feel as though they have the option to close commenting sections, as those are only tangentially related to the original content, for other organizations such as social networks and online games, the communal space is inherent to the platform itself. Moreover, removing the opportunity for users to comment and engage communally negates the opportunity to gain from the greatest affordance of the Internet: the ability to collaborate and learn from each other. According to Johanna Blakely, the director of the Norman Lear Centre, the worst outcome of closing comment sections is that we lose out on the potential of these interactive platforms to learn about each other, collaborate, and grow. Blakely is one of several domain experts from various disciplines interviewed as part of a multidisciplinary effort to identify design solutions to online toxicity. As a researcher who studies the impact of entertainment and media on society, she says,

> just having that archive itself is one of the most valuable things on earth that exist right now. It's not that it suddenly tells us everything about ourselves, but it's this opportunity that we've never had before to at least start interpreting this information about our attention and how we allocate it and our desires and how we record them. (J. Blakely, personal communication, January 3, 2017)

In many cases, the opportunity to share thoughts and perspectives on an issue—be they anything from politics, to pop culture, to hobbies—is part of the motivation to engage in the first place. Removing the ability to comment affects the experience itself: It may take away the motivation to engage with a topic more deeply and to share it with a wider audience (Konnikova, 2013).

The benefit of finding ways to remedy the current toxicity found in online commenting spaces is not just experiential. While there is evidence that the communal element of online interactions is a driving factor in audience engagement, there are financial repercussions to the decision to remove commenting, as well. Just as newspaper readers have transitioned to digital platforms in seek of up-to-date information, television viewers are cutting cords and moving to online sources of content such as Netflix and Amazon (Strangelove, 2015). As such, it would behoove media corporations to foster their online communities. If commenting sections are closed down and users cannot engage on the proprietary platforms where the media on which they are commenting is housed, the result is not that those users will cease to comment, rather, they will comment elsewhere. The net result is that that "elsewhere" will grow, and benefit financially from the activity of those users, while the outlet generating content will suffer based on lower engagement. As media consumption habits become increasingly digital-first, there is a strong business case to be made, to consider the design of commenting features and user engagement, alongside the design of Web and mobile platforms, and the creation of the content itself.

Just as there is a business argument for making the commenting sections of traditional media outlets less hostile, the same is true of digital environments that are innately interactive, such as social networks and online games, says game designer Jeffrey Lin whose credits include the massive multiplayer online game *League of Legends*. Lin was interviewed for this project because of his complementary expertise in game design and human interaction; as a designer with a PhD in cognitive neuroscience, he studies the way players engage with each other and develops applied design solutions based on those findings. According to Lin, the more negative behaviors an individual is exposed to when playing a game, the more likely he or she is to quit and never come back. And so, he concludes, this is an essential—and valuable—problem for companies to solve (J. Lin, personal communication, February 21, 2017).

DESIGN SOLUTIONS: DIGITAL SOCIAL INFRASTRUCTURE

By design, social media can foster toxic behavior. Platforms favor short, quippy remarks, shock value is key to virality (Olsen & Gaude, 2015), and the speed by which timelines scroll past a user's field of vision fuels a sense of ephemerality, whereby users are more likely to comment quickly without necessarily considering the impact of their words. Just as the design of these platforms seems to encourage uncivil discourse, it can be argued that it is through design strategies that this growing toxicity can be combatted.

In *The Design of Everyday Things* (Norman, 2013), the seminal text on the design of everything around us, author Don Norman explains, that "design presents a fascinating interplay of technology and psychology" and that good designers "must understand both" (Norman, 2013, p. 7). He says,

All artificial things are designed. Whether it is the layout of furniture in a room, the paths through a garden or forest, or the intricacies of an electronic device, some person or group of people has to decide upon the layout, operation and mechanisms. Not all designed things involve physical structures. Services, lectures, rules and procedures and the organizational structures of businesses and governments do not have physical mechanisms, but their rules of operation have to be designed, sometimes informally, sometimes precisely recorded and specified. (Norman, 2013, p. 4)

It is understandable that the abuse that is encountered online can make individuals feel defeated and demoralized about the potential for positive change. Based on rampant trolling and flame wars—hostile, aggressive online exchanges—it is not uncommon for the Internet to be understood as the digital equivalent of a giant flood light, bringing into stark relief the worst of human nature. From this perspective, viewing the Internet as a mirror of humanity, it can seem as though there is a sort of inevitability to the toxicity that overflows online. But addressed from Norman's design-centric point of view, the Internet's tendency toward toxicity is neither innate nor unsolvable. Rather, it is an issue of bad design.

To date, the Internet has widely been seen as a digital frontier, a 'Wild West' where anything goes (Schneiderman, 2014), with little enforced regulation. On the one hand, this open sensibility has created an unprecedented arena for the democratization of ideas and ideals, but that is in jeopardy when toxicity strangles the air out of communal online spaces. In this seemingly lawless, ruleless, and often repercussion-less free-for-all, users feel empowered to say, or do, anything without a thought to social tolls. But even offline, when there are no rules, anarchy prevails. This is the premise of the classic work of literature, *Lord of the Flies* (Golding, 1954), in which lawless disorder surfaces, after a group of young boys are stranded on a deserted island without adult supervision, having survived a plane crash. Without rules to abide by, the group's social infrastructure quickly deteriorates into a cruel and dangerous free-for-all. A fable about the fragility of peaceful coexistence from before the invention of the modern Internet, the tale is a precursor to what is common today across much of the online world, wherein harassment emerges when there are no rules, or no enforced social contract.

Offline, society has developed codes of conduct that the majority of the public lives by; agreeing to these design systems or sets of rules helps people to coexist. These design systems, or rules, comprise a "social infrastructure," designed to help people keep themselves and each other free from harm. Laws exist as guidelines, and there are repercussions when laws are disobeyed. Take for example the system by which traffic flows. Traffic control is social infrastructure, a system designed to make our transportation interactions easier and mitigate the potential for damage. While there are repercussions when drivers break established rules, signals such as stop signs and changing colored lights have been designed to help drivers steer clear of wrongdoing in the first place. The traffic system has all of the markers that define what Norman would consider good design: Rules are clearly defined and communicated, and users are aware of what is possible, as well as the repercussions for deviating from the intended behavior. He explains, "good design requires stepping back from competitive pressures and ensuring that the entire product be consistent, coherent, and understandable" (Norman, 2013, p. 263). Perhaps the toxicity we see online is not an "internet issue", but rather a design issue, and online communities would benefit from a system similar to the traffic system, with widely understood and accepted codes of conduct and repercussions for bad behavior. After all, while anonymity is often blamed as the culprit for bad online behavior, in fact, it seems that it is the lack of consequences or repercussions that fosters a hostile or aggressive nature (Birk et al., 2016). As Norman explains, "designers need to focus their attention on the cases where things go wrong, not just when things work as planned" (Norman, 2013, p. 9). If the early vision for the Internet was a hope that it would grow into a communal network wherein individuals could share ideas and co-create solutions, then the evolution of spaces such as open-source communities can be seen to be best-case scenarios. The rampant toxicity that fills forums and social media feeds is the worst-case scenario of an initial utopian vision and as such is ripe for redesign.

DIALOGUE VS DEBATE

In considering the design of a successful online social infrastructure, it is important to keep in mind that aspiring to online civility does not necessitate that everyone be in agreement all of the time, or that comments should be banal and homogenous. Nor does it in any way equate to censorship, or the limiting of an individual's freedom of speech. Rather, the ideal is a system that is designed to encourage dialogue. At its best, the Internet is a tool that democratizes. This is evident in diverse cases, ranging from the Arab Spring, in which digital tools were used to voice the concerns and experiences of the populous, to the anti-establishment celebrity status of early YouTubers, who garnered massive audiences and success despite breaking from traditional entertainment models and gate-keepers (Shirky, 2008).

As Daniel Yankelovitch comments in *I'm Right and You're an Idiot* (Hoggan & Litwin, 2016), "Democracy requires space for compromise, and compromise is best won through acknowledging the legitimate con-cerns of the other. We need to bridge opposing positions, not accentu-ate differences" (Hoggan & Litwin, 2016, p. 7). Author James Hoggan goes on to add, "When we use dialogue rather than debate we gain com-pletely different insights into the ways people see the world" (Hoggan & Litwin, 2016, p. 9). Though neither Yankelovitch nor Hoggan is ref-erencing the Internet expressly, their comments are relevant to this dis-cussion of online civility. After all, the inherent strength of the Internet is its ability to connect users with diverse points of view. The challenge is simply that despite its potential, all too often, open spaces for online dis-cussion are hijacked by disparaging abusers, as opposed to those wishing to acknowledge different perspectives.

A person can be argumentative and still be civil. As long as an argu-ment is made without insulting or offensive language, it can maintain its civility, even if it might not be considered "polite" or "nice" (Ksiazek, 2015). Unfortunately, oftentimes in the worst of online confrontations, there is no attempt at dialogue, let alone civility. As psychologist Daniel Kahneman states, "we can be blind to the obvious, and we are also blind to our blindness" (Kahneman, 2011, p. 48). Or, as Hoggan so aptly named his book, the toxicity of online commenting is due to the phe-nomenon of "I'm right and you're an idiot" (Hoggan & Litwin, 2016). When a user attacks another's views or posts, with comments that target them based on factors such as gender, sexual orientation, or even politi-cal leanings, the intention is to rile that person, rather than to educate or inform.

For Steve Ladurantaye, who at the time of writing was the manager of digital news for *CBC*, overseeing not only the content being posted to the national broadcaster's Web site, but also the strategy for online community and commenting, the hostility that prevents civil online discourse is not a new occurrence. Rather, the industries that are now struggling to remedy rampant online toxicity have fostered a me-versus-you or us-versus-them sensibility for a long time now, in order to provoke responses. In the digital age, the term for this kind of fabricated provocation is "click bait," content that is designed and presented to attract attention, even if it that attention is negative. From his experience working in multiple newsrooms, Ladurantaye explains, "Stories are set up to be provocative and they are deliberately framed as somebody versus somebody... It's sort of the way journalism has worked for the last 100 years." But, he adds, if journalists and media makers can develop a model where they provide context and offer solutions, they can promote conversation. "I think once you start [providing solutions instead of provoking responses] you've taken away the natural inclination to oppose. There's not your side and my side, rather it's 'this is a problem and this is how it might be fixed'" (S. Ladurantaye, personal communication, February 15, 2017).

While the Internet seems to inherently foster incivility, it is not the first platform to encourage debate. While on the one hand, the Internet's open, networked nature makes it uniquely well equipped to help diverse users work together to solve problems, there are lessons that can be learned from other platforms that have managed to facilitate debate while avoiding the pitfalls of harassment and abuse. Charles Shanks is the senior producer of *CBC* radio's national call-in program *Cross Country Checkup*. In his role, Shanks has been designing debates for a long time. For over forty years, the radio program has been taking calls from diverse listeners all across the country on current affairs issues; the strategy is to highlight the places where opposing views might actually coincide or overlap.

> We try to frame it more towards the middle where people are a little more ambivalent, more willing to move and listen to each other's opinions. I think we've worked hard at that over the years and people know that this is not the place you go to see banging heads, this is the place you go to actually talk... Acknowledging similarities, instead of focusing on differences can lay the basis for dialogue versus debate. (C. Shanks, personal communication, March 3, 2017)

And while this strategy has been largely successful for the decades-old radio call-in show, it would appear to be equally beneficial online.

While Ladurantaye and Shanks were interviewed for their perspectives from the trenches of the newsroom, and the potential design solutions that can be gleaned from their experiences interacting with audiences in radio and digital platforms, Sean Stewart was included in this research for his understanding of game mechanics and user engagement, specifically as it pertains to collaboration among users. Stewart is credited as being one of the founders of Alternate Reality Games (ARGs), a breed of collaborative games that take place across a range of platforms spanning the Internet and the offline world. Just as there is wisdom to be gained in terms of making the online environment more civil from the experience of keeping a call-in program like *Cross Country Checkup* on the air for over four decades; likewise, there are design lessons from gaming that can be useful in the redesign of comment sections of news articles and journalistic media. According to Stewart, the key to success in ARGs lays in bringing players together, as opposed to pitting them against each other for the sake of competition. (S. Stewart, personal communication, January 4, 2017). With *The Beast*, for instance, an ARG created to accompany the Steven Speilberg film, *A.I. Artificial Intelligence*, players take responsibility for themselves, from the start, to host their own conversations as a means of pooling knowledge and solving puzzles. "Players communicate with one another, share their knowledge, offer storyline interpretations and gather info necessary to solve the game" (Kim, Allen, & Lee, 2008). In this context, commenting was established not as a means of expressing a polarizing opinion, or attributing value to the content in question, but rather as a means of collaboratively engaging with the content to extend the experience.

"One of the things that was interesting about *The Beast*, which is different from the comments section on *Sports Illustrated* or the *New York Times*, is there was no conversation that we hosted. There was only a conversation driven by the players themselves," says Stewart. "So they took responsibility for it from the beginning. There was no authority against whom to rebel. It was communal" (S. Stewart, personal communication, January 4, 2017). This is an explanation, also, for why niche online communities experience less hostility than platforms with broader scopes. In niche communities or fan sites, the users agree on shared values and interests when they opt in. As a result, says Blakely, these communities are full of constructive dialogue. "Of course there are fights and battles and tiffs. But, generally the interaction is incredibly positive, because people are constantly learning from a community that they did not have immediate geographical access to" (J. Blakely, personal communication, January 3, 2017).

The explanation for this, according to Stewart, is that on a niche site like *Ravelry.com*, a popular knitting community, despite different backgrounds or even levels of prowess, there is a shared assumption that everyone is there to learn, and by default, everyone there is imperfect. This, as a foray into the community, prevents the me-versus-you premise that can so quickly yield toxicity in public forums. "If you are on a site like *Ravelry*, everyone drops a stitch, everyone makes a horrible lumpy thing, everyone admires the work that is hard because they know it's hard and everyone shares their stories of failure," says Stewart. "Anytime there is a community of doers it is also a community of failures, because that's the price of admission" (S. Stewart, personal communication, January 4, 2017). He points out that, with opinion and punditry, the forms of communication that are dominant in many commenting platforms that serve broader audiences, there is no failure. Rather, each time a user speaks, or posts, or tweets, it is coming from a place of authority or certainty.

The takeaway for the brave designers tackling the issue of online civility is to focus on commonalities. For the incivility that emerges in news-based commenting sections, this could be as simple as trying to solve the problems being addressed through an approach such as solutions journalism, which focuses on how people are addressing challenges and gives readers resources to be able to help in a given cause (Curry & Hammonds, 2014), instead of overextending and trying to be everything to everyone. With this approach, users can be actively engaged in a meaningful and purposeful way, without being inflammatory or argumentative, by raising awareness, or contributing funds, for example, to the issue being addressed, through solutions provided by the journalist.

Additionally, there is a benefit to a design that is both top-down, wherein the social infrastructure is designed and enforced by the company, and bottom-up, whereby users create their own rules and community standards. Reiterating Stewart's findings that healthy communities tend to include an element of self-moderation, Lin notes that while many companies choose one approach or the other, either controlling the community or taking a hands-off approach, in fact, a healthy balance is ideal; a design-centered approach (top-down) can solve half the problems, and a community-centered approach (bottom up) can solve the other half. In other words, in addition to whatever mechanism the designers create, the more that the community can take control of the space for themselves, to establish shared goals and values, the more that community will self-enforce civil discourse. While Lin and Stewart cite examples from gaming, the presence of hostility in these environments is no less challenging to contend with than what is found in the comment sections of news and media organizations, and their findings provide practical design solutions that can be applied in other contexts to help foster civil online engagement.

ANONYMITY, CONSEQUENCES, AND REPERCUSSIONS

While the anonymity that is prevalent online, and unique to online discourse, is often cited as the culprit for bad behavior (Cho, Kim, & Acquisti, 2012), there is reason to believe that anonymity alone is not to blame for the rampant toxicity that is expressed online. That said, studies note that by humanizing the Web, and developing strategies whereby posters see other commenters as more than just anonymous generators of text on a screen, the level of civility is increased. For Ladurantaye, initiating human interaction during Facebook live streaming of news programming, whereby a moderator responded to and interacted with the community in real time, made a big difference to the tone of the subsequent audience conversations. The benefit of reminding users that their online peers are also real human beings on the other side of the computer screen is substantial. The risk of forgetting that the profiles people engage with online are also real human beings is a trap that even seasoned professionals can fall into, without a face looking them back in the eye. "Even I have a really hard time thinking of people in the comments section as people," says Ladurantaye. Many outlets have found that the level of civility increases when the author of a post or article engages in the comment section (Stroud, 2014). It should be noted, however, that there is a human toll for wading into an already toxic forum, especially as a self-identified female or minority, wherein the bashing often has little to do with the substance of the original content, and more to do with preconceptions and bias.

While several organizations have tried implementing real name policies, whereby users are required to create online profiles linked to their offline identities, to combat what they consider to be the negative effects of online anonymity, many have yielded better results through the implementation of a code of conduct, with consequences and repercussions for those who step out of line (Lin, 2015). Sometimes, the two are correlated. For example, Ladurantaye explains that the advantage of using Facebook as a platform for commenting is that most people can be held accountable because they use their real names. "You can report toxic behavior and the user can have their account lost.

That level of accountability is important." But as Lin points out, that model is imperfect, as the repercussions are not directly related to the user's goal, which in the case of Ladurantaye's *CBC* audience would be to read and comment on news articles. "Even if I say something super racist, I still get access to the news site, I don't get any repercussions, I don't get punished at all and in fact I kind of enjoy everybody giving me more attention for me being the person that I am on that site" (J. Lin, personal communication, February 21, 2017).

Working as a designer on *League of Legends*, Lin found that by implementing meaningful consequences for bad behavior, negativity was greatly reduced. In broad strokes, "if the community finds that you've behaved inappropriately, you can be temporarily banned from the game," a punishment powerful enough to impact the decisions, behavior, and language of individual players. After a year of research, Lin and his team realized that significant punishment for bad user behavior had never been integrated into the game's design, so users were free to behave badly without consequence, "We had to approach it from a consequences perspective first because the culture had gone to a point where it was out of control" (Lin, 2017). Implementing a system, or social infrastructure, with penalties for negative behaviors was the best way to get what Lin calls "a meaningful and necessary reset." Designers of the game implemented *The Tribunal*, wherein community members can collectively vote on whether a flagged infraction does in fact break the agreed-upon code of conduct, and then they administer a punishment accordingly, often booting players from the game and preventing them from being able to play for a length of time deemed proportionate to their offense. This method was found to successfully mitigate toxic behavior, with a 50% reduction in recidivism after a player is punished for an infringement (Blackburn & Kwak, 2014).

Similarly, the online forum *Reddit*, despite its reputation for xenophobia, has also managed to successfully implement a design strategy that centers on user-led moderation, and repercussions for bad behavior. With "shadow-banning," a user is blocked, but unaware of it; as Lin explains it, "they can keep posting, and they think they are posting so other people can see, but nobody else can. What they learn is if they keep posting this toxic stuff, nobody actually gives them any feedback so they just stop" (Lin, 2017). If the incentive for posting to a platform such as *Reddit* is to be seen and have your comments read, this punishment will incentivize a change of tone or approach, so that the user can stay in the conversation. As Stewart notes, "We are, even the very trolliest among us, social creatures. And if your comments get conclusively down-voted you feel less" (Stewart, 2017).

For this kind of punishment to be most effective, repercussions should be immediate, in order to draw a connection between cause and effect, so that the offending poster is aware of the relationship between their toxic behavior and the resulting punishment. Several companies—including Riot Games, the makers of *League of Legends*, and Google, which has launched a tool called Jigsaw—have now implemented strategies involving machine learning, to pick up negative keywords, with an immediate consequence of 30-second loss of chat or similar repercussions. Lin (2017) explains, "The closer the feedback loop to the actual time of the incident, the much better the results are," adding that the real-time repercussions are far more effective in changing user behavior than punishment after the fact. Granted, systems using artificial intelligence that look for keywords are far from perfect solutions; this approach still has a tendency to identify false positives and punish commenters for their use of flagged words, even when they are not being used in a harmful context. Nonetheless, the premise of delivering repercussions with enough immediacy that users are made aware of their infringement is a lesson that has been shown to yield positive results.

INCENTIVES AND REWARDS

Inevitably, users will not always be in agreement with each other. In fact, it is the diversity of opinions that is meant to be protected, even in cases where individuals are as polarized as they could be—for example, supporters of opposing political parties or ideologies—systems can be redesigned to incentivize good behavior and foster online civility. While Wikipedia, like Reddit, is not immune to sexism and flame wars, according to research from the Harvard Business School, individuals who edit political articles on the platform seem to grow less biased. Users who have a particular political bent tend to edit pages with opposing political positions; a right-wing contributor is likely to edit a left-wing page and encounter different views and vice versa. Because of the collaborative nature of the site, which relies on user-generated content and moderation, no article is ever "complete," and any change to the content of an article can be edited, or deleted, at any time. In a study of 70,000 articles (Greenstein & Zhu, 2014), the researchers found that contributors who started out with extreme political stances developed more neutral language over time, breaking out of their filter bubbles, the echo chamber of like-minded opinions that often manifests in online communities and social networks, due to the necessity to post edits in such a way that they would not be removed by someone with opposing views, thus making all articles more balanced. In other words, inherent in the design of Wikipedia is a reward for presenting content as objectively as possible, as the content that is deemed acceptable by the widest array of users is the content that is most likely to remain visible and not be deleted or edited.

Blakely (2017) notes that some design strategies rely on incentive as much as punishment

> Generally, the incentive on Wikipedia for editors is to edit something and have it stay up... They know that if they just go on an opposing political site and rail, it will be deleted immediately. But if they can find a way to put it in just the right terms that it will slide past the censors, who supposedly hate them, it's a victory for them. And, it's a victory for discourse because suddenly we have an encyclopedia entry that reflects everyone's point of view. Having feedback when they do something right will shape people's behavior.

Stewart experienced similar patterns of behavior in *The Beast*, noting that good outcomes tend to lead to more good behavior. He explains it as a type of cognitive dissonance whereby the mentality of the player is, "I'm working with these people therefore I must like these people" (Stewart, 2017). Stewart points out that the community that played *The Beast* and subsequent ARGs came from movie review sites where they were always engaging in hostile arguments and flame wars. But the ARG designers found that as long as the community was kept busy with challenges and tasks, and felt as though their involvement was necessary, the quality of engagement was really positive. He notes, "It even surprised the players themselves!" (Stewart, 2017).

As an extension of this kind of reward-based engagement, Lin suggests designing a platform where the more a user contributes valuable discussion and content the more privileges he or she can unlock, such as the ability to help moderate the conversation as a super-user. But, the platform must be designed in such a way from the start, before behavior patterns become ingrained. "The behavior you're seeing is the behavior you've designed for," says Shirky (2010, p. 196), who explains that behaviors follow opportunity: Even after a designer decides why users will want to participate in their new service, he or she has to give them an opportunity to do so in a way that they can understand and care about.

CONCLUSION

While for many the term microaggressions is evocative of the toxicity that has become commonplace in online commenting sections across the Internet, perhaps it is not too late to fix this culture of digital incivility.

Just as contemporary society has implemented systems of social infrastructure to help people coexist in their offline lives, so too can design help foster civility online. Through strategies including systems of consequences for breaking established and widely understood codes of conduct, to incentives for pursuing meaningful dialogue in a constructive way, several organizations have started to see positive results in their communities, often when they thought that perhaps the problem had already passed the tipping point.

What is also understood is that the Internet is an innately interactive space; online, no conversation is one way, and no content is static. As such, for new systems to be successful, designers need to consider how the infrastructure can be implemented so as to be both a top-down and bottom-up design, wherein the organization and the community members all have a voice, and a stake, in the success of the community.

REFERENCES

Birk, M. V., Buttlar, B., Bowey, J. T., Poeller, S., Thomson, S. C., Baumann, N., & Mandryk, R. L. (2016, May). The effects of social exclusion on play experience and hostile cognitions in digital games. In *Proceedings of the 2016 CHI Conference on Human Factors in Computing Systems* (pp. 3007–3019). San Jose, CA, USA: ACM.

Blackburn, J., & Kwak, H. (2014). STFU NOOB! Predicting crowdsourced decisions on toxic behavior in online games. CoRR, abs/1404.5. Retrieved from http://arxiv.org/abs/1404.5905.

Cho, D., Kim, S., & Acquisti, A. (2012, January). Empirical analysis of online anonymity and user behaviors: The impact of real name policy. In *System*

Science (HICSS), 2012 45th Hawaii International Conference (pp. 3041–3050). Maui, HI, USA: IEEE.

Curry, A. L., & Hammonds, K. H. (2014). The power of solutions journalism. *Solutions Journalism Network.*

Golding, W. (1954). *Lord of the Flies.* New York: Perigee.

Greenstein, S., & Zhu, F. (2014). *Do Experts Or Collective Intelligence Write with More Bias? Evidence from Encyclopedia Britannica and Wikipedia.* Cambridge, MA, USA: Harvard Business School.

Hoggan, J., & Litwin, G. (2016). *I'm Right and You're an Idiot: The Toxic State of Public Discourse and How to Clean It Up.* Vancouver, BC: New Society Publishers.

Johnson, D. G. (1997). Ethics online. *Communications of the ACM, 40*(1), 60–65.

Kahneman, D. (2011). *Thinking, Fast and Slow.* London: Macmillan.

Kim, J. Y., Allen, J. P., & Lee, E. (2008). Alternate reality gaming. *Communications of the ACM, 51*(2), 36–42.

Ksiazek, T. B. (2015). Civil interactivity: How news organizations' commenting policies explain civility and hostility in user comments. *Journal of Broadcasting & Electronic Media, 59*(4), 556–573.

Konnikova, M. (2013). *The Psychology of Online Comments.* Retrieved from http://www.newyorker.com/tech/elements/the-psychology-of-online-comments.

Labarre, S. (2013). *Why We're Shutting Off Our Comments.* Retrieved from http://www.popsci.com/science/article/2013-09/why-were-shutting-our-comments.

Lin, J. (2015). *Doing Something About the 'Impossible Problem' of Abuse in Online Games.* Retrieved from https://www.recode.net/2015/7/7/11564110/doing-something-about-the-impossible-problem-of-abuse-in-online-games.

McLuhan, M. (1994). *Understanding Media: The Extensions of Man.* Cambridge, MA: MIT Press.

Norman, D. (2013). *The Design of Everyday Things: Revised and Expanded Edition.* New York: Basic Books.

Olsen, C. B., & Gaude, C. (2015). *Show Me What You Share and I'll Tell You Who You Are.* Retrieved from: http://lup.lub.lu.se/student-papers/record/5463392.

Pringle, R. (2017). *Online Hate Might Just Be an Issue of Bad Design.* Retrieved from http://www.cbc.ca/news/opinion/online-toxicity-1.4001767.

Schneiderman, E. (2014). *Taming the Digital Wild West.* Retrieved from https://www.nytimes.com/2014/04/23/opinion/taming-the-digital-wild-west.html.

Shirky, C. (2008). *Here Comes Everybody: The Power of Organizing Without Organizations.* New York: Penguin Books.

Shirky, C. (2010). *Cognitive Surplus: How Technology Makes Consumers into Collaborators*. New York: Penguin Books.

Stroud, N. J. (2014). *Journalist Involvement in Comment Sections*. Report prepared for the Engaging News Project. [online] https://engagingnewsproject.org/enp_prod/wp-content/uploads/2014/04/ENP_Comments_Report.pdf.

Strangelove, M. (2015). *Post-TV: Piracy, Cord-Cutting, and the Future of Television*. Toronto: University of Toronto Press.

Sue, D. W., Capodilupo, C. M., Torino, G. C., Bucceri, J. M., Holder, A., Nadal, K. L., & Esquilin, M. (2007). Racial microaggressions in everyday life: Implications for clinical practice. *American Psychologist, 62*(4), 271.

CHAPTER 17

The Limits of Violence

Toivo Koivukoski

Is it possible that there are kinds of violence not yet recognized as such, in the sense that practices, policies, and social formations taken to be normal and natural today may come to be known as affronts to human dignity in the future? If that is indeed a possibility, then how could one come to know the true forms of violence and aggression both subjectively and systemically, seeing the injustice for what it is even when the social code of justice is not up to that measure?

For human societies get it wrong sometimes; they encode patterns of domination into the very structures of state and institutions, making objects, slaves, and resources of human beings where respect and recognition ought to be the hallmarks of civility derived from humane values.

So why not allow violence, aggression, and domination as bases for social organization? And precisely where does one discern the limits and bounds of that particular "Thou shall not"? A consequentialist argument would propose that violence and aggression, treated as a means to an end, are ultimately impotent; they breed resistance rather than recognition, and compromise the kind of soft-power that would amplify the effects of human accomplishment (Keohane & Nye, 2010). On principle, the use, or

T. Koivukoski (✉)
Nipissing University Peace Research Initiative, Nipissing University,
North Bay, Canada

C. L. Cho et al. (eds.), *Exploring the Toxicity of Lateral Violence
and Microaggressions*, https://doi.org/10.1007/978-3-319-74760-6_17

327

threat of the use of violence against others is unethical, when domination, rather than collectively set goals, is understood as the end of action.

In order to understand that ethical principle in practical terms one would have to know the scope of violence as such in its definition and limits. By knowing violence in terms of its limits and possibilities one would gain an ethical compass by which to judge both actions and institutions according to their ethical rightness, where freedom and equality are the goals of human historical striving (even as we get to know more fully just what is meant by freedom and what by equality); to see deprivations for what they are, so as to make our shared world better at cultivating human dignity as a shared aspiration.

And yet, precisely because the universal recognition of human beings as essentially free and equal is clearly an aspirational goal for humanity, we measure ourselves against standards not yet fully known. And that is the crux of an inquiry where there is the possibility that there may be injustices before our eyes that we do not yet have the words to articulate; that there may be intimations of deprival without register in the dominant sensibilities and institutional orders. For the human being in an inhumane society, it is a kind of voiceless scream incapable of accepting the pointlessness of violence, and yet inarticulate to the loss. It is a loss of a sense of loss itself, like Nietzsche's image of the Last Men, who say "'We have invented happiness,' ... and they blink" (Nietzsche, trans. 1995). That blink is the interval of self-satisfaction, an indication of the lack of a gap between wish and fulfillment, wherein happiness is nothing more than a measure of efficiency in outcomes. Within that technological horizon of a humanity dehumanized by the modern project, what remains for Nietzsche is the trans-valuation of values, and a human good delinked from transcendent sources. That modern technology, conceived as vehicle for human freedom, would also allow violence as a systemic function should hardly be surprising, given that condition of possibility of routinized violence is obscured by a lack of a sense of lack. What is needed then is some epistemological cue by which to discern, in the lexicon of Canadian political philosopher George Grant, an "intimation of deprival" so as to think, feel and act beyond the despair that too often accompanies violent social orders (Grant, 1991).

The challenge is to discern precisely where the bloody terminus of violence lies. Viscerally, there is that boundary of the skin, the threshold that keeps the body and the person intact, and that, when broken or bruised, marks the trespass in blood red. And yet even at that material level, the significance of violence and aggression are culturally encoded, and need interpretation. From combative contests like mixed-martial arts to rap battles in hip-hop music, is the blow to the face a crime or a sport? Are statements of vitriolic disrespect verbal harassment or street art? Can the sublimation of violent antagonisms into competitive ago-nisms (to borrow a term from the political theorist Chantall Mouffe), work to harness diffidence and a sense of superiority into terms of peace-ful coexistence (Mouffe, 2005)? The terms of peace require the speeding up of symbolic orders in order to make sense of a set of meanings more substantial than some demonstration of physical superiority. And even at the ontological level of the act, the materiality of violence must always be interpreted for its meaning in order to register as social reality.

This essay aims to discern the limits of violence through a comparison of two traditions of political thought—one drawn from Hegel, the other from Aristotle—as interpreted through the writings of Judith Butler and Hannah Arendt respectively on the possibilities for political transforma-tion. I will consider Butler's effort to recalibrate Hegel's idea of progress moved forward by negation, so as to recast the concept of negation of the given from a version of history driven by violent revolutions and war, to one that makes progress possible through a recognition of the place of otherness in identity. In light of the challenges to this kind of rec-ognition where there are entrenched patterns of domination, I turn to Arendt's application of the Aristotelian distinction between necessity and freedom as a way to limit violence while admitting its perennial influence in human life and political affairs. While violence may remain attached to the human condition so long as we have bodies and are mortal, Arendt argues that under contemporary political conditions war and violent rev-olution are incapable of advancing historical goals, with domination for the sake of domination relegated to petty tyrannical ambition. Rather, Arendt insists that real power is derived from the possibility of collective action, which requires political forums where mutual recognition can be freely given. Carving out the potential for these kinds of political spaces where consent can be established may be the strongest bulwark against modes of domination, and promises the kinds of historical miracles that signal the realization of freedom and equality as goals for human kind.

We All Bleed

It is interesting that the original text from within the Western tradi-tion, Homer's *Iliad*, a poem of war, introduces the word *psyche*, or what would come to be known as the soul. It appears in some very visceral embodied uses, in instances where the word is used to describe a death, as in: "he had painfully breathed out his soul (*psyche)*" (Homer, trans. 1999). As if the soul—if we can use a poetic translation to make sense of poetry—is the dying breath of a person, the death rattle when life leaves the body. And in another similar use, where the material sense of *psyche* is emphasized, Homer describes a battlefield death where the soul leaves the body in the very blood that spills into the earth, as if the soul were flowing from a wound:

> the end of death enfolded him, his eyes and his nostrils; and Patroclus, set-ting his foot on his chest, drew the spear out of the flesh, and the riff fol-lowing with it; and at the same time he drew out the spear point and the soul of Sarpendon. (Homer, trans. 1999)

This is the stuff that we all have in common, the material basis and soul substance of our shared humanity, that we can all be wounded, and that we will all die. As the doctor-poet Norman Bethune reflects, "In this community of pain, there can be no enemies" (Bethune, 1972). Or, as the political theorist Judith Butler postulates, acknowledging an ethical principle on this basis of community in the precariousness of life itself:

> The reason I am not free to destroy another – and indeed, why nations are not finally free to destroy one another – is not only because it will lead to further destructive consequences. That is doubtless true. But what may finally be more true is that the subject that I am is bound to the subject I am not, that we each have the power to destroy and to be destroyed, and that we are bound to one another in this power and this precariousness. In this sense, we are all precarious lives. (Butler, 2010)

The terms of non-violent relations are spelled out here by Butler with precision and detail. There is the consequentialist reasoning that violence done unto others is likely to be returned. That is the logic that informs, to take an ancient example from Thucydides' *History of the Peloponnesian War*, the rejoinder by ambassadors from the island of Melos to the Athenians when they threaten the Melians with either subjugation or slaughter. The Melians make what would turn out to be a prescient case: that an aggressively imperial foreign policy, which sees the existence of independent cities as threats to Athenian security, would make enemies of others who might then quite rationally choose preemptive defenses of their own, with an escalation of conflict rather than security resulting. Indeed, in Thucydides' telling, the genocide of the Melian people—adult males killed, women and children enslaved, and the island colonized— sets the Athenians on a violently compulsive track that would lead to imperial overstretch, and the ultimate collapse of their empire.[1]

To Butler's finer point on the inter-subjectivity that brings with it a shared sense of precariousness, the notion that "the subject that I am is bound to the subject I am not" pertains in part to the underlying material reality of the human condition. The idea is traceable back to Aristotle, who defined a human being as a *zoon politikon*, an animal whose essence is defined in part by our political nature: because we need and love others to sustain and reproduce our biological lives, at the level of economic necessity, so too do we bond together with others for collective security. Thus we can act towards ends that are in the view of those involved, a good (Aristotle, trans. 1984). This sense of shared purpose allows us, as free political subjects, to identify with others in terms of those shared, apparent goods. For, beyond the necessary, collaborative qualities of political and economic life, there is also a dimension of identity to inter-subjectivity, such that one can identify with "the subject I am not."

At this point in the analysis of our constitutive relations with others, a significant divergence of interpretations is possible. That the "subject that I am" is bound to the "subject I am not" could be understood in the classical sense that would have Aristotle define human beings as *zoon politikon*. Or, it could be understood in an historicist sense, after Hegel, with every identity consisting of a synthesis of opposites, thesis and antithesis. In the second line of thought, the historical dialectic works through a cumulative negation driven by contradiction, where there is a pattern of opposition that sets up a tension that sparks historical change and progress. For example, we can consider perhaps the most influential section from Hegel's *Phenomenology of Mind*, on "Lordship and Bondage," which was so crucial for Marxist interpretations in positing an historical dialectic driven by class-consciousness and contradiction. Therein, it is the slave's consciousness of freedom as consisting in the master—who is free from toil because of the labour of slaves—that sets up the possibility of revolutionary *praxis* that would reclaim that freedom for the oppressed through the overthrowal not just of a particular set of masters (so as to merely flip the relation), but to act in such a way as to transform social relations and the institution of slavery itself.

So, rather than the kind of class conflict that would have been familiar to the Ancient Greeks, with their ideas of an unchanging human nature, and where regimes may change from democracy, to oligarchy, and back to democracy again as power and possessions change hands, instead for Hegel the cumulative negation of a doubled consciousness must alter that relation in a constitutive way. The realization of freedom as both formal idea and substantial condition, whether freedom is seen as outside of self-consciousness (for the slave) or as an external source of being and sustenance (for the master) must do away with slavery as such in the historical march towards the universal recognition of human beings as essentially free and equal beings.[2]

This universal recognition begins with a self-division of the historical spirit in a kind of doubling that would have Otherness belonging to an identity in an essential way, not simply as an Otherness that is somehow 'out there' in the world. For this could not be an identity defined and inscribed by a perimeter that walls off Otherness from identity, such that one knows who one is in terms of an opposition to what one is not. That would, after all, be an impossible epistemological task, there being an endless list of things that any one thing, or person, is not. That kind of difference is external to identity, so long as the relation is indifferent. For example, I could say that I am not an elephant, and neither an elephant nor myself would care about the opposition; I will have gotten no closer to understanding just who I am (with that aim of self-consciousness being core to Hegel's modern enlightenment project).

Rather, it is those kinds of relations, where the Other who I am not is somehow constitutive of my identity that are germane here. For Hegel these would be relations like those between Master and slave, or God and man, or State and citizen. To the extent that there is a division within that kind of relation, there is room and animus for the historical dialectic to unfold. So slaves overthrow the institution of slavery, God is incarnated into an historical human being so that humankind can find communion with Him, and the citizen is recognized as free and equal before the laws of the State. Thus, progress towards a free relation to difference—seeing Otherness inscribed into self-consciousness in an essential way so as to bring the Other in and to identify with them— becomes humanity's shared historical goal.[3] Hegel uses the term *negation* to describe the formative and dynamic relation to difference, where negation of the *given* does not destroy it, but rather freely takes in the apparently determinate *given*:

By means of this self-conscious negation, self-consciousness procures for itself the certainty of its own freedom, and thereby raises it into the truth. What vanishes is what is determinate, the difference which, no matter what its nature or whence it comes, sets up to be fixed and unchangeable. The difference has nothing permanent in it, and must vanish before thought because to be differentiated just means not to have its being in itself, but to have its essential nature solely in an other. (Hegel, trans. 1967, p. 248)

In this sense, an encounter with difference through cumulative negation does not set identities that are opposite by nature against one another, as if there are ahistorical categories and antinomies between things, set apart as irreconcilable. Rather, our terms of opposition must be understood historically, as moments in a dialectic that work by bringing the Other into one's identity, recognizing that the Other is essential to one's being.

Beyond peaceful social relations, or religious communion, or the recognition of citizens' rights by the State, perhaps the clearest instance of such a relation to difference would be in the experience of love, where one recognizes an Other as essential to one's being. Though this kind of intimate encounter with difference may be unique and sheltered at the level of erotic love, the possibility of eros in this sense indicates a fusion of the subjective and substantial aspects of freedom, for no other bond is given more freely, and no other connection is so determining in its significance. In this rare and exceptional bond we experience what an openness to the Other can mean as aspiration for self-consciousness, even if it cannot be institutionalized and scaled up as a civilizational goal.

WE ALL SPEAK

This is one way of understanding the constitutive quality of our relations to difference, that Butler describes as a path to peace as read through the lens of Kojève-Hegel. I would like to put together an alternative frame, to use Butler's language, for understanding how others, and the experience of difference, can make an identity whole, and serve as an ontological basis for peace. As an alternative expression of the inter-subjective aspect of reality, drawing from Aristotle rather than Hegel, Hannah Arendt makes reference to the philosopher's *Nicomachean Ethics*, writing that,

To men the reality of the world is guaranteed by the presence of others, by its appearing to all; "for what appears to all, this is what we call Being", (Arendt, 1958, p. 199)

This is another way of framing how human beings come to belong in a shared identity, with plurality considered as an essential aspect of the human condition. If not entirely an ahistorical given (since one can imagine conditions under which human beings could be deprived of the forums necessary for plurality to be expressed) then it is at least a necessary condition for the assurance of the reality of our shared experiences,

> for without a space of appearance and without trusting in action and speech as a mode of being together, neither the reality of one's self, of one's own identity, nor the reality of the surrounding world can be established beyond doubt. (Arendt, 1958, p. 208)

Here we have a perhaps more realistic alternative to an historicist theory of inter-subjectivity, where self-consciousness is attained not in relation to otherness itself, as in Butler's revised Hegelian formulation, but rather in the relation between a political subject, defined in terms of the rights of citizenship, and other citizens gathered together in a public forum, what Arendt describes as a "space of disclosure". The attraction of this theoretical approach is that it allows one to rather neatly localize those affronts to the freedom of the subject that we find in violence, relegating those to a realm of necessity and material compulsion, the private realm, set apart from a realm of freedom that is predicated on mutual recognition among citizens in a public space. That said, the danger of a theory of inter-subjectivity premised on mutual recognition within a public forum is that it allows for exclusion, i.e. for a group to recognize some as free and equal while not affording that respect to others. Outside of the protection of the political community and its laws, deprivation and disregard remain real possibilities. Indeed, the basis of Aristotle's strongest argument for the naturalness of certain forms of slavery was that, under what we would call the technological conditions of the day, the freedoms associated with Athenian citizenship required liberation from the necessity of labour. To have a class of people capable of devoting days of sun-up to sun-down debate on public matters necessitated another class to toil for them. And while Aristotle imagined circumstances under which slaves would not need masters nor masters need slaves (namely if the tools of production would work under their own direction by intelligent anticipation) still, those basic, related ideas of a condition of plurality supported by mutual recognition inscribes violence into the human condition, though in a limited way (Aristotle, trans. 1984).

For if freedom is conceived as a release from the necessities that attend biological life, what Giorgio Agamben describes as "bare life", and as long as we have bodies prone to hunger, thirst, or some physical compulsion forced onto us by another, then violence will be a part of the human condition (Agamben, trans. 1998). Thus Arendt disavows the notion that violence can ever be removed entirely from human life, and even calls into doubt the hope that it ought to be.

In a series of essays *On Violence*, Arendt writes that "Violence is by nature instrumental; like all means it always stands in need of guidance and justification through the ends it pursues" (Arendt, 1969, p. 51). Here the ends to which violence is a means are also the limit of violence, what Aristotle would call a *telos*, in the sense of a purpose calling for and delimiting its proper means. So, the self-defence of a nation may require violent means, but according to the mutually recognized norms of just war theory and international law, any use of armed force must be limited, proportionate to the threat posed, and recognize the principle of distinction between civilians and combatants.

In this sense, Arendt's view on the limits of violence is a classical position, informed by the sensibility that there is an architectonic form of the human condition, with its constitutive distinctions—as in the distinctions between means and ends, private and public, or necessity and freedom. The ideological aims of transforming human nature so as to allow for progress at the level of our species-being has, through the history of the twentieth century, through totalitarian regimes and the technological fantasy of the mastery of human nature, proven to make life unlivable under those regimes, rather than emancipatory.

Arendt's view on violence—considered along a spectrum of aggressive drives to dominion over others, from micro to macro—is that violence can be a useful means to certain ends, but just that. Neither violence nor aggression can be considered ends in themselves (neither dominion over others nor the use of violence for their own sake) because that is the logic of tyrannical ambition and pointless cruelty. These drives do manifest perennially in human societies, though at the expense of the common sense that is the basis not only for civil society, but also to allow us to collectively grasp reality as such. For a collective grasp on reality requires a space of public disclosure—i.e. the public realm under conditions of plurality—and it is this very possibility that is routinely and characteristically suppressed in tyrannical regimes, which drive towards monopolies on public power and the capacities to speak and to be heard. Thus, the despot aggrandizes himself at the expense of the people's shared sense of truth, and holds onto power through the atomization of subjects, stoking suspicion of others and consolidating dominion on the basis of a terrorized social psyche. The result of this undoing of civil society is a system that Arendt describes as "organized loneliness," an echo chamber of fears that isolates the subject, cutting them off from a condition of plurality, making mutual recognition or collective action among subjects impossible (Arendt, 1951, p. 478).[4] Instead of action properly so-called (which is always grounded in and limited by that condition of plurality, and is characteristically indeterminate in its outcomes, because action requires the cooperation of others), in the despotic dystopia one finds mass movements, where currency in ideas is regulated by reductionist logics, and where political discourse with the Other (however that big Other is defined- racially, economically, in terms of religion or ideology) is impossible. Every tyrant is lonely, and his grip on power depends upon his subjects being made to feel lonely also. So instead of civility, there is hatred. Instead of trust, there is terror. Instead of hope, there is paranoia.

Given advances in technologies of surveillance and war, tyrannical states today are especially frightening in their potentials. And yet at the same time, for Arendt, violence and aggression remain essentially impotent for achieving grand ideological aims. The historical context for Arendt's argument is laid out in her seminal studies on war crimes and totalitarianism, (Arendt, 1951, 1963)[5] but in terms of her lesser-known reflections *On Violence*, it was her experience in American university life in the late 1960s that frames the work against a backdrop of student protests, race riots, and the violent policing of mass dissent. Arendt reflects that the spread of student demonstrations in France and the United States through 1968–1969 may have, as instances of reform rather than revolution, brought to light issues otherwise suppressed in conservative institutional orders (Arendt, 1969, p. 79).

Arendt is no easy thinker to categorize (though her pattern of thought makes heavy use of categories as the scaffolding to her logic), and while there is an affinity with Aristotle as one of her key sources (as in her defence of the private/public division from Book 1 of the *Politics* as architectonic for the human condition) there are also quite radical or seemingly 'progressive' dimensions to her arguments on violence. She notes approvingly the institutional reforms gained by the 1968 student protests at Columbia University. She makes heavy use of Noam Chomsky in *On Violence*, with emphasis on critique of a military industrial complex and a war economy. And against the impotence of violence in advancing historical goals, she emphasizes the miraculous quality of non-violent resistance as a way of engaging in genuine political action. If violence and the drive to domination through aggression promote automatic, routinized responses (whether in the forms of submission or escalation) then the power of action consists precisely in that unpredictable capacity to say 'No!' For,

> When commands are no longer obeyed, the means of violence are of no use; and the question of this obedience is not decided by the command-obedience relation but by opinion, and, of course, by the number of those who share it. Everything depends on the power behind that violence. (Arendt, 1969, p. 49)

In terms of this distinction between power and violence, for Arendt it is not as if, according to the realist dictum, all power is fungible to the sovereign authorization to the use of violence, with power being ultimately reducible to violence[6]; rather, the authority to the legitimate use of violence as a means to certain ends is traceable to power, which Arendt defines as "…the human ability not just to act, but to act in concert" (Arendt, 1969, p. 44).

This is the power behind civil disobedience, and it shows in those instances where sovereignty, understood in the Weberian sense of a monopoly on the legitimate use of organized violence within a given territory, breaks down (Weber, 1961). It is the tipping point of any sovereign state, when orders are given to suppress an uprising and those orders are refused. This has been a hallmark feature of regime-change from within, where in the face of civil disobedience armed forces are ordered to fire on their own people, and instead lay down their arms, choosing the people over the state. As these kinds of political action often accompany constitutional crises, with attendant emergency measures, this has often meant a replacement of police or other internal security forces with the military. However, the military is an institution organized for external defence, enlisted by patriotic duty, or conscripted by force of law, and unaccustomed to turning their weapons towards the homeland. Whereas internal security forces may be in the habit of oppressing rather than protecting their own, a military can find little pride in that, and so the power of the people acting en masse is tested against the violence of a military that must be instrumental to political ends. Violence is no substitute for power. Thus, Arendt concludes on the capacity of civil disobedience that,

> The sudden dramatic breakdown of power that ushers in revolutions reveals in a flash how civil disobedience – to laws, to rulers, to institutions – is but the outward manifestation of support and consent. (Arendt, 1969, p. 49)

It is the possibility of establishing "support and consent" in the absence of patterns of domination that empowers people to act. It is this possibility, considered in light of its tenuousness and the perennial attractions of aggression as a mode of leadership, that makes public life and action so fascinatingly unpredictable. For one can never be entirely sure what will happen when a group of people get together and decide to do something (by contrast, apathy and inaction are numbingly predictable). In Arendt's classification, because it involves new beginnings, and not being a lockstep reaction to determining causes, there is always something unprecedented to action, in the sense that the genuine, free act is not conditioned by the history that made it possible. Things could work out otherwise; so long as the consent of others must be gained in order to act, there remains a core uncertainty as to what another person may decide. One becomes dependent on others through collective action, and however much one builds trust with others through shared actions, it remains a messy and patient business to organize a group of free-thinking and willing individuals towards an end that is, in the view of those involved, a good. Corralling people through coercive means is comparatively straightforward, though such means are ultimately incapable of enlisting the full energies of those involved, or of achieving ends truly belonging to the people as a whole, and, therefore, representing power properly so-called.

THE BONDS OF DOMINATION AND OF HOSPITALITY

It is clear that there is a spectrum of modalities of aggression from micro to macro—understood in general terms as the drive to domination over others—ranging from implied threats, to intimidating stares or gestures, to verbal antagonism, to rough negotiations, to violent "signaling", arms testing, military training exercises, movement of troops, to blockades, invasion, occupation, colonization, and at the nadir of violence, genocide. Now given the expense, in terms of human security on the receiving end of violence, and the opportunity costs of delivering aggression, it is an outrage that the potentialities for collective efforts continue to be wasted in these ways. For we may think ourselves to be more civilized than the Athenian ambassadors who say to the doomed Melians, "the dominant exact what they can and weak concede what they must" (Thucydides, trans. 2009) and yet such patterns of domination are perpetuated, though by perhaps more obscure justifications. If aggression and violence are perennial in human history as instrumentalities, then it is in their uses and ends that they find their proper limits.

This is the core of Arendt's argument on violence, that it is merely instrumental, capable of only short-term advantages, and in a contemporary context limited in its usefulness by the destructive potentials of new technologies of violence. Arendt points to the impotence of the most violent means of destruction that humanity has contrived—nuclear weapons—which served a function only to the extent that they were deployed to deter the actual use of nuclear weapons by other states, thus being useful only in that they made nuclear weapons useless. The history of state violence in the twentieth century, and the new-found possibility of world war, demonstrate the impossibility of using violence to advance world historical goals under contemporary conditions.

And yet, although one can demonstrate the tragic qualities of violence alongside of its futility as an agent of historical change, it is also quite clear that aggression—again, understood along a spectrum of behaviours ranging from micro to macro—can have its demonstrable effects. Aggressive professionals and politicians bully forward agendas suited to their interests. Aggression and patterns of submission deferent to shows of dominance have been deeply encoded in cultural norms and privileges. What then may be the means and ways towards emancipation from those inherited shackles of lordship and servitude, in terms of the Hegelian dialectic? And to what extent may different kinds of violence be appropriate to those ends?

As a means of emancipation, Arendt, unlike Hegel, emphasizes the power of collective action, with its sense of novelty, being necessarily undetermined by the sequence of events that went before (and different in that precise sense from the deterministic qualities of violence, lordship and bondage) such that the free act stands out as miraculous.

Hence it is not in the least superstitious, it is even a counsel of realism, to look for the unforeseen and unpredictable, to be prepared for and to expect "miracles" in the political realm. And the more heavily the scales are weighted in favour of disaster, the more miraculous will the deed done in freedom appear; for it is disaster, not salvation, which always happens automatically and therefore must always appear to be irresistible. (Arendt, 1963, p. 170)

Before contrasting the concept of historical action as event with Hegel's idea of progress as a dialectical unity of form and substance, a comparison can be offered between Arendt's phenomenology of the act and Walter Benjamin's theses on history. We attend particularly to Benjamin's 9th thesis, which describes his idea of progress using the image of a Paul Klee painting, *Angelus Novus.*

The "Angel of the New" is portrayed in shocked awe at the danger-ous violence, historical crises, and human suffering inflicted by a history driven by wars and violent revolutions. For if the Hegelian dialectic were in fact the means by which history moves forward, then indeed, as Hegel argues in contemplating "history as the slaughterbench at which the happiness of people, the wisdom of states, and the virtue of individuals have been sacrificed" (Hegel, trans. 1953, p. 27) then the historical fact of victory would indicate the historical rightness of the victor's logic, at least in their historical moment. It is this paean-like quality of Hegel's phenomenology of history that Benjamin and Arendt critique so deci-sively and clearly. For Benjamin, what is at issue with an historicism that turns on the hinges of war is that it confirms a victor's logic (like that of Athens to Melos), and by consequence justifies subordination to that logic as having been historically necessary. Asking for a pledge of loyalty from historical materialism, Benjamin writes that,

The answer is inevitably with the victor. And all rulers as heirs of those who conquered before them. Hence, empathy with the victor invari-ably benefits the rulers. Historical materialists know what that means (Benjamin, trans. 1968, p. 256)

This is the point of resistance to patterns of oppression encoded in our cultures, our economies, and our technology: the idea that simply because things are a certain way, domination is justified as historical fact. This is akin to Aristotle's circular justification of slavery as social insti-tution, a beyond-racist, biological determinism. That is, people incapa-ble of their own self-defence prove themselves suited to subjugation by nature, and thus need the protection and help of a superior civilization. This self-confirming logic deduces from the mere fact of their having been conquered that they are by nature suited to enslavement:

> For he is a slave by nature who is capable of belonging to another – which is also why he belongs to another – and who participates in reason only to the extent of perceiving it, but does not have it (Aristotle, trans. 1984, 1254b21-4)

Even violence and aggression have to find their reasons with privileges encoded into institutional and discursive orders that sublimate domination into society, that is, into the very common sense that perpetuates the privileges thus attained.

Rather, it is clear that things could be otherwise. Events do arise where the indeterminacy of action comes to bear, where a swirl of shared opinions has its moment to coalesce into a shift in common sense; where the institutional programming of shared memory has its hiccup and it becomes possible to re-think customs and traditions once again. And in those moments, which Benjamin describes in terms of an historical consciousness able "to seize hold of memory as it flashes up at a moment of danger", the truth can be grasped (Benjamin, trans. 1968, p. 255). This is what Benjamin calls "divine violence", as in the image of the shocked apprehension at the wreckage of history piling up at the feet of the Angel of the New—world wars and state violence, carnage and explosions blowing her backwards into the future.

Along similar lines to Benjamin, Slavoj Zizek distinguishes between what he calls a "symbolic violence" embodied in language and its forms of logic; Zizek refers to Heidegger who identifies the forms of language and its logic as a worldview, or in that thinker's ponderous tone, language considered as "our house of being" (Zizek, 2008, p. 1). Beyond the violence of symbolism there is what Zizek distinguishes as "systemic violence", that is forms of violence embodied in the routine functioning of economies and social orders. Zizek then further distinguishes what he calls "subjective violence", that is violence done directly by one or a few persons to others. To the extent that institutions are generally not suicidal, as Noam Chomsky observes (Herman & Chomsky, 1988), there is an overarching focus on instances of subjective violence, which has the effect of distracting from symbolic and systemic forms of subjugation. Zizek proposes an alternative: borrowing from Benjamin the idea of "divine violence", that is, some kind of revolutionary act that registers the truly apocalyptic quality of late modernity, brings the Ancient Greek sense of *apo-calypso* as "out of concealment" to the forefront, and cultivates a new common sense from out of the wastelands of a moribund capitalist culture.

This is what apparently remains of culture in an age of mechanical reproduction, with identities manufactured by mass media deploying terror as the emotional basis of belonging. In response to the morass of a civilization in its end game, Zizek approvingly paraphrases Benjamin's observation that "every clash of civilizations is a clash of underlying barbarisms" (Zizek, 2008, p. 177). So how then do we find out what those underlying barbarisms are, and then take action that would genuinely civilize our perceptions of, and hospitality towards, others?

For in terms of decent dealings with others, this has been the hallmark of civility back to the origins of Western political thought; in Homer, a code of hospitality among the Hellenes was what brought them together as a self-conscious civilization. And it is at the margins of hospitality that civility is delimited also. A fitting image of barbarism as the terminus to civility is the Cyclops in Odysseus' story: what marks the Cyclops Polyphemus as monstrously barbaric is his sheer indifference to others, preferring to live alone, reveling in his deplorable condition, and making meals of his visitors. Hospitality was considered core to civil society, precisely as demonstrated in Odysseus' at once sarcastic and earnest reproach to the Cyclops for eating his friends: that the host could not expect guests if he behaved in such a savage way:

> "Cyclops, have some wine, now that you have eaten
> Your human flesh, so you can see what kind of drink
> Was in our ship's hold. I was bringing it to you
> As an offering, hoping you would pity me
> And help get me home. But you are a raving
> Maniac! How do you expect any other man
> Ever to visit you after acting like this?" (Homer, trans. 2000, 9.343-49)

It is telling just what Odysseus saw as the greatest damage done by the Cyclops' cannibalism—perhaps as stark an instance of subjective violence as one can imagine. According to Odysseus' observation, at its basest cannibalism was an erosion of social trusts at the most basic level of civility: the capacities for hospitality, and to have pity on the traveler, to share with them what they needed, and by consequence, to be civilized. That this might mean the sharing of wine makes the desirability of civilization that much more obvious, at least according to Odysseus' Hellenic sensibilities. For beyond their many gods, the laws of various cities, and their various rites of citizenship, the bare premise that made Hellenic civilization possible for otherwise scattered island dwellers and roving sailors was that one owed something to the stranger at the door. The pattern of indebtedness to others that one witnesses in hospitality was constitutive of that civilization in that it provided a baseline trust in which people could share. It was the formative code of character, touching on that core element of our nature that makes human society possible. One owes hospitality to those who need it. The acceptance of this premise in the Hellenic *ethos* would trace out the high water marks of that civilization, and where it was absent, there was barbarism, i.e. the existence of others to whom one owes nothing.

Thus, upon finding Odysseus shipwrecked, "a frightening sight, disfigured with brine", (Homer, 2000, 6.136) the Princess Naussica instructs her hand-maidens to care for the stranger:

> "At the world's frontier, out of all human contact.
> This man comes here as a wanderer,
> And we must take care of him now. All strangers,
> All beggars, are under the protection of Zeus,
> And even small gifts are welcome. So let's feed
> This stranger, give him something to drink,
> And bathe him in the river out of the wind". (Homer, trans. 2000, 6.210-16)

This is an example of civility approaching the domain of civil religion, where a trust in others is derived from a trans-political source—from Zeus in the case of Naussica's order to civility—with trust in the neighbor and stranger both derived from faith in a god. Thus, how people treat each other at the micro level of our day-to-day, street-level experiences, requires a trust in a common sense, the most basic bonds of which can be described in a simple code along the lines of a golden rule, and transcending religious affiliations. Perhaps further improvement is possible through the replacement of the somewhat presumptuous 'Do unto Others as you would have done unto yourself' with the more critical, open, and fair-minded 'Do unto Others as those Others would have done unto themselves'. This inversion of the golden rule would require first asking what the Other would want, without presuming an identity between one's wishes for oneself and what another may need.[7] So, to bring that Other into the discussion around the relief of their condition is crucial, at least inasmuch as one genuinely feels care for them. This would be a new beginning for ethical relations, premised on non-violent, voluntary association. How we manage to make our communities and institutions more peaceful in this sense of non-violent, non-coercive—that is, free—forms of association, would be a suitable measure of our civility.

NOTES

1. I elaborate on this argument concerning why empires tend to expand with tragic consequences, both for the imperial metropole and for the subjugated hinterlands, in "Imperial Compulsions", from *Enduring Empire: Ancient Lessons for Global Politics*, co-edited by myself and David Tabachnick (2009). Toronto: University of Toronto Press.

2. This reading of Hegel as precursor to Marx is informed by the interpretation of Alexandre Kojève, whose selective approach to Hegel's *Phenomenology of Mind* in his influential seminars and *Introduction to the Reading of Hegel* bring a kind of functionality to the thinker, if at the expense of the fullness of Hegel's intents, through the willful disavowal of his concepts of nature, family and civil religion that are prominent in conservative interpretations of the thinker. See Kojève, Alexandre (1969). *Introduction to the Reading of Hegel*. James H. Nichols translation. Ithaca: Cornell University Press. In that alternative interpretation, instead of a lockstep march towards progress, there is emphasis instead on Hegel's retrievals of unity, the family and of community in response to the deprivals of modernity- the Terror of the French Revolution being foremost on his mind. See for example Newell, Waller R. (2009). "Redeeming Modernity: The Ascent of Eros and Wisdom in Hegel's Phenomenology". *Interpretation*, 37(1), 3–28. Still, considering the impact of Kojève's Marxist reading on Continental philosophy, as an indication of Hegel's legacy the interpretation is formative, if not entirely loyal to authorial intent. On the impact of Kojève's interpretation of Hegel, see Roth, Michael S. (1988) *Knowing and History: Appropriations of Hegel in Twentieth-Century France*. Ithaca: Cornell University Press; Rosen, Stanley (1999). "*Kojève*", *A Companion to Continental Philosophy*. London: Wiley-Blackwell; and Butler, Judith (1987). *Subjects of Desire: Hegelian Reflections in Twentieth-Century France*. New York: Columbia University Press.

3. I elaborate on this reading of Hegel's idea of progress in terms of a free relation to difference in Koivukoski, Toivo (2014). *The New Barbarism: Recognizing an Ethic of Difference*. Lanham: Lexington Books.

4. It is worth noting the distinction that Arendt makes between modern forms of tyranny that combine technology and ideology with that ancient, vicious regime:
   "Totalitarian government, like all tyrannies, certainly could not exist without destroying the public realm of life, that is, without destroying, by isolating men, their political capacities. But totalitarian domination as a form of government is new in that it is not content with this isolation and destroys private life as well. It bases itself on loneliness, on the experience of not belonging to the world at all, which is among the most radical and desperate experiences of man.
   Loneliness, the common ground for terror, the essence of totalitarian government,…" (Arendt, 1951, p. 475)
5. See Arendt's account of a Nazi war crimes trial in Arendt, Hannah (1963). *Eichmann in Jerusalem: A Report on the Banality of Evil*, along with *The Origins of Totalitarianism* (1951).
6. As counterargument, consider Hans J. Morgenthau's 6th principle of political realism in (1948). *Politics Among Nations: The Struggle for Power and Peace*. New York: Alfred A Knopf.
7. This inversion of the Golden Rule is proposed by the Confucian scholar Yong Huang in his 2010 essay "The Ethics of Difference in the *Zhuangzi*", *Journal of the American Academy of Religion, 78*(1), 65–99. I elaborate and build on this inversion in *The New Barbarism: Recognizing an Ethic of Difference*.

REFERENCES

Agamben, G. (1998). *Homo Sacer: Sovereign Power and Bare Life* (D. Heller-Roazen, Trans.). Stanford: Stanford University Press.

Arendt, H. (1951). *Origins of Totalitarianism*. New York: Harcourt, Brace and World.

Arendt, H. (1958). *The Human Condition*. Chicago: University of Chicago Press.

Arendt, H. (1963). *Between Past and Future: Six Exercises in Political Thought*. New York: Viking Press.

Arendt, H. (1963/2006). *Eichmann in Jerusalem: A Report on the Banality of Evil*. New York: Penguin.

Arendt, H. (1969). *On Violence*. Orlando: Harcourt.

Aristotle. (1984). *Politics* (C. Lord, Trans.). Chicago: University of Chicago Press.

Benjamin, W. (1968). Theses on the philosophy of history (H. Zohn, Trans.). In H. Arendt (Ed.), *Illuminations*. New York: Shocken Books.

Bethune, N. (1972). *The Wounds*. Guelph: Alive Press.

Butler, J. (1987). *Subjects of Desire: Hegelian Reflections in Twentieth-Century France*. New York: Columbia University Press.

Butler, J. (2010). *Frames of War: When is Life Grievable?* London: Verso.

Grant, G. (1991). *Technology and Empire: Perspectives on North America*. Toronto: Anansi.

Hegel, G. W. F. (1953). *Reason in History* (R. S. Hartman, Trans.). New York: Library of Liberal Arts.

Hegel, G. W. F. (1967). *The Phenomenology of Mind* (J. B. Baillie, Trans.). New York: Harper.

Herman, E. S., & Chomsky, N. (1988). *Manufacturing Consent: The Political Economy of the Mass Media*. New York: Pantheon.

Homer. (1999). *Iliad* (Murray, Trans.). Cambridge: Harvard University Press.

Homer. (2000). *Odyssey* (S. Lombardo, Trans.). Indianapolis: Hackett.

Huang, Y. (2010). The ethics of difference in the *Zhuangzi. Journal of the American Academy of Religion, 78*(1), 65–99.

Keohane, R., & Nye, J. (2010). *Power and Interdependence* (4th ed.). Toronto: Pearson. Originally published in 1977.

Koivukoski, T. (2014). *The New Barbarism: Recognizing an Ethic of Difference*. Lanham: Lexington Books.

Koivukoski, T., & Tabachnick, D., co-editors. (2009). *Enduring Empire: Ancient Lessons for Global Politics*. Toronto: University of Toronto Press.

Kojève, A. (1969). *Introduction to the Reading of Hegel* (J. H. Nichols, Trans.). Ithaca: Cornell University Press.

Morgenthau, H. J. (1948). *Politics Among Nations: The Struggle for Power and Peace*. New York: Alfred A Knopf.

Mouffe, C. (2005). *On the Political*. London: Routledge.

Newell, W. R. (2009). Redeeming modernity: The ascent of eros and wisdom in Hegel's phenomenology. *Interpretation, 37*(1), 3–28.

Nietzsche, F. (1995). *Thus Spoke Zarathustra* (Kaufmann, Trans.). New York: Modern Library.

Rosen, S. (1999). "*Kojève*", *A Companion to Continental Philosophy*. London: Wiley-Blackwell.

Roth, M. S. (1988). *Knowing and History: Appropriations of Hegel in Twentieth-Century France*. Ithaca: Cornell University Press.

Thucydides. (2009). *The Peloponnesian War* (M. Hammond, Trans.). Oxford: Oxford University Press.

Weber, M. (1961). Politics as vocation. In *From Max Weber: Essays in Sociology*. London: Routledge.

Zizek, S. (2008). *Violence: Six Sideways Reflections*. New York: Picador.

Index